PARTY
POLITICS
IN
AMERICA

FRANK J. SORAUF

University of Minnesota

PARTY POLITICS IN AMERICA

THIRD EDITION

LITTLE, BROWN AND COMPANY
Boston   Toronto

Library of Congress Catalog Card No. 75–41740

First Printing

Printed simultaneously in Canada
by Little, Brown & Company (Canada) Limited

Printed in the United States of America

WITHDRAWN

For My Mother and Father

PREFACE

The purposes and outlooks of this book — even its eccentricities — will be apparent to readers without my alerting them in a lengthy preface. And what prefatory material on parties seemed useful I have incorporated in the introductions to the six parts of the book, where I think it stands a better chance of being read.

Whatever sins of commission I am guilty of are on the pages of the book for readers to see. I hope they will not hesitate to call them to my attention. My sins of omission may, however, require a brief comment. With the scholarly literature on parties expanding so rapidly, I have not been able to refer to all of it, and I have been forced to make difficult, even arbitrary, selections from it. In the interests both of brevity and of logic I have also resisted the temptation to dwell at length on interest groups and on American voting behavior. It is a self-imposed limitation that I think I can defend on intellectual as well as practical grounds.

Finally, I should like to acknowledge some of the debts that I have incurred in putting this book into a third edition. This one bears enough similarity to the first two editions for the debts incurred there to continue here. To the thanks I gave in the prefaces to those editions I should like to add a few more. Large numbers of individual students, friends, and professional colleagues have made useful comments and suggestions for the revision. I hope they will forgive such a brief and collective acknowledgment. Among that group, however, I am especially indebted to John Massaro for pointing out a number of errors in the second edition. I am also grateful for the work of my typist, Marilyn Grosenick, and for the help of my assistants, Larry Bye and Sid Groeneman. Finally, I have appreciated the helpfulness and forbearance of Rick Boyer and his colleagues at Little, Brown.

CONTENTS

PARTY
POLITICS
IN
AMERICA

I

PARTIES AND PARTY SYSTEMS

The open and aggressive pursuit of personal advantage will probably never win the admiration of any society. It certainly has not won the admiration of ours. Yet the things men and women want for themselves and for others — status, authority, justice, and wealth, for example — are in short supply. They compete for them by influencing the people or institutions that will recognize one claimant or another. This striving to win the things one holds desirable — a striving we call "politics" — is therefore as widespread as those desires are.

The pervasiveness of politics is a central fact of our times. We have seen in the twentieth century an enormous expansion of governmental activity, and it seems most unlikely that the tides of governmental authority will soon, if ever, recede. The demands of a complex, increasingly urbanized, industrialized society, and the dictates of a world beset by international tensions, scarcely seem to permit a return to the limited government of the early years of the American republic. For the foreseeable future an increasing proportion of the important conflicts and competitions over the desirable things in American society will be settled within the political system. The really meaningful issues of our time will surely be how influence and power are organized within the political system, who wins the rewards and successes of that political activity, and to whom the processes and decisions are responsible. It will be increasingly within the political system that we will decide, in the candid phrase of Harold Lasswell, "who gets what, when, how." [1]

In the United States these political contestings are directed largely at the regular institutions of government. Few political scientists believe that the real and important political decisions are made clandestinely by murky, semivisible elites and merely ratified by the governmental bodies they control.[2] It may happen, to be sure, that political decisions in a

[1] The phrase comes from the title of Harold Lasswell's pioneering book *Politics: Who Gets What, When, How* (New York: McGraw-Hill, 1936).
[2] C. Wright Mills in *The Power Elite* (New York: Oxford University Press, 1956) offers the best-known example of the elitist interpretations of American politics.

1

local community *are* made by a group of influential local citizens rather than by a city council or a mayor or a school board. Nonetheless, one is reasonably safe in looking for the substance of American politics in the legislatures, executives, and courts of the nation, the fifty states, and localities. The politics of which we have been talking consists of the attempts to influence either the making of decisions within these governmental bodies or the selecting of the men and women who will make them — whether the final formal decision is a law, a treaty, an ordinance, an executive order, a judicial decision, or an administrative rule or regulation.

This struggle for influence, this "politics," is not unorganized, however great the disarray may seem to be. Large political organizations attempt to mobilize influence on behalf of aggregates of individuals. In the Western democracies the political party is unquestionably the most important and pervasive of these political organizations; it is not, however, the only one. Interest groups such as the American Farm Bureau Federation and the AFL-CIO mobilize influence. So also do smaller factions and cliques, charismatic individuals, and nonparty political organizations such as Americans for Democratic Action and the American Conservative Union. We cannot, therefore, use the term *politics* to refer only to the activities of the political parties. A substantial portion of American politics goes on within and through the political parties, but a substantial portion also goes on outside them. Interest groups rather than parties, for example, bring certain issues and policy questions to legislatures and administrative agencies. Nonparty organizations also support candidates for office with money and manpower, sometimes even more effectively than the parties do. Thus the terms *politics* and *political* include not only the activity of the political parties but also the activity of other political organizers.

At this point it may help to step back and survey the entire political system in order to understand the place of parties and other political organizations in it (Figure 1). All these political organizations work as intermediaries between the millions of political individuals and the distant seats of government. Working between the political individual and the policy-making machinery of government, they build influence into large aggregates in order to affect the selection of policy makers and the policies they will make. At the same time they codify and simplify information about government and politics as it moves back to the individual. In a very real sense these political organizers are the informal agents by which individuals are represented in the complex democracies of our time. By joining the individual and small group to other individuals and groups, they permit them to participate meaningfully in the selection of their representatives and in the decisions of a usually re-

FIGURE 1   Political Parties as Organizing Intermediaries
in the Political System

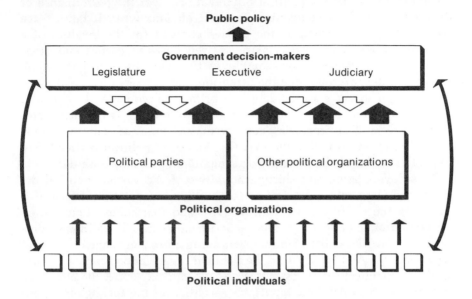

mote government. They are in the broadest sense both the builders and
the agents of majorities.

In any political system the political organizations develop a division
of labor. The political parties concentrate on contesting elections as a
way of aggregating influence. Others, especially the interest groups,
pursue the avenues of direct influence on legislators or administrators.
Still others seek mainly to propagate ideologies or build support on specific issues of foreign or domestic policy. Indeed, the nature of the
division of labor among the various political organizations says a great
deal about any political system and about the general processes of mobilizing influence within it. The division also speaks meaningfully about
the political parties themselves. It is a commonplace, for example, that
among the parties of the democracies the American political parties are
to an unusual extent occupied with the single activity of contesting elections. The parties of Western Europe, on the other hand, have been
more committed to the spreading of ideologies and the disciplining of
legislators. And those of countries such as India have been more involved with the transmitting of political values and information to a
citizenry lacking other avenues of political socialization and communication.

The division of labor among political organizations is, however, neither clear nor permanent. There is always an overlapping — and hence a competition — among political organizations over the performance of their activities. That competition is most obvious when it takes place within the party system, as the parties contend for the loyalties of a fickle electorate. But it takes place as well between parties and other political organizations — for example, in the competition of parties and powerful interest groups for the attention and support of legislators or for the right to name a candidate in a primary election. And the extent to which any one kind of political organization controls or participates in any one kind of organizing activity may change radically over time. Certainly no one would argue that the American political parties today control as much of the business of campaigning as they once did.

These overlapping and shifting activities of the various political organizations lead to a great deal of competition among them. Much of it is among the political parties themselves, and that competition will be considered at some length in the second chapter. Much additional competition, however, is between the parties and a broader range of political organizations. And for what do the political organizations compete? First of all, for political resources: money, skills, and expertise, the efforts of men and women. All these inputs are essential for the fueling of organizational activity, but none of them is in abundant supply in the American polity (or in any other polity). Second, they compete to mobilize individual citizens, to attach their individual loyalties to the goals and symbols of the organization. In short, the parties and other political organizations compete for scarce political resources with which to mobilize the political influence necessary to capture the scarce rewards the political system allocates. They compete for the ability to organize influence in American politics.

Despite these excursions beyond the subject of political parties and into some instant political science, this *is* a book about political parties. The broader survey of politics and political organizations has been necessary as background for two themes that will recur throughout the remainder of the book. The first is that the political party is not the unique political organization we have conventionally thought it is. On the contrary, it is frequently difficult to distinguish from other political organizations, and the difficulties of coming to a clear, agreed-on definition of a political party illustrate that point only too well. When one undertakes any exercise in definition, as we do for the parties in the first chapter, the temptation is always to err on the side of the distinctiveness, even the uniqueness, of the phenomenon one is trying to define. It may well be that the distinctions between parties and other political organizations are not, after all, so great as one might imagine. Parties do have their distinctive qualities — and it is important to know them — but there is little point in denying their similarity to and thus their comparability with many other political organizations.

Second, the broad perspective is essential background for assessing the role and position of the political parties in the American democracy. American writers about the political parties have not been modest in their claims for them. They have celebrated the parties as agents of democracy and as the chosen instruments through which a democratic citizenry governs itself. Some have gone a step further to proclaim them as the originators of the democratic processes which they now serve. E. E. Schattschneider opened his classic, influential study of the American parties this way in 1942:

> The rise of political parties is indubitably one of the principal distinguishing marks of modern government. The parties, in fact, have played a major role as *makers* of governments, more especially they have been the makers of democratic government. It should be stated flatly at the outset that this volume is devoted to the thesis that the political parties created democracy and that modern democracy is unthinkable save in terms of the parties.[3]

For many other scholars, and for many other thoughtful Americans, too, the American democracy presumes the two-party system of today.

Yet, the major American parties have changed and are presently changing — both in the form of their organization and in the pattern and style of their activities. Political parties as they existed fifty years ago scarcely exist today, and the political parties we know today may not exist fifty years hence. In this book a strong case will be made for the proposition that the political parties have lost their preeminent position as political organizations and that competing political organizations now perform many of the activities that have traditionally been regarded as the parties' exclusive prerogatives.[4] If this is indeed the case, we must face the fundamental question of whether political parties are indispensable and inevitable shapers of our politics and our democracy.

These two suspicions — that the parties may be less distinctive and their activities less pervasive than we have thought — add up perhaps to no more than a plea for modesty in the study of the American political parties. It is perfectly natural for both young and experienced scholars to identify with the objects of their study and thus to exaggerate their importance. Medievalists often find the late Middle Ages to be the high point of Western civilization, and most scholars of hitherto obscure painters and philosophers find the object of their study to have been sadly neglected or tragically underestimated. In the case of schol-

[3] E. E. Schattschneider, *Party Government* (New York: Rinehart, 1942), p. 1.
[4] See also Anthony King, "Political Parties in Western Democracies," *Polity* 2 (1969): 111–41.

ars of political parties there are doubtless other reasons for the tendency to overpraise the parties. That tendency results at least in part from an understandable spirit of protectiveness, a desire to defend the parties against what many observers have long thought is a deep antiparty sentiment in American opinion. It also reflects an understandable appreciation of the distinctive features of the American two-party system, especially its stability and long identification with a stable democracy.

The plea here for a modest assessment is also a plea for abandoning preconceptions and great general truths. Reassertions that political parties are essential to or the keystone of American democracy may or may not be true. But simply as assertions they advance our understanding of politics and parties very little. The important questions still are the nature of the parties themselves and the nature of their attempts and successes in organizing American politics.

1

In
Search
of the Political
Parties

Consider the American adults who insist, "I'm a strong Republican," and "I've been a Democrat all my life." It is unlikely that they ever worked within the party organization of their choice, much less made a financial contribution to it. They would be hard-pressed to recall its recent platform commitments, and if they did, they would probably feel no necessary loyalty to them. Furthermore, they probably never meet with the other Americans who express the same party ties, and they would likely find it difficult to name the local officials of their party. In fact, their loyalty to the party of which they consider themselves "members" may be little more than a disposition to support its candidates at elections if all other considerations are fairly equal. Yet, when the interviewers of polling organizations come to their doors, they hesitate not at all to attach themselves to that political party. And we do not hesitate to credit their word, for it is in the nature of the American parties and politics to consider people Democrats or Republicans merely because they say they are.

Are then the major American parties nothing more than great, formless aggregates of people who say they are Democrats and Republicans? Are they nothing more than vague political labels that people attach themselves to? It is perilously easy to conclude so, but the American political parties are also organizations. It *is* possible to join them, to work within them, to become officers in them, to participate in setting their goals and strategies — much as one would within a local fraternal organization or a machinists' union. They do have characteristics that we associate with social organizations: stable, patterned personal relationships and common goals. In other words, they are more than aggregates of people clinging in various degrees of intensity to a party label.

The act of defining the political party, and the American parties in particular, is hampered by the fact that the nature of the political party, like beauty, often rests in the eye of the beholder. The definition is usually a personal perception; it seems to depend on what the individual is looking for, what one hopes to see, what consequences one wants parties to have. (See, for example, the range of definitions in the box that follows.) Any one person's definition is likely to be rooted in a particular time and place and therefore likely not to reflect the diversity of form and activity that marks the parties. But, whatever the reason,

---

A Variety of Definitions of the Political Party

"Party is a body of men united, for promoting by their joint endeavors the national interest, upon some particular principle in which they are all agreed."

Edmund Burke, *Thoughts on the Cause
of the Present Discontents* (1770)

"...We may define 'political party' generally as the articulate organization of society's active political agents, those who are concerned with the control of governmental power and who compete for popular support with another group or groups holding divergent views."

Sigmund Neumann, *Modern Political Parties*
(Chicago: University of Chicago Press,
1956), p. 396; italics omitted.

"...Any group, however loosely organized, seeking to elect governmental office-holders under a given label."

Leon D. Epstein, *Political Parties in Western
Democracies* (New York: Praeger, 1967), p. 9.

"An 'established political party' is hereby declared to be a political party which, as to the state, at the last general election for state and county officers, polled for its candidate for governor more than two per cent of the entire vote cast for governor in the state."

Missouri Statutes (V.A.M.S. §120.140, par. 2.)

" 'Party' or 'Political Party' means any political party, organization or association which elects delegates to a national convention, nominates candidates for electors of President and Vice-President, United States Senator, Representative in Congress, Governor and other offices, and elects a state committee and officers of a state committee by a state convention composed of elected members from each representative district, provided a registered party member is available in each representative district."

Delaware Statutes (15 Del. C. §101.)

neither political scientists nor politicians have achieved any consensus at all on what sets the political party apart from other political organizations.

Despite the absence of consensus, however, the most common definitions fall into one of three main options. Those whose approach is ideological define the parties in terms of commonly held ideas, values, or stands on issues. That approach has not engaged many observers of the American political parties, for ideological homogeneity or purpose has not been a hallmark of the major American parties. Most of the attempts at definition vacillate between two other options. One of these tends to view the political party as a hierarchical organization or structure which draws into its orbit large numbers of voters, candidates, and active party workers. The other approach views the political parties largely in terms of what they do, what their role, function, or activities in the American political systems are. It frequently identifies American political parties with the election campaigns. To those latter two approaches we now turn in order.

THE POLITICAL PARTY AS A SOCIAL STRUCTURE

Large organizations or social structures are people in various roles, responsibilities, patterns of activities, and reciprocal relationships. But which people, what activities, what relationships are we talking about when we speak of the two major American parties? The party leaders and officials, the hundreds of anonymous activists who work for candidates and party causes, the people who vote for the party's candidates, its actual dues-paying members, the people who have an emotional involvement in the fortunes of the party, the men and women elected to office on the party's label? All of them or some of them?

The major American political parties are in truth three-headed political giants, tripartite systems of interactions, which embrace all these individuals. As political structures they include a party organization, a party in office, and a party in the electorate (Figure 1).

The Party Organization

In the party organization one finds the formally chosen party leaders, the informally anointed ones, the legions of local captains and leaders, the members and activists of the party — that is, all those who give their time, money, and skills to the party, whether as leaders or followers. These are the men and women who make and carry out decisions in the name of the party. The organization operates in part through the formal machinery of committees and conventions set by the laws of the fifty states and in part through its own informal apparatus. Here

FIGURE 1   The Three-Party Political Party

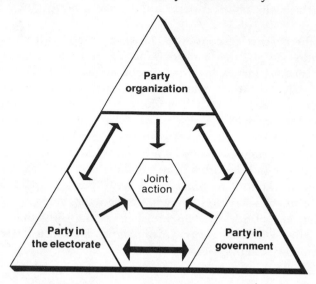

one finds the centers of party authority and bureaucracy, and here also one observes the face-to-face contacts and interactions that bespeak organization of any kind. This is the part of the party that the public, with a good deal of native shrewdness, often refers to simply as the organization, or less flatteringly as "the machine."

The Party in Government

The party in public office is made up of those who have captured office through the symbols of the party and those candidates who seek to do so. The chief executives and legislative parties of the nation and states are its major components. Although in many ways they are not subject to the control or discipline of the party organization, they do in the broadest sense speak for the party. Their pronouncements are the most audible party statements and carry the greatest weight with the public. Theirs is a semiautonomous segment of the party, one that is frequently at odds with the party committees and conventions, and often in competition with the organization proper for political resources and public attention.

The Party in the Electorate

The party in the electorate is the party's most open and least well-defined part. It comprises the men and women who affiliate casually with it, show it some degree of loyalty, and even vote habitually for it. Yet, they do not participate in the party organization or interact with its leaders and activists. Nor are they subject to the incentives and discipline of the party. They are, in effect, the regular consumers of the party's candidates and appeals. As the party's clientele, they make up the majorities necessary for effective political power in the American political system. But their association with the party is a passive one — accepting here, rejecting there, always threatening the party with the fickleness of their affections.

In their three-part structure, therefore, the major American parties include mixed, varied, and even contradictory components. Each party, for example, is a political organization with active, even disciplined participants, but it is also an aggregate of unorganized partisans who may begrudge the party organization even the merest public gesture of support or loyalty. The party thus embraces the widest range of involvement and commitment. It is a reasonably well-defined, voluntary political organization and at the same time an open, public rally of loyalists.

Perhaps the most telling characteristic of the major American parties, therefore, is the integral relationship that their clientele — the party in the electorate — has to them. The other political organizations, such as interest groups and ad hoc campaign organizations, usually work to attract supporters beyond their members and workers; but this wider clientele remains outside the political organization. Not so with the political party. The party in the electorate is more than an external group to be wooed and propitiated. State laws usually permit it a voice in the selection of the parties' candidates in the direct primary, and in many states it helps to select local party officials such as the ward and precinct committeeperson. Consequently, the major American party is an open, inclusive, semipublic political organization. It includes both a tangible political organization and its own political clientele (as well as the party in government, of course). In this combination of exclusive organization and inclusive clientele, of organization and electorate, the political party stands apart from the other political organizations on the American scene and apart from parties elsewhere.

Finally, each major party differs from state to state in the relationships and interactions among its three sectors. The Republicans and the Democrats are so decentralized and so diverse that each state party has its own distinctive mix of the three. Party organizations, for example, differ in form from state to state; in some the party organization dominates the party in government, while in others the reverse is closer to reality. Also, party electorates differ in composition and in the bases of their loyalties; in some states the two parties in the electorate divide roughly along social class lines, but in others they do not. Indeed, much of the distinctive quality of a state party is a reflection of the form and composition of each of the party sectors and of their relationship with each other.

THE PARTY AS A CONGERIES OF ACTIVITIES

From a discussion of the political parties as social structures, we move to a definition of them in terms of activities. We move from what they are to what they do. In varying degrees the competitive political parties of every democracy perform three sets of activities. They select candidates and contest elections, they propagandize on behalf of a party ideology or program, and they organize and attempt to guide the elected officeholders of government. The degree of emphasis that any particular political party puts on each of these individual activities varies within and between countries, but no party completely escapes the necessity of any of them. And by observing the different emphasis that the parties of any two countries give to their activities, one may discover some of the fundamental differences between them. British and continental European parties organize the policy-making machinery of legislatures far more effectively than do the American parties, for example, and therein rests an important difference between them.

Parties as Electors

It often appears that the American parties are little more than regular attempts to capture public office. This electoral activity so dominates the life of the American party that a fever chart of its activity follows almost exactly the cycles of the election calendar. Party activity and vitality reach a peak at the elections, and between elections the parties go into a recuperative hibernation. The parties live to mobilize voter support behind their candidates in elections, for only by winning elections do they maintain the confidence and allegiance of their three sectors. Party activity is goal-oriented, and in American politics most of the general goals as well as the goals of the individual sectors depend ultimately on electoral victory. It is, in fact, chiefly in the attempt to achieve their often separate goals through winning public office that the three sectors of the party are brought together in unified action.

Parties as Propagandizers

Second, the American parties carry on a series of loosely related activities that can perhaps best be called education or propagandization. There is, of course, a school of thought which argues that the American parties fail almost completely to function on behalf of ideas or ideologies. The Democrats and Republicans, to be sure, do not espouse the global, all-inclusive ideologies of a European Marxist or proletarian party. But they do represent aggregates of interests and do stand for different policies on selected issues. At the least the American parties do represent the interests of and the stands congenial to the groups that identify with them and support them. In this quasi-ideological sense they become parties of business or labor, of the advantaged or disadvantaged. Moreover, the events of the 1960s and 1970s suggest that ideology in the pure sense is coming to the American parties. In presidential nominating politics alone one merely needs to mention the Goldwater conservatism of 1964, the Eugene McCarthy candidacy of 1968, and the McGovern liberalism of 1972.

Parties as Governors

Finally, the successful candidates of the American parties organize the decision-making agencies of government. The legislatures of forty-nine states (with the exception of nonpartisan Nebraska) and the United States Congress are organized along party lines, and the voting of their members shows to varying degrees the effects of party discipline and cohesion. To be sure, that cohesion on controversial issues is irregular, sporadic, and often unpredictable in most legislatures. The congressional Democrats, for example, cannot generally count on their southern contingent to support civil rights bills or much welfare legislation. Yet, in the aggregate an important degree of party discipline does exist. In executive branches presidents and governors depend on their fellow partisans for executive talent and count on their party loyalty to bind them to the executive programs. Only the American judiciary largely escapes the organizing and directing touch of the parties.

These, then, are the chief overt activities of democratic political parties generally and of American parties in particular. They are the activities that the parties set out consciously to perform and are mentioned here purely in an introductory sense. Large sections of this or any other book on the American parties must of necessity be devoted to them.

To list the activities of the parties, however, is not to suggest that in the United States the parties monopolize any or all of them. The parties compete with the nonparty political organizations over the ability and the right to perform them. The American parties, having organized the legislatures, battle constantly — and often with little success — against interest groups and constituency pressures in order to firm up party lines for votes on major bills. In attempting to nominate candidates for public office, especially at the local level, the party faces an often insurmountable competition from interest groups, community elites, and powerful local personalities, each of whom may be sponsoring pet candidates. In stating issues and ideologies, they are often overshadowed by the fervor of the minor (third) parties, the ubiquitous interest groups, the mass media, pundits, publicists, and political action groups.

These patterns of party activity also affect the party structure and its three sectors. For example, the emphasis on the electoral activities of American parties elevates the party in government to a position of unusual power, even dominance. It frequently competes with the party organization for the favor of the party in the electorate. In parties more closely allied with issues and ideologies — such as those of continental Europe — party organizations often are able to dictate to legislative parties.

On the other hand, individuals from all three sectors of the party may unite in specific activities. Activists of the party organization loyal to an officeholder may unite with that person, with other individuals of the party in government, and with individuals in the party electorate to return him or her to public office. When the election is won or lost, they will very likely drift apart again. Therefore, one finds within the parties these functional clusters or nuclei, these groups of individuals drawn together in a single, concerted action.[1] Small and informal task groups cut across the differences in structure and goals that characterize the three party sectors. Temporary modifications in structure result from the pattern and pace of party activities.

THE UNPLANNED CONSEQUENCES OF PARTY ACTIVITY

The goal-seeking behavior of any individual or organization has unintended consequences. Congress, by pursuing its legislating activities, may be said to be either resolving or aggravating great areas of social conflict, depending on the observer and his location. Similarly, interest groups, in pursuing their particular goals in the legislative process, are at the same time providing an informal, auxiliary avenue of representation. The search for the unplanned consequences of party activities is an old tradition in the study of the American parties. It produces rich insights into the contributions of the parties to the American political system. Yet it can be frustrating, its findings imprecise and elusive.

When we say that a political party is picking a candidate or organizing an election campaign, we are talking about overt, intended, observable party activity. Not so when we say that the same party is organiz-

---

[1] On the party as a series of task-oriented nuclei, see Joseph A. Schlesinger, "Political Party Organization," in James G. March (ed.), *Handbook of Organizations* (Chicago: Rand McNally, 1965), pp. 764–801.

ing consensus, integrating new groups into society, or giving voice to political opposition. These latter statements describe the activities we *impute* to the parties. They are statements framed in terms of what we perceive the consequences of party activity to be. As such they depend on what meaning, results, or outcomes of action we as individual observers see. Some of our statements are more easily verified by empirical evidence than others. It is surely easier to show that the parties contribute to the political socialization of young Americans than it is to demonstrate that they settle social conflict, because it is easier to observe the process and results of socialization. Perhaps the distinction can best be made by narrowing it to a fine point: it is indisputably true that parties pick candidates for public office, but we only *say* that they recruit leadership for the American political system.

Not surprisingly, then, scholars of the American political parties have seen and recorded wildly differing sets of these unintended consequences. They have usually referred to them as functions, but that semantic convention is virtually the extent of their agreement. It is perhaps foolish to compound the confusion, but what follows is a brief list of some of the most readily identifiable — and thus most frequently mentioned — of these functions or unplanned consequences of party activity.

1. The parties do participate in the *political socialization* of the American electorate by transmitting political values and information to large numbers of voters and future voters. They preach the value of political commitment and activity, and they convey information and cues about the confusing political system. By symbolizing and representing a political point of view, they offer the uninformed or underinformed citizen a map of the political world. They help the citizen form political judgments and make political choices, and in both physical and psychological terms they make it easier to be politically active.

2. The American parties also contribute to the *cumulation of political power*. They aggregate masses of ineffectual political individuals and groups and thereby organize blocs powerful enough to govern or to oppose those who govern. For the confused and confounded citizen they simplify, and often oversimplify, the political world into more comprehensible choices. By using his or her attachment to the party as a perceptual screen, the voter has a master clue for assessing issues and candidates. So both within the individual and in the external political world, the political party operates to focus political loyalties on a small number of alternatives and thus to cumulate support behind them.

3. Because they devote so much effort to contesting elections, the American parties dominate the *recruitment of political leadership*. One needs only to run down a list of the members of the cabinet or even

the Supreme Court to see how many entered public service through a political party or through partisan candidacy for office. Furthermore, the orderly contesting of elections enables the parties to routinize political change and especially change of governmental leadership. More than one commentator has noted the disruptive quality of leadership changes in those countries in which no stable political parties contest in regular elections. And because the American parties pervade all governmental levels in the federal system, they may recruit and elevate leadership from one level to another.

4. Finally, the American parties are a *force for unification* in the divisive American political system. The decentralization, even fragmentation, of government is an incontestably crucial fact of American politics. To the fragmentation of the nation and the fifty states, multiplied by the threefold separation of powers in each, the two great national parties bring a unifying centripetal force. They help to hold together the disparate fragments of government by bringing similar traditions, interests, symbols, and issues to all the parts. They unify with an obviously limited efficiency: for example, they often fail to bind president and Congress together in causes that can transcend the separation of powers. But they do constitute a force for unity, a political adhesive, in an institutional tradition that divides.

There are two chief difficulties with these lists of party functions. First, there is not much agreement among them, a result not only of scholars' different perceptions of the parties but also of their disagreement over what the word *function* means. Some use it to denote the obvious activities of the parties (e.g., their contesting of elections), and others use it, as we do in this text, to describe the unintended consequences or happy by-products of the intended activities of the parties. For yet another group *function* suggests a contribution the party makes to the operation of the broader political system.[2] Additionally, there is the problem of defining or formulating the functional categories so that they can be observed and measured. If, as some writers have argued, one function of political parties is that they organize social conflict or that they articulate important social interests, how do we verify by our own observations whether all parties or some parties do in fact perform those functions? For reasons having to do with both of these problems, this book will look largely at party activity itself, at the more easily observable, intended activity rather than its unintended consequences.

---

[2] Theodore Lowi has brought together a number of various descriptions of party functions in his article "Toward Functionalism in Political Science: The Case of Innovation in Party Systems," *American Political Science Review* 57 (1963): 570–83

THE SPECIAL CHARACTERISTICS OF POLITICAL PARTIES

Perhaps it is time to end these excursions into related topics and narrow the search for political parties. The goal is certainly not a memorable, vest-pocket definition. We seek a succinct understanding of what characterizes the political parties and sets them apart from other political organizations. We need, in other words, a firm grasp of what the political parties are and what they do.

First, political parties, along with other political organizations, exist to organize and mobilize their supporters behind attempts to capture public office and to influence the activities of those already in public office. That much at least they have in common with all political organizations. But if the term *political party* is to have any meaning at all, there must also be differences between parties and other political organizations. Far too much has been made of the differences between the major American parties and other political organizations, especially the large national interest (or pressure) groups. But the differences are there even if they are really only differences among species of the same genus rather than among grossly different genera.

These differences have rarely been explored empirically. V. O. Key in his classic study of southern politics examined the prevailing one-party systems of the American South in the 1940s, and in the process he asked whether the factions and cliques of the dominant Democratic party came eventually to resemble the political parties of two-party or multiparty systems. But the faction proved to be no real substitute for the political party.

> Consider the element of discontinuity in factionalism. Although conditions differ from state to state and from time to time, in many instances the battle for control of a state is fought between groups newly formed for the particular campaign. The groups lack continuity in name — as exists under a party system — and they also lack continuity in the make-up of their inner core of professional politicians or leaders. Naturally, they also lack continuity in voter support which, under two-party conditions, provides a relatively stable following of voters for each party's candidates whoever they may be.

Furthermore, the disorganized politics of factionalism, Key wrote, do not produce the desirable unintended consequences that party activity does. For example,

> loose factional organizations are poor contrivances for recruiting and sifting out leaders of public affairs. Social structures that develop leadership and bring together like-minded citizens lay the basis for the effectuation of the majority will. Loose factions lack the collective spirit of party organization,

which at its best imposes a sense of duty and imparts a spirit of responsibility to the inner core of leaders of the organization.[3]

Even though these factions shared many characteristics with political parties — especially their concern for contesting elections — they lacked the stability, continuity, and degree of responsibility that Key found in the political parties.

We are, however, concerned with the differences between parties and the full range of political organizations. That includes national interest groups such as the AFL-CIO and the American Medical Association, ideological or issue organizations such as those of the new left and the conservative right, organizations concerned only with a single issue such as abortion, and local citizens' groups such as those promoting better schools or fewer taxes. The full range of political organizations includes also individual-candidate followings, ad hoc committees to elect Jones to Congress, and possibly even family dynasties; there were times in the 1960s when it would not have been preposterous to think of the Kennedy family as a political organization.

Above all, the political party is distinguished from other political organizations by its concentration on the contesting of elections. Although the major American parties do not monopolize the contesting of elections, their preeminence in this activity cannot be questioned. Other political organizations do attempt to influence American electoral politics. In many localities interest groups encourage or discourage candidates, work for them within parties, contribute to campaign funds, and get their members to the polls to support them. But other nonparty organizations do little more than attempt to raise funds, organize resources and skills, and recruit workers for some candidate's campaign for public office. The parties, however, are occupied with the contesting of elections in a way and to a degree that other political organizations are not. Their names and symbols, indeed, are the ones the states recognize for inclusion on most ballots.

Not only commitment to electoral activity, but also the organizational consequences of such activity characterize the political party. Since the party chooses to work toward its goals largely in elections, it must recruit an enormous supportive clientele. Although other organizations that attempt to influence legislative committees or rule making in administrative agencies may succeed with a few strategists and the support of only a small, well-mobilized clientele, the political parties, in order to win elections, must depend less on the intricate skills and maneuverings of organizational strategists and more on the mobilization of large numbers of citizens. Party appeals must be broad and inclusive, for the party can ill afford the exclusivity and narrow range of concerns

[3] V. O. Key, *Southern Politics* (New York: Knopf, 1949), pp. 303–04.

Third Force — Not Third Party

The differences and nuances among political organizations are almost infinite. John Gardner, former secretary of Health, Education, and Welfare, founded a group in 1970 called Common Cause and described as a citizens' lobby and a third force. (The first two "forces," apparently, are the Democratic and Republican parties.)

Mr. Gardner hastened to assure potential members, however, that Common Cause would not be a political party. In a recruitment brochure he asserted that it "will not be a third party, but a third force in American life which will uphold the public interest against all comers, particularly the special interests that dominate our national life today. Common Cause will not support candidates; it will confine itself to issues." Common Cause elsewhere described itself as an independent, nonpartisan organization.

Extensive recruitment had by 1974 produced a membership of more than 250,000 and an organization staffed by 85. Common Cause lobbyists and organizers also enjoyed the taste of success for their substantial roles in ending the grip of the seniority system in Congress and in passing new limits on campaign spending.

of many other political organizations. To put it simply, the major political party has committed itself through its concentration on electoral politics to the mobilization of large numbers of citizens in large numbers of elections, and from that commitment flow many of its organizational characteristics.

Furthermore, the major American political parties and similar parties elsewhere are characterized by a full commitment to political activity. They operate solely as political organizations, solely as instruments of political action. Not so the interest groups and most other political organizations, which move freely and frequently from political to nonpolitical activities and back again. The AFL-CIO, for example, seeks many of its goals and interests in nonpolitical ways, especially through collective bargaining. It may, however, turn to political action — to support sympathetic candidates or to lobby before Congress — when political avenues appear the best or only means to achieve these goals. Every organized group in the United States is, as one observer has suggested, a potential political organization.[4] And most of them make good on that potential these days as government grows and involves their interests increasingly in the political process. Still, the interest group almost always maintains some sphere of nonpolitical action.

[4] David B. Truman, *The Governmental Process* (New York: Knopf, 1951).

Political parties are also marked by an uncommon stability and persistence. The personal clique, the faction, the ad hoc campaign organization, and even many interest groups seem by contrast almost political will-o'-the-wisps, which disappear as suddenly as they appear. The size and the abstractness of the political parties, their relative independence of personalities, and their continuing symbolic strength for thousands of voters assure them an impressive political longevity. Both major American parties can trace their histories over a century, and the major parties of the other Western democracies have impressive, if shorter, life spans. It is precisely this enduring, ongoing quality that enhances their value as reference symbols. The parties are there as points of reference year after year and election after election, giving continuity and form to the choices Americans face and the issues they debate.

Finally, the political parties are distinguished from other political organizations by the extent to which they operate as cues or symbols — or even more vaguely as emotion-laden objects of loyalty — for large numbers of citizens. For millions of Americans the party label is the chief cue for their decisions about candidates or issues. It is the point of reference that allows them to organize and simplify the buzzing confusion and strident rhetoric of American politics. As a potent reference symbol, the party label organizes the extensive confusion of American politics *within* the individual American citizen — that is, it organizes his perceptions and structures his choices; it relates his political values and goals to the real options of American politics.

To summarize, the major American political parties exist, as do other political organizations, to organize large numbers of individuals behind attempts to influence the selection of public officials and the decisions these officials subsequently make in office. The parties are set apart from other political organizations by:

1. The extent to which they pursue their organizing through the contesting of elections.
2. The extensiveness and inclusiveness of their organization and clienteles.
3. Their sole concentration on political avenues for achieving their goals.
4. Their demonstrated stability and long life.
5. Their strength as cues and reference symbols in the decision making of citizens.

No one of these characteristics alone sets the political party apart from other political organizations, but when these factors are taken as a whole and the matter of degree is considered, they do set the major political party apart from other types of political organizations.

But, to reemphasize a point previously made, the differences between parties and other political organizations are often slender. Interest groups certainly contest elections to some degree, and the larger ones have achieved impressive stability and duration and also considerable symbolic status. They, too, can recruit candidates and give political clues and cues to their members and fellow travelers. Groups such as the student organizations that attempted to elect peace candidates in the 1970 congressional elections differ from the parties chiefly in size and influence. They participated in the elections, propagated ideologies, tried to influence and organize officeholders. Like the parties, they achieved symbolic status for members and like-minded voters and operated exclusively in the political realm. However, they did not, and probably could not, offer their names and symbols for candidates to use on the ballot. It is only that difference and the whole question of size and degree that separate their activities and political roles from those of the parties.

So similar are the parties to some other political organizations that they resemble them more closely than they do the minor or third parties. In other words, there are political parties and political parties. These minor political parties, called minor because they are not electorally competitive, are only nominally electoral organizations. Not even the congenital optimism of candidates can lead Socialists or Prohibitionists to expect substantial victories at the ballot. Lacking local organization as most of them do, they resemble the major parties as organizations less than do the complex, nationwide interest groups. And their membership base, often related to a single issue, may be just as narrow, just as exclusively recruited, as that of most interest groups. In structure and activities, groups such as the United States Chamber of Commerce and the AFL-CIO resemble the Democrats and Republicans far more than do the Vegetarians and the Socialist Workers.

THE PARTY IN ITS ENVIRONMENT

It is in the nature of a book on political parties to treat them more or less in isolation, to lift them from their context in the political system for special scrutiny. Yet, useful as isolation is, it may give the impression that the political parties are autonomous structures, moving freely within the political system as they and their leaders want. In a too-determined search for the parties alone there is a danger of overlooking the many forces in their environment that shape both their form and their activities.

It is also possible to let analysis and logic run riot and to imagine a party environment that includes virtually every other structure and process in the political system and a great deal outside it. But despite the superficial truth that every social structure or process is related to every other one, clearly some influences on the party are more powerful and insistent than others. It will suffice to limit this discussion to them. Like everything else in this chapter they are set out here as a preliminary guide to the rest of the book.

The Political Institutions

Very little in the American political system escapes the influence of American federalism and the separation of powers. No single factor seems to affect the American legislative parties, for example, so much as the separation of the legislature from the executive. Among the party systems of the world, the legislative parties that have the greatest discipline in voting and the strongest ties to the party organization are found chiefly in those countries with parliamentary systems. The institutions of the parliamentary form lead to the legislative party's cohesive support of (or opposition to) the cabinet, which is drawn from one legislative party or the other. The political parties in American legislatures are under no such necessity of uniting to support or oppose an executive; indeed, support and opposition to executive programs are often cut sharply across party lines.

The decentralization of American federalism has also left its imprint on the American parties. It has ingrained in them local political loyalties and generations of local, often provincial, political traditions. It has spawned an awesome range and number of public offices to fill; thus it has created an electoral politics that in size and diversity dwarfs that of all other political systems. By creating local rewards, local traditions, even local patronage systems, it has created and sustained a whole set of semiautonomous local parties within the two parties. The establishment of these local centers of power has worked mightily against the development of strong, permanent national party organs. The strong centers of influence within the party organizations are still at the state and county levels.

Any discussion of institutional influences on the parties might well consider all the other major American political institutions. It suffices here to add just one more: the executive or administrative institutions. Traditionally the American parties, to an extent unknown elsewhere, have drawn their organizational rewards from the administrative establishments: patronage jobs, high-level cabinet or subcabinet appointments, preferences in purchasing or contracts, special treatment in public services (in building or repairing roads, for example), and special exemptions from public penalties (the fixed ticket, for instance). Those kinds of opportunity and favoritism clearly depend on the nature of the administrative agencies and their vulnerability to the claims of the political executive. Richard Nixon's misuse of administrative agencies such as the Internal Revenue Service was only a recent and especially gross example of an old American practice.

Statutory Regulation

No other parties among the democracies of the world are so bound up in legal regulations as are the American parties. The forms of their organization are prescribed by the states in endless, often finicky, detail. The statutes on party organization set up grandiose layers of party committees and often chart the details of who will compose them, when they will meet, and what their agenda will be. State law also defines the parties themselves, often in defining the right to place candidates on the ballot. A number of states also undertake to regulate the activities of parties; many, for example, regulate their finances, and most place at least some limits on their campaign practices. So severe can these regulations be, in fact, that in some states the parties have developed elaborate strategies to evade the worst burdens of regulation.

Electoral Institutions and Processes

The election machinery in a state may be thought of as an extensive regulation of the parties' chief political activity. At least it is often difficult to determine where the regulation of the party ends and electoral reform begins. Consider, for example, the direct primary. It is both a significant addition to the machinery of American electoral processes and a sharp regulation of the way a party selects the candidates who bear its label in an election. Even the relatively minor differences in primary law from one state to another — such as differences in the form of the ballot or the time of the year in which the primary occurs — are not without their impact on the parties.

The collective electoral institutions of the nation and of the fifty states set a matrix of rules and boundaries within which the parties compete for public office. The various components of these institutions are not neutral, for they give strategic advantages to some of the contestants. The basic American commitment to plurality elections within single-member districts works, as decades of scholars have suggested, in favor of the large competitive parties and against the small weak ones. Similarly, population inequality and gerrymandering in constituencies distort the strength and composition of the party electorates. The institution of the electoral college shapes virtually every aspect of our American presidential politics. Even the smaller details of electoral law dealing with the form of ballots or the use of voting machines make their mark.

The Nature of the Electorate

Because of the importance of the electorate to the political parties, its definition is a central element in the parties' environment. The addition of new groups to the electorate — for democratic electorates expand rather than contract — affects party composition and party appeals. The addition of millions of Americans between eighteen and twenty-one substantially affected both the organization and the activities of the American parties. There are also those less formal changes in the American electorate that result from general changes in American society. Changes in educational levels, in the patterns of political socialization, and in the American class structure all lead to changes in political norms and interests, the level of political involvement, and the information and perceptions of the American electorate.

The Political Culture

It is one thing to specify such tangibles in the parties' environment as regulatory statutes, electoral mechanisms, and even political institutions and electorates. It is quite another, however, to pin down so elusive a part of the party environment as its political culture. The political culture is the all-enveloping network of the political norms, values, and expectations of Americans. It is, in other words, their conglomerate view of what the political system is, what it should be, and what their place is in it. Furthermore, it varies regionally and among different strata or political subcultures of the American population. Party campaign tactics that the big city takes for granted often outrage the nearby country cousins.

The feeling that party politics is a compromising, somewhat dirty business has long seemed to be a major and persistent component of the American political culture. Since the advent of public opinion sampling, the indicators of that hostility toward partisan politics have multiplied. For example, a number of polls have found that American parents prefer that their sons and daughters not choose a full-time political career. Politics as a vocation, in their estimation, compares unfavorably with even the semiskilled trades.[5] In late 1969 *Newsweek* reported a poll of almost eleven hundred students on fifty-seven college campuses across the country. The students were asked to rate the performance of various American institutions. Their ratings follow:

[5] See William C. Mitchell, "The Ambivalent Social Status of the American Politician," *Western Political Quarterly* 12 (1959), 683–99.

Institutions rated	Percentage favorable
Universities	68
Family	58
Business	56
Congress	56
Courts	46
Police	40
High schools	37
Organized religion	33
Political parties	18

Little comment is probably necessary when the police as an institution receive more than twice as much support as parties from a population of college students at the height of campus activism.[6]

A more systematic study of attitudes toward the party system in one state (Wisconsin) points to a curious popular ambivalence toward the parties. There is support for vague salutes to the two-party system and competition. Some 68 percent of the respondents agreed that "democracy works best where competition between parties is strong," for example. But other responses appear to negate a good deal of such support. Some 53 percent agreed that the political system would work better "if we could get rid of conflicts between the parties altogether." Partisan politics in the United States, in other words, may enjoy a somewhat ambiguous support within the American electorate but only at a high level of generality or platitude.[7]

Suspicion of things partisan, however, is only one element in a multi-faceted political culture that shapes the American parties. The views of Americans on such broad points as representative democracy itself are relevant. A prevailing Burkean view of representation, which holds that the representative ought to decide public questions on the basis of his own information and wisdom, certainly retards the development of party discipline in American legislatures. More detailed public attitudes govern even such matters as the incentives for party activity and the kinds of campaign tactics a party or candidate chooses. Indeed, the whole issue of what we consider fair or ethical campaigning is simply a reflection of the norms and expectations of large numbers of Americans.

---

[6] *Newsweek*, December 29, 1969. In spring of 1975 the Gallup Poll asked a national sample of college students to rate the "honesty and ethical standards" of people in a number of vocations. While only 2 percent rated college teachers and 5 percent rated medical doctors "low" or "very low," 53 percent so rated the political officeholders. Only "advertising practitioners" scored below the officeholders, and then by only one percentage point. *Minneapolis Tribune*, May 19, 1975.

[7] Jack Dennis, "Support for the Party System by the Mass Public," *American Political Science Review* 60 (1966), 600–15.

The Nonpolitical Environment

Much of the parties' nonpolitical environment works on them through the elements of the political environment. Changes in levels of education, for example, affect the political culture, the skills of the electorate, and levels of political information. Great jolts in the economy alter the structure of political issues and the goals of the electorate. Education and probably socioeconomic status also seem related to elements of the political culture. The study in Wisconsin just mentioned suggests that less educated Americans accept party loyalty and discipline more easily than the better educated do. Even general social values are quickly translated into political values. Acceptance of a Catholic candidate for the American presidency had to await changes in social attitudes about religion in general and Catholicism in particular.

Whether the impact of the nonpolitical environment is direct or indirect, however, may be beside the point. The impact is strong and often disruptive. The advent of a recession, for example, may have important repercussions on the parties. It may make money raising more difficult; it will certainly make patronage positions more attractive and perhaps even shift the incentives for recruiting the workers on which the party organizations rely. It will also certainly define a very important issue for the electorate. If the crisis is especially severe, as was the Great Depression of the 1930s, it may even fracture and reorganize the pattern of basic, enduring party loyalties.

A PRELIMINARY OVERVIEW

This entire chapter has been sketchy and preliminary. All its points, however, will be discussed at greater length in the chapters that follow. The purpose here has been merely to set out some basic understandings and analytical issues for the reader.

Much of the material in this chapter can be thought of in the schematic way of Figure 2. Political parties both get and spend. They "get" in the sense that they recruit the inputs or resources that they need to function: money, skills, manpower, and loyalty. They spend in the sense that they convert these resources into outputs or party activities: the contesting of elections, organizing of party officeholders, and education on issues or ideologies. All three sectors of the party in their various ways must mobilize resources; only to a limited extent do the recruiting of inputs and the generation of outputs go on in a uniform way among the three sectors.

Enveloping all this party activity, as we have just seen, is the party's context or environment. That environment affects all aspects of the party: its organization and its recruiting of resources (input) and its

FIGURE 2   The Political Party: Structure and Activities

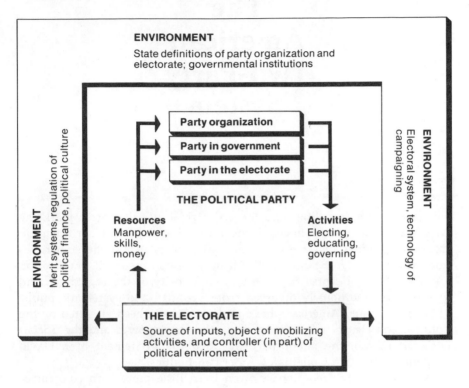

shaping of activities (output). Figure 2 in a sketchy way attempts to bring these concepts together into a unified presentation of the party as a functioning political institution. It cannot include the competings of parties among themselves and with other political organizations. That functioning of the parties in tandem within the party system we take up next. Along with it we consider the nature of party competition and the importance of it and of the two-party system itself for American democracy.

2

The American Two-Party System

The powerful personalities and the eccentric issues that often mark the American minor parties have an uncanny ability to divert our attention from the routines of American electoral politics. Amid the sometimes portentous gravity of those politics it may lighten the spirit to reflect on a political party devoted to the moral superiority of the vegetable. And in a politics traditionally divorced from ideology and systematic public philosophy, many Americans have understandably been attracted by the political conscience of parties such as the Progressives and the Socialists. Often, too, the minor parties added the excitement of a David challenging the two Goliaths of American politics.

What had in the recent past often been little more than colorful or amusing, however, became a matter of considerable seriousness in 1968. In the presidential election of that year George C. Wallace captured almost 10 million votes and came fairly close to throwing the entire election into the unpredictable hands of the House of Representatives. Had he not been struck down by an assassin's bullet midway in the 1972 preconvention campaign he might well have exceeded the 1968 accomplishment. How is it, then, that we refer so glibly to the American two-party system? Why do we acknowledge only two parties and cavalierly disregard the whole array of smaller ones? Like our deceptively simple references to political parties, our references to party systems flow easily — and vaguely. But the mathematics of "two" and the components of a "system" are by no means self-evident.

The conventional terminology we use to describe party systems is based on two related major premises: that parties are primarily electoral organizations and that their electoral activities are carried out in direct competition with other electoral parties. The designation of a one-party, two-party, five-party, or multiparty system simply indicates the number of political parties able to compete for office with some prospect of success. Hence the mathematics rests on a distinction between the competitive major parties and the noncompetitive minor parties. What is called the party system is composed, therefore, only of the electorally competitive parties.

For all its elegant simplicity (and to some extent, because of it) this conventional classification of party systems has a number of significant shortcomings:

1. It focuses solely on one dimension of the competition among political organizations. Consequently, it overlooks the possibility that the major parties compete ideologically or programmatically with minor parties, even though they do not compete electorally.
2. By focusing only on the political parties, it artificially blocks them off — as a separate segment — from the full range of competition among all kinds of political organizations. Even in the business of nominating and electing candidates for public office, a party may face competition from a local interest group or political elite.
3. By dealing exclusively with electoral competition, it ignores any differences in organization the parties may have and centers its measurement on the size of the party's electorate.
4. Finally, it tends to ignore the implications of the word *system*. It overlooks the relationships and interactions one expects in any system and settles merely for the presence of competitive parties and their presumed competings in elections.

But so ingrained in both everyday use and in the scholarly literature is this concept of the party system that one has little choice but to work within its terms.

THE NATIONAL PARTY SYSTEM

Since the Civil War only two political parties, the Democratic and the Republican, have maintained a competitive position in the battle for the American presidency and the American Congress. That fact, exceptional in itself, is overshadowed by the closeness of their competition. Of the twenty-two presidential elections from 1888 through 1972, the Republicans won twelve and the Democrats ten.[1] Of those twenty-two elections only six were decided by a spread of more than 20 percent between the popular vote of the two major parties — that is, in sixteen of them a shift of 10 percent or less of the vote would have given the other party's candidate the lead. And in only four of those twenty-two presidential elections did the winners get more than 60 percent of the total popular

[1] However, the Democrats led the popular vote in eleven elections, losing the election of 1888 in the electoral college despite Grover Cleveland's lead in the popular vote.

vote: Warren G. Harding in 1920, Franklin Roosevelt in 1936, Lyndon Johnson in 1964, and Richard Nixon in 1972. Nine of the twenty-two were decided by a spread of less than 7 percent of the popular vote, and so close have presidential elections been generally that Dwight D. Eisenhower's 57.4 percent of the popular vote in 1956 was widely called a landslide. The shade over 61 percent with which Lyndon Johnson won in 1964 also set a new record for a president's percentage of the popular vote.[2] The 1960s also saw two of the closest presidential elections in American history. John F. Kennedy in 1960 polled only .2 percent of the popular vote more than did Richard Nixon, and Mr. Nixon in turn led the popular vote by only .7 percent in 1968.

As close as the results of the presidential elections have been, the elections to Congress have been even closer. If we move to percentages of the two-party vote for ease of comparison, we quickly note the remarkable balance between the aggregate votes cast for Democratic and Republican candidates for the House of Representatives from all over the United States during the century (Table 1). From 1900 through 1974 only one of the biennial elections to the House of Representatives, that of 1920, saw a difference greater than twenty percentage points in the division of the two-party vote. The median percentage spread between the candidates of the two parties for the House from 1900 through 1974 was 6.2; it was 15.6 for the presidential candidates in the same period. Perhaps even more telling, in every year except 1948, 1960, and 1968 the margin between congressional candidates was smaller than that between the presidential aspirants.

The fineness and persistence of party competition in national politics is, therefore, apparent in even the quickest survey of recent electoral history. Even more impressive, perhaps, is the resilience of the major parties. While from time to time the parties have lapsed from closely matched competitiveness, in the long run they have shown a remarkable facility for restoring balance. The Democrats recovered quickly from the failures of the 1920s, and the Republicans confounded the pessimists by springing back from the Roosevelt victories of the 1930s. And despite the catastrophes of 1964, the Republicans gained forty-seven seats in the House in 1966 and won the presidency in 1968 and 1972.

But is this aggregate record of winning and losing in national elections what we mean by a two-party system? There is ample reason for doubting that it is. Organizationally the national parties are only loose

---

[2] The reader may be confused here about political record keeping. Note that this 61.1 percent for Lyndon Johnson was the percentage of the total popular vote. Other relevant records in presidential elections: greatest electoral college vote, Franklin Roosevelt in 1936 with 523 votes; greatest percentage of two-party vote, Calvin Coolidge in 1924 with 65.2 percent.

TABLE 1   Percentage of Two-Party Vote Won by Republican
Candidates for the Presidency and House of Representatives: 1900–74

	Presidential Election		House Election	
Year	Percentage Republican	Percentage spread between Republican and Democratic candidates	Percentage Republican	Percentage spread between Republican and Democratic candidates
1900	53.1	6.2	52.7	5.4
1902			51.3	2.6
1904	60.0	20.0	56.3	12.6
1906			53.5	7.0
1908	54.5	9.0	51.9	3.8
1910			50.5	1.0
1912	35.6	−28.8	42.9	−14.2
1914			49.7	−.6
1916	48.3	−3.4	51.1	2.2
1918			54.9	9.8
1920	63.8	27.6	62.3	24.6
1922			53.6	7.2
1924	65.2	30.4	57.9	15.8
1926			58.4	16.8
1928	58.8	17.6	57.2	14.4
1930			54.1	8.2
1932	40.9	−18.2	43.1	−13.8
1934			43.8	−12.4
1936	37.5	−25.0	41.5	−17.0
1938			49.2	−1.6
1940	45.0	−10.0	47.0	−6.0
1942			52.3	4.6
1944	46.2	−7.6	48.3	−3.4
1946			54.7	9.4
1948	47.7	−4.6	46.8	−6.4
1950			49.9	−.2
1952	55.4	10.8	50.1	.2
1954			47.5	−5.0
1956	57.8	15.6	49.0	−2.0
1958			43.9	−12.2
1960	49.9	−.2	45.0	−10.0
1962			47.4	−5.2
1964	38.7	−22.6	42.5	−15.0

Continued

TABLE 1 *Continued*

Year	Presidential Election		House Election	
	Percentage Republican	Percentage spread between Republican and Democratic candidates	Percentage Republican	Percentage spread between Republican and Democratic candidates
1966			48.7	−2.6
1968	50.4	.8	49.1	−1.8
1970			45.6	−8.8
1972	61.8	23.6	47.3	−5.4
1974			43.0	−14.0

Source Data from 1900 through 1960: Donald E. Stokes and Gudmund R. Iversen, "On the Existence of Forces Restoring Party Competition," *Public Opinion Quarterly* 26 (Summer 1962): 162. Data from 1962 through 1972: *Statistical Abstract*, 1974. Data for 1974 from *Congressional Quarterly Weekly Report*, November 9, 1974.

coalitions of virtually autonomous state parties, over whom the national party organs exercise very little authority or discipline. The American national parties, to the extent that they exist, are largely loyal electorates whose political concerns are focused on national politics. Even that national electorate, however, chooses a president from a constituency which, as it is defined by the electoral college, is really a weighted sum of the state constituencies. Furthermore, the members of the House of Representatives are chosen from local constituencies in elections contested by local parties on what are frequently local issues.

Paying attention only to national competitiveness raises another danger. It may very well be that what we see as an amazingly close competition on the national level is only an artificial competitiveness — merely a summation of offsetting one-partyisms in various sections of the country. That is to say, statements about national competitiveness gloss over the issue of how unevenly the competitiveness is spread over the states and counties of the country. For these reasons, the term *American party system* must be used in a broad, almost figurative sense. Perhaps it is best thought of, in the words of its chief critics, as "a shorthand expression for the totality of party conflict in the United States." [3]

[3] Austin Ranney and Willmoore Kendall, *Democracy and the American Party System* (New York: Harcourt, Brace, 1956), p. 161.

THE FIFTY AMERICAN PARTY SYSTEMS

All but obscured in the incredible closeness of both presidential elections and the aggregate vote for congressmen is the one-partyism not apparent when one examines only national totals. For example, it was not until 1964 that Georgia cast its electoral votes for a Republican and Vermont voted for a Democrat for the first time since the Civil War. And although one may talk of the aggregate closeness of the biennial elections to the House of Representatives, the aura of competitiveness vanishes in part if one looks at the individual races. Very significant numbers of congressmen win election to the House of Representatives with more than 60 percent of the total vote — in 1970, 71.9 percent of the congressmen did; in 1972, 73.6 percent; and in 1974, 60 percent. In 1972, in fact, thirty-nine members of the House were elected without any competition whatsoever; in 1974 the number was forty-one.

If we are to discuss the varying degrees of competitiveness of the fifty state party systems, however, the practical problem of defining *competitiveness* can be postponed no longer. Logically *competitiveness* refers either to an assessment of the quality of past competition or to a prediction of the possibilities of competitiveness in the near future. In both cases the problems are considerable. First of all, we must decide whether to count vote totals and percentages or simply the offices won. Do we regard a party that systematically garners 40 or 45 percent of the vote, but never wins office, any differently than we do one that hovers around the 20 to 25 percent mark? If we are to make distinctions between parties such as these, where do we draw the fine line between competitiveness and noncompetitiveness? At 25, 30, 35, or 40 percent? An impressive number of scholars settle for the 40 percent figure. Then, too, we must decide whether and how to discriminate between the party that averages 40 percent of the vote and wins office occasionally from the party that averages 40 percent and never wins.

Finally, the classifier of parties and party systems on the basis of competitiveness must determine which offices to consult — the vote for presidential candidates, for governors and senators, for statewide officials (such as the attorney general), for the state legislature, or a combination of them. A state may show strikingly different competitive patterns between its national and its state and local politics. Arizona in the 1950s, for example, voted twice for Eisenhower, elected a Republican governor in three of the five elections, and voted twice for a Republican senator, Barry Goldwater. Yet, during those years the Arizona state senate ranged from 79 to 100 percent Democratic, and the lower house varied from 63 to 90 percent Democratic.[4]

[4] These data come from the *Book of the States* (Chicago: Council of State Governments) for the 1950s and 1960s.

In categorizing the party systems of the American states, one can dismiss the possibility of multiparty systems. To be sure, there are examples of them in the American experience. In Minnesota, Wisconsin, and North Dakota in the 1930s and 1940s, remnants of the Progressive movement — the Progressive party in Wisconsin, the Farmer-Labor party in Minnesota, and the Non-Partisan League in North Dakota — competed with some success against the major parties. But in all three cases the heavy pressures of the national two-party system forced them to disband and send their loyalists into the two major parties. In these and a few other instances of statewide multipartyism in the recent American past, the period of multipartyism was brief and ended with a return to two-partyism.

The range of party system types among the fifty states, then, extends only the short way from the one-party system to the competitive two-party system. Drawing on the work of two other scholars, Austin Ranney recently divided the fifty state party systems into four categories: one-party Democratic, modified one-party Democratic, modified one-party Republican, and two-party (see Table 2). No states fell into a one-party Republican category. The Ranney rankings are based on a composite index of the popular vote for Democratic gubernatorial candidates, percentages of seats held by Democrats in the state legislature, and percentages of all the gubernatorial and state legislative terms the Democrats controlled. The resulting averages of those percentages yielded scores from 1.000 (complete Democratic success) to .000 (total Republican success); the scores are reported with the rankings in Table 2. The rankings are based wholly on state offices; they do not take into account the state's vote in presidential or senatorial elections. To some extent, therefore, they are isolated from the abnormal patterns of national politics that accompanied Lyndon Johnson's sweep in 1964 and George Wallace's incursions in 1968.[5]

[5] Austin Ranney, "Parties in State Politics" (Chap. 3) in Herbert Jacob and Kenneth Vines (eds.), Politics in the American States, 2nd ed. (Boston: Little, Brown, 1971), pp. 84–89. The Ranney categories are based on those of Richard Dawson and James Robinson, "Inter-Party Competition, Economic Variables, and Welfare Policies in the American States," Journal of Politics 25 (1963): 265–89. For other data and measures, see Paul T. David, Party Strength in the United States, 1872–1970 (Charlottesville: University of Virginia Press, 1972), updated with 1972 data in Paul T. David, "Party Strength in the United States: Changes in 1972," Journal of Politics 36 (1974): 785–96; Joseph A. Schlesinger, "A Two-Dimensional Scheme for Classifying the States According to Degree of Inter-Party Competition," American Political Science Review 49 (1955): 1120–28; David G. Pfeiffer, "The Measurement of Inter-Party Competition and Systemic Stability," American Political Science Review 61 (1967): 457–67; and Mark Stern, "Measuring Interparty Competition: A Proposal and a Test of a Model," Journal of Politics 34 (1972): 889–904. Despite the welter of measures and indices reported here, two scholars have found that there is a very high order of correlation among the results of the various measures. See Richard E. Zody and Norman R. Luttbeg, "An Evaluation of Various Measures of State Party Competition," Western Political Quarterly 21 (1968): 723–24.

TABLE 2   The Fifty States Classified according to Degree
of Interparty Competition: 1956–70

One-party Democratic	Modified one-party Democratic	Two-party		Modified one-party Republican
Louisiana (.9877)	North Carolina (.8332)	Hawaii (.6870)	New Jersey (.5122)	North Dakota (.3305)
Alabama (.9685)	Virginia (.8235)	Rhode Island (.6590)	Pennsylvania (.4800)	Kansas (.3297)
Mississippi (.9407)	Florida (.8052)	Massachusetts (.6430)	Colorado (.4725)	New Hampshire (.3282)
South Carolina (.9292)	Tennessee (.7942)	Alaska (.6383)	Michigan (.4622)	South Dakota (.3142)
Texas (.9132)	Maryland (.7905)	California (.6150)	Utah (.4565)	Vermont (.2822)
Georgia (.9080)	Oklahoma (.7792)	Nebraska (.6065)	Indiana (.4450)	
Arkansas (.8850)	Missouri (.7415)	Washington (.6047)	Illinois (.4235)	
	Kentucky (.7170)	Minnesota (.5910)	Wisconsin (.4102)	
	West Virginia (.7152)	Nevada (.5742)	Idaho (.4077)	
	New Mexico (.7150)	Connecticut (.5732)	Iowa (.3965)	
		Delaware (.5687)	Ohio (.3837)	
		Arizona (.5663)	New York (.3835)	
		Montana (.5480)	Maine (.3820)	
		Oregon (.5387)	Wyoming (.3537)	

Source   Herbert Jacob and Kenneth N. Vines, *Politics in the American States*, 2nd ed. (Boston: Little, Brown, 1971), p. 87. Reprinted by permission. The indices are constructed on data for 1956–70.

Useful as they are, such indices again do not fully reveal the complexities of party competition. One rarely finds competitiveness evenly spread throughout the politics of any one state. For example, Illinois in 1960 gave a bare .2 percent more of its popular vote to Kennedy than Nixon, yet more than half of its congressmen were elected in that same year by 60 percent or more of the vote. Or to concentrate on variations within state politics, gubernatorial elections generally reflect a more

intense competitiveness than do elections to the state legislature. Some
sixty governors were elected or reelected in the years 1972–74, and 83
percent of them were elected with less than 60 percent of the vote.[6]
Yet the state legislatures that were elected in the same period revealed
a partisan composition that belied the competitiveness in the election of
governors. Only in 37 percent of the houses of the state legislatures
did the percentage of Democratic legislators fall between 40 and 59
percent (Table 3). To be sure, some of the lack of partisan balance in
the American legislatures may be a result of very skillful drawing of
district lines. Yet with all allowances made, the patterns of competitiveness these data suggest are not the same patterns indicated by the data
from gubernatorial elections of the period.

TABLE 3   Size of Democratic Contingent
in Forty-nine American State
Legislatures: 1973

Percentage Democratic	Upper house	Lower house
0–19	0	0
20–39	8	9
40–59	18	18
60–79	14	12
80–100	9	10
	49	49

Source   Data from Book of the States, 1974–75.
Note   The total is only forty-nine because Nebraska has a nonpartisan legislature.

Thus it is difficult to speak even of a *state* party system. On close
inspection each one is found to be an aggregate of different competitive
patterns. It is not at all unusual for a party — even one that wins most
statewide elections — to have trouble filling its ticket in some local elections. Powerful officeholders can use a long term and the advantage of
office to build a personal following independent of party strength. For
the rest of their careers they may fend off competition and insulate
themselves from the patterns of normally competitive politics in their
states. In fact, nothing dampens two-party competition more effectively
than the power of incumbency, especially when it is exercised in a small
and homogeneous constituency.

[6] The data on the governors were drawn from the 1974 *Statistical Abstract of the
United States.*

THE CAUSES AND CONDITIONS OF TWO-PARTY SYSTEMS

Despite deviations to one-partyism, in its broad outlines the American party system has been and is a two-party system. Beyond all subtle variations in competition, there is the inescapable, crucial fact that almost all partisan political conflict in the United States has been channeled, however unevenly, through two great, enduring political parties. They rise and fall, they establish their own seats of strength, and they suffer their local weaknesses; but no political party since the Civil War has challenged their dualism. Perhaps even more remarkable is the fact that one does not easily find another democracy in which two parties have for so long contained the competitive electoral politics of the country. Even in Great Britain, progenitor of dual parties, three parties — the Conservatives, Liberals, and Labourites — have remained in some degree of competition since the turn of the century. Even in its present weakened position, the Liberal party won fourteen parliamentary seats in the 1974 elections on 20 percent of the popular vote.

The rareness of the two-party system among the democracies and its dominance in American politics have stimulated a very considerable explanatory effort. The question is an obvious one: Why should this one nation among so many others develop the two-party system? In the interests of an orderly attack on the problem, the most frequent explanations have been divided into four groups: the institutional, dualist, cultural, and consensual.

Institutional Theories

By far the most widespread explanation of the two-party system associates it with electoral and governmental institutions. In part it argues that single-member, plurality electoral systems produce two-party systems and that multimember constituencies and proportional representation result in multipartyism. Plurality election in a single-member district means simply that one candidate is elected and that the winner is the person who receives the largest number of votes. There are no second, third, and fourth seats for the trailing parties. In a system of proportional representation, on the other hand, a party polling 20 percent or so of a nation's votes may capture close to 20 percent of the legislative seats. The main purpose of proportional representation is to guarantee minorities representation roughly equal to their strength. That same 20 percent would win very few, if any, seats in the American plurality electoral system.[7] The American election system, therefore, offers

---

[7] Large numbers of states do have multimember districts for one or both houses of the state legislature. The fact that these districts have not altered the two-party system suggests that plurality election is more important than single-member districting in sustaining two-partyism.

no reward of office to any but the plurality winner, and, so the theory goes, the discouragement from repeated inabilities to win pluralities weeds out the chronic minority parties.

Many of the institutional theorists also argue the importance of the single national executive. The American presidency and the governorships, the main prizes of American politics, fall only to parties that can win pluralities. On the contrary, a cabinet in a European nation may be formed by a coalition that includes representatives of minority parties. In the palmiest days of multipartyism in the French Third and Fourth Republics, for instance, a party winning 10 or 15 percent of the national vote could and at times did capture the premiership. Again, in countries with a single national executive, the indivisible nature of the office favors the strongest competitors. Beyond the loss of the executive office, the minor party is denied the national leadership, the focus of the national campaign, the national spokesmen that so increasingly dominate the politics of the democracies. The necessity to contend for a national executive, in other words, works against the local or regional party, even those that may elect candidates in their own local bailiwicks.[8]

Dualist Theories

The dualists maintain that an underlying duality of interest in the American society has sustained the American two-party system. V. O. Key suggested that the initial sectional tension between the eastern financial and commercial interests and the western frontiersmen stamped itself on the parties in their incipient stages and fostered a two-party competition. Later the dualism shifted to the North–South conflict over the issue of slavery and the Civil War, and then to the present urban–rural or socioeconomic status divisions.[9] A related line of argument points to a "natural dualism" within democratic institutions: party in power versus party out of power, government versus opposition, pro and anti the status quo, and even the ideological dualism of liberal and conservative. Thus social and economic interests or the very processes of a democratic politics — or both — reduce the political contestants to two great camps, and that dualism gives rise to two political parties.

[8] The institutional theorists are best represented by Maurice Duverger, *Political Parties* (New York: Wiley, 1954), and E. E. Schattschneider, *Party Government* (New York: Rinehart, 1942).
[9] See, for example, V. O. Key, *Politics, Parties and Pressure Groups*, 5th ed. (New York: Crowell, 1964), pp. 229ff.; and James C. Charlesworth, "Is Our Two-Party System Natural?" American Academy of Political and Social Science *Annals* 259 (1948): 1–9.

Cultural Theories

This school of explanation in many ways smacks of the older, largely discredited national character theories. It maintains that the United States and Britain have nurtured two-party systems because of their "political maturity" or their "genius for government." More modestly, it attributes the two-party systems to the development of a political culture that accepts the necessity of compromise, the wisdom of short-term pragmatism, and the avoidance of unyielding dogmatism. The Americans and Britons, in other words, are willing to make the kinds of accommodations necessary to bring their heterogeneous citizenries into two political parties. Then as they develop the dual parties, their political cultures also develop the attitudes and norms that endorse the two-party system as a desirable end in itself.

Social Consensus Theories

Finally, the American party system has been explained in terms of a wide-sweeping American social consensus. Despite a diverse cultural heritage and society, Americans early achieved a consensus on the fundamentals that divide other societies. Virtually all Americans have traditionally accepted the prevailing social, economic, and political institutions. They accept the Constitution and its governmental apparatus, a regulated but free enterprise economy, and (perhaps to a lesser extent) American patterns of social class and status.

In the traditional multiparty countries such as France and Italy, substantial chunks of political opinion have favored radical changes in those and other basic institutions. They have supported programs of fundamental constitutional change, the socialization of the economy, or the disestablishment of the Church. Whether because Americans were spared feudalism and its rigid classes or because they have had a fortuitously expanding economic and geographic frontier, they have escaped the division on fundamentals that racks the other democracies and gives rise to large numbers of irreconcilable political divisions. Since the matters that divide Americans are secondary, so the argument goes, the compromises necessary to bring them into one of two major parties are easier to make.[10]

In appraising these explanations of the American two-party system, one has to ask some searching questions. Are the factors proposed in these explanations *causes* of the two-party system or are they effects of

[10] See Leslie Lipson, "The Two-Party System in British Politics," *American Political Science Review* 47 (1953): 337–58.

it? The chances are that they are, at least in part, effects. Certainly two competitive parties will choose and perpetuate electoral systems that do not offer entrée to minor parties. They will also channel opinion into alternatives, reducing and forcing the system's complexities into their dual channels. The two-party system will also create, foster, and perpetuate the political values and attitudes that justify and protect itself. It will even foster some measure of social consensus by denying competitive opportunities to movements that challenge the great consensus of the status quo.

Although these factors may be effects of the two-party system, they are also certainly causes. But if they are, why has the two-party system been such a comparatively rare phenomenon? If single-member constituencies and plurality elections explain American two-partyism, why did they not produce a similar outcome in Third Republic France? Moreover, American society is not the first to have an overriding duality of interests in its politics. The socioeconomic class divisions between "haves" and "have-nots" have plagued no small number of democracies without leading to a two-party system. The implication seems clear that no one of these theories alone can explain the virtual uniqueness of the American party system.

At the risk of fence straddling, one may venture to suggest that all four explanations illuminate the development of the American party system. No one of them need exclude the impact of any other. Their unique combination has produced a unique two-party system. At the root of the explanation lies the basic, long-run American consensus on fundamental beliefs. No deep rifts over the kind of economy, society, or government we want have traditionally marked our politics. More than one European observer has remarked on the resulting nonideological character of American politics. Consensus has been fostered by American education and social assimilation, aided by two major parties inhospitable to challenges to that consensus. It is not easy now, of course, to talk confidently of a consensus in American life. But if the consensus has broken down to some extent, it has happened well after the American two-party system was established and deeply entrenched.

Lacking cause for deep ideological divisions and disagreeing on few fundamentals, Americans were easily formed into two conglomerate, majority-seeking political parties. The institutions of American government — such as single-member constituencies, plurality elections, and the single executive — were free to exert their power to limit the parties to two without having to repulse countervailing pressures of social division. So, too, in the absence of deeply felt ideologies, a pragmatic opposition to the party in power was easily able to develop a dualism of the "ins" and "outs." And once the two-party system was launched, its very existence then fostered the values of moderation, compromise, and political pragmatism which ensure its perpetuation. The system created deep loyalties within the American public to one party or the other and deep loyalties to the genius of the two-party system itself.

EXCURSIONS INTO ONE-PARTYISM

To argue the existence of only two competitive parties is not to argue that their competitiveness is spread evenly over the country. There are substantial statewide and local pockets of one-partyism in the United States. The states of the Deep South until recently spent very close to their own "four score and seven" years as the country's most celebrated area of one-party domination. Much the same could be said of the rock-like Republicanism of Maine, New Hampshire, and Vermont. And scattered throughout the country are thousands of one-party cities, towns, and counties, in which city hall or the county courthouse comes perilously close to being the property of one party. Just as important, therefore, as the question of the causes of the two-party system is the question of the causes of one-partyism within it.

One-partyism set within the context of broad, two-party competitiveness normally reflects a "fault" in the distribution of the electorates of the competitive parties. Since the 1930s the major American parties, especially in national elections, have divided the American electorate roughly along lines of socioeconomic status and issues — a point that will be developed later. Suffice it here to note that Democratic loyalties have been far more common among ethnic, racial, and religious minority groups, the urban workers, and lower socioeconomic status (SES) groups in general. The Republicans, on the other hand, have drawn a disproportionate number of loyalists from higher status and rural groups.

One-partyism, first of all, may result from some potent local basis of party loyalty that overrides the SES dualism. In the classic one-partyism of the American South, regional loyalties long overrode the factors that were dividing Americans into two parties in most of the rest of the country. Reaction to the Republican party as the party of abolition, Lincoln, the Civil War, and the hated Reconstruction was so pervasive, even three generations after the fact, that the impact of the SES division was precluded. Even today, the South may be in the process of trading in a one-partyism based on the events of the nineteenth century for a new one-partyism based on more recent racial antagonism. In either event, it is a one-partyism based on isolation from the factors that normally produce two-party competitiveness.

Second, one-partyism may result from a maldistribution of the characteristics that normally divide the parties. The local constituency may be too small to contain a perfect sample of SES characteristics and thus of nationally competitive politics. Hence the noncompetitiveness of the "safe" Democratic congressional districts of the older, lower-middle-class neighborhoods of the cities and the "safe" Republican districts of the more fashionable and spacious suburbs. In other words, the more heterogeneous are its people, the more likely the district is to foster competitiveness.

Empirical studies of one-partyism suggest, however, that its causes are far more complex than these two possibilities. Competitiveness has been associated with general socioeconomic diversity in the constituency — especially with urbanism and its industrialism, higher income levels, and ethnic diversity. Yet the relationships are not always strong or dramatic, and one recent study finds no such relationships at all.[11] We are thus left more or less to conjecture. Perhaps a homogeneous district cut from the middle range of SES factors tends to be more competitive than an equally homogeneous district at either the top or the bottom of the SES spectrum. Alternatively, in some localities the patterns of competitiveness may have little to do with patterns of national SES politics or with any other characteristics of the electorate. They may instead reflect the influences of local personages, of powerful officeholders, of local traditions, or of political conflict such as that between a dominant local industry and its disgruntled employees.

One may also look at these pockets of one-partyism another way. The American party system is made up of two electorally competitive parties, which is really to say that it is formed by two parties competing to enlist a majority of the American electorate. The active, initiating sectors of the party — the party organization and the party in government — recruit and enlist the support of the electorate with assorted appeals. If these two parties were fully competitive in every constituency in the country, they would approach a fifty-fifty division of the electorate. They must, however, compete at various disadvantages, and frequently in some area or locality one party works at a disadvantage

[11] Charles M. Bonjean and Robert L. Lineberry, "The Urbanization–Party Competition Hypothesis: A Comparison of All United States Counties," *Journal of Politics* 32 (1970): 305–21. For a further introduction to the study of the correlates of competitiveness in the American party system, see the Ranney chapter in Jacob and Vines, *Politics in the American States*, 2nd ed., pp. 89–91; V. O. Key, *American State Politics* (New York: Knopf, 1956), pp. 227–46; Heinz Eulau, "The Ecological Basis of Party Systems: The Case of Ohio," *Midwest Journal of Political Science* 1 (1957): 125–35; David Gold and John R. Schmidhauser, "Urbanization and Party Competition: The Case of Iowa," ibid. 4 (1960): 62–75; Phillips Cutright, "Urbanization and Competitive Party Politics," *Journal of Politics* 25 (1963): 552–64; Thomas W. Casstevens and Charles O. Press, "The Context of Democratic Competition in American State Politics," *American Journal of Sociology* 68 (1963): 536–43; and Robert Golembiewski, "A Taxonomic Approach to State Political Party Strength," *Western Political Quarterly* 11 (1958): 494–513. The reader who explores this literature should be aware both of the varying definitions of competition and urbanness and of the difference between competitiveness of states and competitiveness of subdivisions (e.g., counties) within states.

that it never manages to overcome. The result is the ability of the other party to maintain a one-party domination. The understanding of one-partyism, then, requires an understanding of the various kinds of competitive disadvantages a party may face.

The competitive disadvantages may begin with immobile electorates. Voters are not easily moved from their attachments to a party, even though the reasons for the original attachment have long passed. Also, a party trying to pull itself into competitiveness may find itself caught in a vicious circle of impotence. Its inability to win elections limits its ability to recruit resources, including manpower, because as a chronic loser it offers so little chance of achieving political goals. It may even find itself without an effective appeal to the electorate. The Republican party in the South, for example, found for many years that the Democrats had preempted the salient political issues in that region.

Today the would-be competitive party finds the disadvantage taking another form: the formation of party loyalties along lines determined by national or statewide political debate. If the Democratic party is identified nationally with the aspirations of the poor and minority groups, its appeal in a homogeneous, affluent suburb may be limited. Increasingly, national politics may thus rob the local party organization of the chance to develop strength based on its own issues, personalities, and traditions. To the extent that party loyalties and identifications grow out of national politics, patterns of competitiveness (and the lack of them) may be largely determined for the local party organizations.

There are, to be sure, other sources of competitive disadvantage. The dominant party may shore up its supremacy by carefully calculated legislative districting. In the past the southern Democrats stifled potential competitiveness by artificially restricting the electorates to middle-class whites. In other instances majority parties have supported nonpartisanship in local elections as a way of drawing on their one-party consensus. In addition to these institutional buttresses to one-partyism, of course, powerful party organization and sedulous canvasing can maintain superiority. The normal processes of socialization and social conformity also work to the disadvantage of a party trying to become competitive. That force of conformity, a number of observers have argued, works especially against competitiveness in the closely knit, socially sensitive world of American suburbia.

THE "ALSO-RANS": THE THIRD PARTIES

By the middle 1960s it appeared that minor parties in American politics were in a steady, irreversible decline. They garnered only a few more than 200,000 votes in the 1960 presidential elections, and in 1964 their aggregate total slipped to 126,000. The most potent of them in 1964, the

Socialist Labor Party, attracted 45,186 voters, a miniscule .06 percent of the popular vote. In 1964 the minor parties in total accounted for less than .2 percent. In the Johnson landslide they clearly made no perceptible difference. Indeed, since 1924 no organized third party had carried a single state in a presidential election.[12] Thus in the mid-1960s a number of commentators were prepared to bid a nostalgic farewell to minor party influence in American politics. Then in 1968 George C. Wallace swaggered into national attention, frightened the major parties, won over 13 percent of the popular vote, and carried five states. Even though the 1972 minor party vote fell far short of 1968's, it nonetheless was more than ten times greater than in 1964 (see Table 4). In any event, it is now clear that the death notices of the minor parties were distinctly premature.

The very looseness with which we customarily use the term *third party* to designate all minor parties may indicate that third place is as good (or bad) as last place in a two-party system. But it would be a serious mistake to treat the minor parties as indistinguishable. They differ in origin, purpose, and function, and American political history of the past one hundred years affords a rich variety of their activity to illustrate those differences.[13]

Although it is true, first of all, that most minor parties are parties of ideology and issue, they differ in the scope of that commitment. The narrow, highly specific commitment of the Prohibitionist and Vegetarian parties is apparent in their names. In the 1840s the Liberty party and its successor, the Free Soil party, campaigned largely on the single issue of the abolition of slavery. At the other extremes are the parties having the broadest ideological commitments — the Marxist parties and the recent profusion of conservative parties, for example — whose program is the major reconstruction of social, economic, and political institutions. In the middle ground between specific issues and total ideologies, the examples are infinitely varied. The farmer-labor parties of economic protest — Greenback, Populist, and Progressive parties — ran on an extensive program of government regulation of the economy (especially of

---

[12] In 1948 J. Strom Thurmond carried four states, but he won them as the officially listed candidate of the Democratic parties in those states. In 1960 the major parties failed to carry some electors from Alabama and Mississippi, but the winners in all cases ran on unpledged slates.

[13] The literature on American third parties is rich and varied. Among the best contributions are John D. Hicks, *The Populist Revolt* (Minneapolis: University of Minnesota Press, 1931); Richard Hofstadter, *The Age of Reform* (New York: Knopf, 1955); David A. Shannon, *The Socialist Party of America* (New York: Macmillan, 1955); K. M. Schmidt, *Henry A. Wallace: Quixotic Crusade 1948* (Syracuse: Syracuse University Press, 1960); George Thayer, *The Farther Shores of Politics* (New York: Simon and Schuster, 1967); Marshall Frady, *Wallace* (New York: World, 1968); and Daniel A. Mazmanian, *Third Parties in Presidential Elections* (Washington: Brookings, 1974).

TABLE 4   Popular Votes Cast for Minor Parties in 1968
and 1972 Presidential Elections

Parties: 1968	Vote: 1968	Parties: 1972	Vote: 1972
American Independent	9,906,141	American	1,080,541
New	74,435	People's	78,801
Socialist Labor	52,588	Socialist Workers	65,290
Socialist Workers	41,300	Socialist Labor	53,614
Peace and Freedom	36,385	Communist	25,222
Prohibition	14,519	Prohibition	13,444
Communist	1,075	Libertarian	2,691
Scattered	19,606	America First	1,743
		Universal	199
		Scattered	23,959
	10,146,049		1,345,504

Source   The data for both years come from the Associated Press's final compila-
tion of official returns as reported in the *New York Times*, December 12, 1968, and
December 22, 1972.

Note   The American Independent party of 1968 and the American party of 1972
are substantially the same party, although George Wallace was its presidential candidate in 1968 and former congressman John G. Schmitz ran in 1972. The best
known of the other candidates in 1972 was Dr. Benjamin Spock, the presidential
candidate of the People's Party. Finally, it is only fair to note that the collection
and counting of third-party votes leave a great deal to be desired in some states.
There is some reason to think, especially, that the votes of minor parties are under-
counted, at least in some parts of some states.

economic bigness) and social welfare legislation. The Progressive party
of 1948 — at least that part of it separate from the Communist party —
combined a program of social reform and civil liberties with a foreign
policy of friendship with the Soviet Union and reduction of Cold War
tensions.

The minor parties differ, too, in their origin. Some were literally im-
ported into the United States. Much of the early Socialist party strength
in the United States came from the freethinkers and radicals who fled
Europe after the failures of the revolutions of 1848. Socialist strength
in cities such as Milwaukee, New York, and Cincinnati reflected the
concentrations of liberal German immigrants there. Other parties —
especially the Granger and Populist parties and their successors — were
parties of indigenous social protest, born of social inequality and economic hardship on the marginal farmlands of America. Other minor
parties began as splinters or factions of one of the major parties. The
Gold Democrats of 1896, the Progressives (the Bull Moose party) of
1912, and the Dixiecrats of 1948 come to mind. So great were their ob-

jections to the platform and candidates of their parent parties that the Progressives and Dixiecrats contested the presidential elections of 1912 and 1948 with their own slates and programs.

Recent presidential elections have seen the entry of a new variety of minor party: the "nonparty." Found chiefly in the southern states, these nonparties have been dissident movements within the Democratic party that have refused to run as separate parties on the ballot. They have exploited two other strategies instead. In some instances they have attempted to run their own candidate (rather than the one chosen by the party's national convention) as the official presidential candidate of the Democratic party in the state. The only four states which J. Strom Thurmond carried in 1948 for the Dixiecrats were those (Alabama, Louisiana, Mississippi, and South Carolina) in which he, rather than Harry Truman, was the candidate of the Democratic party. George Wallace also captured the Alabama Democratic label in 1968, displacing Hubert Humphrey as the Democratic candidate in that state. In other cases these party movements have run unpledged slates of presidential electors. In 1960 unpledged slates ran in Louisiana as a States Rights party and in Mississippi as the Democratic party (although there was another Democratic party ticket pledged to Kennedy). In 1964 another unpledged Democratic slate of electors ran in Alabama and prevented the Johnson-Humphrey ticket from appearing on the Alabama ballot.

Finally, the third parties differ in their tactics. For some their mere existence is a protest against what they believe is the unqualified support of the status quo that the major parties afford. That position certainly characterized the candidacy in 1968 of Eldridge Cleaver on behalf of the Peace and Freedom party. Operating as a political party also offers a reasonably effective educational opportunity. The publicity of the ballot is good, and with it often goes mass-media attention the party could not otherwise hope for. Many of these parties have indeed freely accepted their electoral failures, for they have by their very nature chosen ideological principles over electoral success. They have refused to make the pragmatic compromises that working within a major party entails.

But other minor parties do have serious electoral ambitions. Often their goal is local, although today they find it difficult to control an American city as the Socialists did, or an entire state as the Progressives did. More realistically today, they may hope to hold a balance of power between the major parties in the manner of the Liberals in New York. In the 1965 mayoral election, for instance, John Lindsay's vote on the Republican ticket was less than that of his Democratic opponent; his vote reached the necessary plurality only with the addition of the votes he won in the Liberal party column. Or a party may, as did the Dixiecrats of 1948 and Wallace's American Independent party of 1968, play for the biggest stakes of all: the presidency. Both parties hoped that by carrying a number of states, most likely southern states, they might prevent the major party tickets from winning the necessary majority of votes in the electoral college and thus throw the stalemated election into the House of Representatives. The Wallace effort of 1968 faltered because Richard Nixon carried a number of large states, although by small margins in the popular vote.

It is certainly these parties of electoral opportunity that have generally enjoyed the minor party successes of recent years. The more traditional, stable parties of ideology, which Norman Thomas and the Socialists so long typified in American politics, do indeed seem in decline. Parties such as George Wallace's American party, which is little more than an extension of the ambition of one man, appear to be the type of minor party presently to be reckoned with. In a similar vein, Eugene McCarthy has also flirted with third-party opportunities since his 1968 rebuff in Democratic politics. The loosening of party loyalties to the two major parties and the ease with which a popular, attractive candidate becomes known through television and the other mass media make these parties feasible.

George Wallace's relations with minor political parties have always been distant and more than a little hesitant. There has, at least, been no sign of attachment or loyalty to one. After his candidacy with the American Independent party in 1968, he backed away from leadership of the party, even discouraging its efforts to broaden its base and to support other candidates. For help and support he turned to a personal staff and organization rather than to any party's leadership. By 1971 Wallace was in fact contesting within the Democratic party for convention delegates when he was shot. Less than four years later Wallace was again planning to contest the Democratic primaries. At the same time, however, he was reported to be maintaining close ties with the Committee on Constitutional Alternatives, a conservative group composed largely of Republicans, which for its part was maintaining ties with Ronald Reagan as a possible alternative to President Gerald Ford. To say the least, George Wallace was keeping his partisan options open. The Wallace history, in fact, has always been one of personal candidacy. The political party has merely been a vehicle, perhaps not much more than the degree of organization required by the states for a place on the ballot.

The more conventional, less purely electoral third party has had some rebirth in recent ethnic and racial politics.[14] The Mississippi Freedom Democratic party had its time of greatest national visibility when it challenged the seating of the regular party's delegation to the 1964

[14] For example, see Hanes Walton, Jr., *Black Political Parties: A Historical and Political Analysis* (New York: Free Press, 1972).

Democratic National Convention. Since then the National Democratic Party of Alabama (NDPA) has become the premier example. Founded in 1968, it nominated a biracial slate of ninety-one candidates in that year, electing twenty-three of them to assorted local offices. Its ticket was headed in 1968 by the Humphrey-Muskie duo; the regular Democrats ran a slate of electors pledged to the presidential candidacy of George Wallace. In 1970 it again supported a slate of candidates, including its own party chairman, Dr. John Cashin, as gubernatorial candidate. Of that group of candidates twelve were winners. More recently in 1972 Chicanos formed their own party, La Raza Unida. It has been slow to achieve electoral success.

The variety is endless, and the future is uncertain. But what have the minor parties contributed in the past to the American political processes? The answer, to be candid, is that they have not assumed the importance that the attention lavished on them suggests. "More interesting than influential" must be the verdict.

One line of argument has persistently maintained that the minor parties' early adoption of unpopular programs has ultimately forced the major parties to adopt them. Its proponents point to the platforms of the Socialist party in the years before the 1930s. The issue is whether or not the Socialists' advocacy of such measures as a minimum wage for twenty or thirty years had anything to do with their enactment in the 1930s. There is unfortunately no way of testing what might have happened had there been no Socialist party. But the evidence suggests that the major parties grasp new programs and proposals in their "time of ripeness" — when large numbers of Americans have done so and when such a course, therefore, is politically useful to the parties. In their prior maturing time, new issues need not depend on minor parties for their advocacy. Interest groups, the mass media, influential individuals, and factions within the major parties may perform the propagandizing role, often more effectively than a minor party. More than one commentator has noted that the cause of prohibition in the United States was far more effectively served by interest groups such as the Anti-Saloon League than by the Prohibition party.

There remains, however, the impact that the minor parties have had on elections. Increasingly that impact depends both on the nature of major party competition and on the distribution of strength of the minor party. Magnitude of strength alone is beyond them; since the Civil War only four minor party candidates for the presidency have polled more than 10 percent of the popular vote.[15] We have already

---

[15] They were James B. Weaver (1892, Populist), Theodore Roosevelt (1912, Progressive), Robert La Follette (1924, Progressive), and George Wallace (1968, American Independent).

mentioned the strategic facts that maximized the opportunities of the Dixiecrats in 1948: regional concentration in the South, the close competition of the two major parties, and the complicating presence (especially in New York) of the Henry Wallace Progressives. In 1912 the impact of the Bull Moose Progressives was sufficient to cut sharply into regular Republican (Taft) strength and permit Woodrow Wilson to enter the White House with less than 40 percent of the popular vote. In 1968, the Wallace candidacy so threatened the majority election of the president that it almost toppled the electoral college itself. In brief, the electoral power of the minor parties depends on special situations in which it can make itself a shifting weight between two massive, finely balanced major parties.

WHITHER THE AMERICAN TWO-PARTY SYSTEM?

George Wallace's lawyers stood before the United States Supreme Court in early October of 1968 to plead that the Court strike down Ohio election law and permit Wallace's name to be printed on the ballot in that state as a presidential candidate. It was a scene awash in irony. Wallace had often excoriated the Court for its willingness to invalidate the laws of states in order to protect the rights of individuals, and now his attorneys were making substantially that request. The Ohio law in question had been passed in 1948 in order to prevent the third-party candidacy of Henry Wallace in that state. The law required that a new and unestablished party collect a number of signatures equal to 15 percent of the votes cast in the last statewide election — a percentage which required the Wallace forces to muster 433,000 signatures in 1968. In addition, the Ohio law required those petitions to be submitted in early February, a time far earlier than most campaigns are mobilized. It also prohibited independent, nonparty candidacies.

In its own defense the state of Ohio did not deny its intentions. The law was intended, the state freely conceded, to work to the very great disadvantage of any other than the two established parties. The state argued that it had a legitimate interest in preserving the existing two-party system, in preventing a division of the vote among a number of parties, and ultimately making sure that minority candidates would not win elections. The discrimination against third parties was, in other words, the avowed policy of the state of Ohio. The argument did not sway the Supreme Court, and by a vote of six to three the Court struck down the Ohio law for violating the equal protection clause of the Fourteenth Amendment. Justice Black, speaking for the Court, asserted that the Ohio law imposed an unconstitutional burden on the rights of voting and association and that it discriminated against supporters of minor parties. And thus with the help of the Supreme Court did George Wallace place his name on the Ohio ballot in November of 1968.[16]

The morals and lessons of the story of Wallace against the State of Ohio are many. To some extent, at least, it marked the end of argument that it is constitutionally proper to support and preserve the two-party system with electoral law that discriminates against third-party competitors. It also signaled the extraordinary success of Wallace in surmounting the obstacles that separate the minor party from effective, competitive status in American politics. Victory over Ohio law gave him access to his fiftieth state ballot in November 1968. Over and beyond all these points, however, Wallace's success suggests answers to the question of the future of third parties in American politics.

The Wallace campaign of 1968 can indeed be viewed as a triumph over virtually all the obstacles that law and circumstance place in the way of minor parties. First of all, he won a place on the ballot of every state, and that took no small amount of organization. To be sure, a number of states presented no particular barriers; a mere three hundred signatures sufficed to get his name on the ballot in Colorado. But heroic efforts were necessary in states such as Ohio and California. California law requires far fewer signatures than Ohio — actually only a few more than 66,000 — but it requires that those supporters reregister as voters and as new members of the American Independent party. That is to say, they must go through the formal step of ceasing to be Democrats or Republicans and listing themselves on the voter rolls of California as members of the new party. As an aftermath of his struggle for ballot position, Wallace also left behind a decision of the United States Supreme Court that will prevent states from passing unreasonable or discriminatory electoral laws in the future.

Second, Wallace in 1968 surmounted what had become extraordinary financial problems for most third parties. Most of them had been squeezed into oblivion by their failure to raise sums large enough to engage in the costly campaigning of the day. Campaigns based on the mass media, on armies of advertising and public relations specialists, and on polls and surveys cost increasingly large sums of money. The Wallace campaign astounded observers of American political finance by raising and spending some $7 million, by far the largest sum ever spent by a minor party campaign in American history. So successful were Wallace fund-raising activities that he left the 1968 campaign with a surplus estimated to be in excess of $1 million.

George Wallace also solved — to some extent — the problem of a minor party's becoming a national party. Almost all the effective minor

[16] *Williams* v. *Rhodes*, 393 U.S. 23 (1968).

party activity of the past century has been intensely provincial. Each of the minor parties has been concentrated in one state or region, or in a city or two, of the country. Socialists came from Germany in the middle of the nineteenth century and established Socialist enclaves in cities such as New York, Milwaukee, and Cincinnati. Or, to take another example, regional agricultural depressions gave rise to Populism and other similar movements of the plains and prairies. Traditionally, third parties fed on local, provincial loyalties, interests, and appeals, but those appeals have increasingly lost out in a mobile society that receives the same political messages via the same radio and television networks, the same magazines, and the same press services and syndicated columnists. In this nationalization of American life, a political party's national image and national leaders increasingly dominate the responses of voters — to the obvious disadvantage of a regional or local party which has no national visibility and no candidates to give it a national presence. Although the only states George Wallace carried in 1968 were five in the Deep South, he did indeed carry his message to all the states as a national political figure of consequence.

What, then, can be predicted as a future for minor parties in American politics? Until the Wallace success of 1968 the future had seemed bleak. No candidate of an organized minor party carried even a single state in a presidential election between 1924 and 1968. Perhaps the Wallace candidacy best indicates the extraordinary difficulties a minor-party candidate has in becoming a nationally important candidate. But the resurgence of some other minor parties marked recent elections (see Table 4). Conservatives and Liberals also appear to thrive in New York, at least in part because of the quirk of that state's electoral law that permits a candidate to run on the tickets of both a minor party and a major party. But only sheer ideological fervor can explain the fact that in 1970 the Conservatives elected a United States senator. It does appear, however, that we are seeing the death throes of some of the oldest and pluckiest of the third parties. The day of the Socialist parties, not to mention the Prohibitionist party, may have passed. We may be seeing the emergence instead of minor parties with concerns and ideologies more closely attuned to the issues of the 1970s.

While the future of the minor parties seems uncertain, one can with confidence point to a second general trend in the American party system: the increasing competitiveness of the major parties. It is probably safe to say that in national and statewide politics we are in a period of the most intense, evenly spread, two-party competitiveness of the last one hundred years. There are no regions of the country, and very few states, that can be thought of as one-party areas. Even the once-solid Democratic South is solid no more. Republican Barry Goldwater in

1964 and Richard Nixon in 1972 carried Alabama, Georgia, Louisiana, Mississippi, and South Carolina; in 1968 George Wallace carried all but South Carolina and added Arkansas to them.

To take the longer view, presidents have been increasingly winning with popular vote percentages that vary less and less from one state to another. Table 5 indicates that the standard deviations of the presidents' popular vote in the states from the national average have been diminishing in this century. In other words, presidents are no longer carrying some states by fat margins while losing others in a similarly lopsided way. As the overwhelming votes of the one-party states are eliminated, presidential candidates tend to amass more nearly uniform vote percentages all across the country. Competitiveness, then, is spreading increasingly across the fifty states.

TABLE 5   Standard Deviations of Presidential Percentages of the Popular Vote in the States: 1896–1972

Year	Standard deviation	Year	Standard deviation
1896	17.5	1936	12.6
1900	14.0	1940	13.4
1904	18.8	1944	12.3
1908	14.9	1948	9.8
1912	15.8	1952	8.5
1916	13.4	1956	8.3
1920	16.1	1960	5.8
1924	16.0	1964	10.3
1928	13.5	1968	9.7
1932	14.0	1972	6.6

Note The standard deviation is a measure of the distance of the dispersal of items from the average. It discriminates, therefore, among the dispersals of the following three series: 3, 6, 9; 4, 6, 8; and 5, 6, 7. Even though the means and the medians of the three series would be identical (6), the standard deviations would decline in the order in which the three series are listed.

This spread of major party competitiveness reflects the same nationalization of life and politics in the United States that threatens local minor parties. It is increasingly difficult for one major party to maintain its dominance on the basis of appeals and traditions quite different from those in the rest of the country — as, for example, the Democrats did in the South from 1875 to 1950. Furthermore, the social and economic conditions that support one-partyism are disappearing. Fading especially are the political monopolies of powerful groups that once dominated the politics of a single state from a base in cotton, copper, oil, silver, or organized labor. As Americans move about the country, as industry comes to formerly agrarian states, as more and varied people move to the urban centers, each state becomes a better sample of the diversity of life and interest that undergirds the competition between the two major parties. National mass media and national political leaders also bring the symbols and dialectics of Democratic-Republican conflict to all corners of the country. Thus the party electorates are increasingly recruited by the appeals of national candidates and issues — regardless of whatever special appeals the local party organization makes.

State party organizations and leaders, conversely, cannot hold out against the political issues and images that engulf the rest of the country. They cannot easily set up their own competitive subsystem. As a result, a creeping competitiveness accompanies the end of one-partyism at the state level. First, the states become competitive in national elections, and then the old one-party ties and fears slowly break down, and competition seeps down to local elections. Pennsylvania, for example, became competitive in presidential politics in the 1930s after forty years of domination by the GOP; by the 1950s and 1960s the state was competitive in state and local politics. In the 1960s and 1970s the same process was under way in a number of southern states.

Ironically, the increasing degree of two-party competition has created a set of vexing problems for the American parties. By eliminating pockets of one-party strength, the new competitiveness eliminates a source of stability in the party system. When a party holds noncompetitive strongholds of its own, it can survive even a catastrophic national loss through victories and continued office holding in its own areas of strength. Without those one-party strongholds to fall back on, a losing party in the future may find its loss more sweeping and devastating. Also the spread of two-party competitiveness expands the scope of party competition and thus makes extra demands for the resources the parties must employ. When one-party areas could be written off in a presidential campaign and election, the area of political combat was reduced. Now the parties must mobilize and organize more resources than ever before, for a presidential campaign has to be fought in fifty rather than in thirty states.

POLITICAL PARTIES, THE PARTY SYSTEM, AND DEMOCRACY

Scholars of the American parties have not hesitated to place them at the very center of the democratic processes. Some, indeed, have proclaimed them the originators of those processes. Such claims often commit the fallacy of "party primacy." [17] In any event, there is no need to press the claim that far. What is incontestable is the fact that political parties are deeply involved in the democratic processes by which large numbers of American adults register their political demands and affect the decisions of government. And what is truly important is that the political party — or any other component of the American political system — can finally be assessed only in terms of its role in the democratic politics of the American society.

At the most fundamental level the American parties, and those of the other democracies, serve democracy by reaffirming and promoting its basic values. The very activities of the two gigantic and diversified American parties promote a commitment to the values of compromise, moderation, and the pursuit of limited goals. They encourage the political activity and participation that a democracy depends on. And they reinforce the basic democratic rules of the game: the methods and procedures of orderly criticism and opposition, change by the regular electoral processes, and deference to the will of the majority. These reaffirmations of the democratic ethos the parties achieve in part by the example of their operations and in part by their clarification and simplification of political choices.

In addition, the parties offer an operating mechanism for the processes of democracy. They are mobilizers of both democratic consent and dissent. By channeling choices into a few realistic alternatives, they organize the majorities by which the country is governed. Because of the parties' simplification of political choices, the average citizen, often distracted by personal worries and limited in background, can participate more meaningfully in the affairs of politics. The party is, moreover, the instrument of compromise among competing claims on public policy. Interest groups generally represent a specific, comparatively narrow interest, but the party must bring together a wider range of interests. To put the matter briefly, the political parties have helped fashion a workable system of representation for the mass democracies of the twentieth century. They have offered the many a vehicle for mobilizing their major political asset, their sheer numbers, thereby permitting them to counter the social and economic advantages of small groups and powerful individuals.

Nothing better illustrates the relationship of the political party to democracy than its origin. The major political parties of the United States and the other Western democracies arose in the late eighteenth and nineteenth centuries as a concomitant of the spread of democratic ideologies and electorates. What had been largely legislative caucuses in the United States expanded shortly after the beginning of the nine-

---

[17] Note the quotation from Schattschneider in Part One, p. 5, *supra.*

teenth century into constituency-based parties as the states expanded
the male suffrage by wiping out property-owning and tax-paying qualifications for the vote. Between 1800 and 1850 the mass convention as a
way of selecting party candidates replaced the legislative caucus, and
state and local party organizations blossomed.

A leading scholar of the origins of the American parties has sum-
marized their genesis well:

Parties proper are, apparently, the products of certain types of social-struc-
tural conditions and ideological configurations which have come to characterize political modernization as it has taken place in western societies. The
relevant social conditions appear to be those which are related to the absence
or dissolution of closed, traditionalistic, and hierarchical social structures and
modes of conducting politics. The relevant ideologies appear to be those which
point to mass or democratic involvement or participation in the political process. In short, parties proper appear to be products of the process of modernization and the emergence of mass or democratic politics, and of democratic
or plebiscitarian ideologies — and at the same time to be themselves steps
toward political modernization.[18]

Thus the political party has been the effect as well as the cause of the
political participation of the great number of adults. Its rise and growth
directly parallel the development of popular democracy not only in the
United States but in Great Britain as well. Shortly after the Reform
Act of 1832 had added some 250,000 voters to the British electorate
and eliminated some of the unrepresentative parliamentary constituencies (the pocket and rotten boroughs), the parties in Parliament set up
registration associations in all the constituencies to mobilize and compete for the new voters. Those constituency associations slowly increased their ties and loyalties to the parliamentary parties, creating the
party structures of contemporary Britain.[19]

As the parties were being formed and shaped by the emerging democratic forces, they also helped democratize the institutions within which
they worked. As agencies of the newly expanded electorate, they trans-
formed the legislature into a truly representative assembly, and at the
local level they became the first public instruments for mass political
participation. Even though they are nowhere mentioned in the elegant

[18] William N. Chambers, "Party Development and Party Action: The American
Origins," History and Theory 3 (1963): 117. See also his book on the beginning
of the American parties, Political Parties in a New Nation (New York: Oxford University Press, 1963).
[19] For an excellent, brief summary of the development of political parties, see Ranney and Kendall, Democracy and the American Party System, Chap. 5. For a pioneering history of the development of parties in Britain and the United States there
is an abridgment of Moisei Ostrogorski's Democracy and the Organization of Political Parties edited by Seymour Martin Lipset (New York: Anchor, 1964).

brevity of the American Constitution, the democratization of that document was in part achieved by the parties. For an example one has only to look at the transformation of the electoral college that party voting wrought. What began as a meeting of notables to pick a leading notable for the presidency soon became merely the instrument for recording the preferences of popular majorities for a party-sponsored presidential candidate through party-disciplined electors.

It is precisely, too, its relationship to democratic processes that makes the two-party system so highly valued. It is the two-party system that mobilizes majorities, makes sure that candidates have the mandate of a majority behind them, and organizes the opposition to the majority in power. Behind the widespread preference for the two-party system lurks the experience of other democracies with multipartyism. The parade of unstable, coalition governments, the endless shifting of majorities, the frequent immobility of governments, the splintered confusion of choices facing voters, the almost prismatic refraction of ideologies into endless hues and colors — these have been the consequences of multipartyism in the experience of many Western democracies. By sheer contrast, and perhaps even by a little smugness, the value of two-partyism seems so great. The fear of multipartyism and the consequences it would have for the American democracy is a recurrent theme in American politics. It, along with less worthy motives perhaps, was behind Ohio's attempt to keep third parties off its ballot. It is also a major reason for hesitance in reforming the electoral college. It is, indeed, an explanation of a great deal of the legislation controlling parties and elections in this country.

The high value we place on a two-party system assumes, of course, that the parties will be competitive in most or all parts of the nation. It is two *competitive* parties that provide the alternatives in candidates and issues on which a meaningful democratic choice depends. Two competitive parties provide the only set of clear, dramatic political alternatives which the voter can grasp and on the basis of which he can act. Furthermore, only the presence of a competitor can impose limits on a party. Each one, then, must tailor its candidates and programs to minimize losses to the other party. The presence of the real alternative is as sharp a limitation, as sure a guarantor of responsibility in the political system, as it is in the economic marketplace. The party that does not have to reckon with the responsiveness and strength of another is less compelled to consider the reactions of its "customers." Thus the *quality* of the competition in the American party system and in American democratic politics depends on its quantity.

One-partyism, on the other hand, shifts the organization of political conflict to factions within the dominant party. The dominant party, for its part, suffers the torments of factionalism. Classic parties of this type, such as the southern Democratic parties until recently, lose whatever cohesion they might have had. They become collections of factions and followings based on personalities, regions of the state, rewards of patronage, or particular interests. Their organization is transient and shifting, and they cannot identify over time with issues or interests. What emerges, in fact, is a caricature of a political party.

The subordinate party in one-partyism lapses into torpor, kept alive only by a few workers hoping for national party patronage or a voice in the national party itself. It cannot attract resources, party workers, attractive candidates, or many loyal voters. The voter, too, is often robbed of his political choice and alternatives. What meaningful choices there are for him can be made only in the primary election of the dominant party. But with primaries serving as quasi elections, the business of nominating is often done earlier and informally by party leaders and factions.[20]

There is a danger, however, that one can be carried away by the euphoria of the salutes to the American political parties. Too many observers of the American two-party system have assumed that it is inextricably bound up with American democracy, that its competitive pulls and tugs are somehow a part of the very essence of the democratic processes. It may be useful here to temper the euphoria with two notes of warning in order to keep the reader alerted to the two problems as he moves through a survey of the American parties.

The first warning note is simply that electoral competition between the two parties is not inherent or inevitable in a two-party system. Competition may break down simply as a result of the collapse of capacity. The atrophy of party organization, the loss of electorates, or even the loss of status may prevent a party from competing. Or competition may break down because people choose not to compete. Through the years of Democratic domination of the South, the Republican parties became merely small circles of seekers after national patronage who could achieve their goals without contesting a local election. In a few other localities in the country, parties have been known to enter a kind of political "restraint of trade," whereby they share or split offices. Even more important, especially at the present, is the possibility that political parties — or at least party activists — will decide that electoral competition is not the major overriding business of a political party. If one party or the other, or even a substantial group within one party, ever decides that the triumph of an ideology is more important than victory in elections, all the assumptions on which the competition of the two-party system rests will have been mightily shaken. An overriding con-

---

[20] See V. O. Key's magistral work, *Southern Politics* (New York: Knopf, 1949) for a picture of the classic one-partyism of recent American history.

cern for ideology — of which there were ample signs in both the 1964 and 1972 elections — does provide exactly that challenge to the competitive assumptions of the two-party system.

And the second cautionary note: It is far too easy to assume that American democracy in its present form cannot exist without political parties, or at least without political parties as we know them. Such a claim is and ought to be a question for evidence and analysis. Very probably the two major parties can continue to dominate the American party system. It is by no means as clear, however, that they can continue to dominate the broader competition of all political organizations. It is not at all inconceivable — not even improbable — that the political parties are changing or will change in the near future in their role as political organizers in our political processes. The practice of democracy changes and evolves, and its needs and demands shift with those changes. In order to mobilize majorities of voters in the 1970s and 1980s, there may be a need for political organizations and processes different from those developed and perfected in the earlier years of the twentieth century.

II

THE POLITICAL PARTY AS AN ORGANIZATION

It is often easier to see the political activity than the actor. The tense excitement of a bitterly fought election, the carnival antics and revival-meeting fervor of national conventions, the wrangling between partisan blocs in a state legislature — these and the other activities of the political parties could not be more obvious. But there is a palpable actor behind the activity — a political party with characteristics not unlike those of large national corporations, trade unions, and fraternal societies. The political party is no mere bundle of activities, no disembodied ideology, no unseen hand in the political process. It is a definable, observable social structure that must itself be organized in order to organize political interests.

Within the structure called the political party, all three sectors — the party organization, the party in government, and the party in the electorate — have stable relationships and a rough division of labor and responsibility. All three have, in other words, the characteristics we associate with an organization of any kind. It is a bit misleading, therefore, to call only one of them the party organization, but such are the semantic vagaries of American politics. In justification of that usage, however, it is true that the party organization alone has the organizational capacity to plan and initiate the major share of party activities. It also has the most systematic network of relationships and roles of all the party sectors. It is the sector that speaks in the name of the party, governs it, and under law is responsible for it. It is the sector in which active partisans work to determine the overall goals and to mobilize resources and make decisions on deploying and expending those resources. In that sense it is that part of the party most concerned with its governance and with setting its priorities.

In concrete terms, the party organization is the formal apparatus of the precincts, wards, cities, counties, congressional districts, and state that results from the legislation of the state itself. In this sense the party organization is the party for the purposes of the state; state laws set up these committees and recognize them collectively as the political party. In addition, the party has set up a national committee, which peaks the pyramid of committees the state has created. The party organization is thus the totality of the machinery operated by party officials, leaders, members, and activists. The three chapters that follow will describe this machinery of the party organization at considerable length.

The public life and activities of the party organization — its espousal of ideas and recruitment of candidates, for instance — will receive separate treatment in chapters beyond these. But party organizations have a "private life" in addition to their public life. It involves the kind of internal relationships and behavior that one might find in any complex organization. The three chapters of this part will examine that private life, especially in these aspects:

1. *The formal structure of the organization:* its committees and machinery; the selection of its leadership.
2. *The centers of power:* the relative centralization or decentralization of power within the organization; the locus of final authority within it.
3. *The patterns of decision making:* the processes by which decisions are made, especially the degree of intraorganizational democracy.
4. *Cohesion and consent:* the maintenance of unity, discipline, and morale within the organization.
5. *The recruitment of resources:* the ability of the organization to attract people, money, and skills and the incentives it uses to do so.
6. *The division of labor:* the various roles and relationships among people within the organization.

The private life of the party is far less obvious than the public. But although we may separate the party organization's private life from its public activities, the two are obviously related. To a considerable extent the internal, organizational characteristics of the party affect its capacity to carry on the external, public activities.

A comparison with the large business organization is, if not pressed too far, a valid one. The party organization competes for political resources — manpower, knowledge, and money — against the powerful inducements of the other political organizations. Its rewards or incentives bring together varied groups of men and women who seek their special, and often differing, goals through the medium of party action. What are rewards and incentives from the "mobilizing" viewpoint of the party organization are merely the goals and ends for which their activists have come together in the party. Many of the party organization's activities, therefore, may be viewed in terms of its attempts to win those goals and thereby reward the faithful for their investment of resources, loyalties, work, and support.

Ultimately, the most important questions about the party organizations concern their effectiveness, vitality, and capacity. These characteristics can be summed up as *strength*, and the strength of the party organization has two dimensions: its ability to hold its own in its relationships with the two other sectors of the party, and its ability to function efficiently and consistently in mobilizing resources and making decisions. The party organization, that is, must function successfully within the political party and within the broader political system.

In its relationships with the party in government and the party in the electorate, the party organization rarely achieves any permanent supremacy within the American political party. All three sectors of the party struggle for control of its symbols and its political capabilities. All three have goals — at times competing goals — and each seeks control of the party as a "means" to its own particular ends. Rarely are the party organizations able to dictate to the party in government. It is far more common for them to be dependent on and even submissive to the party in government. They must also conduct an almost endless wooing of their own party electorate, for even the loyal voter is often willing to split his ticket.

In addition to these strained and often dependent relations with the other sectors of the party, the organization confronts formidable problems in maintaining its internal vitality. Contrary to popular impression, party organizations are not unified, omnipotent monoliths. They have within them men and women of different values and goals, and they have always been plagued with dissidents and competing factions. They or parts of them often display amazing degrees of organizational apathy, inefficiency, ineptness, and even organizational disintegration. It is not unusual, for example, to find entire county organizations of the Democratic or Republican party in total desuetude. Furthermore, their decentralization is the despair of politicians as well as scholars. The national committees of the parties exert very limited power over state and local party organizations.

In both these dimensions of the problem of strength and vitality, there are, of course, many variations within the American parties. The next few chapters will illustrate the varieties of party organization. The basic fact remains that by the standards of political parties of most Western democracies, the American party organizations are comparatively weak and insubstantial. And to a considerable extent the problem is in the very nature of the animal. The party organization is an expression of some very special qualities of the American political party. To understand its special problems and substantial limitations, one should perhaps compare it with party organizations found among the other democracies of the world.

At the risk of considerable oversimplification, one can say that among democratic political parties two types of organization appear most frequently: the cadre and the mass membership. In the cadre party, of which the major American parties are prime examples, the organizational machinery is run by a relatively small number of leaders and activists. These officials and activists perpetuate the apparatus of the organization, make decisions in its name, and pick the candidates and strategies that will enlist large numbers of voters. In the mass membership party, on the other hand, the party organization grows out of and is more continuously responsible to the party membership. In these parties substantial parts of the party electorates are involved in the party organization as dues-paying members and even as participants in year-round activities. The party organization has, therefore, a continuous responsibility to its membership, often providing such benefits as insurance and leisure-time activities. In a mass membership party the three sectors are drawn together, with the party organization often occupying a central, dominant position. What we think of as the party in the electorate becomes an integral, even guiding, part of the party organization, with rights of picking officers and voting on policy questions. Because of its great power in the selection of candidates — no primary elections trouble them — these organizations of the mass membership parties exert far greater control over the party in government. In short, the mass membership party resembles a continuous, participatory organization; the cadre party, on the other hand, is far more a momentary, pragmatic coalition of interests and people brought together in a temporary way to win elections (see Table 1).[1]

Thus American party organizations are what they are because American political parties in general are what they are. The American cadre-style party organization expresses the organizational needs of parties that are preoccupied — indeed obsessed — with contesting elections. It reflects the organizational needs of parties that must appeal to majorities rather than to 10, 20, or 30 percent of the electorate. It reflects the needs of parties that have not been traditionally concerned with ideology, with vast political causes, or even with taking specific stands on political issues. Finally, it reflects a political system in which the electorate is already organized by a wealth of interest groups and other nonparty political organizations. To state these points the other way,

[1] Maurice Duverger in his *Political Parties* (New York: Wiley, 1954) inaugurated the distinction between the cadre and mass membership parties. For an expansion of that analysis and an excellent comparison of the American parties with those of other Western democracies, see Leon D. Epstein, *Political Parties in Western Democracies* (New York: Praeger, 1967).

TABLE 1   Comparison of Cadre and Mass Membership
Party Organizations

	Cadre	Mass membership
Members	Generally few	Many dues-paying members
Activities	Predominantly electoral	Ideological and educational, as well as electoral
Organizational continuity	Active chiefly at elections	Continuously active
Leadership	Few full-time workers or leaders (avocational)	Permanent professional bureaucracy and full-time leadership (vocational)
Position in party	Usually subordinate to party in government	Generally some influence over party in government

the party organization of the American parties does not reflect the politics of a multiparty system, the politics of a political system deeply ideologized, or a political system in which the parties themselves have monopolized the organization of political interests.

So there is an insubstantial and even unimpressive quality about party organization in the American parties. Perhaps for this reason the early classic studies of party organization were written in Western Europe rather than the United States.[2] But the American party organizations are nonetheless there, and they command our attention. Despite whatever weaknesses and episodic failures they may have, they are at the very center of the political party. More than any other sector, they control its life, its name, and its symbols. Any study of the American political parties slights them at great peril.

[2] The major examples are the Duverger book cited in the preceding footnote; Robert Michels, *Political Parties* (Glencoe, Ill.: Free Press, 1949, but first published in 1915); and Moisei Ostrogorski, *Democracy and the Organization of Political Parties*, first published in 1902 and now available in an edition of two volumes edited and abridged by Seymour Martin Lipset (New York: Anchor, 1964).

3

The
Party
Organization:
State and
Local

The semantics of American politics often reflect its most tenacious myths. The entire popular vocabulary touching party organization suggests almost menacing strength. "Machines" headed by "bosses" keep the local "captains" toeing a "party line." Their power or strength has become, in a lately fashionable idiom, their "clout." And yet, even the most cursory experience with American party organization suggests that all the puffery hides a vastly less imposing reality.

In many ways the myth of monolithic party organization — and its related vocabulary and idiom — is itself a part of the greater American fear of politics and politicians. In what has become virtually a conspiratorial theory of American politics, the party organization or "machine" is only the prime conspirator or corrupter in a wider net of political intrigue. The truth about American party organization is, therefore, difficult for many Americans to accept, for it involves not only a recognition of reality about the parties but also the modification of some dim views of politics in general. Perhaps because they carry no such preconceptions, foreign observers have found it easier to see American party organization as it really is. Recognition of the truth may surprise them, but it forces no major reorientation of political values or perceptions.

One of the latest in a long series of distinguished foreign commentators on the American polity, H. G. Nicholas, cut quickly through the major myth of party organization in the early 1950s:

Englishmen who have viewed American elections from three thousand miles across the Atlantic have generally been impressed by the elaborateness of the organizations involved as well as by the magnitude and professionalism of it all. The very language of American politics suggests a planned, powerful, smooth-running and disciplined instrument. Surely, these Englishmen have decided, an American party is the counterpart in the field of politics of the corporation in the field of American business — a great, synthetic, efficient, productive mechanism, smoothly controlled from above and ordering the movement of millions below.

I have discovered in the last few weeks that such an image quickly vanishes when confronted with reality. Even a cursory inspection of the American political scene at election time reveals a wholly different condition of affairs. Far from order, there is a rich and riotous confusion; in place of impersonal "machines," there is every kind of spontaneous organism. The disciplined ward heelers turn out to be an unseemly scramble of enthusiastic volunteers; the symmetrical pyramid we have heard about — from precinct to ward to county to state to nation — is an untidy cairn composed of stones of every conceivable size, with mortar either inadequate or nonexistent, and with an apex whose location shifts according to wherever you happen to be standing at the moment. . . .

The American party organization is a phoenix, burning itself out after each election, soaring with a new (or at least a rewelded) pair of wings after each primary. The effort this must involve for all concerned is something that appalls the visitor; the energy that is given to it excites his admiration; the complexities that result therefrom befuddle his poor comprehension.[1]

So it is that things are seldom what they seem in American party organization. Our main problem may be that we are always shifting among three levels of reality: the party organizations as they are stipulated in state legislation, the party organizations as they are in real life, and the party organizations as large numbers of Americans imagine them to be. Neither the pages of statute books nor the fears of many Americans accurately mirror the reality of party organization.

THE FORMS AND OUTLINES OF ORGANIZATION

While the United States Constitution makes no mention of or even oblique reference to political parties, the constitutions and statutes of the fifty states literally bulge with detailed prescriptions defining the nature of party organizations and the duties they are to perform. The states have, in fact, enacted such a kaleidoscopic variety of legislation on the parties that it defies summary or classification. In scope and extent the laws range from those of Oregon, which specify the structure in detailed and full-blown provisions of more than 5,000 words, to those of Georgia, which dispose of the parties in a few extended sentences. In between are all grades and degrees of statutory specificity — laws that permit the parties to determine the composition of the state central committee and those that not only specify it but set the dates and places of its meetings, those that spell out legislative district organization and

---

[1] H. G. Nicholas, "A Briton Considers Our Bewildering Party Apparatus," *The Reporter*, November 25, 1952, pp. 28–29. Copyright 1952 by Fortnightly Publishing Company Inc. Reprinted by permission.

those that don't, those that leave the running of the parties to the parties and those that even set the agendas of their periodic meetings. Despite the variety of state approaches, however, the cardinal fact remains that the definition and regulation of political party organization in the United States have been left entirely to the states.

The great mass of state legislation on the parties covers an extensive range of subjects. Virtually every state has attempted to define the ways in which parties and their candidates are admitted to the ballot. They usually set vote minima — 5 or 10 percent of the vote cast at the last gubernatorial election, perhaps — or alternatively they prescribe the number of signatures on petitions required for access to the ballot.[2] And they inevitably assign specific tasks to the parties: the replacement of candidates who die during the campaign or the selection of presidential electors, for instance. Yet in many ways the most important statutory provisions are those that outline the organizational form the parties must assume and the procedures they must observe as they organize or reorganize. Often the parties in practice modify or embellish that statutory structure, but they never fully escape its imperatives. An examination of the party organization must begin with it.

The party organizations created by the states have one dominant characteristic in common: They match the voting districts and at least some of the constituencies of the state. They form great step pyramids as they reflect the myriad, overlapping constituencies of a democracy committed to the election of vast numbers of officeholders (Figure 1). At the bottom they are built on the smallest voting districts of the state. The basic functionary in the party organization is the local committeeperson representing a ward, a precinct, or a township.[3] Then, in a confusion of layers, the ward and city committees, county committees, and sometimes even state legislative and congressional districts are piled on top of each other.[4] At the apex of the pyramid there is invariably a state committee, usually called a state central committee in the idiom of these statutes. The degree to which this entire structure is actually specified by the statutes differs from state to state. State statutes generally ordain the county and the state committees; some then mandate the other levels, while others leave the full articulation of the organizational hierarchy to the parties themselves.

[2] See Joseph Starr, "The Legal Status of American Political Parties," *American Political Science Review* 34 (1940): 439–55, 685–99.
[3] Terminology for local party officials is in transition. The majority of party organizations seem to have replaced "committeeman" and "committeewoman" with "committeeperson." Most state statutes, however, hold to the former usage.
[4] Within the same state the various intermediate committees may cover geographical areas of varying sizes and thus occupy different positions in the organizational pyramid. Congressional districts, for example, may be smaller than a city or larger than a county, depending on the density of population.

FIGURE 1   Typical Pyramid of Party
Organization in a State

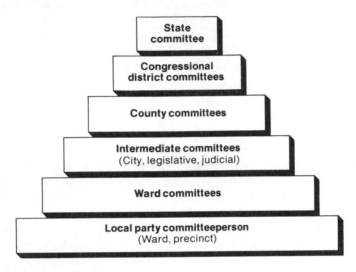

The Elected Committeeperson

Usually the committeeperson is chosen from the local precinct, the smallest voting district in the states, but occasionally he or she is selected from the ward (especially in larger cities) or from the township (in rural areas). Since there are more than 100,000 precincts in the United States, a fully staffed, two-party system would assume the participation of at least some 200,000 men and women. In truth, of course, many of the local committee positions are either vacant or only nominally occupied.

The local committeepersons are generally selected in one of two ways: at local party caucuses or at the primary elections of the party. In those states choosing them at the primaries, any voter may generally place his name in nomination for the party position with a petition signed by a handful of local voters. If, as it often happens, there are no nominees, the committeeperson may be elected by an even smaller handful of write-in votes. In other states the statutes direct or permit the party to hold local caucuses in the wards and precincts to which any voters of the area who declare themselves attached to the party's principles (always unspecified) may come. These party loyalists then elect the committeepersons in the caucus; they also generally elect delegates to county and/or state conventions.

The duties of the local party officials are not often fully spelled out in the statutes. Naturally, in areas where local parties are active, they develop organizational responsibilities that the statutes never mention. The fabled local committeemen or ward heelers of the American political machine knew the local voters, catered to their needs and problems, introduced the party candidates to them, propagandized the parties' issues — all with the ultimate purpose of turning out a bloc of votes for the party on election day. In the less active local parties that are common today the committeepersons may do little more than occasionally campaign and attend meetings.

The Local Committees

A welter of party committees springs from the elected committeepersons. Commonly they collectively make up the city, town, village, legislative, county, and congressional district committees or elect the delegates who do. In a few cases, however, these committees or some of them are chosen at county conventions or by the party's candidates for public office. Regardless of this profusion of committees and the various mechanics of their formation, the chief committee is generally the county committee, although in some states the congressional district committees assume a comparable importance.

The dominance of the county committee in most parts of the country is not difficult to explain. The county as a political division elects not one but a considerable number of public officials. And those officials often control the one major remaining source of political patronage: the county courthouse. Furthermore, many other constituencies — such as congressional districts, state legislative districts, and judicial districts — are defined largely in terms of counties. Then, too, in much of America, life and trade are drawn to the local county seat from the surrounding area. Finally, the statutes of most states recognize the key position of the county committees. Often their members form other parallel committees, and often, too, they send their chairmen or delegates to form the state central committee.

In some metropolitan areas, however, the local party structure is more complex and more diverse. In the Bronx in New York the Democratic county committee is composed of some 3,750 local committeepersons. All of them in each state legislative district (for the state assembly) elect district leaders, who in turn elect the county leaders. Typically, the Democrats of neighboring Brooklyn and Queens have somewhat different organizational structures. In other metropolitan centers the city committees of the large central city assume an unusual importance.

The states, however, do more than create the bare bones of a party organization. They also regulate its activities and its internal processes. Something of the detailed nature of this regulation may be seen in Minnesota's strictures on the operation of its ward and precinct party caucuses. Minnesota statutes specify very precisely:

1. The full details of the public announcement of the caucus that must be made at least twenty days before its convening.
2. The minimum length of the caucus (one hour).
3. The length of time during which the caucus must receive nominations (one-half hour).
4. The procedures for challenging the presence of any of the participants.
5. The use of the secret ballot in all caucus elections.
6. The use of *Robert's Rules of Order* (revised edition) in the caucus deliberations.

Other states spell out equally detailed standards for party operation. They may require that local committees meet within thirty or forty-five days after the primary elections, that they notify the secretary of state or the county clerk of the election of officers within a set period, that they not permit the voting of proxies, that they observe a fixed order of business at their meetings, or that they hold their conventions in certain types of public buildings. Again, the variety of rules is endless, but the point is clear: Under the laws of the states, the political parties are not private organizations.

The State Central Committees

The state central committees of the fifty states are created in almost as many ways as human ingenuity can devise. In some states the lawmakers have left the composition to the decision of the parties, but in most they have decided the matter themselves. Basically, the differences center on two points: the lower party unit from which the state committee members are chosen and the ways in which they are chosen. The unit represented may be the county, the congressional district, the state legislative district, the state convention, cities, or a mixture of them. The methods of choice include election at the party's primaries, election by a lower committee, ex officio representation, or selection by a party convention. The possible number of combinations of the two factors is enormous, and state practice confirms that fact. (See, for example, the state committees outlined in the box.)

The activities of these state committees often are set down in what can only be painful detail. California statutes, for example, provide that the chairman of the state central committee shall serve a two-year term,

The Composition of Six State Central Committees

Illinois: One representative from each congressional district chosen at the primary election.

South Carolina: One representative per county chosen at a convention.

California: Although the two major parties differ in the composition of state central committees, generally speaking the committee is composed of delegates to the party's state convention, party candidates and public officials, state party representatives to the national committee, the chairman of each county committee, and a large number of additional members appointed by county chairmen, party candidates and public officials, and state convention delegates.

Oregon: The chairman and vice-chairman of each county central committee.

New York: Two representatives elected at the primary from each state assembly district.

Wisconsin: At least two members from each congressional district chosen by the state convention.

that he cannot succeed himself, and that the office must be held alternately by residents of the northern and southern halves of the state. It is common to assign the committees responsibility for calling and organizing party conventions, for drafting party platforms, for supervising the spending of party campaign funds, for selecting the party's presidential electors, representatives to the national committee, and national convention delegates and alternates. Regarding the main business of running a party organization and supporting candidates in the primaries and general elections, state statutes are generally silent, except to say occasionally that the parties may make whatever rules are necessary for the conduct of party business. Some do, however, forbid or permit the committees to endorse candidates in the primary. But on these "political" political activities, more commonly the state statutes are silent.

A number of states, especially those endemically suspicious of entrenched party leadership, set up statewide conventions, to which they assign many of the powers and responsibilities that other states leave to the state central committees. They may ordain that the state convention write the platform, select the national committeepersons from the state, nominate presidential electors, and choose delegates and/or alternates to the party's national convention. Indeed, some states provide that the state convention select the state committee itself. Furthermore, in a small number of states the state convention of the party actually nominates candidates for some statewide offices, a reminder of the power of conventions in the days before the direct primary.[5]

Such, then, are the formal organizational structures created for the parties in the states. Three general observations about them are in order. First, one cannot but notice that state legislators view the parties almost exclusively as electoral organizations. The organizational layers relate to voting districts and the constituencies in which public officials are chosen, and the duties assigned to them are almost exclusively concerned with the contesting of elections. The political party organization — as one views it in the statute books of the states — clearly serves as an auxiliary to the state's regulation of nominations and elections. Indeed, the dominant concern in its creation too often seems to be its usefulness in helping the state administer the electoral processes rather than its viability as a healthy, ongoing party organization.

Second, it is clear from the statutes that state legislators have viewed the parties as skeletal organizations — as cadre parties — run by a small number of party officials. There is little evidence that they have entertained the possibility of membership parties, or even of parties attracting the concerns and labors of bands of activists. Indeed, they assume the contrary. By opening the election of local committeepersons (and even of other party officials) to the electorate of the primary election, they have defined the parties' voters as a quasi-membership group. By legislative fiat they have tried to democratize the parties, to open them to the ultimate participation and authority of all voters. The party that results is thus no closed association whose participating members choose its leaders and chart its affairs. It is the semipublic hybrid of which we have already spoken.

Finally, while the formal organization of the parties within the state appears to be strictly hierarchical, it is not. The state party hierarchies have more aptly been described by V. O. Key as "a system of layers of organization." [6] In some states, for example, the state central committee's members are chosen directly by the voters; the committee, therefore, does not grow out of the committees below it. And even when the linkage between the layers of organization is direct, the links move from bottom to top. Such a system would hardly appear to be ideally

[5] No genuinely comprehensive summary of state statutory provisions on party organization seems to be available. The provisions of the laws of any state can be found easily in the state's codified statutes; the material on party organization is usually located under the general heading "elections." For some summarization see *State Party Structures and Procedures: A State by State Compendium* (New York: National Municipal League, 1967), mimeo.

[6] V. O. Key, *Politics, Parties, and Pressure Groups*, 5th ed. (New York: Crowell, 1964), p. 316.

designed to produce the centralization of power at the apex that the very concept of hierarchy presumes. Basically, the party organization is a system of party committees close to and growing from the political grass roots. The result is to build into the party organizational structure a great deal of localism and distaste for statewide direction.

THE SUBSTANCE AND REALITIES OF PARTY ORGANIZATION

These elaborate statutory parties, with their many layers of committees and their armies of committeepersons, conform to the mental images most Americans have of the party organizations. These are the machines, the organizations, the bosses, the ward heelers, and the party cabals of which the great party juggernauts are said to be made. But, in truth, political party organization in many states and localities is weak, undermanned, even torpid. Where statutes and public expectation see active legions of committeepersons and layer on layer of impressive organization, there is often only sporadic activity by a handful of dispirited party regulars.

Disciplined, effective party organization does exist, to be sure. The classic urban political machine is the best example. Its heyday was the turn of the twentieth century, and its promised land was the burgeoning American city. Its annals are replete with the colorful histories of Tammany Hall in New York, the knaveries of the Prendergasts in Kansas City and Frank ("I am the law") Hague in Jersey City, the cheeky threats of Chicago's "Big Bill" Thompson to punch the King of England on the nose, and the genial rascality (and mail fraud conviction) of Mayor James Curley of Boston. The antics of Mayor Curley were in fact immortalized — and somewhat romanticized — in the novel (and movie) *The Last Hurrah*.[7] Recently, however, the urban machine has fallen on bad days; the defeat of Carmine de Sapio and the other organization Democrats of New York in 1961 by Mayor Robert Wagner and the reformers marks its most spectacular loss. And the election of an insurgent mayor in Pittsburgh in 1969 signaled the decline of yet another machine bastion.

Despite its general decline, the classic urban machine is not yet extinct. It is very much alive and well in Chicago and in a number of smaller American cities, chiefly in the Northeast. Bolstered by control over some 35,000 patronage jobs, the Cook County Democratic organization of Mayor Richard Daley continues its control over nominations and elections, over public employment and preferment, and over major public policy in Chicago and the county (see page 74). But not without

---

[7] Edwin O'Connor, *The Last Hurrah* (Boston: Little, Brown, 1956).

difficulty, for even this last of the big city machines has had its recent trials. The violence surrounding the Democratic national convention in 1968 inevitably called attention to the mayor and his organization. (At the 1972 convention Mayor Daley and the delegation he headed were not seated because they had not been selected in accordance with the new party rules.) Recently, too, the machine has had important defections, its image has been tarnished by convictions for corruption, and it lost the 1972 election of a Cook County attorney to a Republican reformer. Even the mayor himself had his first substantial competition in twenty years in the Democratic primary. The resilient strength of the organization triumphed, however, and Mayor Daley won landslide victories first against his Democratic challengers and then against a hapless Republican opponent.[8]

Urban machines such as those in Chicago depend fundamentally on the distribution of patronage jobs. These appointments win the indispensable loyalty and the service of the workers in the machine itself. Their efforts in turn produce the party "vote" — their own votes and those of friends, family, and neighbors. Beyond patronage, local party workers cope with the problems of local residents in their offices or in the clubrooms of local party headquarters. Often those problems are personal — unemployment or a delinquent son — as well as public or governmental. The machine and its men earn political gratitude by finding a social welfare agency for the troubled, jobs for the jobless, contracts for the local merchant, or even the storied Christmas basket or delivery of coal for the needy. Among the more imaginative party organizations, the services of the machine remain strictly up to date. A newspaper account of the Democratic bosses of Brooklyn recently reported that one especially deft leader had within the week "obtained school crossing guards for Our Lady of Peace parochial school, arranged for the admission of a retarded child into a specialized school, and managed an interdepartmental transfer of an employee of Merrill, Lynch, Pierce, Fenner and Smith, a stock brokerage."[9] This politics of gratitude may also be supported by an ethnic, racial, or religious solidarity in the neighborhood. Urban machines have often successfully played on the group solidarity and aspirations of disadvantaged populations, and the machine did indeed often offer them an important avenue to power and affluence.

In all of this, what keeps the ward and precinct workers working? They, too, enjoy the fruits of patronage. As recently as 1970 almost three out of four Democratic committeemen and more than 40 percent

---

[8] For a general survey of the Daley phenomenon, see Mike Royko, *Boss: Richard J. Daley of Chicago* (New York: Signet, 1971).
[9] *New York Times*, June 1, 1970.

Three Views of the Daley Machine

"The money comes from countless sources. From the patronage army, it goes into ward offices as dues, and part of it is turned over to party headquarters. Every ward leader throws his annual $25-a-head golf days, corned beef dinners, and picnics. The ticket books are thrust at the patronage workers, and they either sell them or, as they say, 'eat them,' bearing the cost themselves.

"There are 'ward books,' with page after page of advertising, sold by precinct workers to local businesses and other favorseekers. Alderman Marzullo puts out a 350-page ad book every year, at one hundred dollars a page. There are no blank pages in his book. The ward organizations keep what they need to function, and the rest is funneled to party headquarters.

"Contractors may be the biggest of all contributors. Daley's public works program has poured billions into their pockets, and they in turn have given millions back to the party in contributions. Much of it comes from contractors who are favored, despite the seemingly fair system of competitive bidding."

Mike Royko, *Boss* (New York:
Signet, 1971), pp. 74–75.

"Democratic politics in Chicago is a close-knit, almost tribal affair, in which many of the major participants trace their lineage through several generations of office holders or political influentials.

"The sons of aldermen inherit their fathers' seats, the offspring of ward committeemen or precinct captains go on to bigger things, the sons of judges get lucrative part-time appointments as lawyers for the transit authority....

"In a city less than 10 percent Irish, nearly all of the major jobs are held by men of Irish origins; since 1933 all of the Mayors have come from the same neighborhood, the Bridgeport area of Chicago."

John Kifner, *New York Times,*
December 11, 1972.

"...At least once a week, Daley meets with his 'director of patronage' to peruse every application for every city job, right down to the lowliest ditch digger's. If and when the mayor stamps his approval, the successful job winner almost by definition joins The Machine (or organization) and assumes the responsibility of working one of Chicago's 3,412 voting precincts come election time. That sort of quasimilitary arrangement continues to produce virtual blitzes at the ballot box....

"One of the most withering experiences in a ward boss's life comes on election night when he must bring his tally downtown to party headquarters at the Sherman House Hotel. Somewhat in the manner of a schoolboy presenting his report card to a stern father, each of the 50 meets alone with Daley to submit his precinct-by-precinct vote. According to one insider who has observed the ritual, Daley sits at a desk and silently studies the tallies. If they please him, he rises and vigorously pumps both of the successful committeeman's hands. If they displease him, Daley gives the miscreant a blistering tongue-lashing. On one such occasion, the mayor was so incensed with a non-producer that he reached across his desk and began shaking him by his necktie."

Newsweek, April 5, 1971.

---

of the Democratic committeewomen in Pittsburgh held public jobs, chiefly with the Pittsburgh city government and the Allegheny county government.[10] Additionally, the faithful enjoy the social and psychological rewards of power and of nearness to greater power. Their political positions bring them into social circles and to economic opportunity that would otherwise be denied them. For some of them service to the organization yields chances to run for public office since the machine often chooses its candidates from among the active faithful. But what the machine giveth, the machine can take away. The dissident or unproductive party worker may quickly find himself stripped of honors and rewards, for the reward can quickly be converted to the sanction.

The classic urban machine is the acme of party organization in the United States. It develops a continuous, year-round existence as it meets a vast range of problems and needs of the urban dweller. It is part electoral organization, part "informal government," part social service agency, and part route to success. In these ways and in its highly structured, articulated, and bureaucratized army of workers, it resembles the local organization of a European mass membership party. It would probably not delight Mayor Daley to learn that in many of these ways the Chicago Democratic machine resembles a local Communist party organization in northern Italy. But there are, of course, differences. The American machine has no membership base, and it has few, if any, ideological concerns. Its focus on the immediate needs of its constituents has driven the urban machine to look almost completely inward and to ignore the issues and ideologies of the political world beyond. It is provincially concerned with the city, and its politics are almost completely divorced from the issues that agitate our national politics.[11]

---

[10] Lee S. Weinberg, "Stability and Change Among Pittsburgh Precinct Politicians, 1954–1970," *Social Science* 50 (1975): 14.

[11] The literature on the American urban machine is staggering in its size. Among the best pieces are Edward Banfield and James Q. Wilson, *City Politics* (Cambridge: Harvard University Press, 1963); Harold Gosnell, *Machine Politics: Chicago Model* (Chicago: University of Chicago Press, 1939); and Raymond E. Wolfinger, "Why Political Machines Have Not Withered Away and Other Revisionist Thoughts," *Journal of Politics* 34 (1972): 365–98.

Yet, the machines of the big cities have never been and are not now typical of party organization in the United States. The other extreme — virtually unrepresented in the scholarly or popular literature because it offers so little to study — is virtual disorganization. In these cases, most of the committee positions in the party's county unit are unfilled or held by completely inactive incumbents (who may have been elected without their consent by four or five write-in votes). A chairman and a handful of loyal party officials may meet occasionally to carry out the most essential affairs of the party, or the affairs that state statutes require of them. Their main activity occurs shortly before the primary elections as they plead with members of the party to become candidates or offer themselves as candidates in order to "fill the party ticket." They are largely without influence or following, for often their party is a chronic minority party. They meet infrequently, raise little money for election campaigns, and create little or no public attention. The extent of such organizational weakness is difficult to estimate, although it is the rule rather than the exception in much of rural America.

Most American party organization lies between these two extremes. But "between" encompasses a great organizational distance. It might be accurate, however, to say that the average local party organization comes closer to the pole of disorganization than to the pole of maximum organization. In some instances, in fact, local party leaders will fight the strengthening of party organization lest new party activists challenge their little arena of power and claim their patronage rewards. Even where the recruitment of party leaders and activists is open, fluctuations in popular involvement work toward a modest party organization. In 1972, for example, the open precinct caucuses of the Minnesota Democratic party attracted some 50,000 partisans; the average attendance in metropolitan precincts was well above 100, but the rural precincts averaged only a handful. Two years earlier, however, the party had attracted only an average of about ten people per precinct. The greater participation of 1972, it is safe to say, reflected interest in that year's presidential politics, not in building local party organization.

It is not easy to locate the "average" city or county organization, but it probably shares these characteristics:

1. An active chairman and executive committee, plus a few associated activists, who in effect make most of the decisions in the name of the party, who raise funds, who seek out and screen candidates (or approve the candidates who select themselves), and who speak locally for the party.
2. A ward and precinct organization in which only a few local committeepersons are active and in which there is little door-to-door canvasing or other direct voter contact.

3. The active participation in organizational matters of some of the party's elected public officials, who may share effective control of the organization with its official leadership.
4. A distinctly periodic calendar of activities marked by a watchful waiting or general inactivity at other than election times.

Here one does not find the serried ranks of party foot soldiers. The leadership operates not with threats and iron discipline but with pleading and cajoling. There are few incentives and rewards left in the hands of these parties with which to recruit all the effort and manpower the statutory structures seem to assume.

Such a sketch of the "average" local party organization cannot, of course, begin to suggest the many forms that local parties take in the United States. It takes no account, for instance, of the oligarchic rural or small-town machines, in which a few local notables (who may or may not hold party or public office) dominate a political organization with a variable combination of patronage, local prestige and status, friendship, kinship, and private economic power. (It is one of the most durable — and least supportable — myths of American politics that political muscle, and even corruption, must always be urban.)

A sketch of the "average" takes no account either of urban party organizations operating at a level of considerable effectiveness, albeit a level or two below that of the prototypic machine. A recent study of parties in the Detroit area defined the precinct committeeperson's three "critical" tasks to be the registration of new voters, the canvasing of the already registered (by phone or personal visits), and the roundup of voters on election day. Only 17 percent of the Democratic precinct leaders and 25 percent of the Republican leaders performed all three tasks, but another 38 percent of the Democrats and 22 percent of the Republicans carried out two of the three.[12]

THE EXTRALEGAL ORGANIZATION

The forms and types of party organization just discussed operate largely within the formal outlines set down in state statutes. But the parties have made organizational embellishments that go beyond the words, sometimes the clear expectations of many state statutes.

The embellishments are of two kinds, auxiliaries to party organizations and alternatives to them. Among the auxiliaries, women's organizations and caucuses have sprung up in a number of states. In addition

[12] Samuel J. Eldersveld, *Political Parties: A Behavioral Analysis* (Chicago: Rand McNally, 1964), pp. 349–50. David Olson has made one of the few systematic attempts at categorizing county party organizations in his article "Toward a Typology of County Party Organizations," *Southwestern Social Science Quarterly* 48 (1968): 558–72.

to helping the regular organization in fund-raising and organizational work, they work to promote increased participation in party affairs by women as well as to support candidates sympathetic to women's rights and other feminist issues. And a good many parties have experimented with youth organizations; at various times in the recent past both parties have had both national youth organizations and groups of college youth affiliates. However, with the advent of the eighteen-year-old suffrage and reform attempts to involve young people in the party itself, the various youth auxiliaries have declined in membership and vigor. In general, the Democratic and Republican parties at present have fewer auxiliaries than they have ever had before, a tribute perhaps to the parties' attempts to involve all their loyalists and groups in their main units and to the desire of special groups to have their own, nonparty organizations.

However, partisans in a number of states have effected greater transformations in party organization than the mere addition of auxiliaries. They propose, in effect, an alternative to the regular party organization.

The Democratic Reform Clubs

Democratic reform clubs were formed in New York to break the power of Tammany Hall. They draw an educated, upper-middle-class and avocational party activist committed to liberal policies and to the reorientation of organizational politics to issues and ideology. In their organizational reform they have attempted to substitute a club-style membership for the usual cadre organization of the regular party. Within the party they have sought to replace both the traditional reliance on patronage and the hierarchical authority of the party leader (i.e., "boss"). More than anything else, however, theirs is a rebellion against the essentially issueless politics of personal reward and ethnicity that typified big city politics for so long. Similar groups sprang up in Illinois, the most persistent and long-lived of them being the Independent Voters of Illinois (IVI). Both sets of groups continue their reform fights into the 1970s, the New York reform clubs against the regular party leadership in New York and the IVI and allied groups against the Cook County organization of Richard Daley.[13]

The Wisconsin Voluntary Organizations

In the 1920s the conservative wing of the Wisconsin Republicans, repeatedly the losers in primaries to the La Follette progressive wing,

[13] See James Q. Wilson, *The Amateur Democrat* (Chicago: University of Chicago Press, 1962). On New York reform politics see the bittersweet account of Edward N. Costikyan, *Behind Closed Doors* (New York: Harcourt, Brace, 1966).

formed a separate, extralegal party organization to represent its ideology and support its candidates in the GOP primary. When the progressives left the Republican cover in the 1930s and formed their own state party, the "regular" Republicans found it easier to operate through their voluntary party organization than through the carefully regulated statutory organization. The Democrats, casting about for a more effective party organization, followed suit in the 1940s and 1950s. Both parties operated through these duplicating but separate voluntary organizations until 1974, keeping a separate and docile statutory organization to perform the mandated statutory duties. In 1974 the Wisconsin legislature brought developments full circle by abolishing the statutory committees and vesting in the voluntary committees the functions that state statutes require to be performed.[14]

The California Clubs

The splendid profusion of club-style party organizations in California began in the 1930s when liberal Republicans founded the California Republican Assembly to revive the faltering Republican party. A conservative competitor, the United Republicans of California, sprang up in the early 1960s to oppose the liberals of the CRA, but conservatives captured the CRA just a short time later. In 1965 the liberal Republicans repaired to a new set of organizations, the California Republican League. On the Democratic side, the older of the organizations, the liberal California Democratic Clubs, was founded in 1953 with the remnants of the 1952 Stevenson supporters. In both parties these clubs have featured some separate local organizations, a hard core of dues-paying members, and a series of tumultuous conventions at which the clubs' ideologists have endorsed candidates for support at their party's primary. Although the clubs' combined membership of approximately 70,000 constitutes a notable roll of activists, in neither party have the organizations been able to develop the scope or unity to match Wisconsin's control of the statutory organization.[15]

Finally, while other states have not equaled this degree of extralegal party organization, some state parties have in a limited way grafted membership organizations onto the regular statutory organization.

[14] For an account of the Wisconsin voluntary organizations in their flower, see Leon D. Epstein, *Politics in Wisconsin* (Madison: University of Wisconsin Press, 1958). By the late 1950s the two parties' voluntary organizations had enrolled some 20,000 dues-paying members.

[15] By far the largest number of the members are enrolled in the California Democratic Clubs. See Robert L. Morlan and Leroy C. Hardy, *Politics in California* (Belmont: Dickinson, 1968), pp. 26–33.

Other state parties have begun to hold special endorsing conventions apart from the formal conventions they are required to hold. In other states, too, the outlines of party statutory organization are sufficiently loose to permit the parties to shape an organization as they please.

The development of these voluntary organizations speaks volumes about the inadequacy of the conventional statutory party organization within which the parties must operate. The voluntary clubs have arisen in part because the inflexible statutory organization cannot accommodate the new middle-class style of organization with its emphasis on ideological and avocational activists and greater participation by dues-paying members. Furthermore, most reflect the problems that statutory party organizations have in controlling their party's primary. In Wisconsin the old statutory party conventions were required to convene *after* the primary, and in California the statutory party organizations are forbidden to make endorsements in the primary. In other ways, too, the voluntary organizations provide a release from state regulation of parties; in Wisconsin, for example, the voluntary structure enabled the parties to elude the state's severe restrictions on campaign spending by statutory organizations. Finally, the voluntary organizations are often instruments of factional warfare that is almost always ideological. Fervent ideologists have used them to combat other ideologists or non-ideologists within the party.

THE LOCUS OF POWER

It remains to ask what in reality is the locus of power within these party organizations. Is the hierarchical chain of authority really maintained? Most scholars feel that in most states the major locus of organizational vitality, and thus of organizational authority, is the county committee. Most state party organizations are merely federations — and loose ones at that — of semiautonomous or autonomous local baronies and baronial county chairmen.

The Democratic party of Ohio exemplifies these loosely knit, decentralized state party organizations. Writing of it in the early 1960s, one observer noted,

There was, in fact, no statewide Democratic party in Ohio. The state's Democratic party was an aggregation of city machines which had little or no interest in statewide elections unless the candidate was from their city. Ray Miller, the Cuyahoga County (Cleveland) Democratic boss, explicitly maintained that his organization was an independent entity with neither legal nor moral ties with a state Democratic party." [16]

[16] John H. Fenton, *Midwest Politics* (New York: Holt, Rinehart, Winston, 1966), p. 137.

This kind of decentralization is often accentuated by factionalism within the party — regional factions, those centering on personages, liberal-conservative factions, or a mixture of factional lines. Every state party has such factionalism; its effect depends on its relative strength.

To build a powerful state organization, in other words, is to build one that can dominate the city and county organizations and overcome the grass roots localism of the statutory party organizations. Not many state organizations succeed. Indiana's Democratic party, for one, has maintained its strength and reputation as one of the country's most powerful state organizations. It dispenses a considerable amount of patronage — estimates vary from 10,000 to 20,000 jobs — and most of the ninety-two county chairmen find a position within it. Its strength is also augmented by an old tradition in which grateful patronage holders return 2 percent of their salaries to the party coffers.[17] However, even so enduring a state organization as the Byrd machine in Virginia has recently suffered a rapid decline. The state fiefdom of former Democratic senator Harry F. Byrd was in the lord-in-the-manor style. The size of the salaries of six officials in each Virginia county depended on the decisions of a single board appointed by the governor, and state officials also controlled the county patronage. A limited suffrage, a homogeneous rural conservatism, and the active support of a social and economic oligarchy buttressed the Byrd organization. However, it was crippled in the 1966 elections, largely by an electorate swelled by new black and urban voters. By 1969 his son and successor, Harry F. Byrd, Jr., had lost control of the state organization and chose to run for reelection as an independent rather than as a Democrat.

To some extent the success of state party organizations in establishing their control over local organizations depends on personal virtuosity. There are great, masterful party chairmen, just as there are great orchestra conductors. But party resources play an important role, too. The powerful state organizations have often been those with great amounts of patronage to confer. All the better for them, too, if the patronage holders can be induced to return part of their salaries. It is no coincidence either that state party organization has flourished in the states in which the primary elections are least inclusive, such as Connecticut and Indiana. In those states the state party organization still determines much more directly who the statewide and congressional candidates will be. But when these advantages are neutralized, the result

---

[17] For some of the flavor of Indiana's Democratic party, see Robert J. McNeill, *Democratic Campaign Financing in Indiana, 1964* (published jointly by the Institute of Public Administration, Indiana University, and Citizens' Research Foundation, 1966). For an account of a state in which governors do at times centralize party control, see Malcolm E. Jewell and Everett W. Cunningham, *Kentucky Politics* (Lexington: University of Kentucky Press, 1968).

in most states is the usual decentralization of authority and power within the state organization. Only the county and city organizations are ongoing political organizations with grass roots support. They alone develop a base of power directly in the electorate, and that is powerful leverage within the party organization.

The question of the locus of power in state organizations — the question of centralization or decentralization — is an important one because of its consequences for the party. The centralized state party organization, for example, has vastly greater power over candidates for statewide office and far greater capacity for enforcing discipline in its party in the state legislature. It can control party finances and through them the conduct of election campaigns. The decentralized alternative undermines the entire possibility of party cohesion in the legislature and prevents the development of statewide issues or campaigns. Instead of a "state politics" conducted by a state party organization, there prevails a fragmented politics of local interests under the aegis of autonomous local organizations and leaders.[18]

TRENDS AND CHANGES

Party organization must and will reflect the political culture and the socioeconomic conditions of the time. As they change, the parties also change. No case better illustrates that fact than the decline of the city machine in American politics. Civil service and merit systems have gradually robbed it of the patronage jobs with which it rewarded its workers and officers. The ethnic minorities who supported it in its dominant days have been increasingly integrated into American life. Greater education and literacy have created a political awareness and sophistication that rebels at being led, sheeplike and docile, to the polls in a "delivered" vote. The values of the times demand participatory rights for individuals in all organizations. The growth of the welfare state, too, has provided freely and openly the welfare services that the urban machine "gave" only to its deserving patrons. And the growth of national, ideologized politics and national candidates has helped to break down the isolated localism and the essentially issueless politics of the machine.

Small wonder, then, that the old-style machine organization has fallen on bad days. One increasingly hears its style and ethics condemned. Its military discipline and central authority — its bossism — do not sit well with middle-class Americans in the 1970s. Nor do its issueless politics or patronage ethic. But perhaps all this is only to say that as

[18] Duane Lockard, *New England State Politics* (Princeton: Princeton University Press, 1959), pp. 325–26.

an organizational mode and style the urban machine has outlived its appointed time. And in our tendency to dismiss it, too often we forget that the urban machine was once one of the few agencies integrating the newly arrived city dwellers into American life and softening their often desperate condition in strange surroundings. It was also an instrument of popular democracy, the means by which the majorities of the cities first won control of their cities from old, aristocratic, and largely Anglo-Saxon elites.

Where something approaching the old-style urban machine persists today, it is in circumstances not unlike those the new immigrant faced in American cities at the turn of the century. The black and Puerto Rican newcomers to the northern cities, for example, face the same (or more severe) problems of poverty, discrimination, political powerlessness, ethnic isolation, and inability to cope with the life of the city. Many of the older political incentives and organizational styles "work" in their neighborhoods. The old-fashioned political machine survives, for instance, in Jersey City, New Jersey, a city in which less than 30 percent of the people have completed high school and in which more than one-quarter of the population lives in substandard housing.

The young, the educated, the middle-class people have been moving out. To some degree, they have been replaced by poor blacks and Puerto Ricans — though the "nonwhite" population makes up only 13.5 percent of the city's 269,000 people. The rest are poor Irish, Italian, and Polish families, with no one but the political ward leaders to turn to for jobs or other favors.[19]

The new middle-class politics of affluence has little to offer the citizens of the new ghettoes, and its middle-class styles and values are those of an America into which they have not yet been welcomed.

It is not easy to measure the decline of the urban machine or of the full range of conventional American party organization. The Survey Research Center reported, for example, that in the 1972 campaign only 29 percent of American adults had been contacted by someone from one of the parties. Most of the voting electorate, in other words, were reached exclusively, if at all, by the mass media. The candidate projecting his image and message through the media and personal appearances need not depend on the political party as the chief organizer and persuader of voters. Unquestionably this revolution in campaigning has also undermined the power of the party organizations. They are no longer the indispensable instrument for election to office. The candidate may now purchase the information and skills necessary for the campaign from the pollster and the public relations specialist. Several gen-

[19] Martin Arnold, *New York Times*, November 22, 1970.

erations ago he would have had no alternative but to get them from the party organization — at the party's price.

The chief contemporary changes in party organization, therefore, are the sporadic development of both candidate-centered campaign organizations and a club-style membership organization to accommodate the middle-class ideologists. What we have today in American party organization is far removed from the a priori organizational hierarchies that state legislatures have stipulated. The statutory models do exist here and there across the United States, but they are not — and probably never were — the norm in American party organization. State and local party organizations are today looser and more flexible. They can more accurately be seen as a coalition of political groupings and a pool or reservoir of party-oriented personnel. The county organization may, in other words, be a loose coalition of:

1. The statutory organization (or that part of it actually manned).
2. A cluster of related, satellite organizations (the auxiliaries, the clubs, and the personal followings of candidates and officeholders).
3. Allied, nonparty political organizations (the chamber of commerce, trade unions, other local interest groups, civic organizations, or nonparty liberal and conservative groups).
4. Active and potentially active individuals, attracted by candidates, by issues, and by the party itself.

The party is, in other words, a pool of active groups and candidates. They are recruited for different reasons, and they are activated by different candidates, different issues, and different elections. A hotly contested election of local officials, especially those controlling local patronage, will activate one cluster of partisans, and a congressional campaign in which the chief issue is the environment will activate another. What we have thought of as the party organization is really an organizational nucleus, a continuing core of organization and activists, around which are formed the shifting organizational coalitions that speak and act in the name of the local party.

In searching for change in American party organization, however, it is easy to lose sight of what does not change. Despite recent trends, the American parties remain largely skeletal, cadre party organizations, run generally by small numbers of activists and involving the great masses of their supporters scarcely at all. The shift away from the hierarchical organizational forms inherent in the statutes of the states has largely been a shift from a tight, hierarchical cadre organization to a loose cadre organization. For despite the brave appearance of some membership clubs, the American parties are still a long way away from becoming mass membership parties, and they are still some distance from achieving the continuously active, year-round tempos of those parties. By the standards of the parties in the rest of the world, American party organization continues to be characterized by unusual fluidity and evanescence, by failure to generate activity at nonelection times, and by the ease with which a handful of activists and public office-holders dominate it.

4

The Political Party of the Activists

Behind the imposing facades of the statutory party structures are the living, organizational realities of the political parties. The statutes do not reckon with the men and women of the party, their goals and motives, their interactions and relationships, the contributions they make to the organizations, the price they exact for those contributions. Yet the activity and motivations of those men and women are closer to the real world of party politics than all the statutory paragraphs put together.

We may easily accept the bemused cynicism of Will Rogers about the organizational condition of the American parties: "I don't belong to an organized political party. I'm a Democrat." But however disorganized they may be, they *are* purposive, goal-seeking organizations. As the most completely electoral parties in the democracies of the world, they are vastly committed to the winning of elections. Additionally, they may seek any number of short- and long-run goals: the spread of an ideology, the enactment of a set of public policies, or the easing of regulations affecting their activities. But whatever the goal or goals, the political party must select means and strategies for achieving them, always choosing with the knowledge that the other major party and other political organizations are similarly trying to attain competing goals of their own.

As an organization, therefore, the major political party is a mechanism for uniting adherents in the pursuit of goals. It recruits and mobilizes the resources and skills for political action. In the employment of those resources it works out a division of labor and a hierarchy of authority. Like any other complex organization it has its leaders and followers, its own specialization of role and function, its own internal system of communication. And it is a decision-making apparatus in which choices must be made about the mobilization of resources, the setting of strategies, and the deployment of assets. These internal processes are what the private life of the political party is all about. They are the processes by which the party organization converts the raw materials of people, resources, and expertise into the goal-oriented activities of the parties.

Goal seeking also goes on within the party organization on a personal, individual level. Individual party leaders, workers, and members are in the party organization for some identifiable, if covert or implicit, set of reasons. There must, in other words, be rewards or incentives — "payoffs" in the broadest, nonliteral sense of the word — for devoting one's time to party activity rather than to the service of Kiwanis or the PTA or the improvement of one's golf game.

THE SYSTEM OF INCENTIVES

The American political parties have never operated primarily in a cash economy: They have rarely bought or hired the millions of man-hours of labor they need. Even today paid staffs are small or nonexistent in most party organizations, and it is a rare party chairman who draws even a pittance of a salary from the party organization. The great number of Americans active in the parties receive no cash in return for their considerable time and skills. Even the earthy old custom of paying precinct workers on election day is vanishing. What is it, then, that induces party workers to lavish their hours and efforts on the affairs of the parties? If the parties' payments are not made in cash, in what coin are they made? [1]

Patronage

Patronage, the use of appointive governmental positions to reward past party work and induce future labors, is hardly unique to the American political parties. Even today the municipal services of the Italian cities swarm with the partisans in power. But very probably no other party system over its history has relied as systematically on patronage as the American. The easy confidence of the Jacksonians that no public task was so complex that it demanded experience and their matching conviction that "to the victors go the spoils" set the ethic early in the nineteenth century. From then to the present a vast array of public jobholders — from elevator operators and charwomen in city hall to American ambassadors in foreign capitals — have owed their appointment to political worthiness and the right political sponsorship.

Despite the explosive growth of government bureaucracy in this century, the amount of patronage available to the parties has declined precipitously. The expansion of civil service and merit systems has been

---

[1] For a somewhat different categorization of incentives, see James Q. Wilson, *Political Organizations* (New York: Basic Books, 1974).

the chief reason. What was once a flourishing federal patronage — historians write of the hordes of ill-mannered job seekers overrunning presidential inaugurations — has by now dwindled to well below 1 percent of the federal establishment. There still remain the United States marshals, the collectors of customs, and the rural mail carriers, to mention a few of the classic federal patronage posts, but theirs is a shrinking roster.[2]

Similar declines have come, albeit more slowly, to the states and localities. Any number of states, counties, and cities — the great majority probably — have virtually abolished patronage, moving to merit systems of some sort. In a number of states the governor has no patronage available beyond his own immediate staff. Patronage does, of course, continue to flourish in a minority of states. New York, for example, has some 40,000 positions available for party patronage. But in recent years even some of the vaunted centers of patronage have seen the merit principle make new and severe inroads. Kentucky legislation in 1960 reduced the number of year-round jobs available for patronage from 16,000 to 4,000, about 75 percent of them on the highway maintenance crews.[3] Pennsylvania, which had almost 50,000 patronage positions as late as 1970, lost a sizable number in collective bargaining. In 1971 some 17,500 workers, most of them also with the highway crews, negotiated a contract in which the state agreed not to discriminate against any employee on the basis of political affiliations. The contract also forbids the state to require workers to make political contributions or to engage in political activity. All sides agreed that it marked the beginning of the end of patronage in Pennsylvania. Actually, the cities and counties remain the chief centers of patronage. Chicago and Cook County, as we noted earlier, provide Mayor Richard Daley's Democratic organization with about 35,000 patronage jobs.

The unavailability of patronage is, however, only a part of the parties' problem. There are administrative problems as well. A recent survey of county chairmen in Ohio finds that they achieve only a partial return in party work or contributions from their patronage appointees.[4] The problems the parties encounter in using the available patronage jobs are legion. Patronage seekers may not meet the skill requirements of the job; heavy-equipment operators are hard enough to find without adding a set of political credentials. Also, the politics of patronage has always worked best among the depressed and disadvantaged; most patronage

[2] On the federal patronage see Harvey C. Mansfield, "Political Parties, Patronage, and the Federal Government Service," in *The Federal Government Service* (New York: American Assembly, 1954).
[3] Malcolm E. Jewell and Everett W. Cunningham, *Kentucky Politics* (Lexington: University of Kentucky Press, 1968), p. 43.
[4] W. Robert Gump, "The Functions of Patronage in American Party Politics: An Empirical Reappraisal," *Midwest Journal of Political Science* 15 (1971): 87–107.

positions do not tempt the educated, "respected" middle-class leadership the parties would like to attract. Furthermore, elected executives may use patronage to build their own political followings rather than the party apparatus. Finally, the parties may not be able to use the patronage available to them. Especially when they win power after years of failure, they do not have the necessary administrative machinery, the list of job seekers, or even the will to fire ruthlessly the opposing partisans and replace them with loyal followers.[5]

Perhaps in response both to the shrinking availability of patronage and to the party's shrinking need for it, recent years have seen the development of a new patronage variant: the political nonjob:

> The members of the new elite corps of American politics — the fund raisers, the intellectual counselors, "media coordinators," and leaders of the growing citizen's movements — are profitably employed already, with better pay and working conditions than government can offer. To them, the most appealing aspect of a public job is the prestige which sometimes accompanies it.
>
> Happily, political leaders have devised ways to bestow the status symbols of high office without the job itself. At Democratic national headquarters in Washington, where many such split-level appointments are routinely requisitioned and cleared, the new institution is known as "the honorary." Elsewhere it has been dubbed the patronage non-job, and it can range from nomination to a White House advisory committee to an invitation to be an honored member of an Air Force civic inspection tour of California, arranged at the behest of your local Congressman.[6]

So although by 1961 count there were only 133 full-time appointive jobs available for patronage use in the Interior Department (many of them carrying, moreover, skill and experience qualifications), the Department had 49 advisory committees and commissions with a total membership of about 800, 52 of them presidential appointments, with which the recipient received a parchment certificate signed by the president. The development is not a novel one. In Britain the king or queen's Honors List has served the same function for some time, and Kentucky has been appointing colonels for almost as long.

Political Career

Elective political office has the income, responsibility, prestige, and excitement — not to mention the power — that most patronage positions do not. And since the political party offers an efficient, and in some cases the only, avenue to elective office, it is inevitable that the pos-

[5] On patronage see Daniel P. Moynihan and James Q. Wilson, "Patronage in New York State, 1955–1959," *American Political Science Review* 58 (1964): 286–301; and Frank J. Sorauf, "State Patronage in a Rural County," *American Political Science Review* 50 (1956): 1046–56.
[6] Don Oberdorfer, "The New Political Non-Job," *Harper's* (October 1965), pp. 108ff.

sibility of an elective political career should recruit new party activists or sustain activity after other incentives have worn off. In the middle 1950s, for instance, about half of a group of Wisconsin party officials from both parties said they had been either elected or defeated in a past try for elective office; 21 percent declared that they "intended" to run, and 35 percent "desired" to make a race for office.[7]

There are party organizations with such disciplined control over their primaries that they can and do "give" public office, especially at the state and local level, to loyal party workers. If the party dominates the politics of the area, control of the primaries makes public offices an "elective patronage." The candidate is offered the chance to run and then does little more as the party organization runs up the necessary majorities. That degree of control over nomination and election to office is, however, vanishing along with patronage. Both the party and the would-be candidate feel the impact. The party must look for candidates with some appeal and qualities beyond their service to the party. The candidates know that, useful though the advantage of party support may be, it is rarely sufficient by itself.

What then does the candidate get from the support of the party? He needs advice, know-how, manpower, and money, and in most parts of the country the party still remains a likely source of them. Service in the party, then, yields the skill, experience, connections, approval, and resources that any candidate needs. It is, of course, possible for the candidate without party ties to seek election, but for every one who does, there are hundreds of successful office seekers who have party ties. And for the partisan who already holds office there is no easier way to ensure reelection or to move to a more attractive office than by work in the party. So sedulous are the party's officeholders in currying the support of the party organizations that speculation over their ambitions and "moves" remains a favorite intraparty recreation.

Preferments

The tangible, material rewards of politics may take forms other than appointive or elective office. The active partisan or the financial "fat cat" may, for example, seek preference in the awarding of public contracts. In this respect, it is no accident that the leaders of the construction industry are so active politically in the states and localities that spend millions every year on roads and public buildings. Preference may take other forms: a tolerant or haphazard application of regulatory or inspection policies, unusually prompt or efficient public services (snow and garbage removal, for example), a forgiving instrument of the law (e.g.,

[7] Leon D. Epstein, *Politics in Wisconsin* (Madison: University of Wisconsin Press, 1958), pp. 91, 187.

the fixed traffic ticket), or the granting of a scarce public service (admission to crowded mental hospitals, for instance). It may also involve the granting of scarce "opportunities" such as liquor licenses or franchises. By "preferment," in other words, one means special treatment or advantage, and it is dependent usually on the party's holding the decision-making positions in government. It is partly in this sense that parties talk of "controlling" city hall, the county courthouse, or the state capitol.

Preferments: An Old and a Recent View

Preferments available to the party faithful change with time. So, too, do the terms that describe them and the justifications that support them. But whether it's "honest graft" or an extended definition of patronage, the incentive is the same.

"There's an honest graft, and I'm an example of how it works. I might sum up the whole thing by sayin': 'I seen my opportunities and I took 'em.'

"Just let me explain by examples. My party's in power in the city, and it's goin' to undertake a lot of public improvements. Well, I'm tipped off, say, that they're going to lay out a new park at a certain place.

"I see my opportunity and I take it. I go to that place and I buy up all the land I can in the neighborhood. . . .

"Ain't it perfectly honest to charge a good price and make a profit on my investment and foresight? Of course it is. Well, that's honest graft."

George Washington Plunkett in William Riordan's
Plunkett of Tammany Hall (New York: Dutton, 1905), p. 3.

"This is the stuff of modern political patronage:

"Insurance premiums on government property. For example, Erastus Corning 2d, the Democratic Mayor of Albany, is president of an insurance company that receives $100,000 in annual premiums to insure the property of Albany County.

"Bank deposits of state funds. For example, John J. Lynch, chairman of the Brooklyn Democratic party, is chairman of a bank that has $3-million in state funds deposited by Controller Arthur Levitt. . . .

"Mr. Corning said his company received $100,000 in premiums annually for insuring the property of Albany County. This business was obtained without competitive bidding, because the uniform insurance rates are fixed by law by the State Department of Insurance and no insurance company can undersell another.

"Asked whether there was a conflict between his public and private offices, the Mayor replied in an interview: 'I'm in no way a county official. The question of conflict of interest has never been raised.' "

Martin Tolchin, *New York Times*,
June 17, 1968, pp. 1, 30.

One particularly unappealing form is the "preferment" given activities that operate on the shady side of the law. It may involve a calculated ignoring of prostitution, bookmaking, the numbers game, or traffic in drugs in return for some form of political support. In other forms it has involved the parties' taking a share of protection money or the proceeds from crime, vice, or the rackets. The link between crime and politics in New York, write Glazer and Moynihan, was "complex."

The politicians of course needed money; and political protection was on the whole more important to illegitimate than to legitimate businessmen. Other elements were mixed in. There was ethnic pride, which motivated a Frank Costello as much as it did a businessman who had not become rich as a bootlegger. There was a desire to help out relatives and friends. There was the fact that bootleggers, politicians, lawyers, judges, and policemen had all grown up on the block together, and had never lost touch. How was one to sort out the influences, and decide the significance of the fact that judges and ex-bootleggers and gamblers all sat around the same table to raise money for an orphan's home? [8]

The prevalence of such an incentive to party effort is understandably difficult to estimate. Perhaps it suffices to say that it is probably less vital than the political cynics think and more important than the Pollyannas admit. The chances are, though, that what nexus there is between organized crime and government goes on through mechanisms other than the political party. And when it touches the party and electoral politics, the influence of crime is probably felt more through campaign contributions than directly in the party organization. In 1960 Alexander Heard estimated ("a guess — and that is what it is") that underworld money accounted for 15 percent of the campaign expenditures at state and local levels.[9]

Socioeconomic Mobility

Political activity offers easy publicity (or notoriety) and contacts for those who seek them: young lawyers trying to build a practice, owners of food and watering spots, insurance and real estate brokers, storekeepers, and the socially ambitious. Party activity opens up the contacts that lead to prosperity in a business or profession, to a new job or business opportunity, even to an elevated social status.

Writes one observer of the Philadelphia organization men:

One explanation of their motivation would locate the "boys'" essential urge in the factor known as "prestige." The truth is, many intellectuals and many

[8] Nathan Glazer and Daniel P. Moynihan, *Beyond the Melting Pot* (Cambridge: MIT Press, 1963), pp. 210–12.
[9] Alexander Heard, *The Costs of Democracy* (Chapel Hill: University of North Carolina Press, 1960), p. 163.

members of the upper class who have come in contact with politicians argue that, for the Irish, Jewish, Italian bright boys who pursue it, politics is a "status-conferring" occupation. The Bill Greens and the Victor Blancs and the Aus Meehans, they point out, could no doubt have earned wealth and even the respect of their fellow-men by selling insurance, practicing law, and the like. But the one thing that they could not earn in these ways is "place" in the community. Politics gives them that.[10]

In the tired American phrase, some people join the active ranks in the parties to "get ahead," whether they define getting ahead in terms of upward social or economic mobility.

Social and Psychological Satisfactions

The personal, nonmaterial rewards of party activity are not easy to identify and certainly not easy to measure. But one can sense the social rewards of politics in the camaraderie of the gang at party headquarters or the courthouse. It is evident at a party dinner as the workers press around the great and near great of the party, hoping for a word of greeting or a nod of recognition. In the new-style political clubs the attractiveness of the social life and friendship circle is explicit. "Many volunteers are rootless, transient newcomers searching the city for a means of associating with like-minded people." But while the parties' clubs rely on the social incentives, those incentives are probably secondary:

Although many clubs in various cities offer their members reduced air fares to Europe on charter flights, a full schedule of social events, forums featuring prestigious speakers, and the opportunity to play the political game, and although some members join simply to find a mate quickly or get to Paris inexpensively, if the clubs should cease to define themselves as organizations devoted to liberalism or reformism or similar worthy causes, they could not for long sustain the interest of any but the handful who simply enjoy the company of others or like being district leader.[11]

At a more general level, almost all the reported research on the motivations of party activists finds that large numbers of them reply that they "like people" or that they "like politics."

Social satisfactions merge almost imperceptibly into the psychological. "Like the theater, politics is a great nourisher of egos," writes one observer. "It attracts men who are hungry for attention, for assurance that somebody loves them, for the soul-stirring music of their own

[10] James Reichley, *The Art of Government: Reform and Organization Politics in Philadelphia* (New York: Fund for the Republic, 1959), p. 104.
[11] James Q. Wilson, *The Amateur Democrat* (Chicago: University of Chicago Press, 1962), p. 165.

voices." [12] Party work may also offer the individual a cause or an enterprise with which to identify, a charismatic leader to follow, a round of activities that can lift him above the personally unrewarding tasks of the workaday world. The party may be a small island of excitement in a sea of routine. It may even offer an occasion for the manipulation or domination of others, a chance to decide or command, even an avenue for the projection of aggressions and hostilities.

Ideology and Policy Issues

Even the most casual soundings of party rhetoric these days indicate an increasing identification of partisans as "liberals" or "conservatives." Behind these phrases lies a potent motivation to party activity: a commitment to clusters of related attitudes about government and politics, especially about the proper role of government in contemporary society. On a more modest and limited scale the spur to activity may be concern for a single issue or interest (tax cuts, the war in Vietnam, the maintenance of local schools, the well-being of a neighborhood or racial or ethnic group) or a single area of policy concern (foreign policy, civil rights, local planning). The "cause" may, indeed, be the reform or rehabilitation of the political party itself.

Just as the importance of the immediate, material, personal rewards of politics has recently declined, that of issue and ideology has increased. Even in Manhattan, long the fief of Tammany Hall, the trend is evident:

There is a "new look" among today's political activists. They are "respectable," solid middle-class citizens. The party "hack" of fiction, films, and the traditional literature is hard to find among the young, well-educated, affluent, and socially acceptable committeemen — and women — of the nineteen-sixties. Concomitantly, both the nature of political motivation and the character of political activity have changed. The contemporary politician considers his party organization an instrument for effectuating policy rather than a haven of personal security. He tends to be more interested in social reform than in catering to individual constituents. [13]

In national politics the country in 1964 witnessed the capture of the Republican national party by partisans whose chief criterion for candidate and platform was frankly ideological. And in 1968 and 1972 the ideological left organized around the presidential candidacies of Eugene McCarthy and George McGovern, deeply affecting the presidential politics of the Democrats. [14]

The party activist may also be drawn to the party by a more general

[12] John Fischer, "Please Don't Bite the Politicians," *Harper's* (November 1960), p. 16.
[13] Robert S. Hirschfield, Bert E. Swanson, and Blanche D. Blank, "A Profile of Political Activists in Manhattan," *Western Political Quarterly* 15 (1962): 505.
[14] Party ideology will be considered more fully in Chap. 16.

civic commitment. A sense of obligation and duty as a citizen, a belief in the democratic values of citizen participation, may impel him. Scholars who have questioned party workers about their motives for service in the party know the familiar answers. They were "asked" to serve, and they assented because it was their civic duty. Often that response, in whatever words it may be couched, merely masks what the respondent feels are less acceptable motives. Often, however, it is an honest reflection of deeply ingrained civic values. Often, too, it may be combined with general, even vague, commitments to "good government" and political reform.

The Party Itself

Two final varieties of incentive, both essentially related to the party per se, must be mentioned. First of all, as a party activist works within the party, the well-being of the party itself becomes an incentive for work. He attaches many of his loyalties and aspirations to the party, and its health becomes an end in itself. The party's wins and losses become issues in and of themselves, and attacks on it are far more than attacks on its policies and activities. Second, it may be, as Robert Salisbury suggests in his study of St. Louis politicians, that large numbers of party activists participate "because they were brought up in a highly politicized atmosphere." The party "participant per family socialization was probably not exposed to involvement in other kinds of organizations, any more than a devout young communicant of the church would necessarily be taught to carry his devotion into other organizational settings." [15] In other words, party workers may gravitate to the party because they are accustomed to it and because through years of socialization they have invested loyalties in it.

No party organization depends on a single incentive, and very few partisans labor in the party for only one. Most party organizations rely on a variety or system of incentives. A residuum of patronage workers may coexist with workers attracted by policy issues or by a middle-class sense of civic responsibility. The mixture of incentives may vary between urban and rural areas, or between different local political cultures. One study suggests that at least in New York's Nassau County, issues and ideologies are a less potent incentive in the majority than in the minority party.[16] The mix may even vary within the same party

[15] Robert H. Salisbury, "The Urban Party Organization Member," *Public Opinion Quarterly* 29 (1965–66): 562, 564. For additional intergenerational data see David R. Derge, *Public Leadership in Indiana* (Bloomington: Indiana University Institute of Public Administration, 1969).
[16] Dennis S. Ippolito and Lewis Bowman, "Goals and Activities of Party Officials in a Suburban Community," *Western Political Quarterly* 22 (1969): 572–80.

organization. Eldersveld reports that in Wayne County, Michigan, the precinct chairmen depend heavily on the rewards of social contacts, whereas the party's higher leadership seeks a combination of immediate economic gain and ideological-philosophical rewards.[17]

For all the subtleties of the mix and variety of incentives, however, general comments about their overall frequency *are* possible. Scholarly evidence on the point comes from sporadic studies of parties in scattered parts of the country, but what evidence there is points to the dominance of ideological or issue incentives. Put very simply, the desire to use the party as a means to achieve policy goals appears to be the major incentive attracting individuals to party work these days.[18] And even though similar data are unavailable for earlier periods, there is ample reason to believe that this generalization was far less true of party workers a generation or two ago.

Indeed, incentives may change even for any one individual — that is, the incentive that recruits a person to party activity may not sustain him in that activity. Several studies suggest that a shift in incentive takes place in those party activists attracted by the purposive incentives — those who seek to achieve issue, ideological, or other impersonal goals through their party activity. To sustain their involvement in party work, they tend to depend more on incentives of social contact, identification with the party itself, and other personal rewards and satisfactions.[19] Perhaps an electorally pragmatic party — one traditionally committed to the flexibilities necessary to win elections — has difficulty providing the ideological successes to sustain the worker whose incentive remains ideological for any length of time.

THE PROCESSES OF RECRUITMENT

The mere existence of incentives for work in the party organization will not automatically produce a full roster of active workers. In the political party, as in any other large organization, the organization itself must recruit actively in order to ensure for itself useful and compatible recruits. For his part, the potential activist may lack either the knowledge of the opportunity or the stimulus to act or both. There must, therefore,

---

[17] Samuel Eldersveld, *Political Parties: A Behavioral Analysis* (Chicago: Rand, McNally, 1964), p. 278; see also all of Chap. 11.

[18] Lewis Bowman, Dennis Ippolito, and William Donaldson, "Incentives for the Maintenance of Grassroots Political Activism," *Midwest Journal of Political Science* 13 (1969): 126–39; Charles W. Wiggins and William L. Turk, "State Party Chairmen: A Profile," *Western Political Quarterly* 23 (1970): 321–32.

[19] Among others, see M. Margaret Conway and Frank B. Feigert, "Motivation, Incentive Systems, and the Political Organization," *American Political Science Review* 62 (1968): 1159–73.

be some process of recruitment that will join the opportunity and the stimulus to the incentives in order to attract the activists.

However, the parties find it difficult to undertake this recruitment and thus to undertake their own continuing renewal. Frequently their incentives are not attractive enough to compete even with the modest pleasures of activity in the local PTA. They lack any effective mechanism for recruiting new personnel and may even lack the awareness of the necessity. Furthermore, state statutes often take at least part of the recruitment process out of their hands; open party caucuses and the election of party officials at primaries tend to encourage self-recruitment at the expense of party initiatives and control. Above all, the chronic need for personnel of any kind disposes the parties to accept whatever help is available. Even patronage-rich organizations in job-poor communities tend not to be rigorous in recruiting new activists. Friendship and contacts within the party organization may speed the entry of the new activist more effectively than political skills or promise of performance.

In the absence of regular, rigorous party-recruitment procedures, opportunities for party work come in a haphazard way. Initially, a certain degree of awareness of and information about the parties is necessary, plus some strong political goals and commitments. Then at the time of recruitment there must also be some more immediate occasion or stimulus for the individual to enter party work. Sometimes that stimulus is internal, and the individual in effect recruits himself. In other cases the stimulus is external, most often the invitation or persuasion of some individual. Activists tend to ascribe their initial recruitment largely to these external stimuli; two studies of local party workers have set the self-starters at only 10 and 29 percent of the interviewees.[20] In view of the favorable myth of the office seeking the individual, however, it may be that the party activists protest too much.

In sum, then, we have an extensive, informal recruitment system — a complex of interrelated factors that selects out of the American population a particular group of men and women. Among its elements are:

1. The motives, goals, and knowledge of the men and women with the kinds of skills and assets the parties want to recruit.
2. The incentives to party activity which the party can offer.
3. The external factors which alter the value of the incentive (e.g., the impact of employment levels on the value of patronage) or the ability

---

[20] Phillip Althoff and Samuel C. Patterson, "Political Activism in a Rural County," *Midwest Journal of Political Science* 10 (1966): 39–51; and Lewis Bowman and G. R. Boynton, "Recruitment Patterns among Local Party Officials," *American Political Science Review* 60 (1966): 667–76. On the initial recruitment to party work in general see also Eldersveld, *Political Parties*, Chap. 6.

of the individual to accept it (e.g., laws such as the Hatch Acts, which forbid active party work by U.S. civil servants).

4. The factors which determine the party's recruitment role (e.g., the election of precinct workers at primaries).

5. The contacts, overtures, opportunities, and persuasions that are the immediate, proximate occasions of recruitment.[21]

The components of this system change constantly, and as they do they affect the supply of personnel entering the organization and thus the organization itself. Recruitment in whatever form, though, is a matching of the motives and goals of the individual with the incentives and expectations of the party organization. The immediate act of recruitment is either the catalyst or the occasion for the matching.

An auxiliary recruitment system may also work within the organization to promote especially successful party workers to positions of greater responsibility. What data we have on the political careers of party activists, however, do not suggest that party workers uniformly inch up a career ladder in the party, position by position. For example, only about one-third of a recent group of county chairmen and cochairmen in Oklahoma had ever held any other party office, and half of them had never held any public or party office at all.[22]

On the other hand, Detroit area party leadership tends to rise almost exclusively through the avenues of party and public office; one group comes up through the precinct positions, another through the auxiliary organizations (i.e., the women's groups, youth organizations, political clubs), and a third and smaller group moves from the race for public office to a career within the party.[23] In general, the way stations of a political career vary with and reflect the nature of the political organization. In those party organizations of relatively open access and easy mobility, careers in the party are easily, almost spontaneously, developed. In the disciplined, hierarchical party organization, the party activist works up the hierarchy in carefully graded steps and expectations.

THE PARTIES' RECRUITS

Since recruitment patterns both change over time and differ from locality to locality, it is difficult to generalize about the activists they recruit into the party organization. Note, for example, the differences between

[21] For an alternate but similar recruitment model, see the Bowman and Boynton article cited in footnote 20. C. Richard Hoffstetter in "Organizational Activists: The Bases of Participation in Amateur and Professional Groups," *American Politics Quarterly* 1 (1973): 244–76, also concludes that individual participation is based on considerations much broader than simply responses to incentives.

[22] Samuel C. Patterson, "Characteristics of Party Leaders," *Western Political Quarterly* 16 (1963): 343–44.

[23] Eldersveld, *Political Parties*, pp. 142–43.

the local committeemen and committeewomen of the Democratic parties of Pittsburgh and Manhattan and how those differences are related to fundamental differences in the incentive and recruitment systems:[24]

	Pittsburgh (1970)	Manhattan (1959–60)
Patronage holders	74% of men, 42% of women	Approximately 5% "on public payroll"
Education	17% attended or graduated from college	67% attended or graduated from college
Age	15% under 40	28% under 35
Occupations	Overwhelmingly governmental	19% business executives and professional; 24% small businessmen

This is not to suggest that any single factor in the recruitment (in this case the presence or absence of the patronage incentive) fully explains the differences between the Democratic activists of these two city organizations. Differences of this sort may also reflect the kinds of personnel the organization wants and needs, differences in organizational roles and tasks (as between dominant and minority parties or between machine and club-style parties) or even differences in what the local community considers acceptable motives and incentives.

American party activists, despite all the variations in recruitment systems, do have in common two characteristics that set them apart from the general population of adults. First, they tend rather uniformly to come from families with a history of party activity. Study after study indicates that large numbers of party activists had in their immediate family an adult party activist as they were growing up. Second, activists are marked by their relatively high socioeconomic status (SES), whether one measures SES by income, by years of formal education, or by occupation. The highest SES among the active partisans can be found, as one might expect, in the top leadership ranks of the parties. Consequently, the parties attract men and women with the time and financial resources to afford politics, with the information and knowledge to understand it, and with the skills to be useful in it. Only some local organizations, and especially their precinct workers, have been exceptions; in general, only in patronage-oriented, favor-dispensing machines in the center cities are the party workers at all representative of the populations in which they work.[25]

[24] Hirschfield, Swanson, and Blank, "Political Activists in Manhattan," and Lee S. Weinberg, "Stability and Change Among Pittsburgh Precinct Politicians, 1954–70," *Social Science* 50 (1975): 10–16.
[25] Minor parties may also be an exception to the relatively high SES of party activists. See, for example, James M. Elden and David R. Schweitzer, "New Third Party Radicalism: The Case of the California Peace and Freedom Party," *Western Political Quarterly* 24 (1971): 761–74.

In most parts of the country, however, Republican activists come from higher SES groups than do their Democratic counterparts. One table in the Eldersveld study of the Detroit area parties (Table 1) illustrates clearly this SES difference between the two parties (and between each party's middle leadership and precinct workers as well). The Republicans' higher SES undoubtedly reflects their policy and ideological sympathies for higher income and status groups over the last generation or more. One exception to the general SES ascendancy of the Republicans does appear around the country. In one-party Democratic areas the dominant Democratic party attracts high-status leadership, probably

TABLE 1   Income, Occupation, and Education for Middle and Lower Level Party Leaders: Wayne County, Michigan, Study

	Republicans		Democrats	
	Executive board	Precinct leaders	Executive board	Precinct leaders
Income				
Under $4,000	0%	15%	0%	7%
$4,000–$5,000	10	10	0	16
$5,000–$10,000	52	35	100	53
Over $10,000	38	35	0	17
Not ascertainable	0	5	0	6
Education				
Elementary only	9	11	0	14
High school	30	38	75	60
College (other than business college)	61	51	25	26
Completed college	52	22	18	14
Occupation (head of household)				
Professional	43	19	18	16
Manager, proprietor	17	36	29	10
Clerical and sales	9	14	6	17
Blue-collar (craftsman, foreman)	30	16	41	35
Blue-collar (semiskilled and unskilled)	0	15	6	22
Number of cases	23	143	18	138

Source   Samuel J. Eldersveld, *Political Parties: A Behavioral Analysis*, © 1964 by Rand McNally and Company, Chicago, Table 3.1, p. 52.

because it is both "respectable" as the party of power and inviting as the party of opportunity.[26]

Within this overloading of high-status activists, one special dominance — that of lawyers — is too obvious to be overlooked and too well known to bear much elaboration. Lawyers are the high priests of the American political cult. Studies of county chairmen in Oklahoma, Kansas, North Carolina, and Wisconsin show a median percentage of attorneys among county chairmen somewhat above 20 percent. Recently more than 40 percent of the state chairmen around the country were also attorneys.[27] To an extent unduplicated in other democracies the lawyer in American society is the professional political careerist. Lawyers have cultivated skills of oratory and debate, and they are occupationally concerned with the actions of government, schooled in public issues, and practiced in parliamentary procedures. Naturally they appear to many Americans ideally suited to assume political leadership. They generally also have the necessary community contacts and flexible time schedule for party activity; their professional income and stature also stand to gain from political activity. The major parties even reserve for them a special type of political reward: the elective or politically appointive judgeship.[28]

Workers in the two parties tend also to vary in religion and ethnic background. In a significant number of localities across the country, the Democratic party organizations have larger percentages of Catholics and Jews, those of the Republican party higher percentages of Protestants. Similarly (and very much relatedly), Democratic workers more frequently than Republicans come from Irish and Southern and Eastern European national and ethnic stock. Republicans come more frequently from Northern and Western European backgrounds and from old Yankee families.[29] These interparty differences again reflect the basic voter coalitions of the two parties. Of course, there is a strong tendency for the activists of both parties to reflect the ethnic, racial, national, and religious composition of a homogeneous area. They are the sons and daughters of the locally dominant or prominent groups. While they are

[26] Patterson, "Characteristics of Party Leaders," pp. 332–52; and William J. Crotty, "The Social Attributes of Party Organizational Activists in a Transitional Political System," Western Political Quarterly 20 (1967): 669–81. On the more general SES differences between workers of the two major parties, see Richard J. Heuwinkel and Charles W. Wiggins, "Party Competition and Party Leadership Attributes," American Journal of Political Science 17 (1973): 159–69. It is also important to note that while party leaders do come from upper SES groups, by and large they do not come from the very highest, elite SES circles.

[27] Patterson, "Characteristics of Party Leaders," p. 339; Crotty, "Social Attributes," p. 677; Wiggins and Turk, "State Party Chairmen," p. 325.

[28] One cannot begin to summarize the literature dealing with lawyers in American politics. As an example, see Heinz Eulau and John D. Sprague, Lawyers in Politics (Indianapolis: Bobbs-Merrill, 1964).

[29] For example, see Weinberg, "Stability and Change."

thoroughly representative of these groups, their education, income, and occupation (especially of the Republicans) will still be well above the average SES for the area.

So much for the social characteristics of the organizational activists. There remains the tantalizing and elusive question of their personalities and their psyches. On a common sense level, one can say without fear of contradiction that party activists are often gregarious and extroverted. Yet, that fact is apparent almost by definition alone, for party activity is not apt to appeal to the introvert or the misanthrope. But Harold Lasswell and others have argued that there is a special "political personality," that political life attracts men and women with personal tensions that can be easily projected on public objects or with personal needs that can be sublimated or satisfied in political activity.[30] No convincing evidence exists, however, that the parties attract activists with any different or more pressing personality needs than the American population as a whole. One study does find, in fact, that the incidence of "authoritarian personalities" is not high among party workers. (The few authoritarians do tend to favor both disciplined, hierarchical party organizations and nonideological party goals and activities.)[31]

It goes without saying that people are the parties' chief organizational resource. But different people bring different expectations, goals, skills to the party. To a considerable extent the goals and activities of a party organization reflect the men and women its incentives are able to recruit. The differences in organizational characteristics between Democrats and Republicans in any locality — or between reformers and regulars within a party — begin with differences in the party workers themselves, their backgrounds and skills, their personal goals and motives, their perception of their rights and roles as party activists, and their understanding of the ultimate goals and priorities of the party and its representatives.

VITALITY OF THE PARTY ORGANIZATION

The party organization is an apparatus for recruiting political resources and mobilizing them in the pursuit of political goals. Its organizational capacity results from the specialization of roles and skills employed in the achievement of common political objectives. The diversity in American party organization produces diversity of organizational goals, styles, and activities. For decades the American model or "ideal" in local party organization has been the classic urban machine. Its organizational hierarchy, its full range of year-round services and activities, and its army

[30] Harold Lasswell, *Psychopathology and Politics* (Chicago: University of Chicago Press, 1931), and also his *Power and Personality* (New York: Norton, 1948).
[31] Louise Harned, "Authoritarian Attitudes and Party Activity," *Public Opinion Quarterly* 25 (1961): 393–99.

of eager workers in the wards and precincts have represented organizational perfection to many party leaders. It is an organizational form in which the personal attention, service, friendship, and persuasiveness of the local party worker are directed at the local electorate. All its activities through the year are geared to earn the support of that electorate and thus enable the activists and office seekers of the party to deliver its vote and achieve their political goals through victory at the polls.

As the last chapter suggested, the ideal has never been the norm. The classic machine organization was never widespread in either of the two major parties in the United States. Its chief and indispensable ingredient, the local ward or precinct worker, has too often been inactive or completely absent. Recent evidence, even in the American cities, has begun to mount:

1. Of party activists in St. Louis, some 27 percent do not perform "any significant amount of political or electioneering tasks." [32]
2. Only about one-fourth of a group of workers in Massachusetts and North Carolina perform all four "critical" campaign tasks (door-to-door canvasing, telephone campaigning, transporting people to the polls, and talking to voters about the election); only one-half of them perform any three.[33]
3. In the Detroit area only 13 percent of the Democratic precinct workers and 3 percent of the Republicans meet criteria of organizational efficiency close to the model of the well-organized political machine.[34]

Were there comparable data on rural and small-town party organization, they would surely suggest even greater disorganization.

However, the organizational problem extends beyond inert or underactive committeepersons. Parties often cannot maintain the nexus of roles and relationships on which the organizational paragon depends. Eldersveld's study of the Detroit parties offers the fullest analysis. Communication lines in the parties, he found,

were not a perfect pyramid; communication was highly voluntaristic and noncoercive. From one-fourth to two-fifths of the precinct leaders did not have contacts with their district leaders, and from 10 to 15 percent seemed almost completely isolated. Further, the content of communication in the party seemed highly preoccupied with "vote getting" and campaign tactics.

Nor were authority relationships pyramided, for

the vast majority of precinct leaders were "little oligarchs," running their operations alone or with "friends and neighbors," with limited contact and

---

[32] Salisbury, "Urban Party Organization Member," p. 557.
[33] Lewis Bowman and G. R. Boynton, "Activities and Role Definitions of Grassroots Party Officials," *Journal of Politics* 28 (1966): 132-34.
[34] Eldersveld, *Political Parties*, p. 348.

involvement in district-level operations, and with limited reasons for self-consciously adjusting their work patterns and plans to perceive district-level demands.[35]

Throughout the Detroit parties, in fact, there was only diversity whereas the ideal assumed monolithic homogeneity. Local workers entered and remained in party service for a splendid variety of motives. They carried out different tasks, even within the same party. They had differing political values and differing perceptions of political reality — even different views of their own and the opposing party. And they differed greatly in the way they perceived their roles as precinct leaders. The parties "did not communicate one particular role conception to rank-and-file leaders. The party line, if there was one, was confused and poorly communicated." As a result, some 45 percent saw themselves chiefly as vote mobilizers, 24 percent as ideological leaders, 18 percent as welfare promoters for local residents, and 10 percent appeared to have formulated no role at all.[36]

Yet the ideal or the myth of American party organization persists. Party organizations across the country are judged against it, and hopeful party leaders aspire to it. Almost every concept of organizational strength employs it. It is, however, in many ways a late nineteenth-century ideal; it reflects the methods of campaigning and the nature of the American electorate in that era. Perhaps as an organizational type it is either not necessary in view of today's campaigns and elections or not feasible in view of today's political resources. Certainly it is not easily compatible with the participatory demands of the new reformers and activists. Very possibly voters can be reached — or will have to be reached — by means other than the ubiquitous precinct worker. No one form of party organization (and no one kind of organizational incentive or activist) is best or optimal. Different political traditions, resources, and styles demand different kinds of party organization.

Leaving judgments of strength and weakness aside, American party organizations do differ in their distance from the classic organizational type. And it is possible to generalize roughly about the conditions under which they do or do not approach it.

Urban-Rural Differences

The close proximity of people in urban residential neighborhoods makes possible the intense political activity, the intricate organizational life, and the stable political loyalties of the highly developed political organizations. So, too, do the problems of the cities and the presence of the

[35] Ibid., pp. 377, 408.
[36] Ibid., pp. 254, 270. No roles were ascertained for 3 percent of the leaders.

unassimilated minorities there. Door-to-door campaigning, election rallies, party headquarters, even regular contact with the voters — all the
signs of strong and vigorous party organization — make far less sense
in rural America. Party nominating and electioneering differ there, and
so do the incentives for and the amount of party activity. Not surprisingly, then, the acmes of party organization have been reached in the
urban, especially in the metropolitan, centers.[37]

Differences in Political Cultures

The expectations that citizens have about political party organization
differ. The persistent canvasing by committeepersons and their frank
questions about voter preferences may be taken as a matter of course in
some quarters but not in others. Similarly, patronage and the political
organization founded on it may be respectable in some states or localities but not in others. What may seem a benevolent party organization
in Chicago may offend a good many sensibilities in down-state Illinois.
These differences in political culture tend to follow urban-rural lines, but
there are also regional and social-class differences in norms and expectations for the parties.

Differences in Two-Party Competitiveness

Unquestionably the great number of defunct party organizations occur
in the long-term minority parties. The Republican parties of the Deep
South until the 1950s served for a long time as their classic illustration.
Badly demoralized and shorn of both influence and hope, the minority
party easily lapses into organizational feebleness. It can provide none of
the rewards, tangible or intangible, that induce individuals to give their
time, skills, or money to a party organization. Its activists often lack
respectability, much less influence in the community.[38]

Differences in State Statutes

The statutory forms and regulations of some states are more burden-
some than those of others. All other things being equal, for example, a
party is handicapped by a state requirement that all party functionaries
be chosen at the primary. Even within a single state, inflexible statutory

---

[37] See Frank J. Sorauf, *Party and Representation* (New York: Atherton, 1963), especially Chap. 3. For a somewhat different approach to this issue with results not
altogether different, see Paul A. Beck, "Environment and Party: The Impact of Political and Demographic County Characteristics on Party Behavior," *American
Political Science Review* 68 (1974): 1229–44.
[38] V. O. Key, *Southern Politics* (New York: Knopf, 1949), Chap. 13.

provisions limit the local parties that wish to innovate in forms of organization.

Differences in Primary Laws

In a number of states with efficient party organization (Indiana, Connecticut, and Delaware come to mind) the organizations still nominate candidates for statewide offices and some local ones at conventions. That is, the direct primaries of those states are among the least comprehensive in the country, and in the case of Connecticut the primary did not come into being until 1955. Consequently, the party still had a vital nominating role left to it, a purpose and need for maintaining organizational capacity. Lockard wrote of the Connecticut parties before the primary:

In the absence of a primary the opportunity for political advancement lay with the organization, not through independent appeals to the electorate in a primary election. Local organizations had reason to exist even where there was little hope of winning an election for their party, for there were state conventions biennially in which important decisions were made. In contrast to many states in which the primary has been employed, there has been no appreciable withering away of the party organization in local areas.[39]

V. O. Key, in fact, has argued that the introduction of the direct primary into American politics in this century is primarily responsible for the atrophy of local party organization throughout the country.[40]

This list of explanations is not intended to be comprehensive. The availability of patronage or other rewards of preference explains the development of some powerful local and statewide organizations, although in other settings there appears to be no relationship between the incentive a party worker responds to and the extent of his party activity.[41] In other instances flourishing organization may simply reflect the effort and skill of a particular party leader or group of leaders. Hard work and organizational ability are as easily felt in the parties as they are in any other large social group.

POWER AND DISCIPLINE IN THE ORGANIZATION

Organization implies discipline — at least enough discipline to coordinate its parts and to implement its decisions. It also implies some well-established system of authority for making those decisions. The organi-

[39] Duane Lockard, *New England State Politics* (Princeton: Princeton University Press, 1959), pp. 325–26.
[40] V. O. Key, *American State Politics* (New York: Knopf, 1956), Chap. 6.
[41] M. Margaret Conway and Frank B. Feigert, "Incentives and Task Performance Among Party Precinct Workers," *Western Political Quarterly* 27 (1974): 693–709.

zational myths of American politics, if anything, have overreacted to these implications and posited the presence of virtually authoritarian control within the party organization. Some leader generally identified as the boss has widely been thought to wield absolute power over its minions. Much like a Renaissance despot, he was said to rule by reason of cunning, bravery, and sheer force of will. The boss, in fact, became something of an American folk hero, feared for his ruthlessness and admired for his rascality and intrepid daring. He has been celebrated in the public arts,[42] and if he had not existed, it might have been necessary to create him, if only to justify the political cynicism of generations of Americans.

Very few organizational leaders ruled or now rule absolutely by personal magnetism, tactical adroitness, or the use of sanctions. Even in the era of boss rule, the boss's power was shared with influential underlings, and the terms of that sharing were deeply rooted in all of the hierarchical traditions of the organization.

The persistent attacks on "Boss rule" have misrepresented the nature of power in the old machine system. Power was hierarchical in the party, diffused in the way it is diffused in any army. Because the commanding general was powerful, it did not follow that the division generals were powerless. Tammany district leaders were important men, and, right down to the block captain, all had rights.[43]

Yet, it does remain true that in many of the classic political organizations, power and discipline were greatly centralized and largely removed from the control of workers and activists in the wards and precincts. The local leader had his rights, but they were bounded by the greater rights and authority of his superiors.

Much of that centralization was possible because the foot soldier in the ranks accepted the hierarchical system of authority. If he was a Catholic, and many were, the party's hierarchy may have seemed as natural and inevitable as that of the Church. Furthermore, his goals were clear and simple. If he received his patronage job, he cared little about what the party did or did not do. More recently, however, the party activist has come to demand a voice in the affairs of the party. He is an ideologist, and a goodly portion of his ideological fervor may be directed at reforming the party's authoritarianism and bossism. He is committed to the norms and imperatives of democracy, at least in part because of his higher level of education and political information. His commitment to intraparty democracy also follows logically from his desire to move the party to ideology, because the achievement of his own political goals

[42] For example, note Edwin O'Connor, The Last Hurrah (Boston: Little, Brown, 1956), and Robert Penn Warren, All the King's Men (New York: Harcourt, Brace, 1946).
[43] Glazer and Moynihan, Beyond the Melting Pot, p. 227.

The Boss in Cartoon

American artists at the turn of the century caught for all time the enduring American view of the urban political boss. Thomas Nast's portrait of Tammany joined a moneybag head to the body of Boss Tweed. Walter Clark's image needs no explanation.

Thomas Nast, "The Brains." From *Harper's Weekly,*
October 21, 1871. Metropolitan Museum of Art, New York.

Walter Appleton Clark, "The Boss."
From *Collier's Weekly,* November 10, 1906.

From Ralph E. Shikes, *The Indignant Eye* (Boston: Beacon Press, 1969), pp. 312, 321.

hinges directly on the party's achieving congruent ones. So he must re-form the American parties if he is to reform American society.[44]

It is not only participation, however, that is cutting into the discipline of the party organization. Discipline depends also on the ability of the organization to withdraw or withhold its incentives. Much of the dis-cipline of the classic machine resulted from the willingness and ability of party leaders to manipulate the material rewards of patronage and preferment. The recalcitrant or inefficient committeeman sacrificed his public job or his hope for it. The party controlled, even monopolized, these rewards; what it had given it could take away. The newer incen-tives, however, cannot so easily be given or revoked. The party is only one among many organizations pursuing policy or ideological goals; and given the party's very imperfect control of its legislators, it may not even be the most efficient means to these ends. The ideologically ori-ented activist may find substitute outlets for his activities in interest groups or nonparty political associations such as neighborhood associa-tions, the Americans for Democratic Action, or the John Birch Society.

Whether or not concentrated, irresponsible power has been a fact within the party organizations, large numbers of Americans think that it has. The American political culture is almost haunted by the fear that a few men, responsible to no one, will control the selection of public officials and set the agendas of policy making in "smoke-filled rooms." Understandably, the search for mechanisms with which to control that power has been a long and diligent one. The results fall into two broad categories: mechanisms that impose controls outside the parties and those that look to internal controls.

External Controls

The theory of political laissez-faire suggests that two competitive parties will set limits to each other's exercise of organizational power by their very competition. The argument, of course, directly parallels the argu-ment of the self-regulating effects of economic competition in the free marketplace. If one party offers the electorate a shoddy political product or if it overprices its political goods, it will lose its political consumers to its competitor. Indeed, the current spread of two-party competitiveness may make that hope more credible. But one-partyism — the monopoly of the political system — negates the automatic corrective action as-sumed in laissez-faire theory; and some of the centers of greatest orga-nizational power are without serious two-party competition. Mayor Richard J. Daley and his Democratic machine won reelection in Chicago with 78 percent of the vote in 1975.

[44] Wilson, *The Amateur Democrat*, Chap. 5.

The states have generally preferred statutory controls on party power to the unseen hand of competition. However, their disappointments have outnumbered their successes. In those states in which voters at the primary pick precinct committeepersons and other party officials, there are rarely contests for offices. Frequently there is not even a single candidate. And in other states the attempts to regulate the holding of party caucuses and conventions have not always guaranteed access to all qualified comers. At the 1964 Democratic national convention the members of the Mississippi Freedom Democratic party charged that they had not been admitted to the party meetings that elected county convention delegates and that when they were elected delegates, they had not been seated at the conventions.

The effect of any of these external controls is extremely difficult to gauge. The most outrageous and blatant uses of party organization power in the United States have occurred in the one-party cities or regions. In many states statutorily protected access has opened the organization both to the competitions of other factions or oligarchies and to reinvigoration by new party personnel. And in all the states the direct primary has at least forced the parties to face the scrutiny of voters on one key decision: the nomination of candidates for office. In addition to these two mechanisms, the mass communications media and the other political organizations — by their watchfulness and readiness to criticize — set other limits on organizational power. But, to be realistic, the major sources of control must come from within the party itself.

Internal Controls

In his sweeping "iron law of oligarchy," Robert Michels declared sixty years ago without qualification that majorities within organizations are incapable of governing themselves. Organizations, he argued, are by their nature oligarchic or "minoritarian," for only the active minority has the experience, interest, and involvement necessary to manage the affairs of complex organizations.

Organization implies the tendency to oligarchy. In every organization, whether it be a political party, a professional union, or any other association of the kind, the aristocratic tendency manifests itself very clearly. The mechanism of the organization, while conferring a solidity of structure, induces serious changes in the organized mass, completely inverting the respective position of the leaders and the led. As a result of organization, every party or professional union becomes divided into a minority of directors and a majority of directed.[45]

[45] Robert Michels, *Political Parties* (Glencoe, Ill.: Free Press, 1949; originally published in 1915), p. 32.

To the extent that we are all believers in the myths of the bosses, the smoke-filled rooms, and the deals between oligarchs, we are all children of Michels.

The kind of intraparty democracy that Michels lamented, however, has little relevance to the nonmembership, cadre organizations of the American major parties. For who are the participating members, the ineffective majorities, here? The party in the electorate, which the states permit to choose some party leaders, are members in only the loosest sense. Only in isolated parts of the country have the parties developed bona fide membership organizations. There is, in the meaning of Michels, really no inactive majority within the American parties. The party organization is the cadre, and it is made up of activists — active in varying degrees, of course — who are reckoned as being "of" the party simply because they *are* active as workers, officers, leaders, or even hangers-on. Control of party power must, therefore, come largely from within the party cadre. The relevant question is not really so much one of control as distribution of power within the organizational leadership.

The distribution of power within most American party organizations can be described in Samuel Eldersveld's apt term *stratarchy*. It is "the enlargement of the ruling group of an organization, its power stratification, the involvement of large numbers of people in group decision-making, and, thus, the diffusion and proliferation of control throughout the structure." [46] Various levels of party organization operate at least semi-independently of other levels, even superordinate ones. Precinct committeemen, district leaders, even county officials freely define their own political roles and nourish their separate bases of party power. So "although authority to speak for the organization may remain in the hands of the top elite nucleus, there is great autonomy in operations at the lower 'strata' or echelons of the hierarchy, and . . . control from the top is minimal and formal." [47]

What accounts for stratarchy and the failure of top party leaders to centralize organizational power in the hierarchy? One might suppose that the lowest party strata, in view of their relatively low levels of activity, would pose no barrier to that centralization. Indeed, significant numbers of precinct leaders may not even want or expect a voice in party affairs. Experience and expertise are surely on the side of the top party leadership, and so, too, is the organizational need for tactical flexibility. So, too, is the power to manipulate some of the party's incentives to centralize power.

---

[46] Eldersveld, *Political Parties*, p. 99. The term "stratarchy" comes from Harold Lasswell and Abraham Kaplan, *Power and Society* (New Haven: Yale University Press, 1950).
[47] Eldersveld, *Political Parties*, pp. 99–100.

Yet, weighing against the pressures for the development of a central-ized party oligarchy are these factors:

1. *Participatory expectations.* Large percentages of the new party activ-ists — accustomed to being beneficiaries of the democratic ethos in their service or fraternal clubs — expect to find it also in the political party in which they have chosen to work. The party, therefore, may have to tolerate or even "create" intraparty democracy (or consulta-tion) to maintain organizational vitality, to lift morale, and to achieve cohesion.

2. *Controls of lower party levels over the higher.* Most notably the chieftains of the lower-level party organizations collectively make up the conventions or consultative bodies that select the levels of party officialdom above them. Patterson, for example, brings together data on the percentages of county chairmen from Oklahoma, Kansas, and Wisconsin who were delegates to state conventions (Table 2). Clearly, the county chairmen in these states are forces to be reckoned with in the state party organizations. Similarly, precinct workers or delegates often form city or county committees.

3. *Internal competition.* Party organizations rarely are unified monoliths. They often embrace competing organizations or factions. Differences in goals and political styles produce continuing competitions in the selecting of party officials and the mapping of party activities. In 1956 and 1957 in Wisconsin, at least some county party offices were contested in 39 percent of the Republican organizations and 59 per-cent of the Democratic.[48]

4. *Organizational insufficiencies.* This theme is sounded repeatedly in the study of the Wayne County, Michigan, party organizations. The mutual role perceptions of various party leadership levels do not "square"; there is no "neat overlap . . . between role perceptions. This divergence and lack of unanimity suggest no clear understanding or expectation in the party hierarchy as to specific tasks of those in pre-cinct and executive board positions, either as perceptions by others or among themselves."[49] Communication among levels of the hier-archy is sporadic and discontinuous. Motivational and ideological structures differ widely and even conflict, both among levels in the hierarchy and from area to area in the organization.

Diffusion of power marks all but the exceptional party organizations. Top party leaders engage in much mobilizing and wooing of support within the organization; their consultations with middle-level leadership are endless. Even the ward or precinct leader with a small electoral fol-

[48] Epstein, *Politics in Wisconsin*, p. 90.
[49] Eldersveld, *Political Parties*, p. 111.

TABLE 2   Percentages of County Chairmen Serving
as Delegates to State Conventions

	Oklahoma	Kansas	Wisconsin
Democratic delegates to state convention	89.8	71.2	95.3
Republican delegates to state convention	86.7	84.3	100.0

Source Data from Samuel C. Patterson, "Characteristics of Party
Leaders," *Western Political Quarterly* 16 (1963): 346.

lowing and a single vote at an important convention must be cultivated.
And, above all, party leaders in the eras following "patronage and preferment" no longer command, for their commands no longer carry potent sanctions. They plead, they bargain, they cajole, and they reason —
and they even learn to lose gracefully on occasion. They mobilize party
power not so much by threats as by the solidarity of common goals and
interests.

American party organizations have probably never commanded incentives and rewards at all equal to their organizational goals and ambitions. In that sense, they have been chronically "underfinanced." They
never have been able to recruit the kinds of resources they would have
to have in order to flesh out the party organization that the state statutes
create. The thousands of inactive precinct workers and unfilled precinct
positions testify to that poverty of incentive. The parties, therefore, have
no alternative but to establish organizational forms that permit them to
live within their means.

5

National Organizations: The Uncertain Summit

So extreme are the traditional observations on the decentralization of the American parties that one is tempted to dismiss them as empty rhetoric or pure hyperbole. One noted scholar of the American parties has written:

Decentralization of power is by all odds the most important single characteristic of the American major party; more than anything else this trait distinguishes it from all others. Indeed, once this truth is understood, nearly everything else about American parties is greatly illuminated.... The American major party is, to repeat the definition, a loose confederation of state and local bosses for limited purposes.[1]

Is it possible, one wonders, that these disparate, often disorganized, local party organizations are not subordinated to or coordinated by some higher party unit? Are the local and state organizations free to use the name and traditions of a nationwide political party for their own local, parochial interests without any control by the national party? Closer examination of the American parties reveals that what seems to be hyperbole is merely a statement of reality. Power and authority in the party organizations are precisely that diffuse, and this fact colors virtually every aspect of party activity.

State and local party organizations of the major parties pick their own officers, nominate their candidates, take their own stands on issues, and raise and spend their own funds without interference from any manifestation of the national party. Every four years they come together as a national party to select a presidential candidate and write a platform, but they have historically been careful to leave only an enfeebled national organization behind as they break camp. What appears to be a pyramiding of state party committees into a single, integrating national

[1] E. E. Schattschneider, *Party Government* (New York: Rinehart, 1942), pp. 129, 132–33; emphasis omitted.

party authority, therefore, is in reality nothing of the kind. Often the national committees serve only as arenas for the bargaining and jockeying among the powerful local and state organizations and presidential candidates within the party. The authors of the leading study of the national committees chose pointedly to title it *Politics Without Power*.[2] Indeed, it has often been said that in reality there are no national parties, that what we blithely call the national parties are merely hydra-headed coalitions of jealous, wary, and very diverse state and local party organizations.

Decentralization is hardly a precise term. It is, furthermore, a highly relative one, for one party system's decentralization may be another's centralization. What standards we have can be found only by looking at the status of national party committees and executives elsewhere. In 1957, for instance, the national executive committee of the Congress party of India refused to renominate almost one-third of the party's incumbent members of Parliament because it wanted instead to recruit younger candidates. Although that degree of control over the nomination of local candidates is rare, it is not uncommon for national parties to influence and even occasionally to overturn local nominations. It is also common for national party committees to attempt to enforce party policy on the party's members in the legislature. Socialist parties in Western Europe have for decades held their parliamentary parties to the party positions laid down by the national party executives, occasionally expelling the legislator who refused to be so bound. The Democratic and Republican national committees have no such disciplinary powers, no such ability to control local nominations, nor even the power to speak on behalf of the party on the issues of the day.

Ironically, this organizational decentralization persists at a time when most other aspects of American life are becoming more centralized. The mass media bring the same reporters, TV images, and columnists and commentators into homes in all parts of the country. Government in the American federal system has by any measure been increasingly centered in Washington in the past generation. Even the other two sectors of the party have been "nationalized" in the past few decades. The party in the electorate responds increasingly to national issues such as the war in Vietnam, to national candidates (especially those for the presidency), and to national party symbols and stands on issues. With that nationalization of politics, attention now centers also on the national parties in government: on the president for the party in power and on the congressional leadership of both parties. Yet decentralization in the party

---

[2] Cornelius P. Cotter and Bernard C. Hennessy, *Politics Without Power: The National Party Committees* (New York: Atherton, 1964). Although the Cotter and Hennessy book is somewhat out of date on details, the general point of view and interpretation are still valid.

organization persists. Moreover, it persists despite a concerted attempt in the 1970s to develop a stronger national membership organization within the Democratic party. While the Democratic ferment may have shaken somewhat the autonomous power of the state organizations, it left the main contours of that autonomy undisturbed.

THE NATIONAL COMMITTEES AND NATIONAL OFFICERS

Technically, the nominating convention that each party holds midway in the year of a presidential election is the party's supreme national authority. But the convention's constructive role goes only slightly beyond the selection of presidential and vice-presidential candidates and the formulation of party platforms. It does ratify the selection of national committeemen, and it does specify the structure and powers of the national committees. But since the convention adjourns sine die (i.e., without setting a time for a future meeting) until four years later, it can exercise no continuing supervision over the national organizational apparatus of the party.

The national committees of the two major parties were for years similarly composed. The drastic revision of the Democratic body in 1972 changed that (Table 1). The Democratic National Committee has now become twice the size of its Republican counterpart. More importantly, the Democrats have abandoned the confederational nature of the committee. Traditionally each state has been represented in both national committees on an approximately equal basis, regardless of the size of its electorate or the extent of its support for the party. States, not populations or number of partisans, were represented, much in the way that the United States and the Maldive Islands have equal representation in the United Nations General Assembly. That representational system overrepresented the state organizations of the smaller states, and it also gave roughly equal weight in the national committees to the winning and the losing parts of the party. The practical consequence was to strengthen the conservative wings of both parties, the southern and western segments of the Democratic party and the Taft-Goldwater areas in the GOP. The newly restructured Democratic National Committee, however, will give weight both to population and to party support; New York and California each have eighteen members on the committee, and Nevada has four. That altered representation at the least establishes one necessary condition for revivifying the national committee and for centralizing authority in the party.

Formally, the national conventions select the members of the national committees, but that action merely ratifies decisions made within the states and state parties. The state parties differ from each other in mak-

TABLE 1   Composition of Democratic and Republican
National Committees

	Members
Democratic National Committee	
Chairperson and next highest ranking officer of opposite sex from each state, D.C., Puerto Rico	104
200 members apportioned to states on same basis as delegates to national convention (minimum: two per state)	200
Chairman of Democratic Governors Conference, and two additional Democratic governors	3
Democratic leader and one other person from each house of Congress	4
Chairman of Democratic Mayors Conference, and two additional Democratic mayors	3
President and two other representatives of Young Democrats	3
Up to 25 additional members	0–25
	317–42
Republican National Committee	
Chairman, national committeeman, and national committeewoman from each state, D.C., Guam, Puerto Rico, and Virgin Islands	162
	162

ing their decisions, and in many states, the two parties choose their national committeemen and committeewomen differently. Among the four main methods — selection by state party convention, by the party delegation to the national convention, by the state central committee, and by election at a primary — the first is the most popular in both parties. In this welter of selection processes one point is worth noting. Although the parties' state organizations can usually control the selection of national committeemen when they are chosen by the state committee and by the state conventions, when they are chosen in primaries or by national convention delegates the selection may be less controllable. Especially in states that choose convention delegates in presidential primaries, the delegation may represent voter support of a momentarily popular candidate more than it represents the leadership of the state party. A number of Democratic delegations in 1972, for example, were composed of party newcomers and mavericks who were pledged to George McGovern; the old-line party leaders in the state had supported other contenders and thus failed to be delegates.

The chairmen and other officers of the national committees do not have to be — and often are not — members of the committees. They are elected and removed by the committees. Immediately after the conventions, however, tradition recognizes the right of the parties' presidential candidates to name the national chairmen for the course of the presidential campaign. The committees ratify their choices without question. And since the party of the president will continue to respect his choice of a national party chairman after the election, only the committee of the "out" party in effect selects its own national chairman. The committees generally have much greater freedom to select other committee officials — vice-chairmen, secretaries, and treasurers — many of whom come from the committee itself. In addition, both national committees select executive committees, which include the officers and from ten to fifteen other members of the committee.

Within this apparatus — supplemented, of course, by the national committees' permanent staffs — the chairmen dominate. The full committees meet only two or three times a year, and occasionally even less than that. As Cotter and Hennessy report:

Collectively the national committee is not much more than a categorical group. . . . The national committee members have very little collective identity, little patterned interaction, and only rudimentary common values and goals.

Except for occasional meetings — largely for show and newsmaking purposes — the national committees may be thought of not so much as groups, but as lists of people who have obtained their national committee memberships through organizational processes wholly separate in each state.[3]

The other officers of the party are not especially influential, and the executive committees meet only a little oftener than the full committees. Like the full committees, they are men and women whose concern is state (and even local) organizational work rather than the building of a strong national party apparatus. So, traditionally the national chairman, with the permanent staff, has in effect been the national party organization.

There may be some change in the traditional role, however, especially in the Democratic party. The party in 1974, for the first time in either party, adopted a party constitution (the Democratic Party Charter) which gives ongoing status to the national committee and the national officers. Furthermore, the new composition of the party's national committee shifts influence to the organizations of the populous, most solidly

[3] Ibid., p. 39.

Democratic states, and thus to the ideological and reformist wings of the party. All of that, plus the new attention given more generally to the national party, may lead to a role beyond the usual one of arranging the national conventions and participating marginally in the presidential campaigns. Indeed, the new Democratic Charter specifically lists among the duties of the national committee that of "formulating and disseminating statements of party policy." It also charges it with "conducting" the presidential campaign. The 1976 presidential election will doubtless provide the first tests for the hopes of the Democratic reformers.

In reality, the role of the national committees is flexible. If theirs is the party of the president, they may be little more than managers of the president's campaigns and builders of his political support. Indeed, during the Nixon years, the president and his staff managed his political matters, and Rogers Morton and Robert Dole, the Republican national chairmen, did little more than serve as liaisons between the president and party leaders around the country. Occasionally a president such as Dwight Eisenhower will shift the burden of distributing the federal patronage to the national committee and chairman. In the party out of power the chairman and committee must often bind up wounds, heal intraparty squabbles, help pay debts from the losing campaign, raise new money, and revivify the party organization around the country. The chairman of the opposition party may also speak for the party and as an alternative to the president's party.

As the role of the committee and its chairman shifts, so, too, do the job specifications for a national party chairman. Within the party of the president, he or she must be congenial to the president, representative of his ideological stance, and willing to be loyal primarily to the president. Within the opposition party, the chairman will often be congenial to — or at least trusted by — the various factions or segments of the party. Frequently he or she is chosen for ideological neutrality or lack of identification with any of the individuals seeking the party's next presidential nomination. Often he is chosen for his experience in the nuts and bolts of party organization. It is significant that the Republicans after the 1964 defeat replaced Dean Burch, a Goldwater ideologue, with an organizational pragmatist, Ray Bliss, the Ohio party chairman. The Democrats did likewise after their catastrophe in 1972, replacing McGovern's choice, Jean Westwood, with an old party "pro," Robert Strauss. As the job specifications vary, so do the hunting grounds for prospective chairmen. Historically, the parties have most frequently found their chairmen among state party leaders, although the parties have lately shown an increasing tendency to select members of Congress (see Table 2).

TABLE 2   National Committee Chairmen of the Major Parties: 1955–75

Name	Years	Political position at appointment
Democrats		
Paul M. Butler	1955–60	National committeeman from Indiana
Henry M. Jackson	1960–61	U.S. senator from Washington
John M. Bailey	1961–68	State party chairman in Connecticut
Lawrence F. O'Brien	1968–69	U.S. postmaster general
Fred R. Harris	1969–70	U.S. senator from Oklahoma
Lawrence F. O'Brien	1970–72	Former national party chairman
Jean Westwood	1972	Active in McGovern preconvention campaign
Robert Strauss	1972–	Democratic national treasurer
Republicans		
Leonard W. Hall	1953–57	Party leader, former congressman from New York
Meade Alcorn	1957–59	State party chairman in Connecticut
Thruston B. Morton	1959–61	U.S. senator from Kentucky
William E. Miller	1961–64	U.S. representative from New York
Dean Burch	1964–65	Active in Barry Goldwater campaign
Ray C. Bliss	1965–69	State party chairman in Ohio
Rogers C. Morton	1969–71	U.S. representative from Maryland
Robert J. Dole	1971–73	U.S. senator from Kansas
George Bush	1973–74	U.S. Ambassador to the United Nations
Mary Louise Smith	1974–	Cochairman of Republican National Committee

Despite the shifting roles of the committees and their chairmen, the committees have fairly stable, ongoing structures and activities. Each has its research division, which charts trends and projections in election data. Each has a number of divisions working with a special segment of the party's clientele: women, minorities, intellectuals, and young people. Each is also prepared to offer advice to state and local organizations on running campaigns, maintaining good press and public relations, raising funds, selecting winning candidates, and keeping the party organization in repair. And each has a fund-raising arm with its finance chairman. In fact, staff and programs of the national committees now absorb annual budgets of between $1 million and $3 million.[4]

[4] For a good brief section on the Republican National Committee and its operations, see Charles O. Jones, *The Republican Party in American Politics* (New York: Macmillan, 1965).

On Selecting a National Party Chairman: 1971

The necessity of finding a new national chairman fell to the Republicans in late 1970 and early 1971 with the appointment of the incumbent chairman, Rogers C. B. Morton, as secretary of the interior. Two reports in the *New York Times* revealed some of the problems and rituals in the selection. There is no reason to think they are not typical of such decisions in the president's party.

"Washington sources said yesterday that the Nixon Administration was finding it difficult to replace Representative Rogers C. B. Morton of Maryland as chairman of the Republican National Committee, partly because at least some potential candidates considered the job to offer no real power. . . .

"It is widely assumed in Washington that Mr. Nixon's re-election campaign will be managed not by the national chairman but by Attorney General John M. Mitchell, who is expected to resign later this year or early in 1972 to return to full-time political work for the President.

"Such an arrangement would leave the national chairman with only a minor role. Much the same was true this year, when basic Republican planning was done by Robert H. Finch, a counsellor to the President, by Murray Chotiner, Mr. Nixon's long-time political tactician, and by the President himself.

" 'I might be interested,' said one of the candidates for party chairman, 'but not if it means being water boy for John Mitchell and Murray Chotiner.' "

R. W. Apple, Jr., *New York Times,*
November 27, 1970.

"President Nixon has selected Senator Robert J. Dole of Kansas as the new chairman of the Republican National Committee, sources at the committee and the White House disclosed today. . . .

"Mr. Morton . . . announced through his Washington office today that he was choosing a 12-man selection committee to recommend a new chairman to the national committee at its annual meeting here, starting Jan. 15.

"A source at party headquarters conceded, however, that no selection committee would have been chosen unless Mr. Nixon had already made up his mind. The selection committee, which will be composed of members of the national committee, 'will ask who Nixon wants and ratify his choice,' the source said.

"He compared the process — which will probably include a meeting with the President on Jan. 14 — "to 'the mating dance of the egret.' "

R. W. Apple, Jr., *New York Times,*
January 6, 1971.

THE SUPPORTING CAST OF NATIONAL GROUPS

Clustered around the national committees are a set of more or less formal groups that also purport to speak for the national party or some part of it. Some of them are creatures of the national committees, but their independent voices often undermine the authority of national committee pronouncements and actions.

The Regional Organizations

Within recent years both parties have begun to develop regional party organizations. The Republicans have systematically divided the country into a number of regions. The regional groups, composed chiefly of state party officers and executive directors, meet periodically to discuss issues and election strategy. During the Nixon and Ford years those meetings often included briefings by officials of the administration. In the past the Democrats in some areas of the country met more sporadically on their own initiative and outside of the auspices of the Democratic National Committee. The new Democratic Charter of 1974, however, instructs the national committee to create regional organizations. As of the present, however, neither party's regional groups have staffs or ongoing responsibilities. They are therefore a long way from being an intermediate level of organization between the state parties and the national committees.

The Women's Groups

The national headquarters of each party has a women's division. The Office of Women's Activities within the Democratic party serves the Democratic women's clubs chartered by the various state committees. There is, however, no national women's organization in the Democratic party. The Republicans have a women's division within the national office and also in the same building the offices of the National Federation of Republican Women, whose officers are elected by the federation's own convention. So of the two parties, only the Republicans have what might be or might become an autonomous women's organization. In reality, however, the federation has always been responsive to the cues of national party leadership, and to find any instances of striking independence on its part would be difficult indeed.

These women's divisions and organizations now face a very uncertain future. They are in many ways monuments to the subordinate position women long occupied in the parties. Women have increasingly entered regular leadership positions in the parties within the past decade. A woman has now chaired each party's national committee for the first time in history (Table 2), and both parties showed a marked increase in the number of women at the 1972 national conventions. Both parties have also eliminated the designated offices for women — for example, the party vice-chairwoman positions — which for so long confirmed their separate but unequal status. For their part, the more activist women want a role in the regular party organizations, or else they prefer to become active in nonparty organizations (such as the National Women's Political Caucus). Certainly they do not have in mind the docile, subordinate role that the parties' auxiliaries traditionally had. Consequently, there has recently been much malaise within the women's organizations and much searching for a new and proper role.

The Youth Groups

The Young Republican National Federation and the Young Democrats of America are both national federations of state and local youth groups. Both meet biennially in conventions to elect national officers and to debate and pass resolutions. "Young" in both instances means men and women to the age of 35; indeed, the Democrats did not retreat from a maximum age of 40 until 1971. Both parties also have federations of college organizations (College Young Democrats of America and the College Republican National Federation), which are similarly organized. In addition, the Republicans have attempted to set up high school units (Teen Age Republicans), and there is again a national federation of them. But in this proliferation of groups, the first set is clearly the most important. Both the Young Democrats and the Young Republicans are represented on their party's national committee, and both clearly have the major staff and funding help, provided in substantial part by the senior party.

Unlike the women, the organized youth of both parties have been neither docile nor compliant. At local, state, and national levels they have often taken stands and supported candidates that embarrassed the senior party organization. The Young Republicans, for instance, had a long infatuation with Goldwater conservatism, continuing long after the regular leadership of the party tried to reflect a more centrist position. In the late 1960s and 1970s, their loyalties turned increasingly to the conservatism of Governor Ronald Reagan of California. The Young Democrats often stand to the left of their senior party organization. In 1969, for instance, their national convention called for repeal of all legal limits on abortion, for liberalization of marijuana laws, for recognition of Cuba and Communist China, and for an "immediate and total withdrawal of all American troops in Vietnam." That was, to put it mildly, a far cry from the platform that the Democratic National Convention had adopted a year earlier in Chicago.

The future of the youth organizations in both parties, like that of the women's auxiliaries, has been clouded by recent events. The adoption of the eighteen-year-old vote and the youth activism of the 1960s and 1970s brought thousands of young people into the main business of the parties and made them less willing to accept the status of tutelage which the youth organizations imply. Many of them had brought the Eugene McCarthy campaign to major contention in 1968, and many also went as delegates to the 1972 conventions of both parties. In any event, membership in all of the party youth groups has fallen off; between 1968 and 1975, for example, official party estimates of membership in the Young Democrats of America fell from 1 million to 100,000. Signs of apathy are evident in all quarters. It may, indeed, be no exaggeration to say that the youth and women's groups are in good measure victims of the parties' willingness and ability to involve those very individuals in their central business.

The Party Governors

The state governors inevitably speak with authority in the councils of their national party. They have the prestige both of high office and of electoral success. Many lead or command the support of state party organizations. Many also head state delegations to the party's national conventions, and a few inevitably contend for their party's presidential nomination.

The organization of the gubernatorial presence in the national parties, however, is relatively recent. The Republicans were first. Led chiefly by the liberals after the Goldwater defeat of 1964, the Republican governors wanted primarily to create a counterweight to the party's conservatives. A few years later they established a full-time Washington office with financial help from the party's national committee, but their influence waned after the Republican victory of 1968. Like many of these groups within the national parties, the governors operate most tellingly in the power vacuums of an opposition party. Their declining numbers in the 1970s — there were only thirteen Republican governors by 1975 — also undermined their influence within the party.

By the 1970s the Democratic governors began to press for a role in national party politics. Their ranks bolstered by victories and their party even more disorganized in opposition than is usually the case, they sought a more prominent voice in the decisions of 1972. By 1974 they had achieved that voice and won representation, although in modest numbers, on the national committee. They had also demonstrated their strength in the adoption of the new party charter. Meeting only a month before the national party conference in December of 1974, the governors threw their support behind the compromise reform proposal that ultimately passed in the conference. All in all, their position in the party reflected their political position — a large, strong, and politically success-ful voice in a disarrayed party of opposition.

The Party Notables

Both the Democrats and Republicans possess a group of party notables who exert informal but very real power in national party councils. Often they are distinguished citizens, former officeholders, captains of finance or industry, holders of famous names, or long-time contributors to the party coffers. Sometimes — as in the case of a distinguished Democrat, Averell Harriman — they are all those things at once. Sometimes they combine contacts in business or finance or distinguished military careers with service to the party. What the notables have in common, of course, is that they are notable, that they have visibility, entrée to important circles inside and outside of politics, and a vast reservoir of experience in public life or service.[5]

To say that these notables exist in each party and that they are in-fluential, however, is not to say that they are organized or that they self-consciously function as an elite or establishment within the parties. The most concrete charges made about them in the last generation have been made by conservative Republicans against the domination of GOP affairs by an "eastern establishment" which was said to include old and famous names in law, finance, and journalism. Fear of its power dogged the personal ambitions of Nelson Rockefeller, widely seen as its most recent representative.

The Ideologists and Issue Framers

Those partisans concerned primarily with issues and ideology have not found it easy to organize their concerns within the national parties. Groups with a tangential relationship to the formal organizations of the national parties have, however, sprung up from time to time. For ex-ample, the Ripon Society — named for the city in Wisconsin that claims to be the birthplace of the Republican party — in recent years has served as a voice for liberal Republicanism. The society, composed chiefly of young, East Coast academics and professional people, won considerable

---

[5] It can be argued that the stars of entertainment now more active than ever in party politics constitute a new group of "notables." Shirley MacLaine and Paul New-man of the Democrats and John Wayne of the Republicans are among the best known. They and their colleagues, however, are largely without experience in public office and probably without influence in the councils of the party.

attention in early 1970 with a demand for the dismissal of Attorney General John Mitchell.[6] At the other end of the Republican spectrum, a group calling itself United Republicans of America continues to raise money for the support of conservative Republican candidates for Congress. The New Democratic Coalition, composed largely of the remnants of the McCarthy crusade, sprang up in the wake of the Democratic fiascos of 1968, but by the mid-seventies it was no longer a force in Democratic politics. After the Democratic loss in 1972 the Coalition for a Democratic Majority attempted to speak for a centrist, perhaps even nonideological, position.

These external ideological voices have largely been the work of outsiders, of partisans who have seen the party captured by an ideology, or a lack of ideology, unacceptable to them. On the other hand, the national committees have struggled since the 1950s to create policy-making bodies that could and would define stands on public issues for the broader party.

The most recent of them — the Democratic Policy Council — will serve as an illustration. Composed of sixty-six members, it was established in 1969 by the Democratic National Committee and designed primarily to make statements on national issues. Hubert Humphrey, the party's defeated presidential candidate, became its chairman. It quickly found itself between the stone and the hard place. The former supporters of the Eugene McCarthy and Robert Kennedy campaigns were suspicious of its old-style, centrist liberalism, whereas the party's congressional contingent was not happy when it took positions to the left of congressional preferences. The life and times of groups such as the Democratic Policy Council are complicated by the fact that they are not merely instruments for enunciating policy. A tip-off to their deeper purposes is found in the fact that they exist only in opposition parties. Their supporters generally intend them to prevent the party's congressional party from acting as the only spokesman of the opposition party. That desire to compete with the congressional party stems mainly from disapproval of the relative conservatism of the party's congressmen. In the Kennedy and Johnson years the moderates within the GOP formed an All-Republican Conference with General Eisenhower its honorary chairman. The Republican congressional leadership accepted membership with good grace if not with enthusiasm, but Senator Barry Goldwater, speaking as a conservative and as a seeker after the 1964 nomination, criticized it as a splinter group and an untimely reincarnation of

---

[6] The attorney general was widely quoted as having dismissed the Riponeers as "little juvenile delinquents." A good deal of the society's work is, however, less dramatic and more scholarly than this exchange might suggest. See, for example, its report on the 1968 presidential elections, *The Lessons of Victory* (New York: Dial, 1969).

the citizens' groups that had led to the Eisenhower draft of 1952. After the loss of 1964, the party set up a similar Republican Coordinating Committee.

The latest idea in mechanisms for coping with national issues and ideologies is the party conference held midway between the regular nominating conventions. The Democrats held the first one in American party history in late 1974, and their new charter offers the hope of future ones. (The charter does, however, use the verb "may" rather than "must.") The 1974 Democratic conference was a modest one and probably something of a disappointment to some partisans. It was held in December of 1974 in order not to intrude on the congressional election campaigns. Then, also out of deference to congressional fears that it would pass irresponsible (i.e., excessively liberal) statements, it was limited to a policy statement on the faltering economy. That statement, though, was widely reported, and so was the more general news that the Democrats had held the conference and addressed equity in the selection of delegates to the 1976 convention without inflicting lasting damage on the party. So the midyear conference has yet to prove that it will become a means for the injection of issues into national politics. But it is now available, if wanted, for the task.

None of these subordinate groups has been more than a small supporting character in the drama of American national politics. None of them generates much influence or speaks for large numbers of party voters or activists. But so relatively weak are the national party committees that the presence of these groups tends to diffuse and disperse the modest aura of authority the committees attempt to maintain. By far the greatest challenge to the authority of the national party organizations, however, comes from the party's powerful members in office — its party in the Congress and in the White House. To that battle for control of the party we now turn.

WHO SPEAKS FOR THE PARTY?

Among the political parties of the rest of the world, it is not difficult to find examples of powerful, authoritative national committees. It is the rule that the national committees of political parties dominate the national presence and image of the political party. In most party systems, the national committee and its executive committee enunciate the ideology and the policy views of the party. The national committee is also the national center of authority within the party organization, maintaining substantial control over such matters as party finance and the running of party campaigns. That model of the highly centralized party is not, of course, even remotely applicable in the United States.

Within the two major American parties, the national organizations —
the party's national committees — long ago failed in their attempt to
speak for the national party to the party's officeholders.

It is no exaggeration to say that national party organizations in the
United States have been crippled in a collision with the American presidency. So pervasive has the influence of the presidency been on the
national parties that the problem of control can best be divided in two:
the situation in the party holding the presidency and that in the party
out of power. When the party holds the presidency, the president's
program and record of decisions become the party's. It is the president
who interprets the party's platform and the mandate of its voters. His
preferences, whether embodied in the formal measures of the State of
the Union address or tossed off more casually at a press conference,
impose a policy on his party. He may consult the party chairman or
other party worthies, but no one mistakes the presidential initiative.

Presidential relations with the national committee and its chairman
differ, of course, with the experience and inclinations of the president.
Dwight Eisenhower, totally without experience in party politics, preferred to leave the national committee a free hand in patronage and
organizational matters. Under John F. Kennedy, the Democratic National Committee and its officers declined in importance as the president,
his brother Robert, Lawrence O'Brien, and other Kennedy aides took
over the keeping of contacts with state party leaders, the mapping of
electoral strategy, the raising of party funds, and the issuing of party
pronunciamentos. Initially in the administration of Lyndon Johnson
there was a period of dominance of the national committee by Johnson
men, many of them old Texas associates. Late in 1965 and 1966, however, President Johnson began to replace committee operations with
those of his own White House advisers (chief among them were Marvin
Watson, formerly a chairman of the Texas Democratic party, and Postmaster General Lawrence O'Brien).

The vitiation of the national committee and its apparatus reached
new levels in the presidential years of Richard M. Nixon. In the early
Nixon years an active and well-financed national committee staff worked
closely with the president and the White House staff. Increasingly, however, national Republican strategy was formulated in the White House.
The president's immediate political advisors — men like Harry Dent and
Murray Chotiner, for instance — and even his immediate staff became
directly involved in political party decisions. The White House tapes
revealed that John Ehrlichman and H. R. Haldeman were repeatedly
involved in the business of the 1972 campaign. That campaign was in
fact headed by a Committee for the Re-Election of the President (the
so-called CREEP) with another administration figure and old political
crony, John Mitchell, at the helm. The national committee and its chair-

man, Senator Robert Dole, were pushed to the margins of party activity — far enough, indeed, for them to be completely ignorant and innocent of all of the Watergate activities.

This White House dominance of the national party does not necessarily please the state and local organizations of the party. While they want a weak national party and headquarters, they want one that will offer them patronage, campaign help, and organizational advice and services. A vigorously political president, on the other hand, often wants the national apparatus to serve *his* interests. He wants its organizational skills to promote his political future, its pronouncements to assist his program, its dealings with Congress to help his dealings with Congress. He sees in the limited federal patronage an opportunity to achieve the goals of his administration or his political career rather than a set of rewards for workers in the state and local parties. Quite simply, it is not always in the interest of the president that the national committee attend to the wants of local party organization.

By contrast, in those four long years after presidential defeat, a national party suffers an almost incessant jockeying for the right to lead. The defeated candidate, the party's legislative leadership, the national chairman, and other party notables may all purport to be the voice of the party. This contention, furthermore, is over much more than policy positions and initiatives. It is also part of the continuing struggle to define the party's strategies and pick its next presidential candidate.

The formal traditions of American politics rather pretentiously label the defeated presidential candidate the "titular head" of his party. Whatever the term may mean, a losing presidential candidate must fight to maintain even a precarious influence in his party. How effective a voice he has in party policy depends on his own base of power within the party. All other things being equal, a candidate who lost by a few hundred thousand votes will maintain his control better than one who lost by several million. His political skills, his policy orientations, his control of a state party, his taste for party conflict, even his own ambitions, also affect his power. In 1967 Richard Nixon, a Republican loser once removed, probably came closer to being a spokesman for the Republican party than did its most recent loser, Barry Goldwater. Similarly, Hubert Humphrey maintained a greater leadership role after his narrow defeat in 1968 than did George McGovern after the landslide of 1972.

More commonly, however, the leadership of the "out" party falls to its leaders in Congress. The congressional party, simply because its legislative responsibilities force it to take policy stands, formulates the party position and challenges the program of the president. Indeed, in the early 1960s the periodic television appearances of Republican congressional leaders Senator Everett M. Dirksen and Representative Charles Halleck (the programs were jocularly called the "Ev and Charlie

Show") came to symbolize the organized Republican opposition. The series continued in a slightly changed format after Representative Gerald Ford replaced Halleck as the Republican floor leader in the House in early 1965. Since 1968 Democratic congressional domination has been less apparent, perhaps because of the age of Speaker John McCormack and the less assertive style both of his successor, Carl Albert, and of Senator Mike Mansfield.

Neither in the party of the president nor in the party of the opposition, then, does the national party apparatus become the policy voice of the party. In part that failure stems from the almost suffocating influence of the president. In part it stems from the fact that the American parties have not been parties of ideology. If their organizations had large numbers of members and party activists who subscribed to a set of principles, the national committee of the party might more easily be able to speak on behalf of party principles and policies. But within the American party organizations such policy statements find little support among the activists and loyalists of the party. To put it succinctly, within the American party organizations there is simply no large clientele expecting and listening for ideological pronouncements by the party organization itself.

Failing to fill the role of enunciator of policy and issue positions, the national committees might more modestly be expected to function as coordinators of campaigns and party organization. But even in those electoral tasks, the national committees have not found a lasting role. What role they have generally centers on the presidential election. For that reason the organizational and activity level of the national committee is, like most other party committees in the United States, definitely periodic. It comes to life for elections and then sinks back into some degree of inactivity. Presidents and other national party leaders tend to view the national committee as one more party campaign organization, this one for the presidential conventions and campaigns of every four years. For their part, state organizations want a national committee that will render campaign assistance without imposing organizational or ideological control.

Even in the congressional elections the national committees defer in great measure to the powerful campaign committees that each party has organized in each house of Congress. These four party campaign committees — often referred to as the Hill committees — exist for only one purpose: the election of the parties' candidates to the Congress. They assist incumbent senators and representatives by providing speech-preparation services, television and radio tapes and scripts, press releases, legislative histories and roll-call research, photographic services, and campaign literature. For nonincumbent candidates — especially those in closely competitive districts — they provide campaign assistance that ranges from money and research on the record of the opponent to organizational help in the district and advice on the skillful use of press, radio, and television.

The Hill committees compete in a number of important ways with the national committees of their respective parties. While the national committee deals with the party's national candidates, national image, and national issues, the Hill committees minimize national issues and candidates if it is prudent to do so in the essentially local elections with which they are concerned. And always there is competition for money. Even though the Republicans have created a supraorganizational finance committee to coordinate the fund raising of the national committee and the two Hill committees, it has not succeeded in imposing its budgetary control over the Hill committees. The Republican Congressional Campaign Committee continues, for example, to maintain its Boosters Club, in which a membership "fee" of $1,000 or more entitles one to the occasional company and camaraderie of the House Republicans. Competition among the Democratic organizations is less intense, probably because their Hill committees have on the whole been less imposing organizations.

THE NATIONAL PARTIES: TROUBLES AT THE SUMMIT

Like so many groups in American life — the American Bar Association, the American Medical Association, the United States Chamber of Commerce, the large, international trade unions, to mention only a few examples — the organizational structure of the Democratic and Republican parties follows the lines of American federalism. Above the state organizational units the parties have erected a single national committee. But unlike so many federated organizations, the parties' national committees have never surmounted the autonomous power of the state and local organizations. They remain relatively powerless victims of the decentralization of American politics. The hierarchical form of American party organization deceives once again.

The causes of national committee weakness are many. Like all American parties the national committee is a skeletal organization without any base of mass membership; but unlike state and local organizations it lacks even the circles of workers and loyalists that sustain the cadre parties. Furthermore, it must depend on financial levies on the state parties (quotas) to help pay its staff and expenses, and state organizations may fall quickly into arrears on their payments when miffed or disappointed. Also, the national committees lack the full-time attention of their members, whose main concern is state and local politics. Even the national chairman may be preoccupied with his own business or profession, with his role in state party affairs, or with a cabinet office or a seat in Congress. Even if he devotes full time to the job, the chairman rarely stays long enough to master the complexities of the national committee operations; from 1955 to 1975 the Republican and Democratic chairmen both averaged less than two and a half years on the job.

Furthermore, the national committees have no sanctions over state and local organizations or over rebel congressmen and senators. They cannot control or even greatly influence nominations in the states. Even if the traditions and mores of political localism did not prevent such intervention, the direct primary would. Nor can the national committee control the selection of local party officials; custom and state law prevent it again. And so far the national committee has not been able to develop the power of the purse as a weapon of national party authority. Above all, there is no consensus, no unity, among the state party organizations which a national committee might reflect and which it might use as a base of power.

Consequently, therefore, the party in government dominates the national parties even more than it dominates the state and local parties. Incumbent presidents commonly turn them into auxiliary personal organizations, and in the party which lost the presidential election they serve, however wanly and uncertainly, as an alternative to or a critic of the president and his administration. Thus the national party is in effect a presidential party. It reflects the national constituency of the president rather than the aggregate of local, far less "national" congressional constituencies. It exists to nominate and elect a president, and it is allied against the locally rooted, decentralized outlook of the Congress. And ironically, it is the national committee's victory in the presidential election that signals its own lesser role as the handmaiden of presidential power.

Is there then no hope of raising the stature and influence of national party committees? They might well expand their role under either one of two conditions. They would certainly be strengthened if they could win control of some of the rewards and incentives of partisan politics. If the national committee were to control the distribution of party and electoral resources — campaign funds, for example — the present distribution of power within the parties would be sharply altered. Already the campaign finance reforms of 1974 may bolster the national party somewhat, even though public funds will go to the presidential campaigns rather than to the parties themselves. Furthermore the national committees have developed a growing repertory of fund-raising schemes with which to support themselves. The splashy Democratic telethons from Los Angeles featuring the glamorous Democrats in the movie and TV industries are an obvious example.[7]

Alternatively, the national party apparatus would certainly be strengthened by the continued turn of party electorates and party activists to a politics of issue or ideology. Already men and women are increasingly brought to political activity by a concern for issues, and those issues and the ideologies related to them are more and more national in scope. Coverage by television and the other mass media focuses attention on national events, national issues, national personalities. State parties find it more difficult to isolate themselves from the currents of national politics and to base their appeals on local issues and traditions. Even such general ideological labels as "liberal" and "conservative" have meaning only in issues of national scope, and increasingly they have the same meaning in all parts of the country. Ultimately, if a national party were to be unified behind a national ideology or posture on issues and were to be peopled by activists loyal to it, it would inevitably express that unity in stronger national party organizations.

The centralizing forces are clearly more vigorously at work in the Democratic party in the mid-1970s. The McCarthy bid for the party nomination in 1968 and the McGovern candidacy of 1972 brought new ideologists into the party ranks. The Democrats have also tightened national control over the selection of delegates to the national conventions, a degree of national control over state practice unimaginable several decades ago.[8] The Democrats have also adopted a new constitution and held their first national midterm party conference in 1974. Both were less vigorous than their original proponents had planned, but they nonetheless may be portents of things to come. Most striking of all, two committees of the party set up in 1968 and chaired finally by Congressmen James O'Hara and Donald Fraser actually included a national membership party for the Democrats in the proposed charter. They envisioned a national party in the European mode with personal membership (with dues from those who could afford them), a vital national organization, and party conferences that would write party policy for the party in government. The charter as it finally passed in 1974 contained none of this, of course. But for the moment the failure may be less important than the fact of the attempt.

In short, there is already within the Democratic party more sentiment in favor of national party strength — or at least against the traditional

---

[7] The recent changes and reforms in campaign finance will be discussed fully in Chap. 13.

[8] See Chap. 11 for a description of the recent battles in both parties over the nature of representation in the national conventions.

localism of the parties — than there has ever been. Much or most of it is issue-centered. If it continues to grow, we may well expect increased support for proposals similar to those of the Fraser and O'Hara committees. If it does not grow and still persists, the question of reform and nationalization will continue to divide the party. All of these trends are, to be sure, less evident at the moment within the Republican party. It has been the presidential party in the early 1970s, and these reforms are the phenomena of parties out of power. But it is hard to believe that nationalizing trends can or will strike only one of the two major parties. Both parties must respond in the long run to the same imperatives of the political climate and culture.

A FINAL NOTE ON PARTY ORGANIZATION

We have come to accept large-scale organization as an important social reality in this century. In business, government, universities, and voluntary organizations, it is a time of complex social structures and of the bureaucrats and "organization men" who have become their symbols. We have every right to include the parties among them, but it is an inescapable fact that the parties, almost alone among our major social institutions, have resisted the development of large, centralized organization.

Even by the standards of the parties of the other democracies, the American party organizations cut an unimpressive figure. They lack the hierarchical control and efficiency, the unified setting of priorities and strategy, and the central responsibility we associate with large contemporary organizations. Instead of a continuity of relationships and of operations, the American party organizations feature only improvisatory, elusive, and sporadic structure and activities. And whereas the party organizations of the rest of the Western democracies have had a permanent, highly professional leadership and large party bureaucracies, the American organizations have generally done without a professional bureaucracy or leadership cadre.[9] One does not make a career in the administration of the American parties. The business of American party organization is largely in the hands of part-time activists, which is perhaps to say that its business and its organizational relationships require no specialists and no full-time professional care.

One is compelled to wonder at the reasons for the stunting of American party organization. In part it results from statutory limits and prescriptions. Traditional fears of political parties and party strength have certainly contributed as well. (There is little in American political val-

[9] On party bureaucracy, see the perceptive article of Charles E. Schutz, "Bureaucratic Party Organization Through Professional Political Staffing," *Midwest Journal of Political Science* 8 (1964): 127–42.

ues that would welcome an efficient or "businesslike" operation of the parties.) In large part, however, the underorganization of the American parties results from their fundamental character. They have been pragmatic electoral parties, involved chiefly in supporting candidates for public office and active mainly during campaigns. As such they have long been led and dominated, not by career bureaucrats, but by public office seekers and holders. Perhaps, too, the degree of pragmatic flexibility to which Americans have carried their party politics rules out the routine and the fixity of a large organization. Organization is to some extent routine and unchanging, and it is therefore more compatible with the party of unchanging ideology or principle than with one committed to the adjustments necessary for electoral success. So the electoral preoccupations of the American parties have tipped the scales in favor of parties in government and against the party organization.

III

THE POLITICAL PARTY AS AN ELECTORATE

In very few party systems is the gulf between the party organization and the party in the electorate[1] as great as it is in the American party system. Unlike most of the parties of the European democracies, the American party organizations have not been able to integrate the party's most loyal supporters into the party organization. Throughout the 1960s and into the 1970s the Italian Communist and Christian Democratic parties by themselves enrolled about 10 percent of Italian adults into party membership. On the other hand, membership groups within the American parties are very small and comparatively rare.

Nor have the American parties mounted any substantial programs to educate their loyal electorates into the programs and traditions of the party. The cadre organization of the American parties remains apart from even the most loyal portion of the party electorate. It views even the most sympathetic voters as a clientele to be wooed and reinforced anew at each election. Those sympathetic voters, for all their protestations of loyalty to the party, also stand apart. They consider their obligations to the party amply filled if they support its candidates in a substantial majority of instances.

This party in the electorate, unlike the party organization, is largely a categorical group. There is no interaction within it, no structured or stable set of relationships, no organizational or group life. And like any categorical group it is an artifact of the way we choose to define it. There is common scholarly agreement, however, that the party in the electorate is characterized by its feelings of loyalty to or identification with the party. In the American political context its people are the men and women who consider themselves Democrats and Republicans; they

---

[1] The term was popularized by V. O. Key in his *Politics, Parties, and Pressure Groups*, 5th ed. (New York: Crowell, 1964), p. 164. Key, however, attributed the term to Ralph M. Goldman.

may even, in the loose usages of American politics, consider themselves "members" of one political party or the other. In practical, operational terms they are the partisans who answer either "Republican" or "Democrat" to survey questions such as, "Generally speaking, do you usually think of yourself as a Republican, a Democrat, an independent, or what?" [2]

The size of the American parties in the electorate depends, of course, on the measures of them we employ. The 1972 data of the Survey Research Center (SRC), for example, indicate the following breakdowns of party identifications within the American electorate: [3]

Strong Democrats	14.8%
Weak Democrats	25.6
Independents	34.6
Weak Republicans	13.1
Strong Republicans	10.3
Others (no answer, apolitical, other party, etc.)	1.7
	100.1%

If one groups all the partisan identifiers together, he defines two party electorates that account for almost two-thirds of American adults (63.8 percent). A more reasonable alternative might be to accept only the "strong" identifiers, totaling 25.1 percent of the American adults, as approximations of the two parties in the electorate.

Such estimates of the size of the party electorate, it should be emphasized, are exceptionally arbitrary. One can imagine other acceptable ways of measuring the party in the electorate. One might, for example, identify it with the party's regular voters, regardless of what loyalty they may or may not declare. (In 1972 about 35 percent of the SRC's national sample declared that they had always voted for the same party since they began to vote.) But there are good reasons for preferring the criterion of party identification. Strong party identifiers do tend to be the party's faithful voters. But they are more than straight-ticket voters. They have a degree of loyalty and emotional attachment to the party that substitutes in some measure for the formal act of membership in a party system in which membership is not common. They are

---

[2] The question is the chief one the Survey Research Center of the University of Michigan uses to determine party identification. The Gallup Poll (American Institute of Public Opinion) uses the following similar question: In politics, as of today, do you consider yourself a Republican, Democrat, or independent?

[3] The identifications here were developed in response to the question above and to a follow-up question which separated the partisan identifiers into strong and weak groups. The independents were also broken into the following subgroups on another question: independent Democrats, 11.1 percent; independents, 13.1 percent; and independent Republicans, 10.4 percent.

also more apt to be active workers in the party. In short, the party identifiers bring fairly predictable votes to the party, but in addition they bring loyalty, activity, and even public support to it.[4]

Despite their expressions of party loyalty, the members of the parties in the electorate are fickle and sometimes waver in the support of the party of their choice. The party organizations and candidates know that even their electoral support cannot be taken for granted; other appeals and loyalties may on occasion override even the staunchest party loyalties. And some loyalists — probably a minority — express a loyalty that is little more than an empty formula. They may be Democrats or Republicans in the same sense that many individuals call themselves "members" of a religious denomination when they have not stepped inside a church for years. And yet for all of this, the members of the party electorates do vote for the candidates of "their" party and support its public positions with a faithfulness far beyond that of the rest of the total electorate. They tend, in other words, to be the party regulars and straight-ticket voters. They are the men and women who, in the argot of Madison Avenue, display the greatest partisan "product loyalty."

For all its uncertainties the party in the electorate does provide the party organization and candidates with a stable, hard core of electoral support. The reliability of this electorate releases the organization and its standard-bearers from the intolerable burden of convincing and mobilizing a full majority of the electorate in every campaign. But the party in the electorate performs additional services for the party. It is a reservoir of potential activists for the organization. Its members may also make financial contributions to the party, or they may work in a specific campaign. Those people who attend party rallies, who talk about politics and persuade friends, or who express any form of political enthusiasm in the community very probably come from its ranks. Its members are most active in perpetuating the party by socializing their children into loyalty to it and possibly activity in it. In sum, they give the party a substance, an image, a presence in the community, and the most involved among them constitute something of an auxiliary semiorganization that supports the exertions of the loyal party organization.

The party in the electorate is an alarmingly diverse group largely because the simple gesture of loyalty that defines it — a word or two in response to a stranger asking questions — means so many different things to different people. (Notice that we include people in the party electorate on the basis of their own attribution of attachment and not

[4] For an examination of the alternatives in identifying party adherents, see Everett C. Ladd and Charles D. Hadley, "Party Definition and Party Differentiation," *Public Opinion Quarterly* 37 (1973): 21–34.

on the basis of actual voting, or activity, or contribution to the life of the political party.) Understandably, the boundaries of the party electorate are indistinct. Individuals also move freely in and out of it, either to or from the more active circles of the party organization or the less committed circles of the electorate at large (or even in rare instances into the electorate of the other party). A compelling, charismatic candidate, for example, may move adults across the group lines. Both Eugene McCarthy and George McGovern brought a large number of new activists into the Democratic party.

But a party in the electorate is more than a categorical group or even a quasi organization. It is also an aggregate of cognitive images. It is, in other words, a system of impressions, or an object of opinion and judgment, *within* large numbers of individual voters. It is a loyalty or identification ordinarily so strong that it assumes a dominant position in the individual's political cosmos. It is the "party *in* the elector." It acts as a reference symbol, a political cue-giver, and a perceptual screen through which he sees and evaluates candidates and issues. Loyalty to a political party is, therefore, often a dominant factor in the subtle calculus by which the American political animal sees, reacts, decides, and acts. And for voters and citizens, the political party of their cognitions may be far more real and tangible than any overt political activity or any observable political organization. For they react to what they perceive. The political party of their perceptions may be only a loosely codified set of judgments and impressions of men, issues, and events, but for them it may be more real than the party of leaders, platforms, and organizations.

Since the American parties are still cadre parties without important membership contingents, the party in the electorate gives the party its mass, popular character. It is to the party in the electorate that people generally refer when they speak of Democrats and Republicans. It is certainly to the party in the electorate that the casual observer refers when he says, for example, that the Democratic party is the party of the disadvantaged or that the Republican party is the party of the small towns. Many of the differences in the programs and the public images of the major parties spring from differences in the segments of the American electorate that they are successful in enlisting. In fact, the interplay between the appeals of the party (i.e., its candidates, issues, and traditions) and its loyal electoral clienteles — each one shaping and reinforcing the other — comes very close to determining who and what the parties are.

All of this is not to suggest that the rest of the American electorate is of less concern to the American party. At no time can a party or its candidates find within its party electorate the majorities needed for election to office. Even though the voters outside the loyal party electorates have lighter commitments to party and issue, as well as lower levels of political involvement and information, competition for their support is keen, for the two American parties are ever aware of the need for majority support. They cannot, as can some of the parties of the parliamentary democracies, fall back on a safely committed and heavily ideological 15 or 25 percent of the electorate. So they must mobilize majorities in part from vast, fluid, heterogeneous, often disinterested voters beyond the parties in the electorate.

The individuals of the American electorate, therefore, range along a continuum from heavy, almost blind commitment to a political party to total lack of commitment, not only to a political party but to *any* political cause or object. The competitive American parties do not ignore or take for granted any segment of that total electorate. The three chapters of Part III examine the electorate's variety and importance. Chapter 6 deals with the amorphous parties in the electorate, asking who are the Democrats and who are the Republicans. It is concerned, as we earlier suggested, with the party electorate as a categorical group. Chapter 7 takes up the party *within* the elector, the party as a set of cognitive images. It deals with the impact of party loyalty or identification on the political behavior of the individual. Chapter 8 focuses on the legal and self-imposed restrictions on the total electorate that limit the parties' attempts to activate their loyalists and recruit new supporters.

6
The
Loyal
Electorates

For millions of Americans unconcerned with the intricacies of party organization, the group of party loyalists we call the party in the electorate *is* the political party. Much of the written history of American parties and politics has reinforced that impression. It has concentrated on the wins and losses of the parties in their competitions for the presidency and the Congress. It has recorded the successes of the parties, not in terms of party organization, strategy, or activity, but in terms of the enduring blocs of voters supporting them. Thus the parties have been defined at various times as parties of the East or West, the North or South, the city or country, the rich or poor, the white or black.

This visibility of the party in the electorate, even though it is only a loosely defined categorical group, is one of the major sources of its importance. Its interests and involvements contribute significantly to the public image of the party, and its life-styles and political values will inevitably be impressed on it. The importance of that impact, however, is matched by a second. Within the cognitive mechanism of American voters, loyalty to or identification with a political party has long been the single most important influence on their political behavior. It colors judgments of candidates and issues, and it guides decisions on how to vote.

TWO-PARTY DIVISIONS IN THE ELECTORATE

In the period since 1860 the two major parties have each enjoyed a time of long-run ascendancy. From 1860 through the presidential election of 1928, Republican presidential candidates won fourteen out of eighteen times. Their supremacy was broken only by the two victories of Grover Cleveland, each won by an eyelash margin, and by the two of Woodrow Wilson. Moreover, Wilson's initial victory in 1912 was built on less than 40 percent of the popular vote, a result of the fact that Teddy Roosevelt's Bull Moose candidacy split a sizable chunk of Republican votes from the regular Republican candidate, William Howard Taft. Furthermore, in this period the Democrats managed to set one record in futility; in the election of 1924 they won only 34.8 percent of the two-party popular vote for president.

Since the 1930s the Democrats have enjoyed a period of similar dominance. Of the eleven presidential elections from 1932 through 1972 the Democrats won seven, losing two to Dwight D. Eisenhower and two to Richard Nixon. Furthermore, in this latter period the Republicans set two records of their own in futility. In 1936 they won only eight electoral votes, the smallest number for a major party in modern times, and in 1964 Lyndon Johnson rolled up a record 61.1 percent of the total popular vote at their expense.

The same two periods of dominance are reflected even more dramatically in party control of the two houses of Congress (Table 1). The very fact that the cycles of control of Congress follow those of the presidency so closely lends further support to the conclusion that these are cycles of *party* ascendancy. Since the Civil War, in fact, on only three occasions (1956, 1968, and 1972) did a winning president see the opposing party carry both houses of Congress in a year of his election.

TABLE 1   Partisan Control of the Houses of Congress, 1861–1931 and 1931–75

	House of Representatives		Senate	
	Dems.	Repubs.	Dems.	Repubs.
1861–1931 (37th–71st Congress)	12	23	5	30
1931–75 (72nd–94th Congress)	21	2	20	3

Behind the striking dominance of the Republicans from 1861 to 1930 and the Democrats from 1930 to the present lies the great probability that each party was in the time of its ascendancy the majority party. That is, during the period of its successes the dominant party commanded the partisan loyalties of a majority of Americans. Its loyal, supportive party in the electorate was large enough to guarantee victory in the great percentage of elections. The minority party could win only sporadically by overriding the dominant party loyalties with an uncommonly attractive candidate or an especially salient issue. That the Republicans were such a majority party before 1930 we must take more or less on faith; more precisely, we make that assumption in a

projection backward of what we have learned about the American electorate and the power of party loyalty through public opinion surveys
since the 1940s.

With an amazing regularity for the past generation, the American
adult population has been preferring, identifying with, or expressing
loyalty to the Democratic party.[1] Table 2 indicates the persistence of
the Democratic party's superiority among the party identifiers.[2] It also
illustrates the remarkable stability of party identifications in the United
States — a stability so great in recent years that not even a popular
president of the minority party, General Eisenhower, could jar it. Nor
did Richard Nixon's sweeping victory in 1972 add any loyalists to the
Republican ranks. Finally, it should be clear that such data on party
identification do not assess patterns of voting but rather the fundamental loyalties to or preferences for party, regardless of the specific
candidates and issues in an election campaign.

TABLE 2   Party Identification of American Adults: 1952–72

Identification	Oct. 1952	Oct. 1956	Oct. 1960	Oct. 1964	Oct. 1968	Oct. 1972
Strong Democrats	22%	21%	21%	27%	20%	15%
Weak Democrats	25	23	25	25	25	26
Independents	22	24	23	23	29	35
Weak Republicans	14	14	13	13	14	13
Strong Republicans	13	15	14	11	10	10
Others	4	3	4	2	2	2

Source   Survey Research Center of the University of Michigan; data made available through the Inter-University Consortium for Political Research.

But more important than the question of how many Democratic and
Republican identifiers there are is the question of who they are. From
what educational backgrounds, what regions, what occupations, what

---

[1] For the basic procedures and assumptions underlying this concept of party identification, see Angus Campbell et al., *The American Voter* (New York: Wiley, 1960).
[2] The data of the Gallup Poll (American Institute of Public Opinion) are very similar, even though the questions and categories are a little different.

	1960	1964	1968	1972	1974
Democrats	47%	53%	46%	42%	44%
Independents	23	22	27	31	35
Republicans	30	25	27	27	21

Gallup data for early 1975 show further Republican erosion to 22 percent. Democratic strength at 46 percent, and the independents inching to 32 percent.

religions, what social groups come the Democrats and the Republicans? On what bases of loyalty do the parties attract supporters and voters? Or, conversely, what experiences and values shape the decisions of Americans to align themselves with one party rather than the other? Why do some Americans identify with one party and others with another?

THE ACQUISITION OF PARTY LOYALTIES

It is a commonplace among Americans to say that one is a Democrat or a Republican because he was born one, just as he was born a Methodist, a Catholic, or a Christian Scientist. The processes of political socialization begin early in life as the child begins to become aware of political parties and absorb judgments about them. He soon realizes that one of the parties is the family's party, that it is "good," that it is "our" party. Even in later life many Americans recognize the early origins of their party loyalties:

I'm a borned Republican, sister. We're Republicans from start to finish, clear back on the family tree. Hot Republicans all along. I'm not so much in favor of Eisenhower as the party he is on. I won't weaken my party by voting for a Democrat. . . .

I was just raised to believe in the Democrats and they have been good for the working man — that's good enough for me. The Republicans are a cheap outfit all the way around. I just don't like the Republicans, my past experience with them has been all bad.[3]

Even though they do not often consciously indoctrinate their children into loyalty to a political party, parents are the prime agents of political socialization in the American culture. Their casual conversations, their references to political events, and the example of their political activity are sufficient to convey their party loyalties to their children. And so stable are the results that the intergenerational similarities in party loyalty persist even when the children reach adulthood (Table 3).[4] Furthermore, parents with consistent, reinforcing party loyalties are more likely to produce strong party identifiers among their children. Those without party loyalties or with mixed loyalties produce offspring who are more likely to be independents. Interestingly, too, a number of studies have found that the relationship in party preferences between generations is greater than the relationship in political attitudes. Thus, as one writer has put it, "We have suggestive evidence that the social-

[3] Angus Campbell, Gerald Gurin, and Warren Miller, *The Voter Decides* (Evanston: Row, Peterson, 1954), p. 92.
[4] Campbell et al., *The American Voter*, p. 147.

TABLE 3   Intergenerational Similarities in Party Identification: 1972

Party identification of offspring	Party of Mother and Father				
	Both Democrat	Both Republican	Both independent or apolitical	Father Democrat, mother Republican	Mother Democrat, father Republican
Strong Democrat	23.5%	2.9%	5.3%	15.5%	1.4%
Weak Democrat	38.0	6.7	9.3	22.5	27.1
Independent	27.2	31.0	72.0	40.8	41.4
Weak Republican	6.6	27.6	10.7	15.5	15.7
Strong Republican	4.2	31.2	2.0	5.6	12.9
Apolitical, etc.	.5	1.6	.7	—	1.4
	(N = 1083)	(N = 520)	(N = 150)	(N = 71)	(N = 70)

Source Survey Research Center of the University of Michigan; data made available through the Inter-University Consortium for Political Research.

Note The table omits the instances in which one parent had a party identification and the other was independent, apolitical, or allied with another party.

ization of the individual into a *party* is a much more direct process than the socialization of the logically congruent area of ideology." [5]

That the acquisition of party loyalties comes surprisingly early and easily is also one conclusion of a study of schoolchildren in New Haven, Connecticut.[6] More than 60 percent of the fourth-grade children were able to state a party preference — a percentage, the author notes, close to the percentage the SRC data showed for the twenty-one- to twenty-four-year-old segment of its national adult sample. At this age, however, few of the children support their identification with much information about party leaders, issues, or traditions. Not until they are eighth-graders do they develop the supportive knowledge that permits party identification to become fully operative in the political world. At that age, for example, they begin to associate the parties with general economic interests or groups — with business or labor, with the rich or the poor. So, this abstract party loyalty is much more easily acquired than information about political issues and ideology. Moreover, lower SES children identify with a party just as frequently as children from higher SES backgrounds.

Every indication, therefore, points to the family as the chief socializer into party loyalty. The strong correlation of the child's party identification with that of his parents suggests this conclusion. So, too, does the fact that the identification is present before the child reaches the grades in which teachers and curricula usually touch on politics. Some offspring do, of course, leave the party of their parents. Those whose initial identification is weak are more apt to change than those whose first party commitment is strong. But, by and large, people hew to the first party loyalty, and the intergenerational agreement persists a long time.

Despite that stability of the initial party identification, we do know that the process of socialization, including the development of party identification, is no single, one-shot influence. At the least it involves a life-long series of refinements and reinforcements of the initial socialization. It may also be weakened or altered during adulthood by cataclysmic events, such as the Civil War, the Great Depression of the 1930s, or the unrest and upheaval in social values in the 1960s and 1970s. Although changes in occupation alone seem not to affect party identification, a change in life-style, peer groups, or basic social attitudes often does. Individuals may, of course, react to far less dramatic

---

[5] Herbert Hyman, *Political Socialization* (Glencoe: Free Press, 1959), p. 74. The high degree of intergenerational similarity in party identifications is reaffirmed and explained in Paul A. Beck and M. Kent Jennings, "Parents as 'Middlepersons' in Political Socialization," *Journal of Politics* 37 (1975): 83–107.

[6] Fred I. Greenstein, *Children and Politics* (New Haven: Yale University Press, 1965). See also Robert D. Hess and Judith V. Torney, *The Development of Political Attitudes in Children* (Chicago: Aldine, 1967), especially pp. 80–81.

events. Beneath the stability of the aggregate totals of party identifications in the country (Table 2), there are individuals moving in some
direction across party lines at every moment. In the late 1950s and
1960s, at least, some 10 percent of the American electorate was shifting party identification between one presidential election and the next.[7]

In part the stability of these party loyalties results from the relative
absence in the American political system of other agencies of political
socialization that might challenge the early influences of the family.
Schools in the early grades often avoid political studies, and the main
conscious educational attempt at political socialization — the high
school civics course — may not have the impact planned for it. One
recent national study concludes that there is no evidence that the
courses have a significant effect on the political orientations of the great
majority of high school students.[8] American churches generally steer
clear of partisan commitments — contrary, for example, to the willingness of many European churches to support the various Christian Democratic parties of Europe. The American parties themselves engage in
very little direct socialization; they do not maintain the youth groups,
the flourishing university branches (which may have offices, lounges,
and eating facilities), the social or recreational activities, or the occupational organizations that their European counterparts do.[9] Business and
worker groups — especially trade unions — do engage in this kind of
socialization, but often with a gingerliness one would not find as often
in their European counterparts. Indeed, it has long been a maxim of
American middle-class gentility that one does not discuss either religion
or politics in polite social circles.

Thus the adolescent and young adult finds that his party loyalty is
supported by a homogeneous political environment of family, friends,
and secondary groups into which no new political socializers threaten
to intrude. Even as a young adult his friends, associates, relatives, and
spouse have the same partisan loyalties that he does. In short, most individuals are "anchored in a matrix of politically harmonious primary associations — a result, to some extent, of conscious selection and of the
tendency for the social environment to bring together people of like

---

[7] See Douglas Dobson and Douglas St. Angelo, "Party Identification and the Float-
ing Vote: Some Dynamics," *American Political Science Review* 69 (1975): 481–90.
[8] Kenneth P. Langton and M. Kent Jennings, "Political Socialization and the High
School Civics Curriculum in the United States," *American Political Science Review*
62 (1968): pp. 852–67.
[9] The new Democratic Charter promises new Democratic activity in this area. Article Nine sets up a National Education and Training Council and provides: "In order
to encourage a lifetime of meaningful political participation for every Democrat,
the National Education and Training Council shall attempt to reach every young
citizen as they [sic] enter the electorate at 18 years of age." It remains to be seen
if the Democrats can carry out those plans.

views." [10] But when individuals are not so anchored, they may alter the party identification. For example, when the parents' party identification is not congruent with their general social class characteristics — that is, when the political signals are not harmonious or homogeneous — their children are more apt to develop an identification with the other party. [11]

Party identification in the United States, therefore, has traditionally been acquired early and lingered late. For most Americans it has remained long after the stimuli for its formation were forgotten. But what has always been need not always be. At least one recent study suggests that the processes of initiation into party identification may be changing. [12] A recent national sample of twelfth-graders shows a lower than expected correlation with the party loyalties of their parents. That same group also contained a higher percentage of independents than one finds in the adult American population. It may well be that changes in family life and in the relationships between generations have reduced the effectiveness of the family as a socializer, or it may be that the mass media and other sources of information to which high schoolers are exposed have broken the family's monopoly on political socialization. Either possibility would presage a new set of socialization processes. It would probably also herald greater instability in the patterns of party identification in American politics.

SOCIAL CLASS AND PARTY IDENTIFICATION

The processes of political socialization do not, however, explain the distribution of party loyalties in the United States. They describe how rather than why the individual acquires his particular party loyalty. At best, explanations of socialization, resting as they do on parental influences, in most instances merely push the question back a generation.

The search for an explanation of these party loyalties should very likely begin with social class. It is probably true, as Seymour Lipset has asserted, that the principal generalization one can make about loyalties to the democratic parties of the world is that they are primarily based on social class. [13] We have referred before to social class and to socioeconomic status, and a fuller explanation of the terms is probably overdue. Much of the literature uses them interchangeably (or almost interchangeably), but the preference here is for the latter term and its

---

[10] Herbert McClosky and Harold E. Dahlgren, "Primary Group Influence on Party Loyalty," *American Political Science Review* 53 (1959): 775.
[11] Arthur S. Goldberg, "Social Determinism and Rationality as Bases of Party Identification," *American Political Science Review* 63 (1969): 5–25.
[12] M. Kent Jennings and Richard G. Niemi, "The Transmission of Political Values from Parent to Child," *American Political Science Review* 62 (1968): 169–84.
[13] *Political Man* (New York: Anchor, 1963), p. 230.

conventional abbreviation, SES. Socioeconomic status is simply the relative ranking of the economic and/or social deference the individual can
command. But regardless of the rubric one chooses, status differences
underlie the party electorates of the mature, industrial democracies with
which one can most reasonably compare the United States. The very
nature of economic and political development, and thus of the class
differences of industrialized economies, seems to transcend the older
party lines based on ethnic, racial, religious, or regional differences.

The signs and marks of SES conflict are scattered throughout American history, even in the preindustrial decades. James Madison, one of
the most knowing observers of human nature among the Founding
Fathers, wrote in his famous tenth paper of *The Federalist* that economic differences are the most common source of faction.[14] Social and
economic status differences clearly underlay the battle between the
wealthy, aristocratic Federalists and the less privileged Jeffersonian
Democrats. Then, almost a century later, William Jennings Bryan made
the Democratic party the vehicle for the protests of the Grangers, the
emerging Socialists, the Greenbackers, the Knights of Labor, and the
Populists — all of them composed largely of the discontented and disadvantaged. Bryan ("the Great Commoner") came to the Democratic
convention of 1896 as the voice of prairie Populism. He challenged the
conservatism of Grover Cleveland in his celebrated attack on the gold
standard and hard money. ("You shall not press down upon the brow
of labor this crown of thorns. You shall not crucify mankind upon this
cross of gold.") Stirred by the Nebraska prophet, the convention re-
pudiated its conservative leadership and picked Bryan himself as its
candidate. Despite his defeat, the Democrats twice (1900 and 1908)
returned to him as their presidential candidate for the crusade against
corporate wealth, eastern banking interests, and what Bryan liked to
call the "plutocracy."

In many ways Bryan and the Democrats of 1896 appear to be the
harbingers of modern American politics. Bryan captured the Democratic
party for the rural and agrarian interests in their fight against the new
industrial and financial interests. The Republicans became the party
committed to the pursuit of industrialization. Woodrow Wilson's "New
Freedom" and its reforms reflected the Democrats' identification both
with agrarian interests and increasingly with urban, immigrant, industrial have-nots. In the suffusing prosperity of the 1920s many of the
class differences between the two parties were greatly muted. But in
the elections of 1928 and 1932 they erupted again.[15]

[14] See Madison's tenth *Federalist* paper: ". . . the most common and durable source
of factions has been the various and unequal distribution of property."
[15] See the excellent account of this section of American party history in Everett C.
Ladd, *American Political Parties* (New York: Norton, 1970), Chap. 4.

The SES stamp on the parties became more vivid in the 1930s. The migration to the cities and the crushing impoverishments of the Great Depression were the events out of which Franklin Roosevelt rebuilt the Democratic party more firmly than ever as a party of social and economic reform. This intensification of the SES lines between the two parties was his "revolution" in party politics. His New Deal programs — labor legislation, social security, wages and hours laws — solidified the Democratic party's image as the party of the relative have-nots. Even groups such as the blacks, long allied with the Republicans as the party of Lincoln, were lured to the Democratic banner; the strength of SES issues even kept them as allies of southern whites in the Roosevelt coalition. In brief, Franklin Roosevelt buttressed the class divisions of industrialism by adding to its conflicts the consequent response of government: the Welfare State. Its programs and expenditures heightened the stakes, and thus the commitments, of socioeconomic status politics.[16]

All of this is not to argue that only socioeconomic status differences divided the major American parties in this century. But the evidence is very strong that it did constitute an important and possibly the overriding difference between them. However, only since the 1940s and the advent of reliable public opinion polling has it been possible to make fairly precise and confident statements about the attitudes, the SES, the party identifications, and the votes of individual Americans. Much of our analysis of electorates before World War II, therefore, rests on indirect evidence.

The relationships between party and SES in the 1970s are apparent in the nature of the two party electorates in 1972 (Table 4). The relationship lurks even where it is not obvious. The implications of the partisan differences in educational levels, for example, cannot be taken at face value. There seems little reason to suspect that the intellectually liberating experiences of formal education lead young men and women overwhelmingly to the true path of Republicanism. It seems more reasonable to suppose that the positive relationship between years of education and Republicanism results from the intermediating SES variable (i.e., a higher percentage of upper SES parents send their sons and daughters to college, and the college degree leads to higher SES jobs). Also, given the higher SES of Protestants in the United States, their relationship with Republicanism unquestionably reflects in part those status differences. And there certainly is no need to elaborate the enormous SES differences between whites and blacks in the United States.

---

[16] Among the histories of the American parties see Wilfred Binkley, *American Political Parties* (New York: Knopf, 1962); George H. Mayer, *The Republican Party: 1954–1964* (New York: Oxford University Press, 1964); William N. Chambers, *The Democrats: 1789–1964* (Princeton: Van Nostrand, 1964); and Arthur M. Schlesinger, Jr. (ed.), *History of United States Political Parties*, 4 vols. (New York: Chelsea, 1973).

TABLE 4 Social Characteristics of Party Identifiers: 1972

	Strong Democrat	Weak Democrat	Independent	Weak Republican	Strong Republican	Others	Totals
Race							
White	12.5%	24.6%	36.0%	14.3%	11.1%	1.6%	100.1%
Black	36.3	31.1	22.8	3.7	3.7	2.3	99.9
Other	9.8	46.3	26.8	4.9	4.9	7.3	100.0
Occupation							
Professional	10.8	20.7	38.5	17.4	11.8	.8	100.0
Manager, official	9.0	20.5	34.0	19.1	16.6	.8	100.0
Clerical, sales	14.9	24.8	37.6	12.7	8.4	1.6	100.0
Skilled, semiskilled	16.6	27.3	36.5	9.8	8.2	1.7	100.1
Unskilled, service	16.1	32.7	32.1	8.6	7.7	2.7	99.9
Farmer	14.1	27.3	20.2	19.2	16.2	3.0	100.0
Other (retired, etc.)	21.1	24.8	26.4	14.5	10.3	2.9	100.0
Religion							
Protestant	13.4	24.4	33.0	15.2	12.4	1.6	100.0
Catholic	19.1	31.3	34.4	8.0	5.9	1.5	100.2
Jewish	26.2	24.6	37.7	8.2	1.6	1.6	99.9
Education							
None through 8 grades	23.8	26.2	22.7	13.2	10.4	3.8	100.1
9 through 12 grades	14.0	26.9	37.3	11.6	9.0	1.2	100.0
Some college	11.3	26.0	37.0	11.7	12.0	2.1	100.1
Baccalaureate degree	5.7	21.0	39.3	20.2	13.7	—	99.9
Advanced degree	17.4	14.1	38.0	19.6	10.9	—	100.0
Income							
$0–$2,999	20.4	25.9	27.7	13.1	9.1	3.6	99.8
$3,000–$5,999	17.5	27.9	32.0	10.2	11.0	1.5	100.1
$6,000–$8,999	14.3	28.6	34.9	11.7	8.5	1.9	99.9
$9,000–$11,999	13.7	26.9	37.6	12.4	7.6	1.8	100.0
$12,000–$19,999	13.3	24.4	35.8	13.5	12.4	.8	100.2
$20,000 and over	8.6	17.6	35.6	21.3	16.1	.7	99.9

Source Survey Research Center of the University of Michigan; data made available through the Inter-University Consortium for Political Research.

Yet, the lines of SES difference between the American parties are less distinct than their rhetoric and campaigns might lead one to expect. They are certainly less clear than comparable ones in European party systems. In a comparison of party identifiers in the United States and Norway, Campbell and Valen report:

> In both countries the occupational distribution of identifiers differs among the parties. In the United States, the differences are rather small. The Democratic Party draws 30 per cent of its adherents from the white-collar occupations, 46 per cent from the blue-collar. The Republicans come 36 per cent from the white-collar occupations and 39 per cent from the blue-collar. The occupational differences are very much greater among the various Norwegian parties. Of the Labor Party identifiers 79 per cent are blue-collar workers, 17 per cent are white-collar; among the Conservatives the proportions are 19 per cent and 76 per cent.[17]

Even the two Norwegian parties of the center, whose ideologies are not primarily economic, are more distinctive in their division of occupational groups than are the American parties. Furthermore, SES differences between the two parties are deteriorating at an increasing rate. As recently as 1968 almost 60 percent of the unskilled and service workers identified with the Democratic party; by 1972 it was only 48.8. Similarly, the 62.8 percent of those with a grammar school education or less who identified with the Democratic party in 1968 shrank to 50 percent in 1972.

So we approach the conclusion of most observers of the American parties: that socioeconomic status and party loyalty are not so closely associated in the United States as they are in a number of the other Western democracies.[18] Both American parties have within their loyal electorates an important number of representatives from upper, middle, and lower status groups. Consequently, they find it difficult to formulate overt class appeals or to enunciate ideologies that reflect sharp class or status differences. The heterogeneous nature of their loyalists is perfectly consistent with the parties' pragmatic, relatively nonideological tone, and with their mission as brokers among diverse social groupings. Thus the lines of SES division between the major American parties are indistinct and overlapping, and while SES is one explanation of interparty differences, it is by no means the only one.

The weakness of SES differences between the two party electorates may result partially from the imperfect translation of SES differences into differences in party identification. Among the influences muting

---

[17] Angus Campbell and Henry Valen, "Party Identification in Norway and the United States," *Public Opinion Quarterly* 25 (1961): 514–15.
[18] See Robert R. Alford, *Party and Society* (Chicago: Rand McNally, 1963), Chap. 8.

the translation of status differences into political ones the following may be the most important:

1. *The shifting SES lines of American federalism.* SES lines differ from state to state, and it is difficult and somewhat misleading to make aggregate, national comparisons using identical categories. The distribution of SES groups in Montana, for example, differs greatly from that in New York. Some large and powerful groups in New York — blacks, Jews, and urban laborers come to mind — are considerably less numerous and important in Montana. The Republican parties of the two states, therefore, recruit electorates that greatly differ in SES composition. By the sheer necessity of remaining competitive, the Republicans of New York will amass a more heterogeneous electorate than the Republicans of Montana may feel compelled to.

2. *The suppression of SES differences.* Some state and local party leaders may obliterate SES lines (with decreasing success, probably) by fostering an issueless politics of localism and loyalty to personalities. For years the Democratic parties of the southern states were classic examples of that kind of determinedly non-SES politics. Furthermore, the ascendancy of non-SES issues such as the war in Vietnam inevitably mutes SES issues and differences.

3. *Diffidence about class politics.* American mores do not encourage a politics of class or socioeconomic status. Many Americans do not see class divisions or conflict in the American society; at most they see themselves as members of a very broad and inclusive middle class. Explicit class appeals would probably antagonize one group of Americans and bypass another classless group. Furthermore, American uncertainty and naïveté about class lead some voters to perceive their class differently than the objective indicators suggest. The owner of a modest home, because of that ownership, may identify with SES groups somewhat above the one to which all educational, occupational, and income indicators point.

4. *The slowness of SES translation into politics.* The loyalties of party identification tend to respond only slowly to changes in SES. Many party loyalties formed early as a result of family influences, in fact, are responses to SES one or two generations late. The young man or woman raised and socialized into the Democratic party by a working-class father may cling to that party identification long after graduating from college, entering the business world, and reaching the country club. Also, party loyalties shaped as SES responses to depressions, recessions, or prosperity may remain long after the event.

ALTERNATIVES TO THE SES BASIS OF LOYALTIES

In view of the relatively weak SES divisions between the Democratic and Republican electorates, there must clearly be additional explanations for the distribution of party loyalties in the United States.

Sectionalism

The greatest challenge to the SES interpretations of American politics came historically from the school that ascribed the primary differences between parties to sectional differences.[19] The sectional theories hold that the varying geographic areas or sections of the country have separate, identifiable, and deeply felt political interests, which when honored and favored by a political party unite large numbers of otherwise differing voters behind its standard.[20] Thus in the sectional explanations one speaks of the Republicans' and the Democrats' building national coalitions behind presidential candidates by joining the votes of one section to those of another, or of parties' dominating the loyalties of this or that section of the country.

Unquestionably the most enduring sectionalism in American party history was that of the Democratic party in the South. Even before the Civil War the interests of the South in slavery and in an agriculture geared to export markets had unified it as a political section. The searing experience of that war and the reconstruction that followed made the South into the Solid South and delivered it to the Democrats. United by historical experience and by a desperate defense of a way of life, the eleven states of the Confederacy cast their electoral votes for Democratic presidential candidates in every election from 1880 through 1924, except for Tennessee's defection in 1920. Al Smith's Catholicism frightened four of them into the Republican column in 1928, but the Roosevelt economic programs reinforced the region's economic interests — and in no way greatly challenged its way of life — and brought the South back to the Democratic party for the four Roosevelt elections. Only with the successes of the Dixiecrat ticket in 1948 did the South begin to move away from its traditional party loyalties.

Similarly, strong East-West differences have periodically marked American party conflict. In the early years of the Republic, the fading Federalists held to an ever-narrowing base of eastern seaport and financial interests, while the Jeffersonians expanded westward with the

---

[19] For example, Arthur N. Holcombe, *Our More Perfect Union* (Cambridge: Harvard University Press, 1950).
[20] For a somewhat different and excellent essay on the nature of sectionalism, see V. O. Key, *Politics, Parties, and Pressure Groups*, 5th ed. (New York: Crowell, 1964), pp. 232–33.

new settlers. Jackson, too, pointed his party appeals to the men of the frontier, and the protest movements that thrust William Jennings Bryan into the 1896 campaign sprang from the agrarian discontent of the western prairies. Many of the Populists' loudest complaints were directed at eastern capitalism, eastern bankers, and eastern trusts. Indeed, the geographical distribution of the presidential vote of 1896 is striking affirmation of sectional voting (Figure 1).

FIGURE 1   States Carried by the Democratic Party in the Presidential Election of 1896

States carried by the Democratic party
in the presidential election of 1896

Sectionalism can best be identified by its most obvious characteristic: sectional one-partyism. When sectional loyalties have been strong enough to override all the other sources of party loyalty, they have unified the section behind a single party. When the sectionalism has endured, it has reinforced the one-partyism both socially and psychologically. Young voters learned that the dominant party was the party of the section because it was the defender of the style and quality of its life.

The pull of sectionalism has declined steadily within the past several generations. The isolation and homogeneity of life in the old sections have yielded to a nationalization of life and interests in the country. One-party areas or sections are breaking down into two-party competitiveness, and that in itself is the best clue that sectional loyalties no longer have the power they once did. Sectional loyalties, of course, have not completely disappeared. Southern sectionalism awakened in a new guise in 1964 as five states of the Deep South supported Barry Goldwater, the Republican presidential candidate. They were the only states he carried beyond his own home state of Arizona. Then in 1968 George Wallace carried only five states on the American Independent ticket: Alabama, Arkansas, Georgia, Louisiana, and Mississippi. But elsewhere sectionalism now appears to have receded into a secondary position in the development of political party loyalties.

In retrospect, it is difficult to say what force sectionalism had even at its zenith. The great difficulty with the sectional explanations is that the term "section" may simply be an obscuring shorthand for a geographic concentration of other identifiable interests — ethnic, racial, or possibly SES. Much sectional voting in the past, for instance, reflected conflicts among crop economies in the various agricultural sections. Thus the central question: Are the sections themselves the basic source of sectional interests, or are they merely categories or concentrations of voters who identify with a party for other reasons? It means little to say that the Midwest supported Franklin Roosevelt in 1936 or that the West backed Eisenhower. To be sure, the South has been more than a descriptive category; its political behavior has been sectional in the sense of unified interests and an awareness of the region and its distinctiveness. But the case for sectional explanations weakens greatly as soon as one looks beyond the South.[21]

Urban-Rural Differences

For a considerable portion of the twentieth century there was a conventional wisdom that, especially outside of the South, the Democrats were the party of the cities and the Republicans the party of the small towns and countryside. And it was probably so. The big city political machines were overwhelmingly Democratic, and it was largely in the urban centers that the Democratic blue-collar workers and racial and ethnic groups lived. The Republican commitment to individual self-reliance and a limited role for government appealed to the less complicated ways of rural America. Beginning in the 1960s, however, the urban-rural division between the major parties became progressively blurred and muted. By the 1970s there is only an indistinct division in which, while the largest metropolitan areas show some preference for the Democrats,

---

[21] It may well be that the sectional interpretations were a reflection of the fact that before the late 1940s the only electoral data for analysis were the gross, aggregate totals in which the units of analysis were geographical areas of some sort. Since then the data of the public opinion surveys have made the individual the unit of analysis.

there are no real differences by party in any of the other urban or rural categories. And what differences remain can clearly be explained on other than urban grounds, especially on the obvious SES ones.

As the United States becomes increasingly urban and metropolitan — almost three-fourths of the American population in 1970 lived in some urban place or urbanized area — the question ceases to be one of urban versus rural America. It becomes one of distinction within the urban sectors, between different kinds of cities and different parts of metropolitan areas. Selective migration out of the older center cities promises to leave them ethnic, racial, and low-SES enclaves and thus inclined to be Democratic. Urban diversity and two-party competitiveness may move to the suburbs and urban fringe areas (Table 5).[22] But two related points seem clear on urbanism and the division of the two-party loyalties. First, what differences there are along or within urban-rural lines are largely socioeconomic, and as those SES differences in American party loyalties decline, so too will the urban-rural ones. Second, while a case can indeed be made that there are genuinely urban or rural or small-city interests in American politics, they have never stamped themselves on the division of party identifications.

TABLE 5   Party Support in 13 Minneapolis Suburbs

Suburbs divided by median incomes (1970 Census)	1974 median vote for Democratic congressional candidate[a]
Seven suburbs with highest median incomes	40.4%
Six suburbs with lowest median incomes	48.1%

[a] The median for all 13 suburbs was 43.0%.

Religion

Even when income, education, and occupation are held constant, Catholics and Jews tend to support the Democratic party and non-Southern Protestants the Republican party. Again, however, the statistical relationships are only that; they do not necessarily identify cause. Perhaps despite the holding of some SES factors constant, there remains an SES factor; a Jew of high income, lengthy formal education, and professional occupation (the usual formal characteristics of high SES) may be

---

[22] See also Benjamin Walter and Frederick M. Wirt, "The Political Consequences of Suburban Variety," *Social Science Quarterly* 52 (1971): 746–67.

denied by prejudice the status he might otherwise expect. The same illustration applies to some Catholics, but presently not with the force it had a generation or two ago when anti-Catholic bias was greater and when Catholic identification with the Democratic party was at its strongest.

Yet, it does appear that religion — both as theology and as group identification — is involved here.[23] A Jewish internationalism and concern for social justice, rooted in the religious and ethnic traditions of Judaism, disposes many Jews to the Democratic party as the party of international concern, support for the state of Israel, and social and economic justice.[24] In the case of American Catholics, the tie to the Democratic party is in great part a tie of personalities and political organization. The political machines of the cities were traditionally led by Catholics, and their patronage and largesse often went to the newly immigrated Catholics from Europe. The roll call of Catholics in Democratic leadership, furthermore, extends beyond the local bosses. All but three of the national chairmen of the Democratic party since the late 1920s have been Roman Catholics, and it has also been the party of the two Catholic candidates for the presidency: Al Smith and John F. Kennedy. The ties of Protestantism to Republicanism are less obvious, probably in part because of the enormous diversity of sects that Protestantism embraces. Very possibly, however, the theological individualism of more conservative Protestantism disposes individuals to Republicanism; at least there has been a clear relationship in recent years between Protestant fundamentalism and political conservatism.[25]

Race

Not too long ago the Republican party, as the party of Lincoln, the Civil War, and the hated reconstruction, was associated with racial equality in the minds of Americans both black and white. In the generation between 1930 and 1960, however, the wheels of racial politics turned 180 degrees. It is now the Democratic party, the Kennedy and Johnson administrations, and Democratic Congresses that blacks see advancing racial equality and integration. Blacks identify with the Democratic party in overwhelming numbers and regardless of any other set

[23] David Knoke, "Religion, Stratification and Politics: America in the 1960's," *American Journal of Political Science* 18 (1974): 331–45.
[24] Lawrence Fuchs, *The Political Behavior of the American Jews* (Glencoe: Free Press, 1956).
[25] The 1960 presidential election occasioned a spate of works on the religious factor in American party loyalties and voting behavior. See Scott Greer, "Catholic Voters and the Democratic Party," *Public Opinion Quarterly* 25 (1961): 611–25; and Philip E. Converse, "Religion and Politics: The 1960 Election," in Angus Campbell et al., *Elections and the Political Order* (New York: Wiley, 1966), pp. 96–124.

of social characteristics. The 1972 SRC data show that 67 percent of black adults identify with the Democratic party and only 7 percent with the Republicans. All other indications suggest that the same overwhelming preference marks the loyalties of Chicanos, Puerto Ricans, and American Indians.

Traditionalism

Attachments to a political party need not be associated with an interest, a set of goals, or a group need. It is sufficient for some Americans that their party is the party of their parents, their friends, or their locale. Or that it is the party of their fellow workers or worshippers. For these identifiers it suffices to say, for example, "Everyone around here is a Democrat (or a Republican)." In some sections of the country the prevailing homogeneity of party identification may still reflect the loyalties of the original migrants into the area. Southern Illinois, settled by Democrats from the South, inclines to the Democratic party even today.[26]

Party Leadership and Personalities

Individuals may identify the political party with a particular leader or group of leaders within it. They may attach themselves to the Democratic party as the party of Franklin Roosevelt or John F. Kennedy, or to the Republican party as the party of Dwight D. Eisenhower or Barry Goldwater. For them the party is little more than an extension of an attractive, compelling personality, and their loyalty to it in great part reflects an affection for that personality. Such an explanation of party identification, however, is probably easily overestimated. President Eisenhower, despite the magnitude of his victories and personal popularity, made little dent on long-run loyalties, even of those Democrats who voted for him.

Issue Involvement

Well-informed citizens who are involved in political issues and ideologies will possibly identify with a political party because of the policy positions it takes. For most of this century, for example, the Democratic party has been more willing than the Republican to espouse American commitments abroad, beginning with entry into the League of Nations and continuing today over questions of foreign aid. Republicans have on the whole been more chary of foreign involvement,

---

[26] For a discussion of these traditional loyalties resulting from patterns of migration, see V. O. Key, *American State Politics* (New York: Knopf, 1956), Chap. 8.

more nationalistic, and more prone to isolationism. Other short-run policy differences may have had an equal impact. The issues of prohibition and the Noble Experiment of the Eighteenth Amendment have by now receded into the mists of American history. But in the 1920s and 1930s the question divided the two parties and probably some of their identifiers. The "drys," who supported the experiment, were largely in the Republican party, and most of its "wet" opponents worked in the Democratic party.

In the 1970s party identification seems related most closely to individual stands on the social issues — on those questions concerning government programs that guarantee a minimum standard of living or security for all Americans (Table 6). These are the issues of the Welfare State, the ones touching government medical care or insurance, guaranteed levels of income, social security or welfare programs. Fundamentally they are questions of the redistribution of wealth, for the government taxes income progressively to provide programs of greatest proportional advantage to lower income groups. They are SES issues, one might say, because they propose different benefits for people of different SES.

TABLE 6   Opinions of Party Identifiers on Government Guarantee of Jobs and Standard of Living: 1972

Opinions on government role in guaranteeing jobs, standard of living	Strong Demo- crats	Weak Demo- crats	Inde- pen- dents	Weak Repub- licans	Strong Repub- licans
Strongly positive	36.5%	20.1%	18.0%	11.1%	9.9%
Moderately positive, neutral, and moderately negative	46.6	53.3	47.1	45.2	49.5
Strongly negative	16.9	26.6	35.0	43.7	40.6

Source Survey Research Center of the University of Michigan; data made available through the Inter-University Consortium for Political Research.

Note The table here is a collapsing of a seven-point scale of reactions (three positive, three negative, and one in the middle) between the two polar positions: that the government should have the responsibility for jobs and standard of living, and that each individual should get ahead on his own. It is also important to note that only 34 percent of the adult sample responded with informed, useable responses.

So, *this* is the SES connection in American politics. Clearly much of the partisan rhetoric and conflict of American politics runs along SES lines — whether it is a congressional debate over a poverty program or medicare, a presidential campaign debate on labor-management relations, or a state or local clash over a sales tax. The American electorate, even in its distribution of partisan loyalties, responds to it. But the response comes not cleanly or clearly as the response of specific social classes or groups; it comes from individuals who for one reason or another have come to hold attitudes or views about the role of government and its social responsibility for the less advantaged in American society. Americans develop what appear to be SES sympathies that are not necessarily congruent with their own SES. There may be at work some feeling for the socioeconomic underdog, or some deference to the socioeconomic overdog, or some residual loyalties to a status or class of some years before. There may even be operating some view of a secure and stable society. So, the relationship is not between socioeconomic characteristics and party identification; it is between attitudes and party. And in politics, after all, it is the operational attitude, not the origin, that is important.

The force of issues on party identification is very likely more complex than all of this suggests. For one thing, the attitudes on SES-type issues are for many voters absorbed in broader liberal and conservative (and other) ideologies. As one might expect, there is a considerable correlation between self-described liberals and Democrats, and conversely, between conservatives and Republicans (Table 7). And second, we clearly see the new and rising importance of non-SES issues in recent elections — issues of the war in Vietnam, violence and crime and thus of "law and order," protests and rapid change and reform, racial and sexual equality, and the new moral issues such as those of abortion and sexual freedom. Most of them cut across present party lines. Many of them have influenced a good many presidential votes in recent years. What we do not yet know is whether any of them will be of sufficient intensity, duration, and breadth of appeal to shake very many party loyalties.

PARTY IDENTIFICATION IN FLUX

Party loyalties in the American electorate are more fluid than ever. The old ties to socioeconomic backgrounds, and even to attitudes or preferences on SES issues, are declining. It becomes harder and harder to say to what party identification relates and from what more basic attachments it springs. Fewer and fewer individuals, indeed, will declare it; the independents in the electorate rise inexorably. There is some evidence that changes in it are occurring more rapidly, and perhaps more casually, than ever. And even among those who still hold to some measure of party loyalty, that attachment seems to affect less and less of their political perceptions and behavior.[27] Furthermore, the consequences

---

[27] This point and its ramifications will be examined in the next chapter.

TABLE 7 Relationship between Ideological Self-Perception and Party Identification: 1972

Voters' description of own position	Strong Democrat	Weak Democrat	Inde-pendent	Weak Repub-lican	Strong Repub-lican
Liberal	23.8%	14.2%	17.2%	8.8%	5.4%
Moderate	18.5	24.3	21.3	22.3	19.8
Conservative	9.0	16.9	19.5	33.3	39.9
Don't know, no answer, can't say, etc.	48.8	44.6	42.0	35.6	34.9
	100.1	100.0	100.0	100.0	100.0

Source Survey Research Center of the University of Michigan: data made available through the Inter-University Consortium for Political Research.

Note The three categories above represent a collapsing of a seven-point scale on the original question. "Liberal" here embraces three options: extremely liberal, liberal, and slightly liberal. "Conservative" includes answers to three parallel options. "Moderate" reports answers to that single option; 37 percent of the total replies in these seven options were "moderate."

of these changes for the American parties can scarcely be exaggerated. Since the stability of the two major American parties has been grounded in the party as a symbol or a cognitive image, the decline of that symbolic strength "within" the American voter poses the most serious threat imaginable to the parties and to their traditionally central position in American politics.

The American party electorate has always been distinctive in that it is a group defined primarily by that loyalty and not by loyalty to an ideology or a class position (in which the party is merely a means to those ends). This very "partisan-ness" and heterogeneity of the American party electorates made them staunch allies of the two-party system, as Campbell and Valen have observed:

The strength of these party attachments and the general weakness in the American electorate of ideological interest both serve to maintain the two-party system. The failure of various attempts to launch third parties appealing to the special interests of the farmers or the urban working class reflects the conserving force of these two attributes of the American party system. Deriving from the two-party system, they have become important factors in its preservation.[28]

What was most important, in other words, was not the composition of the two parties in the electorate but the durability of the allegiances be-

[28] Campbell and Valen, "Party Identification," p. 524.

hind them. It was precisely this willing loyalty on the part of so many Americans that undergirded the stability of the two-party system. As the quantity and quality of that loyalty declines, the change in the parties and in American politics will be fundamental.

For the present, however, the American parties in the electorate are still impressive, even if complex and troubled. They are perhaps best thought of as multilayered aggregates, each stratum having a different reason for party loyalty and each experiencing different consequences as a result of it. One might with a little imagination see them as thick sheets of plywood, each drawing its strength from the many different layers with their grains all running in different directions. Thus the coalitions that compose the Democratic and Republican electorates at any one time are built from complicated sets of influences. Among them are both SES and non-SES factors, those that relate to specific social interests or philosophies and those that are related to old traditions, to family preferences, or to group solidarity. It is, therefore, too simple to speak in dichotomies of rich and poor, black and white, city and farm. It is too simple even to look for single categories of explanation, single sets of influences.

Especially because party loyalties are enduring, one must look not only at the complex influences of the day but also at those of past days. Party loyalists are added to a party's electorate in successive stages, in buildups of layer on layer. To understand those coalitions requires, therefore, a kind of political geology that explores the political strata of the past. Indeed, Walter Dean Burnham, who originated the study of political geology, finds that issues of the 1964 presidential election — especially those with racial resonances — awakened in New York state some old electoral alignments of the nineteenth century. Granted that a dominant or overt cleavage or set of cleavages characterizes the two party electorates at any one time,

there are also latent or suppressed cleavages which may endure for decades without losing their capacity to influence voting outcomes. . . . [There] is the strong likelihood that American voting behavior in the present era is crosscut with a far richer mixture of overt and latent cleavages, cleavages of "ancient" and "modern" vintage, than has hitherto been supposed.[29]

Whatever may be the overt configuration of party loyalties at any time, there is no reason to think it will last for all time. It is thoroughly possible that a major American military loss or a crippling international oil embargo would elevate defense or foreign policy issues to a new power in determining party identifications. It is equally possible that a serious depression or a galloping inflation would reawaken and sharpen

[29] Walter Dean Burnham, "American Voting Behavior and the 1964 Election," *Midwest Journal of Political Science* 12 (1968): 32.

the old SES divisions. The determinants of party loyalties are themselves shifting, dynamic, and vulnerable to change. When they shift radically, we have those great and rare rearrangements of party loyalties called realignments. Historically these shifts have been triggered by the conjunction of presidential elections and cataclysmic events — the Civil War, panics, depressions, and foreign wars. Most recently the events of the Great Depression of the late 1920s and 1930s established the basic SES coalitions that still persist in parties today. (Realignments will be more fully discussed in the next chapter.)

Not all the changes in the party electorates, of course, are sharp, fundamental, long-time realignments. Individual voters change their party loyalties at all times of the political season. In the shorter run the parties struggle to hold the loyalties of their voters in the face of shifts within the range of the current divisions between them. The American population ages, and the parties must appeal to a new group, the nation's senior citizens. Migrations to the West and to the cities alter the distribution of the state electorates and therefore of the parties in the electorate. And a raging war in Vietnam threatens many party loyalties. Moreover, there are signs that these short-run forces are more and more active. Not too long ago, estimates put at less than 20 percent the number of individuals who shifted their party identification at some time in their lives. The 1972 data, however, report that 26 percent of the SRC's sample had changed their party (or independent) preference at least once in their adult lives.[30]

Perhaps the most trenchant illustration of the short-run changes possible in the American party electorates is in the electorate under thirty. There are already ample signs that these voters do not distribute themselves between the two parties in the usual ratio. Evidence has existed for some time that the percentage of voters between twenty-one and thirty who call themselves independents is higher than the percentage for the adult population as a whole. The trend was reinforced with the addition of voters between eighteen and twenty-one. Also, it is clear in the data (Table 8) that those who do pick a party are less inclined to the Republicans than older voters. Furthermore, it is the younger voters who less and less translate their social class directly into a party choice.[31] As young voters enter the party electorates — or do not enter them — the shape of American party coalitions is drastically changed.

[30] The estimate of less than 20 percent is for the late 1950s and comes from Campbell et al., *The American Voter*, p. 48. The jump in the comparable percentage from 1968 to 1972 is only from 25 to 26 percent, but the significance is doubtless greater when one considers that a vast number of new and very young voters (who had less of a "lifetime" for which to report a change) had entered the electorate in the same period.

[31] See Paul R. Abramson, "Generational Change in American Electoral Behavior," *American Political Science Review* 68 (1974): 93–105.

TABLE 8   Percentage of Partisans and
Independents in Two Age Segments
of the American Electorate: 1972

	18–29	30 and over
Democrats	33.2	43.7
Independents	51.3	29.3
Republicans	15.4	27.0
	99.9	100.0

Source Survey Research Center of the University
of Michigan; data made available through the Inter-
University Consortium for Political Research.

Amid this change and decay in the composition of the party electorates, there *are* discernible shifts in them that will surely alter the
bases of two-party competition. There is, first of all, the persistent rise
in the percentage of independents. The Democrats also appear to be
losing support in the South as the Republicans gain it there. Working-
class identification is also declining among the Democrats and rising
among the Republicans. Conversely, the Democrats are attracting new
partisans from the middle and upper-middle classes, especially from
professional and intellectual groups in them. Both parties are annexing
those voters who respond to what they see as the Democratic or Republican position in any one issue or a group of them. The party electorates
cut across socioeconomic, ethnic, regional, and occupational categories
ever more sharply. The effect is to create two even more diverse and
fluid party electorates. They are electorates so diverse that the parties
will in the future surely find it difficult to propitiate all sectors of them.
At the very least, the candidates of the parties will find it a challenge to
unite them at any one election.

That the bases and divisions of the party electorates seem less and
less clear is perhaps only an analytical nuisance. That only a shrinking
percentage of Americans is willing to join a party electorate is a challenge to party politics as we have recently known them. But the possibility that the force of the party "in" the voters is weakening, that the
effect of party loyalties on their political perceptions and decisions matters less, threatens the very future of the American two-party system.
To that question we now turn.

7

The
Party within
the Elector

The hyperactive world of American politics is difficult to understand at best. The periodic contentions of parties and candidates, the overlapping layers of party organization, the hyperbole of political charge and countercharge may baffle even the highly politicized and active party workers. The confusion is inevitably greater among the less experienced and involved members of the party electorate. Their best guide to this trackless political world is their party identification. Donald Stokes has written:

> In view of the fact that very few Americans have very deep interest in politics, it is a mild paradox that party loyalties should be so widespread. A partial key to this puzzle is that these identifications perform for the citizen an exceedingly useful evaluative function. To the average person the affairs of government are remote and complex, and yet the average citizen is asked periodically to formulate opinions about those affairs. At the very least, he has to decide how he will vote, what choice he will make between candidates offering different programs and very different versions of contemporary political events. In this dilemma, having the party symbol stamped on certain candidates, certain issue positions, certain interpretations of political reality is of great psychological convenience.[1]

The political party, therefore, exists in two forms for the individual. Obviously he can see the party of the real world — the party of conventions, candidates, campaigns, and organization. But he comes also to depend on a cognitive party — the party of his attitudes, goals, and loyalties, the party *within the elector*. This party is an organizing point of view, a screen or framework through which he sees political reality and in terms of which he organizes it in his own mind. We all perceive the world about us selectively, and for the committed partisan, the member of the party electorate, party loyalty is the key to the selectivity. Because the party identification will very likely be his most enduring

[1] Donald E. Stokes, "Party Loyalty and the Likelihood of Deviating Elections," in Angus Campbell et al., *Elections and the Political Order* (New York: Wiley, 1966), pp. 126–27.

political attachment, it serves as something of a political gyroscope, stabilizing his political outlooks against the buffetings of changing political currents and appeals.

Before we go on to a discussion of the influence of party identification, three general points ought to be established about the party identification itself. First of all, it is remarkably unchanging, despite all the flux of American politics. The distribution of loyalists between the two parties has been very stable (see Table 2 of Chapter 6). Since 1952 the Democratic identifiers have remained between 41 and 52 percent. And individuals' own identifications have stayed firm. SRC data for the 1972 election show that only one out of four independents and party identifiers had had different loyalties at any earlier time in their lives.

Second, the force or effect of the party identification cannot easily be understated. It is the major key to the political behavior of the American adult. Knowing that one fact about a person or a group tells us more about their political perceptions and political activities than does any other fact. It is the single most important influence on the political behavior of the American adult.[2]

Third, party identification, still powerful though it may be, is today less dominant than it was ten or twenty years ago. In fact, the 1972 election was, according to SRC analysis, the first presidential election in its experience in which party identification was less important than issues in determining the outcome of the election. So, while we can say that party identification remains the major key to American political behavior, we are less certain than we once were that it will continue to be.

IDENTIFICATION, PARTY, AND POLITICAL ACTIVITY

The stronger the party identification, the greater is the probability that the individual will be active in politics generally and active in a political party in particular. The individuals with the strongest party identifications are more likely

1. To evince an interest in coming elections and to express a concern about their outcome (they think it definitely makes a difference who wins).
2. To expose themselves to the newspaper, magazine, television, and radio reports about politics or a campaign and to the events of the campaign themselves.

---

[2] This chapter is concerned only with party identification and its influences and impacts. It is by no means an attempt to deal with the entire range of American political or voting behavior.

3. To talk with their friends about the election and to try to persuade them to support this or that candidate. For example, in 1972 the "strong" party identifiers were almost two times more likely to be "very much interested" in the election campaign as were other American adults.

To put these relationships in more general terms, the men and women whose political interest and activity place them within or very close to the activists of the party organization come in disproportionate numbers from these identifiers.[3]

Also, short of activity in the parties, the "strong" party identifiers see the parties in sharper terms than do the "weak" identifiers and the independents. They certainly see the parties as more committed to sharply differentiated liberal and conservative positions, and they are more apt to spot "extremism" in the other party (Table 1). They also are surer that there are important differences between the parties on specific policy issues.[4] And, not very surprisingly, the party electorates tend to have stronger positive and negative views about the two parties and their abilities to govern for the benefit of the nation.

TABLE 1   Perceptions of Party Identifiers about the Ideological Positions of the Two Major Parties: 1972

	Strong Demo- crats	Weak Demo- crats	Inde- pen- dents	Weak Repub- licans	Strong Repub- licans
Perceptions of Democrats					
Extremely liberal, liberal	15.8%	14.5%	15.1%	28.8%	34.2%
Slightly liberal, moderate	25.3	27.1	30.9	24.5	19.0
Perceptions of Republicans					
Extremely conservative, conservative	24.8	15.4	16.1	20.0	18.3
Slightly conservative, moderate	15.6	27.1	29.8	34.2	34.3

Source Survey Research Center of the University of Michigan; data made available through the Inter-University Consortium for Political Research.

[3] Data on the political activity and involvement of party identifiers can be found in virtually all studies of American voting behavior. Among others, see Angus Campbell et al., *The American Voter* (New York: Wiley, 1960), especially Chap. 6; and Sidney Verba and Norman H. Nie, *Participation in America* (New York: Harper and Row, 1972).

[4] Gerald M. Pomper, *Voters' Choice* (New York: Dodd, Mead, 1975), Chap. 8.

Such relationships by themselves are no reason to leap to the conclusion that party identification somehow produces greater party activity
or a sharper issue image. Party activity — or any political activity, for
that matter — appears to be the result of a complicated set of recruitment, access, incentive, and availability factors. That one of these factors is probably loyal commitment to a party seems clear. But it is
equally clear that party identification is not the only condition necessary
for party activity.

JUDGMENT OF CANDIDATES AND ISSUES

Party identification and the loyalty and commitment it represents operate as a screen through which individuals select political information
from the welter of political messages that assail them. It also serves as
an aid to help one evaluate information. The effect of party identification on judgments of the parties can easily be surmised. But the effect
of that identification on the individual's perceptions of candidates and
political issues bears greater scrutiny.

Party identification provides a perceptual screen or predisposition
through which the voter sees the candidates. "The stronger the voter's
party bias, the more likely he is to see the candidate of his own party
as hero, the candidate of the other party as villain." [5] In the 1960 presidential election, however, a powerful set of competing perceptual predispositions was also at work. Catholics tended to perceive John F.
Kennedy more favorably than did Protestants. Nonetheless, party identification kept its organizing power. When religious loyalties were held
constant, party identification had its effect on the perception of Kennedy.
And when party identifications were held constant, the religious loyalty
had *its* effect. When one says, therefore, that a candidate is attractive or
compelling, he is saying something about the electorate as well as about
the candidate.

The control that party identification exercises in the perception of
candidates may, however, be somewhat selective. In any event, that is
the conclusion of a study of a sample of Detroit voters.[6] The partisan
perception appears to extend to the candidate's political traits but not to
such purely personal matters as his personality, appearance, or social
characteristics (e.g., his religion). The partisan view of candidates is
selective in another sense: It is not without limits. Before the 1972 elec-

[5] Donald E. Stokes, "Some Dynamic Elements of Contests for the Presidency,"
American Political Science Review 60 (1966): 23. The material of this paragraph is
drawn from the Stokes article.
[6] Roberta A. Sigel, "Effects of Partisanship on the Perception of Political Candidates," *Public Opinion Quarterly* 28 (1964): 483–96.

tion, for instance, Democrats joined Republicans in viewing Richard Nixon more favorably than George McGovern.

The impact of party identification on political issues is not as easy to determine as its impact on candidate perception. The candidate is a tangible person, but an issue is an abstraction with far more subtle symbolic components. It is easy to show that party identifiers of the two parties take more sharply defined positions on public policies than the nonidentifiers (see Table 6 in Chapter 6). They are also more apt to have an issue or ideological position congruent with the one generally associated with the party of their choice. (That effect, it should be noted, has become less and less apparent as the American electorate has increasingly identified the positions of the parties correctly.) Party identification may, of course, provide that congruence in the first place by guiding some party loyalists to their party's position on issues. For other party loyalists the congruence is the result of an ideology that predated and governed the choice of party. The issue, and thus the uncertainty, is in the relationship between the formation of issue stands and party loyalty.

PARTY IDENTIFICATION AND VOTING

So powerful and stable has party identification been in the voting behavior of American adults that the Survey Research Center organizes its main typology of American presidential elections around the question of the role that party loyalties played in them. Thus the SRC describes three chief election types:

1. The *maintaining* election, in which the party attachments of the recent past prevail without any great change; the elections of 1948, 1960, and 1964 would appear to be examples.
2. The *deviating* election, in which the basic distribution of party loyalties is not changed but in which short-run forces (such as an attractive candidate or issues of great salience) cause the defeat of the majority party; the Republican successes of 1952, 1956, 1968, and 1972 are examples.
3. The *realigning* election, in which a new distribution of party loyalties emerges and governs the outcome; the elections of 1928 and 1932 offer the most recent examples.[7]

These latter realigning elections are distinguished by "the presence of a great national crisis, leading to a conflict regarding governmental poli-

---

[7] See Angus Campbell, "A Classification of the Presidential Election," in Campbell et al., *Elections and the Political Order*, pp. 63–77. See also V. O. Key, "A Theory of Critical Elections," *Journal of Politics* 17 (1955): 3–18.

cies and the association of the two major parties with relatively clearly contrasting programs for its solution." [8]

Implicit in this typology is another useful trichotomy to which we have already referred. Scholars of voting behavior find it useful to break the influences on the voting decision into three main categories: party identification, candidate, and issues. And of the three, party identification has usually dominated not only because it has such depth and endurance but also because it affects perceptions and judgments of the other two. Only very appealing candidates and issues overturn the power of the long-run party identification (in what would be a deviating election). The case of the 1972 presidential election is a classic example. President Richard M. Nixon, the candidate of the minority party in party identifications, won over George McGovern, the majority party candidate, on two grounds. He was the more credible and respected of the candidates (in October 1972, of course), and his party's positions on issues such as the war in Vietnam were more acceptable to the majority of voters. It was the first time among recent elections in which the issues weighed more heavily than party identification in determining the votes of the electorate.[9] The 1972 election also brought to three the total of "deviating" elections in the post-World War II years, one more than the total of "maintaining" elections! Along with the election of 1968 it illustrated in one more way the declining strength of party identifications.

The stronger the party identification, however, the less likely it is that the voter will be deflected from support of his party by the short-run appeals of candidates or issues (Table 2). And the stronger the identification, the more likely it is that the voter will make that most tangible gesture of party solidarity — vote the straight ticket (Table 2). The evidence of these statements in the 1972 elections, clear and dramatic as it is, can be duplicated for earlier presidential years. In fact, in earlier years the relationships were even stronger. In 1968 the percentages of the various categories of identifiers were an average of 9.1 percent higher than in 1972.

[8] Angus Campbell, in Campbell et al., *Elections and the Political Order*, p. 76. For an extended debate on an alternative, four-part scheme, see Gerald M. Pomper, "Classification of Presidential Elections," *Journal of Politics* 29 (1967): 535–66, and Walter Dean Burnham, *Critical Elections and the Mainsprings of American Politics* (New York: Norton, 1970), pp. 32–33.
[9] A note of clarification is in order. When we speak of the power of party identification here, we speak of its ability to affect large numbers of vote decisions. It is possible for it to be the prime determining force in the sum of the vote decisions and yet at the same time for the majority party to lose an election (as in 1952 and 1956). The margin of such electoral victories is small, and the great majority of voters may still be responding to party cues. In 1972, however, there was both a minor party victory and the eclipse of the total effect of party loyalty in the electorate.

TABLE 2   Vote Decision and Ticket Splitting among
Party Identifiers: 1972

	Strong Demo-crats	Weak Demo-crats	Inde-pen-dents	Weak Repub-licans	Strong Repub-licans
Vote for President: 1972					
Democratic	46.3%	27.7%	17.1%	6.2%	2.5%
Republican	16.8	29.5	33.6	63.6	73.4
Other, no answer, etc.	2.5	2.6	3.7	2.0	1.1
Didn't vote	34.5	40.2	45.6	28.2	23.0
	100.1	100.0	100.0	100.0	100.0
Straight ticket vote in state, local elections: 1972	38.8%	20.5%	14.0%	26.6%	43.9%
Voted for same party since began to vote: 1972	67.0	33.4	17.0	32.2	61.5

Source Survey Research Center of the University of Michigan; data made available through the Inter-University Consortium for Political Research.

The 1960 presidential race between Richard M. Nixon and John F. Kennedy affords a fascinating instance of the clash of party loyalties and of another potent set of social loyalties — those of religion. In this sense Kennedy's Catholicism was more than an issue or a candidate; it was the stimulus for another, largely nonpolitical, perceptual predisposition. The effect of those loyalties on the perceptions of Kennedy himself we have already assessed. But despite the strength of the religious loyalties, Philip Converse concluded after an examination of attitudes and voting in the 1960 election that in casting their votes, "Protestant Democrats were more likely to behave as Democrats than as Protestants, and Catholic Republicans were more likely to behave as Republicans than as Catholics." [10]

These observations on the impact of party identification on the voter largely reflect decisions in national or statewide elections. Party identification may have either more or less impact in state and local elections. Where the voter has personal, face-to-face contact with the candidates in a rural county, his evaluation of them may be so strong that it overrides party loyalties. Or some voters may find the application of party loyalties inappropriate to the less partisan campaigns for local office,

[10] Philip E. Converse, "Religion and Politics: The 1960 Election," in Campbell et al., *Elections and the Political Order*, p. 123.

especially when the office appears to have little policy-making responsibility (e.g., the local clerk of the court or the registrar of deeds). On
the other hand, voters in local elections may have to rely even more
than in national elections on the guidance of party. In a large city, the
voter having to make choices on a long ballot of city, county, state, and
other officers may have no alternative to reliance on the party label. In
these elections his or her information on issues and candidates may be
only a fraction of what it is in a presidential election.[11]

THE MYTHS OF THE INDEPENDENT

That party loyalties should govern so much political behavior in a political culture that so warmly celebrates the political independent — the
voter who "votes for the best man rather than the party" — is too
striking a paradox to have escaped attention. On the basis of the data
of the SRC, it has been easy to puncture the myth of the American political independent. But before the myth is finally put to rest, we ought
perhaps to be clear what myth we are burying.

If by the term *independent* we mean those Americans who refuse to
identify with a political party, then the myth *is* a casualty of survey
research. While it is true that the self-styled independent splits his
ticket more frequently, waits longer in the campaign to make his voting
decision, and shows a moderate level of interest in government generally, he falls short of the picture of the independent in most other
respects. He is less concerned about specific elections than identifiers
are, less well informed and less active politically than they are. And he
is more apt than they not to vote at a given election (Table 2). He is, in
short, less politically active and involved than the party identifier and
in many respects less the "good citizen."

There is no reason, however, why we cannot define the political independents in terms of their behavior or activity. In his last work, published posthumously, V. O. Key attempted to reclaim the independents
from their current obloquy by dealing not with the self-styled independents but with voters who switched their party vote in a consecutive
pair of presidential elections.[12] The picture of the American voter that
emerges from American political folklore and the new electoral studies,
Key noted, is not a pretty one; it is one of an electorate whose voting
decision is determined by deeply ingrained attitudes, perceptions, and

---

[11] For another view of the differential effect of party identification on vote choice,
see Barbara Hinckley, Richard Hofstetter, and John Kessel, "Information and the
Vote: A Comparative Election Study," *American Politics Quarterly* 2 (1974): 131–58.
[12] V. O. Key (with the assistance of Milton C. Cummings), *The Responsible Electorate* (Cambridge: Harvard University Press, 1966).

loyalties without its having grasped the major political issues and alternatives.

Key's search for electoral "rationality" centers, therefore, on the switchers, the voters who do *not* keep voting for the same party in consecutive elections. Key's switchers, by the usual criteria, come much closer to the image of the independent than do the self-described independents. He finds their levels of political interest no lower than those of the stand-patters who remain firm in their voting allegiances. By definition, of course, the switchers are not nonvoters. Above all, they are marked by an issue-related rationality that well fits the usual picture of the independent. They agree on policy issues with the stand-patters toward whom they shift, and disagree with the policies of the party from which they defect.[13]

Changes under way in the American electorate may, in fact, force us to rewrite some of the other myths about the independent. The numbers of self-styled independents are increasing among American voters (Tables 2 and 8 of the last chapter). Indeed, among the electorate under thirty the percentage of independents exceeds 50 percent. There are also signs that recent additions to the group have altered its composition. Many of the new independents are from higher educational and SES levels than the older ones, giving the independents a more heterogeneous social composition.

Independents' behavior and attitudes in presidential elections have shown some inclination to change. They recently have appeared as interested in the general affairs of government and politics as party identifiers (Table 3). And in 1968 the independents voted in the same percentage and were as attentive to the campaign as were the party loyalists. It may have been that the range of options in 1968 — from Eugene McCarthy through George Wallace — drew them, if briefly, into more sustained contact with American politics, for in 1972 they reverted to older patterns of lower involvement. More generally, we now seem to have

at least *two sets* of independents: "old independents," who correspond to the rather bleak classical survey-research picture, and "new independents," who may have declined to identify with either major party not because they are relatively politically unconscious, but because the structure of electoral politics at the present time turns upon parties, issues, and symbolisms which do not have much meaning in terms of their political values or cognitions.[14]

Even though this second group may not quite meet the criteria for the classic American independent, it comes closer than the independents did

[13] A concept of the independent as ticket-splitter is developed in Walter DeVries and Lance Tarrance, *The Ticket Splitter* (Grand Rapids: Eerdmans, 1972).
[14] Burnham, *Critical Elections and the Mainsprings of American Politics*, p. 127.

TABLE 3   Levels of Interest in Government and Public Affairs
Shown by Party Identifiers and Independents: 1972

Respondent follows government and public affairs	Strong Democrats	Weak Democrats	Independents	Weak Republicans	Strong Republicans
Most of the time	44.3%	29.1%	36.0%	37.5%	45.6%
Some of the time	31.1	40.3	37.1	35.2	33.8
Only now and then	13.3	17.8	15.9	15.8	13.9
Hardly at all	11.3	12.8	11.1	11.5	6.8
	100.0	100.0	100.1	100.0	100.1

Source Survey Research Center of the University of Michigan; data made available through the Inter-University Consortium for Political Research.

earlier. And the American political independents thus evolve into a group as diverse and stratified as the party identifiers.[15]

THE LOYAL ELECTORATES IN CHANGE

The leaders of the party organizations scarcely know the men and women of the party's loyal electorate. They know them largely in the same way that political scientists do: in some abstract, aggregate profile. They know that members of the party in the electorate see the issues and candidates through party-tinted glasses. They know that the party electorate has a unified and reinforcing view of politics, that it is more likely to vote the party ticket, and that it is easier to lure into activity for the party or a candidate. Party strategists know, in other words, that it is a reliable hard core of party supporters. In a general if vague way, they see — as do political scientists — that party identification is a commitment strong enough to affect other commitments and pervasive enough to color and codify perceptions of political reality.

Much of the strategy of American political campaigning is based on these assumptions about loyal party electorates. The general strategy is often to stimulate and reinforce the party loyalties of one's own partisans while making candidate and issue appeals to independents and partisans of the other party. When in 1968 workers and union members threatened to bolt the Humphrey ticket, labor leaders drove hard to reinforce old labor loyalties to the Democratic party and to hammer at

[15] William H. Flanigan and Nancy H. Zingale suggest another kind of diversity among independents based on whether or not they lean to one party or the other in their *Political Behavior of the American Electorate*, 3rd ed. (Boston: Allyn and Bacon, 1975).

the issues of wages and employment that would reinforce those ties. (As it turned out, they succeeded in bringing back a large number of strays to the Democratic fold by election day.)

Furthermore, the sizes and compositions of the two party electorates determine the more specific strategies. It appears that the present pattern of party loyalty, for example, requires the Republicans to minimize party-stimulating appeals, party identifications, and SES issues. Their hope presently rests with attractive candidates and nonclass issues. It is surely not coincidental that both Barry Goldwater in 1964 and Richard Nixon in 1968 and 1972 emphasized a large number of issues that met those specifications: crime and morality, local responsibility for civil rights and racial equality, defense and foreign policy, and the war in Vietnam.

So great has been the controlling and stabilizing force of these two great, unchanging party electorates in American politics that it is hard to imagine what politics would be like without them. But many signs indicate that we may know without having to let our imaginations loose. As the percentage of independents rises, of course, the number of people expressing a party loyalty declines. But the signs of trouble for the parties are more extensive than declining numbers. Party identifications are losing some of their old control over the judgments and decisions of the American voter. Even party loyalists are splitting more tickets, showing more attention to issues, and voting less consistently for the party's presidential candidate.

The nature of the recent changes can best be seen against the backdrop of the traditional stability of American party lines and party identification. Because large numbers of people had party identifications, because they rarely changed in a lifetime, and because those identifications strongly governed their voting decisions, patterns of voting support for the two parties have been extremely stable. In election after election, individual voters in large numbers voted straight party tickets. And the patterns of party support remained stable geographically. A party's pattern of state-to-state support (and county-to-county support within states) remained steady election after election. And when the votes *have* shifted — enough to tip balances of victory and defeat — they have shifted so evenly as not to alter greatly those overall patterns of support. A party's state-to-state profile of support has been raised or lowered but not greatly changed.

Only periodic party realignments, such as the ones of 1928 and 1932, jolted this long-term stability. At such times a new pattern and distribution of party loyalties was established and its continuities persisted until the next realignment. But in the late 1960s and well into the 1970s we began to experience instability without realignment. Split-ticket voting is on the upsurge and increasing faster than the growth rate of self-described independents. The comfortably high correlations of presidential vote from one election to another have disappeared. The elections of 1964, 1968, and 1972 saw the parties putting together coalitions that bore little resemblance to the coalitions of their supporters in 1960 and the years before. In visual, maplike terms, the profile of the parties' areas of strengths and weaknesses in those elections differed sharply from earlier ones and from each other.[16]

It is just possible that we are teetering on the edge of party realignment. A strong third-party movement — such as that of George Wallace — has usually preceded realignments in the past. A number of observers have suggested that the Democrats may build a new coalition by combining the young, the disaffected, the minority groups, the disadvantaged, and a goodly portion of the successful and affluent. The Republicans would thus become the party of a working-class and middle-class conservatism — the party of the middle America or silent majority of whom Republican orators speak.[17]

But there still remains the alternative possibility that we are seeing only the declining effectiveness of party identifications and that that explains the greater number of independents, the increased rate of switching party identifications and splitting tickets. In the past we ignored the possibility that alignments might stay relatively fixed while their force declined. But is it possible that ultimately many voters will not take their party loyalties seriously enough to change them? Will they merely clutch them halfheartedly or slip from them into independence? Or is is possible that American adults will shift loyalties gradually on an individual basis, and that instead of the quick and sharp realignments of the past we will have a continuous realignment?[18]

For a glimpse of an alternative to the vaunted stability of American parties and voting patterns, one need look only to France. A comparative study of French and American political socialization reveals the relative absence of party loyalties in France. The authors link that fact to French political instability, noting that in France there is available "a mass base for flash party movements. . . ."[19] It is, therefore, not only the stable two-party system that would be threatened by the continued

[16] On the 1968 election, see Philip E. Converse et al., "Continuity and Change in American Politics: Parties and Issues in the 1968 Election," *American Political Science Review* 63 (1969): 1083–1105.
[17] James L. Sundquist, *Dynamics of the Party System* (Washington: Brookings, 1973).
[18] Many of these themes are developed more fully in Burnham, *Critical Elections and the Mainsprings of American Politics*, Chaps. 5 and 6.
[19] Philip E. Converse and Georges Dupeux, "Politicization of the Electorate in France and the United States," in Campbell et al., *Elections and the Political Order*, p. 291.

decline of the number and force of party identifications. That development would challenge the stability of *any* party system.

In a subject (and chapter) filled with paradoxes, it may be fitting to
conclude with one more. It has often been said that the source of the
weakness of the American parties is their refusal to make commitments
to ideology, their inability to take distinctive policy stands. They have
been pragmatic, brokerage parties without programs to attract mass
followings. Yet, it is precisely this relative absence of political ideology
in American politics that has made the parties in the electorate as strong
as they are. In the United States it is the political party and loyalty to
it that guide the individual. The party itself, not a class-based ideology
or some other social loyalty, structures political reality and decisions. In
the American context the political party is, therefore, closer to the cognitive and behavioral center of the American voter and his judgments.
It has many organizational competitors in the recruitment of resources
and clienteles, but the major American party is without serious competition as a force in organizing the world *within* the American voters.

8

The American
Electorate

Much of the history of the political parties of the Western democracies can be written in terms of their responses to the expansion of the suffrage. The parties began as essentially aristocratic instruments mobilizing very homogeneous and limited electorates, and they have had to alter their organizations and their appeals as the electorates expanded to include virtually all adults. In multiparty systems in the Western world, new parties often rose to represent new groups admitted to the suffrage. The European Socialist and Labor parties, for example, catered to the newly enfranchised industrial workers. The stability of the American two-party system, however, has ruled out such an accommodation of new electorates. The two major American parties have had to expand their hospitality to new groups winning the vote.

Since the American parties are overwhelmingly electoral parties, any changes in the size, composition, or activity level of the American electorate affect all their aspects. From the electorate's total dimensions they recruit and establish their own, especially loyal, party electorates. They also recruit from it the workers, skills, and money for the party organizations and for their candidates and campaigns. And, above all, they seek in it the majorities they must mobilize if they are to win elections.

Unfortunately, it is not entirely clear just who constitutes the American electorate. Obviously it is something less than the total number of American adults. The "something less" is generally the result of two kinds of factors: (1) the restrictions placed on it (or, if one prefers, the definitions of it) by the states, and (2) the unwillingness of the eligibles either to register or to vote. Just how and why these limitations operate, on whom they fall, and the numbers they disenfranchise are not easy matters to settle. It is impossible, for example, to give anything more than an educated guess about the number of Americans who actually meet the legal requirements for voting in presidential elections in the fifty states. That guess is made especially difficult by the fact that the requirements differ from state to state. The task is really the definition of fifty electorates.

If the American electorate — either in its legal or its self-defining (turnout) dimension — were an accurate sample of the adult American population, the issue of its dimensions would be far less important. But the effective electorate is nothing of the sort. It overrepresents some groups in the American society and underrepresents others. Given the preference of various groups for one party or the other, the composition and possible enlargement of the electorate are matters of the greatest consequence for the parties. Since American blacks identify largely with the Democratic party at present, for example, various attempts to bring them into the American electorate affect the nature of the parties' loyal electorates and the patterns of their competition.

THE ELECTORATE: THE PROBLEM OF MEASUREMENT

After every presidential election, commentators on American civic values don sackcloth and ashes to note that as usual a relatively small percentage of American adults stirred themselves to vote. In 1968, for instance, a campaign of unparalleled cost and scope — and one that included the liveliest third-party candidacy in more than forty years — attracted only 61 percent of the "potential electorate" to the polls. A two-way race between less than usually attractive candidates attracted only 55.7 percent in 1972. The lowest turnouts in 1972 were the 31.5 and 37.8 percent in the District of Columbia and Georgia; South Dakota and North Dakota led at 70.8 and 69.8 percent.[1]

These and similar turnout percentages, regardless of what elections happen to be involved, depend on two categories of data, one fairly reliable and the other highly suspect. Given the generally accurate counting and reporting of vote totals that prevail in most localities, the figures on actual turnout (the numbers of voters voting) are fairly reliable. However, the base figures of total possible voters (on the basis of which the turnout percentages are calculated) are questionable. Whether the base is called total voters, potential voters, or the potential electorate, it usually turns out to be a total of all persons of voting age in the states (by count of the United States Census Bureau). Thus the widely quoted 55.7 percent turnout for the 1972 presidential election was computed on such a base of some 139,643,000 "potential voters."

Such reckonings of so-called potential voters are essentially misleading because they fail to take into account the restrictions on the suffrage other than that of age. Nor do they consider the number of voters made ineligible to vote by their failure (where required) to go through the administrative processes of registration. The reasonable remedy, therefore, is to substitute for the concept of potential voters some measure of eligible voters, but that total is precisely what is so hard to come by.

[1] Data from *Statistical Abstract of the United States: 1974*, 95th ed. (U.S. Bureau of Census: Washington, 1974), pp. 437–38.

The outer limits to the American electorate are not hard to determine. The electorate can be no larger than the number of adults of age in the country and no smaller than the number of actual voters (categories 1 and 3 in Table 1). But the intermediate estimate of the eligible electorate (category 2 in Table 1), the one so badly needed for accurate estimates of turnout percentages, is the puzzle. Until we have that figure, the easy availability of the larger number of total adults (the potential electorate) will dictate the use of that figure, and we will continue to manufacture inaccurately low (and unflattering) turnout percentages.

TABLE 1   Categories of Potential, Eligible, and Actual Voters: Presidential Elections of 1960, 1964, 1968, and 1972

	1960 presidential election	1964 presidential election	1968 presidential election	1972 presidential election
1. The so-called *potential electorate:* individuals who met the minimum age requirement for voting	108,459,000	113,900,000	120,006,000	139,643,000
2. The *eligible electorate:* individuals who met state requirements and who registered (where required)	?	?	?	?
3. The *turnout:* individuals who actually voted in election	68,839,000 (63.5%)	70,642,000 (62.0%)	73,198,000 (61.0%)	77,719,000 (55.7%)

The size of the effective American electorate (whether one defines it as the eligible or the actual electorate — categories 2 and 3 in Table 1) results from the impact of forces internal and external to the individual. The external influences include the legal restrictions of the states, their application by the administrative machinery of the state, and the informal restrictions of force or economic and social sanction. The internal influences refer to the values and goals, the motivational levels, the role perceptions, the sense of civic responsibility within the individual. The external definitions of the American electorate are clearer because they are more tangible, and we turn to them first.

LEGAL DEFINITION OF THE ELECTORATE

The decentralizing influences of the American federalism touch almost every important aspect of American electoral politics, and the electorate itself is no exception. The definition of the American electorate over the past 150 years has expanded through the curiously American interlacing of national and state action. The four chief expansions have been these:

1. In the early nineteenth century the states themselves gradually repealed the property and tax-paying qualifications for voting by which they had so severely restricted the male suffrage. By 1860 there remained no states that required property holding and only four that required substantial tax paying as a requisite for voting. About a century later the Twenty-fourth Amendment and the Supreme Court finally ended even the small poll tax as a requirement for voting.
2. By the mid-1870s women began to work through the states for their right to vote, and in 1890 Wyoming became the first state to grant the full franchise to women. Progress slowly bogged down, especially in the eastern states, and women shifted their hopes to the United States Constitution. The Nineteenth Amendment, forbidding states to deny the vote on grounds of sex, was finally ratified in 1920.
3. The expansion of black suffrage began by state action in some of the states of New England before the Civil War, but it culminated after the war with the passage of the Fifteenth Amendment. Congress and the federal courts from that time to the present have periodically attempted to enforce its clauses on some reluctant states.
4. In the 1960s a movement of young people met varied success in their attempt to lower the voting age to eighteen or nineteen by state constitutional amendment. Then the United States Congress in June 1970 passed a law extending the suffrage to eighteen-year-olds in both state and federal elections. Less than a half year later the Supreme Court decided by a five to four vote that the act was constitutional as it applied to federal elections but unconstitutional as it applied to state and local elections. Congress then passed and sent to the states for ratification an amendment to the Constitution lowering the age to eighteen for all elections. That amendment, the Twenty-sixth, was ratified by June 1971, well in time for the 1972 elections.[2]

---

[2] The Supreme Court decision was in *Oregon* v. *Mitchell*, 400 U.S. 112 (1970). The chief section of the constitutional amendment states: "The right of citizens of the United States, who are eighteen years of age or older, to vote shall not be denied or abridged by the United States or by any state on account of age."

None of the major expansions in the American electorate, therefore, was accomplished without national limitations on the power of the states to define the electorate. But despite these and other limits to their power, the fifty states long held the major initiating control in defining the electorate.[3]

Undoubtedly it was the intention of the Founding Fathers to vest that major control in the states. At least that outcome was ensured by writing Article I, Section 2, which provides that for elections to the House ". . . the electors in each state shall have the qualifications requisite for electors of the most numerous branch of the state legislature." And that was as much as they said on the suffrage in the entire constitutional document. No more was necessary, for senators were to be elected indirectly by state legislatures, and the president and vice-president by a genuinely deliberative electoral college. As for the selection of electors to the electoral college, Section 4 of Article I stipulated that each state was to "appoint in such manner as the legislature thereof may direct, a number of electors. . . ." When the Congress and the states converted the election of senators to a direct and popular election, they wrote into the Seventeenth Amendment the same formula that applies to the House: "The electors in each state shall have the qualifications requisite for electors of the most numerous branch of the state legislature."

So, contrary to the traditions of other countries and even of other federal systems, initiative in formulating voting requirements was left to the states. The inevitable result was the absence of a uniform national electorate even for national elections. The constitutional authority of the United States government, therefore, has until very recently been limited to the passive role of saying in three amendments that the states shall not deny citizens the vote solely and explicitly on grounds of race or color (Fifteenth), sex (Nineteenth), or failure to pay a tax (Twenty-fourth). Furthermore, the Fourteenth Amendment's equal protection clause ("no state shall make or enforce any law which shall . . . deny to any person within its jurisdiction the equal protection of the laws.") has been interpreted by the Supreme Court to prevent a state from discriminating against blacks in defining its electorate. Presumably that same clause would similarly protect ethnic, religious, occupational, regional, or other social groups in the unlikely possibility that a state should deny the suffrage to, say, Presbyterians, Italian-Americans, or government employees.

In recent years, however, the national government, through both the Congress and the Supreme Court, has expanded its role in defining the

[3] For background on the early development of the American electorate, see Kirk H. Porter, *A History of Suffrage in the United States* (Chicago: University of Chicago Press, 1918).

American electorate. The Congress by ordinary statute — rather than by constitutional amendment — extended the vote to younger voters in federal elections; banned literacy, understanding, and character tests for registration; and waived residency requirements for voting in presidential elections. The newly expanded congressional authority appears to rest on the Supreme Court's interpretation of Article I, Section 4, the section on the control of congressional elections.[4] The Court itself has expanded its own application of constitutional guarantees, that expansion culminating in 1972 in its decision sharply restricting state residence requirements.[5]

Between the constitutional territory of the states and that of the nation there is a tiny no-man's-land, the District of Columbia. For almost all of American history the citizens of the district have remained voteless, even in their own local affairs. However, since the passage of the Twenty-third Amendment to the Constitution in 1961, the District of Columbia has had three votes (the minimum) in the electoral college. It also elects a nonvoting delegate to Congress and a series of local officials on the authorization of the Congress.

THE AMERICAN ELECTORATE TODAY

Despite their freedom under the Constitution, the states have developed legal definitions of the suffrage that are surprisingly similar. In part, the negative controls of the constitutional amendments have hemmed them in. So, too, have the political pressures for universal adult suffrage, the examples of other states, and increased supervision by the Congress and Supreme Court. In any event, it is now possible to deal with the state definitions of the suffrage in a small number of categories.[6]

Minimum Voting Age

As recently as the 1968 elections, all but four states fixed the minimum voting age at twenty-one. It was eighteen in Kentucky and Georgia,

[4] Section 4 of Article I is as follows: "The Times, Places and Manner of holding Elections for Senators and Representatives, shall be prescribed in each State by the Legislature thereof; but the Congress may at any time by Law make or alter such Regulations, except as to the Places of choosing Senators." Every reader can be his own constitutional expert in deciding whether questions of suffrage are what the Founding Fathers had in mind in writing this section of Article I.
[5] For the citation to this case, see footnote 10. For a full and excellent study of the legal and constitutional issues in defining the electorate, see Richard Claude, *The Supreme Court and the Electoral Process* (Baltimore: Johns Hopkins University Press, 1970).
[6] For a general survey of state laws defining the electorate, see Constance E. Smith, *Voting and Election Laws* (New York: Oceana, 1960).

nineteen in Alaska, and twenty in Hawaii. But thanks to the 1970 Voting Rights Act and the Twenty-sixth Amendment, the minimum age became eighteen for all elections beginning in 1972.

Citizenship

All states now require that voters be citizens of the United States. As surprising as it may seem, in 1900 there were still eleven states that permitted aliens to vote, even though some states required the individual to have begun to seek American citizenship. But in 1926 Arkansas, the last state to capitulate, closed off the alien suffrage. More than any other single factor, the end of mass and open immigration into the United States signaled the end of the vote for noncitizens.

Poll Taxes

Until 1964 five states — Alabama, Mississippi, Texas, Vermont, and Virginia — continued to require the payment of a poll tax (i.e., a head tax or a per capita tax) as a qualification for voting.[7] The tax amounted only to one or two dollars a year, but its disenfranchising effect was often increased by stipulations that it was cumulative, that it had to be paid well in advance of the election, or that the taxpayer had to keep the receipt and present it at the polling booth. In 1964 the Twenty-fourth Amendment to the Constitution, however, invalidated taxpaying as a condition for voting in national elections. A year later, in the Voting Rights Act of 1965, Congress legislated a finding that poll taxes in *any* election are discriminatory. It instructed the attorney general to bring a test case in the federal courts challenging their constitutionality. In March 1966, the Supreme Court declared the Virginia poll tax ($1.50) to be in violation of the equal protection clause of the Fourteenth Amendment. In wording clearly broad enough to include the other state poll taxes, the Court noted that a state violates the Constitution "whenever it makes the affluence of the voter or payment of a fee an electoral standard." [8]

Residence

For most of the history of the Republic, the states were free to require that citizens live for a certain period of time in the state and locality before they could vote. Most, indeed, devised three-layer residence requirements: a minimum period of time in the state, a shorter time in the

[7] In Vermont's case the poll tax was a qualification for voting only in local town affairs; the state repealed it early in 1966.
[8] The 1966 case was *Harper* v. *Virginia State Board of Elections*, 383 U.S. 633 (1966). On the poll tax generally, see Frederic D. Ogden, *The Poll Tax in the South* (University: University of Alabama Press, 1958).

county, and an even shorter period in the local voting district. Traditionally the longest residence requirements were those of the southern states (where they disenfranchised migrant and mobile farm labor), but long waits for eligibility were not uncommon elsewhere. In 1970, in fact, the median residence requirement among the fifty states was one year in the state, three months in the county, and one month in the voting district.[9]

Substantial residence requirements began to crumble in the 1950s and 1960s, however, largely in response both to the demands of a physically mobile society and to the society's rising democratic expectations. States lowered their residence requirements, and many also set up even lower ones for newcomers wishing to vote in presidential elections. Congress in 1970 settled the latter issue by establishing a national uniform residency requirement of thirty days within a state for voting in a presidential election. Then, the Supreme Court in 1972 struck down Tennessee's one-year residence requirement for voting in state and local elections, indicating then a strong preference for a thirty-day limit. The Court later accepted a fifty-day requirement, but in doing so it noted that such a period "approaches the outer constitutional limit."[10] Consequently, almost half of the states have dropped residence requirements altogether, while most of the rest have fixed them at thirty days.

Disqualifications

Virtually all the states restrict the suffrage for reasons of crime or mental incompetence. Institutionalization for insanity or severe mental illness temporarily removes an individual from the suffrage in all states, and in the great majority of states so do convictions for certain categories of crimes, the most common being felonies and electoral corruption. The disqualification for mental illness is limited generally to the time of illness or incapacity. The disqualification for felonies, however, lasts indefinitely in some states, even after release from prison. Only gubernatorial pardon or some formal administrative or legislative action will then restore the franchise.

Literacy Tests

Twenty states in early 1965 — before the passage of the Civil Rights Act of that year — required that the applicant for the suffrage demonstrate his literacy. Often the test, especially when administered by an

---

[9] *Book of the States 1970–71* (Lexington: Council of State Governments, 1971).
[10] *Dunn* v. *Blumstein*, 405 U.S. 330 (1972), and *Burns* v. *Fortson*, 410 U.S. 686 (1973). See also Richard J. Carlson, "Election Legislation," *Book of the States 1974–75*, pp. 24–52.

election clerk, constituted little more than a test of the ability to scrawl a signature. In other states one proved literacy by filling out application forms for registration. In a few states the test was more substantial: In New York a comprehensive test, drafted and administered by educational authorities, included questions to test the reader's understanding of brief expository paragraphs. In Alaska the applicant could demonstrate his facility in English either by reading or speaking it. Furthermore, it had been customary for literacy to mean literacy in English; only Hawaii offered an alternative: Hawaiian.

Associated with these literacy tests were tests of understanding or interpretation. Originally the states intended them as alternatives to literacy tests. If the individual could not read or write, he might qualify for the franchise by demonstrating his ability to explain some aspect of the governmental system or some section of the state constitution. In other states such as Louisiana and Georgia, the local voting registrar could permit an illiterate person to register if he was convinced the individual was of "good character." Mississippi, home of the interpretation test, required this ability in addition to literacy and good character. Local voting registrars selected one of the 286 sections of the state constitution for the applicant to read and interpret; the registrar, of course, was the judge of the adequacy of the interpretation.

The literacy tests and their various accouterments were suspended by the Voting Rights Act of 1965. Under the automatic trigger of that law, the literacy tests of any state and county were automatically suspended if less than 50 percent of the voting age population was registered or voted in November of 1964. Immediately after the passage of the act, the attorney general moved to ban the use of the tests in Alabama, Georgia, Louisiana, Mississippi, South Carolina, and twenty-seven counties of North Carolina. Then in the Voting Rights Act of 1970 Congress suspended the use of literacy, understanding, and character tests anywhere as a prerequisite for registration to vote. It reasoned that, regardless of the states' various intentions, the tests had worked discriminatorily against minority groups. The Supreme Court agreed.

Federal Reservations

Traditionally, the states have refused to recognize citizens living on federal reservations — military posts, national parks, and veterans hospitals, for instance — as citizens of the state for the purpose of voting. Only three states — California, Utah, and West Virginia — give them a vote. Hence the great majority of Americans living on one or another of the five thousand separate pieces of land over which the national government exercises exclusive jurisdiction are without a vote. The one exception is the residents of the District of Columbia.

THE SPECIAL PROBLEM OF THE MINORITIES

Throughout these past paragraphs there runs a repeated theme: the special limits placed on racial and ethnic minorities. Take the case of American blacks. Despite the protections of the Fifteenth Amendment, they would be at a disadvantage were it only for the vote qualifications that apply to all Americans. The residence requirements penalized them for poorly paid jobs as itinerant farm laborers, jobs which often prevented them from educating their children. Nor is it unfair to say that black disenfranchisement is a major reason why the poll tax persisted in the South, why residence requirements were more stringent in the South, why criminal disqualifications are broadest in the South, and why literacy, interpretation, and understanding tests were most common in the South.

But beyond all these explicit limitations, blacks traditionally found themselves blocked by the administration of registration and election law. Endless delay, unavailable registrars, niggling technicalities, double standards — these have been their greatest barriers in recent years. The hearings of the United States Civil Rights Commission document the problem with ample detail. Charles C. Humpstone, staff attorney of the Commission on Civil Rights, reported on the leniency of registrars in Issaquena County, Mississippi, in evaluating the interpretations of white applicants:

A number of inadequate answers were accepted. For example, one white applicant asked to interpret section 35, which reads, "The senate shall consist of members chosen every 4 years by the qualified electors of the several districts," wrote only, "equible wrights" . . . and passed.

Mrs. Mary Oliver Welsh of Humphreys County, Mississippi (who was on old-age assistance and receiving government surplus commodities), recounted her attempts to register to vote:

Well, when I went to register, the registrar asked me what did I come down there for. I told him "to register." He said "Register? For what?" I told him, "To vote." He said "Vote? For what?" And I told him I didn't know what I was coming to vote for. He hollered at me and scared me so, I told him I didn't know what I came to vote for. I was just going to vote. . . . He told me I was going to get in trouble, and he wasn't going to give me no commodities. That's what he said.[11]

These extralegal barriers are in many ways the highest. They are at least the most elusive, the most unpredictable, and ultimately the most demoralizing. Whether they are the physical intimidations of the Ku Klux

---

[11] Hearings before the U.S. Civil Rights Commission, I (held in Jackson, Mississippi, on February 16–20, 1965), pp. 49, 53, 95–96, 131–32.

Klan, the economic reprisals of local whites, or the closed doors and glacial speeds of unwilling registrars, they are the hardest to stop.

In the beginning the struggle for the black franchise began in the classic American way as a legal and constitutional issue. For years after the end of reconstruction, in fact, the states and the United States Supreme Court played a grim game of constitutional "hide and seek." The states would devise a scheme of disenfranchisement, the Court would strike it down, and the states would find another — ad infinitum. The states sometimes were careful not to disenfranchise poorer whites along with the blacks — hence their devising of grandfather clauses, which automatically registered all persons whose ancestors could vote at some specific date before the ratification of the Fifteenth Amendment. The manic quality of this constitutional chase is perhaps best illustrated by the white primary cases. The white primary was simply a party primary in which blacks were forbidden to vote; it arose at a time in which the candidate who won the Democratic primary in southern states was assured of victory in the general election against an enfeebled Republican party. It expired finally, but only after twenty-one years of litigation and five cases before the United States Supreme Court.[12]

Court action, however, is not nearly so well adapted to dealing with informal administrative evasions. Increasingly the most useful remedies are legislative and administrative, a fighting of fire with fire. The civil rights acts of 1957, 1960, 1964, 1965, and 1970 (some are also called voting rights acts) all make this kind of an attack on discrimination against the would-be black voter. Among their many provisions are these:

1. The *attorney general* has been authorized to seek injunctions against individuals preventing blacks from voting in primaries or general elections. In those instances in which he can convince a federal court that a "pattern or practice" of discrimination exists in a district, the court may order registration and send referees to the area.
2. The *Justice Department* has acquired authority to supervise voting procedures in states and counties in which less than 50 percent of potential voters voted in the recent presidential election. Interpretation tests and other similar qualifications have been suspended, and the attorney general may send in federal voter registrations and election observers. Any changes in voting procedures (such as in election districts) must be approved by the attorney general or the United States District Court in the District of Columbia.
3. *Local registrars* have come under greater regulation and control. They must keep voting and registration records for twenty-two months,

---

[12] The end of the white primary is recorded in *Smith* v. *Allwright*, 321 U.S. 649 (1944).

and they must not apply voting requirements unequally. Nor are they permitted to seize on immaterial errors or omissions in the application process as a reason for refusing registration.

It is both inaccurate and unjust to treat all the states of the South as if they were of a single piece. They vary greatly in the formal requirements for registration, and they vary, too, in the extralegal bars they raise. Those differences are reflected in the data of Table 2, which shows the percentages of voting-age blacks, registered in the South. Furthermore, there are substantial differences within different states, some of which reflect different racial ratios, socioeconomic characteristics, and political traditions.[13] Also, it should be made clear that black registration and voting percentages in the rest of the country are consistently below those of whites. The former residence requirements and literacy tests of the northern states also effectively disenfranchised groups of blacks. What has set the South apart are the systematic and explicit attempts to keep blacks out of the electorate.

TABLE 2   Registration by Race in States Covered by the Voting Rights Act: 1965–72

	1965		1967		1972	
	White	Black	White	Black	White	Black
Alabama	69.2%	19.3%	89.6%	51.6%	80.7%	51.7%
Georgia	62.6	27.4	80.3	52.6	70.6	67.8
Louisiana	80.5	31.6	93.1	58.9	80.0	59.1
Mississippi	69.9	6.7	91.5	59.8	71.6	62.2
North Carolina	96.8	46.8	83.0	51.3	62.2	46.3
South Carolina	75.7	37.3	81.7	51.2	51.2	48.0
Virginia	61.1	38.3	63.4	55.6	61.2	54.0
Total	73.4	29.3	79.5	52.1	67.8	56.6

Source   The Voting Rights Act: Ten Years After, report of the United States Commission on Civil Rights (January 1975), p. 43.

The major instrument in the lengthy fight for the black franchise has unquestionably been the 1965 Voting Rights Act. Its life was extended in 1970 and once again in 1975, the latter time with only minimal congressional opposition. Certainly a major part of the changes recorded in

[13] Articles on black voter registration in the South by Donald R. Matthews and James W. Prothro, American Political Science Review 57 (1963): 24–44 and 355–67. See also H. Douglas Price, The Negro and Southern Politics (New York: New York University Press, 1957).

Table 2 result from it.[14] Moreover, in the 1975 extension of the Act the Congress broadened the protection to include linguistic minorities, that is, any political subdivision in which more than 5 percent of the adults belong to such a minority and in which more than half of the adults failed to register or vote in the preceding presidential election. Those districts would also be required to provide bilingual election materials and officials. The United States government is thus on the threshhold of extending its concern for voting to American Indians, Alaskan natives, Asian-Americans, and Spanish-speaking Americans. And in one more way the freedom of the states to define the American electorate has been limited.

THE CUMULATIVE EFFECT

The voting requirements of the fifty states whittled down the 1972 American electorate well below the 139,643,000 persons of voting age shown in Table 1. Just how many American adults they pared off that figure is a matter of informed estimate at best, especially since residence requirements were very much in flux in 1972. Probably the best data one can find on the size of the American electorate come from the Census Bureau's study of the 1974 electorate. On its basis we might reconstruct Table 1 for 1974 in this fashion: [15]

Individuals meeting the minimum age for voting	141,300,000
Individuals eligible to register	128,000,000
Individuals registered	87,900,000
Individuals voting in 1974	63,450,000

Using these data, then, one finds that only 72 percent of the registered electorate and 49 percent of the eligible electorate voted in 1974. In the presidential election of 1972, the Census Bureau estimates, about 87 percent of the registered voters voted, and in the more comparable congressional election of 1970 some 80 percent did.

While the total number of individuals of voting age creeps upward, the percentage of them who are registered drops. The percentage reg-

[14] For a full review of progress and problems under the Voting Rights Acts of 1965 and 1970 see the report of the U.S. Civil Rights Commission cited as the source for Table 2. It is uncommonly well organized and well written, especially as the reports of governmental commissions go.

[15] U.S. Bureau of the Census, *Voter Participation in November 1974*, Series P-20, No. 275 (January 1975). The reader should also know that only three of the four figures above are Census Bureau estimates; the one on individuals eligible to register is mine, based on Census data. Also, the datum on individuals registered includes adults eligible to vote in those states and localities without formal voter registration systems. For an attempt at a similar calculus, see William G. Andrews, "American Voting Participation," *Western Political Quarterly* 19 (1966): 639–52.

istered was well over 70 percent in 1972, but it had sunk to 62 percent in 1974 by Census Bureau count. That fact is all the more striking when one realizes that the passing of literacy tests and the diminution of residence requirements have sharply increased the eligible electorate. In considerable part the decline results from the slowness of eighteen- to twenty-one-year-olds to enter the electorate; their registration and voting percentages are the lowest of any age segment in the American elector- ate. So, the active movement to enroll American voters is shifting from the breaking down of state barriers to the facilitating of registration. States are increasingly adopting mail registrations, and at least two (Minnesota and Maryland) send registration forms even to those not requesting them. (The United States is still some distance from some European countries in which voters are registered automatically without the individual's requesting or aiding the process.) The U.S. Senate in 1972 killed a national system of voter registration by postcard in a close vote won by a coalition of Republicans and southern Democrats. It is clear, nonetheless, that the newest frontier in the expansion of the Amer- ican electorate is the registration process. If it does not push forward, it will be the first time in the American experience that the expansion of the electorate has been halted.

TURNOUT: POLITICAL VARIATIONS

Turnout levels vary widely among the states, even at presidential elec- tions. In 1972 the turnout percentage (i.e., the number of voters taken as a percentage of the total adults of voting age) of South Dakota was more than 40 percentage points higher than the District of Columbia's. The greatest variations, however, occur between different kinds of elec- tions. That fact itself suggests that there are important political limita- tions on turnout inherent in the American political system itself. Clearly, the attention and interest of American voters flag as they face the four- year cycle of American politics, and many of them respond only to those elections of greatest prominence. Probably no electorate in the demo- cratic world is more frequently driven to the polls than the American. Within a four-year cycle it confronts national, state, and local elections for legislative and executive officeholders (and for the judiciary in a majority of the states), not to mention school boards and assorted other local authorities. Most of these elections are preceded by primaries; and initiatives, referenda, and even an occasional recall election further complicate the calendar. So while the British voter in a four- or five-year cycle may go only twice to the polls — once for a parliamentary election and once for the election of local officials — civic obligation may call his beleaguered American counterpart to the polls for six to ten primaries and general elections.

Size of Constituency

In the first place, voter participation varies substantially with the size of the constituency. It is generally greatest in presidential elections and smallest in local elections. While the voting percentage in presidential elections runs now between 50 and 65 percent (of all the adults of voting age), it is less for the gubernatorial elections that come in the nonpresidential years. The congressional elections, too, draw considerably fewer voters in the years between the presidential elections (see Figure 1). And in elections limited to local officials, turnout drops even further.

FIGURE 1   Percentage of Adults Voting in Presidential and Congressional Elections: 1920–72

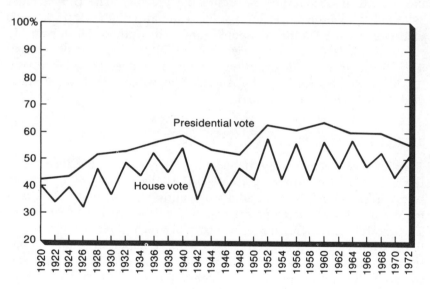

Source   Statistical Abstract of the United States, 1974 (95th ed.).

The reasons for this phenomenon are not hard to imagine. The greater intensity of the campaigns for the presidency and the governorships unquestionably sparks greater voter interest and involvement. The personalities are famous or at least well-known, and the issues seem more momentous. Furthermore, party fortunes are involved and party loyalties are inflamed — contrary to the case in many nonpartisan local and judicial elections. To put it very simply, one should hardly be surprised that a presidential election in which two national political figures and two national parties engage in a three-month mass-media campaign draws three or four times more voters to the polls than does a nonpartisan judicial campaign in which the candidates talk discreetly and a bit dully of the efficient administration of the courts. The wonder is that it is not eight or ten times the number.[16]

The Neglected Primary

Generally throughout the United States, voting in primary elections falls far short of that in general elections. It is not unusual for primary turnouts to be half or less of the turnouts in general elections — more precisely, only 20 or 25 percent of the adults of voting age (the so-called potential electorate). Key's work on gubernatorial primaries marks some of the dimensions of primary voting:

> In a sample of 15 nonsouthern states over the period 1926–1952, in three out of four primaries not more than 35 percent of the potential electorate voted in the primaries of one or the other of the major parties. That is, the total Democratic primary vote plus the total Republican primary vote did not exceed 35 percent of the number of citizens 21 years of age or over. In about one of six primaries the voters in Democratic and Republican gubernatorial primaries did not exceed 20 percent of the number of citizens 21 and over. At the extreme of high participation in only one out of twelve primaries did more than 50 percent of the potential vote turn up at the polls. Most often between 25 and 35 percent of the potential electorate voted in the primaries.[17]

Among primaries for the same office, turnout tends to increase under two circumstances. It increases with competition in the primary and the usually lively campaign that attends a contested primary. It also increases sharply within the dominant party of one-party states. In the southern one-party states, voter turnout in the Democratic primary historically exceeded even the voter turnout of the general election.

Issues and Referenda

Elections to decide issues — referenda and constitutional amendments, chiefly — do not attract the same turnout as do ordinary elections. Even when these issues are on the ballot of regular elections, fewer voters choose to vote on them than for the candidates at the top of the ballot. Very possibly the absence of a personal clash in these questions reduces their interest and immediacy. Perhaps, too, their frequent complexity confuses many would-be voters. But having made these general statements about issue elections, we should note that voter turnout among referenda fluctuates greatly. An emotionally charged and relatively clear issue such as a referendum on nondiscriminatory housing, daylight sav-

[16] See, for example, Howard D. Hamilton, "The Municipal Voter: Voting and Non-voting in City Elections," *American Political Science Review* 65 (1971): 1135–40.
[17] V. O. Key, *American State Politics* (New York: Knopf, 1956), p. 134.

ing time, or the sale of alcoholic beverages will attract far more voters than esoteric questions of taxing bonds or reorganizing state administrative agencies.

The Political Factors

Turnout does vary, therefore, from one kind of election to another. But there are other influences that affect it. Interparty competition in a constituency — whether it is a state or a council district in a city — also increases voter turnout. It does so, furthermore, even when all differences in SES characteristics of the electorate and all historical voting trends in the district are held constant.[18] Understandably, voters seem to be stimulated politically by the excitement of closely contested elections and by the fact that their votes may well affect the outcome. Conversely, there is little appeal in trying to undo a foregone conclusion.

At the same time the details and curiosities of state election law all work their effect on turnout. Partisan elections stimulate larger turnouts than nonpartisan ones. Some states make absentee voting more difficult with longer residence requirements, more complex registration systems, shorter voting hours, and less attractive or convenient voting places. In some instances the use of voting machines — with their mechanical mysteries and intimidation — may discourage voting.[19]

TURNOUT: THE PERSONAL EQUATION

All Americans, however, are more or less confronted by the same plethora of elections and the same complexity in local election procedures. The crucial point is that some of them show voter fatigue more quickly than others. It is also true that all American voters are subjected to the same immediate political "causes" of nonvoting (the uninteresting campaign or the obscure issue, for example), and all face the same immediate personal ones (sickness, forgetfulness, bad weather). But, again, these cumulative hardships or discouragements affect only some citizens' intentions to vote.

Nonvoters in the United States are part of a broader group of political nonparticipants and apathetics — that is to say, they resemble the citizens who abstain from all forms of political activity, whether it be voting, discussing politics, working for a candidate, joining a political party or other political organization, or attending political speeches, rallies, or dinners. Voting turnout is higher in American elections among

[18] C. Richard Hofstetter, "Inter-Party Competition and Electoral Turnout: The Case of Indiana," *American Journal of Political Science* 17 (1973): 351–66.
[19] Norman C. Thomas, "Voting Machines and Voter Participation in Four Michigan Constitutional Revision Referenda," *Western Political Quarterly* 21 (1968): 409–19.

men, higher income groups, the better educated, the middle-aged, Jews and Catholics, whites, and those with high-status occupations. Behind most of these differences there is once again the factor of socioeconomic status (SES). Indeed the relationship between voting and these SES characteristics is generally stronger than that between voting and non-SES traits (e.g., differences in sex). But whether SES factors or not, individual social characteristics taken together explain a great deal of the voting and nonvoting in the United States. One recent study, in fact, finds that individual differences in race, age, income, and educational level together explain more than half of the total variation in voter turnout among the American states.[20]

Furthermore, regular voters have, not surprisingly, higher levels of political interest and involvement than nonvoters. They know the candidates and the burning issues. They are also more apt to be strong party identifiers, and they tend to believe that politics and elections are important and that it really does matter which candidates win the elections. They have strongly ingrained beliefs about the duty to vote, and they possess strong feelings of political "efficacy." That is to say, they think that they can shape the decisions of government and important political outcomes. They engage more often in political discussion, and they tend to be more voracious consumers of newspapers, magazines, and political programs on TV. In fact, by their SES, their own perception of their place and worth in society, their sense of efficacy within it, and their acceptance into its group life, regular voters enjoy a secure place in the community. Conversely, the low-status nonvoters, poorly educated and economically disadvantaged — and possibly further handicapped by racial or ethnic prejudice — have feelings of powerlessness, alienation, and anomie. Rarely sharing in the prosperity or esteem of the community, they believe that they are not influential in it and that those who are care little about what they think or want.[21]

Indeed, if one seeks explanations of nonvoting by focusing on the nonvoters rather than the voters, another possibly important point stands out beyond the fact of alienation and a low sense of political efficacy. Voting is often a threatening activity for the citizen who decides not to vote. In the case of the black in some counties of the deep South it may

[20] Jae-On Kim, John R. Petrocik, and Stephen N. Enokson, "Voter Turnout Among American States: Systemic and Individual Components," *American Political Science Review* 69 (1975): 107–23, with a supplementary comment following it by Douglas D. Rose. For general works on political participation, including voting, see Robert E. Lane, *Political Life* (Glencoe: Free Press, 1959) and Lester W. Milbrath, *Political Participation* (Chicago: Rand McNally, 1965).
[21] On political efficacy, see Angus Campbell et al., *The American Voter* (New York: Wiley, 1960): 96–110, and on the related subject of political cynicism there is Robert E. Agger, Marshall N. Goldstein, and Stanley A. Pearl, "Political Cynicism: Measurement and Meaning," *Journal of Politics* 23 (1961): 477–506.

be overtly threatening. But more commonly the threat is psychological. For the adult who knows little of politics, of the candidates, or of the issues, the act of voting exposes his own ignorance and threatens his own sense of confidence and self-esteem. For the citizen whose political cues are mixed — who was, for example, raised as a Democrat but has Republicanism urged on him by a persuasive spouse, or who favors the ideology of one party but the candidate of the other — the necessity of voting threatens turmoil. Rather than resolve these conflicts the citizen may escape the difficulties of deciding and not vote at all.[22] Conversely, it may be no exaggeration to say that for many habitual voters it is *nonvoting*, with its attendant feelings of guilt, that is threatening.

Finally, voting or nonvoting may reflect the passive or nonparticipatory political culture of a particular group in American life. There is still a lingering feeling in some parts of the country that woman's political place is in the home. Especially in some oriental and Eastern and Southern European ethnic groups in the United States, the female role still shares something of the "kinder, kirche, kuchen" tradition. To take another example, black adults who have for years been taught their own political inferiority and "place" do not easily become active voters even when the opportunity presents itself. Or recently emerging counter-cultures among younger citizens may reject voting as part of a broader rejection of "the system" or the major American institutions.

CONSEQUENCES FOR THE POLITICAL PARTIES

The American parties, therefore, must operate within an American electorate that constantly shifts in size and composition — but that, regardless of its momentary size and composition, is never a sample of either the full American adult population or that segment of it eligible to vote. Much of the strategy of the parties in pursuing their goals, especially the contesting of elections, must take account of those facts.

Long-range Consequences

The long-run consequences for the parties of changes in the electorate spring from basic changes in its legal definitions. Since electorates in democracies expand rather than contract, the changes invariably result from the addition of new groups to the eligible electorate. At the moment, the American parties are witnessing the addition of two major groups: previously disenfranchised American blacks and young citizens between eighteen and twenty-one. Despite the earnest and increasingly

---

[22] For example, see Morris Rosenberg, "Some Determinants of Political Apathy," *Public Opinion Quarterly* 18 (1954): 349–66.

competitive efforts of Republicans, these new electorates will be Democratic ones at least in the foreseeable future.

All the SES characteristics of the black electorate predispose it to the national Democratic party. So, too, do the national Democrats' support of black equality and aspirations. About two-thirds of the black electorate identifies with the Democratic party, and the black vote in both 1964 and 1968 was more than 90 percent Democratic. It was 84 percent in 1972. Between 1964 and 1972 that overwhelmingly Democratic group grew by 1,150,000 in the states of Alabama, Georgia, Louisiana, Mississippi, North Carolina, South Carolina, and Virginia alone.

The effect of this expanding black suffrage on the parties and their electoral competition has already been felt, especially in the South. By 1974 over 1,600 blacks held elective office. Alabama had eight black mayors, and sixteen blacks were serving in the Georgia legislature. In Texas the combination of the abolition of the poll tax and the passage of the 1965 Voting Rights Act — plus some vigorous registration drives among blacks and Chicanos — added well over 400,000 voters between 1964 and 1968. Not accidentally, perhaps, the Humphrey-Muskie ticket carried Texas in 1968.[23]

The impact of the youngest voters entering the electorate for the first time is apt to be more complex. They are somewhat more Democratic than the rest of the population, and they are also much more frequently ideological liberals, regardless of party preference. But they are also more likely to be independents, to split their tickets, and indeed, not to register or vote in the first place. In 1972 the class of newly eligible voters was larger than ever (aged eighteen to twenty-four) because of the lowering of the minimum voting age beginning in that year. More than 25 million young voters entered the electorate in that year, and approximately half of them voted. That eighteen- to twenty-four-year-old group preferred George McGovern over Richard Nixon by a margin of 51 to 49 percent. Mr. Nixon won 66 percent of the votes of those twenty-five and over.[24]

Long-run consequences for the parties also stem from changes in the composition or distribution — rather than the size — of the American electorate. Population growth and migration offer an example. The parties of Alaska, Arizona, California, Colorado, Florida, Maryland, and Nevada all faced increases in state populations in excess of 25 percent between 1960 and 1970. Similarly the aging of the American population creates a larger group of over-sixty-five voters in each successive presidential election. Again, the important point is that these shifts and

23 On black voting and nonvoting, see Donald R. Matthews and James W. Prothro, *Negroes and the New Southern Politics* (New York: Harcourt, Brace, 1966).
24 The voting data come from Gerald M. Pomper, *Voters' Choice* (New York: Dodd, Mead, 1975), p. 93.

growths are differential — the groups (and their goals) added in each case are not a sample of the entire American electorate.

One more striking datum should suffice to conclude these remarks about the consequences of participation and nonparticipation for the parties. There were still some 50 million adults of voting age in 1972 who were not registered to vote — whether for reasons of disqualification or their own unconcern. We have every reason to suspect they are heavily Democratic in their inclinations. Legislation to begin national postcard registration thus became a partisan issue in the Senate in 1972, with liberal Democrats supporting it and conservative Democrats and Republicans in opposition.

Short-range Consequences

In addition to the long-range consequences of changes in the basic structure of the eligible electorate, the political parties must react to the short-range consequences of changes in turnout from election to election. Since increases or decreases in turnout are unlikely to benefit all parties and candidates equally — because nonvoters as a group have different political characteristics from voters (Table 3) — these matters, too, have potent political consequences for the party. The increasing or decreasing of voter turnout and the exploiting of variations in turnout between various elections frequently become focal points in party strategy. The somewhat innocent campaigns of Boy Scouts and Leagues of Women Voters to "get out the vote" sometimes miss this point. Getting out the vote may be tantamount to getting one or the other party into office.

TABLE 3   Comparison of Strong Party Identifiers, Voters in Presidential Election, and Nonvoters in Presidential Election: 1972

	Strong party identifiers	Presidential voters	Presidential nonvoters
Percentage male	43%	45%	37%
Percentage white	83%	90%	86%
Median age	48 years	44 years	39 years
Median education	12th grade	12th grade	11th grade
Percentage "very much" interested in campaign	49%	39%	17%

Source Survey Research Center of the University of Michigan; data made available through the Inter-University Consortium for Political Research.

The conventional wisdom of American politics has it that big turnouts favor the Democrats. With the general truth of that maxim there is little room to quarrel. The greatest percentage of nonvoters in the United States comes from the groups ordinarily disposed to the Democratic party. It is for this reason that effective registration or get-out-the-vote campaigns help the Democrats more often than not. The truth of the maxim explains the money and manpower that organized labor spends in registration campaigns. It explains the ancillary maxim that rainy weather is Republican weather. And it also suggests why in some states Republicans prefer an electoral calendar in which the gubernatorial elections are held in the nonpresidential years and, therefore, in a smaller electorate a bit more favorable to Republican candidates.

Despite the general truth of the maxim linking big turnouts with the Democrats, the relationship is a more subtle and complicated one. Dwight D. Eisenhower, for example, won the presidency as a Republican in two high-turnout elections, and what's more, the nonvoters in 1956 were disposed also to the Republican candidate (Table 4). The Eisenhower success seems to force a clarification. High turnout works to a Democratic advantage only in elections in which party loyalty is a chief or overriding factor. A heavy turnout may be stimulated by a candidate (Eisenhower) or an issue that works to Republican advantage. Especially since the nonvoter is less partisan, he may be more responsive to the momentary, dramatic appeal of issue or candidate. Therefore, the maxim works best in elections or party systems in which the SES factors underlie the division of party loyalties and in which party loyalties remain the chief key to the decisions of voters.

TABLE 4   Postelection Preferences of Nonvoters: 1952–68

	1952	1956	1960	1964	1968	1972
Would have voted Democratic	52%	28%	51%	80%	45%	35%
Would have voted Republican	48	72	49	20	41	65
	100	100	100	100	86 [a]	100 [b]

Source   Angus Campbell et al., *The American Voter* (New York: Wiley, 1960), p. 111. (Campbell's table has been updated by SRC data.)

[a] Fourteen percent would have voted for George Wallace's American Independent party.

[b] The 1972 data are the preferences of respondents who did not intend to vote in the election; the SRC apparently did not try to question nonvoters after the election in 1972.

Party strategists cannot fail to consider the likely voting electorate as they prepare their campaigns. They nourish the often fragile hope that turnouts can be affected selectively and differentially, and they attempt, therefore, to mold the size and makeup of the participating electorate itself in the campaign. When they must contest a primary election, they may hope by discreet and selective campaigning to minimize the turnout, for (generally) the smaller the turnout, the larger will be the proportion of it accounted for by the party's own loyal electorate. In general elections the strategists may try to concentrate campaigns in areas of known party strength and thus maximize that turnout. And the individual planning a congressional career always confronts the fact that he will seek reelection by different electorates in alternate elections — the large turnout of the presidential election followed by the smaller turnout of the midterm elections two years later.

THE BROADER ISSUES

The democratic ethos assumes the desirability of full popular participation in the affairs of democratic self-government. All the instructions of civics courses and all the canons of good citizenship stress it. The case for democracy itself rests on the wisdom of the widest possible sharing of political power and political decision making within the society. And it is precisely this ethos that is offended by the relatively low voting percentages of American adults. The affront to the democratic ethos seems all the greater in view of the fact that voting percentages are higher in countries that Americans would like to think have less stable and responsive democracies.

Widespread nonvoting also casts some doubt on the effectiveness with which the political parties — the political organizations primarily concerned with contesting elections — manage to mobilize the support and involvement of the total eligible electorate. Presumably the parties, heralded so often as the instruments of democratic politics, should maximize political participation in the American society. The political parties themselves are, after all, the results of the expansions of democratic electorates; they are the political organizations that developed to mobilize the new democratic masses and all of whose capabilities are directed to recruiting large political aggregates. Much of the case for their superiority as political organizations rests on that ability.

Related to all these expectations is the additional one that a vigorous two-party competition will result in the widest possible mobilization of the American electorate. Competition abhors a vacuum, we assume, and the two major parties will rush to enlist the support of all possible voters. It is unquestionably true, in fact, that political activity of any kind is greater in the presence of party competition and widespread attitudes of party identification and involvement. Drawing on that fact, a presidential commission appointed by John F. Kennedy to ponder again the problem of American nonvoting reported in 1963 that:

> A great ally of education in the long-range fight against apathy is politics itself — the two-party system. Effective two-party competition prompts political involvement, spurs interest in politics and campaigns, and strengthens a person's feeling that his vote counts. We believe that two-party competition is essential to build and maintain interest in public affairs, and consequently leads to greater voter participation. It is no coincidence that the growth of the Republican party in the South has impelled many more voters of both parties toward the polls.[25]

And yet, making allowances for the relationship between two-party competitiveness and higher turnouts, the fact remains that many of the low turnout percentages that shock observers prevail in areas of considerable competitiveness.

The record of the parties in mobilizing and involving the American electorate is a mixed one. We can point to many examples of effective competition for the support of new groups entering the electorate; the two parties of the South in various areas, despite the strength of old racial mores, have recently made room for black voices in party councils and have made more moderate appeals to the new black electorate. Furthermore, one can hardly blame the parties for the legal limits on the suffrage or for the poverty, illiteracy, and alienation in American society.

Even so, the hands of the parties are not completely clean. They often appear not to relish the challenges of new electors, especially those of low status. The experience of political power has made them (and especially their parties in government) sympathetic to the comfortable status quo of two-party competition. Party leaders and officeholders themselves have been largely recruited from high-status groups in American society and easily accept prevailing norms and institutions. They do not welcome the uncertainties that a radical alteration in the electorate would bring. The party in government, which will have to make the changes in the formal definition of the electorate, has won office with the support of the electorate as it now exists, and it is understandably not anxious to alter it greatly. Furthermore, some state parties in one-party areas have entrenched themselves in power largely by restricting the electorate; in many southern states the Democratic party until recently stayed in power with the aid of an artificially homogeneous suffrage. Not unex-

[25] President's Commission on Registration and Voting Participation, *Report* (Washington, 1963), p. 24.

pectedly, then, the history of women's suffrage and the end of black disenfranchisement indicate that the parties were not in the vanguard of either movement to expand the electorate.

Do the parties also carry a share of the responsibility for the voluntary disenfranchisement of the American nonvoter? They have been blamed for suppressing participation by their failure to interest large numbers of Americans in the dialectics and personalities of politics. E. E. Schattschneider, for example, has argued that to 35 million nonvoters the rituals and choices of American politics are virtually meaningless.[26] The trouble with the Schattschneider thesis is its assumption that nonvoters are rational, informed, and careful surveyors of the political scene who decide they find it irrelevant to their goals. All that we know about the American nonvoters indicates quite the contrary. However, our data on the nonvoter suggest only what he is, not how he happened to become what he is. Thus it is possible to argue that the political parties are one of a number of important political and social institutions that fail to socialize and involve various sectors of the American society.

The American parties, therefore, work within an artificially homogeneous "active" electorate. That electorate reduces the totality of political conflict and the range of political interests the parties must respond to. In every way the parties' political job is easier because of the cumulative restrictions (regardless of how they are imposed) on the American electorate. The parties find it easier to be moderate and pragmatic because the electorate to which they respond is largely settled in and committed to the present basic social arrangements. Compromise and tactical movement come more easily when the effective electorate is homogeneous and in agreement on fundamentals. In brief, while it has been fashionable to say that the moderate, pragmatic, nondoctrinaire American parties are the result of an electorate agreed on the fundamental questions, it is probably also true that the pragmatic, majoritarian parties in a two-party system do not easily draw into their ambit the low-status, alienated, dissident individuals who are not a part of that moderate consensus.

In this state of affairs, reform probably means changes for two sharply different groups of nonvoters. For the largest groups — the marginally interested — changes in definition and administration of the suffrage would at least remove the hurdles to registration and voting. Certainly a great deal of the difference in voting percentages between the United States and the nations of Western Europe results from the fact that voting is more difficult here. If we, too, had automatic and

[26] E. E. Schattschneider, *The Semi-Sovereign People* (New York: Holt, Rinehart and Winston, 1960), Chap. 6.

uniform registration of all citizens by government initiative — as do many other countries — the percentage of registered adults would obviously rise. And vote turnout would as surely be increased by our holding national elections on a holiday or for several days.[27]

The second group of nonvoters — the much smaller number of independents disaffected by the moderatism, caution, and similarity of the two major parties — might possibly be wooed into participation by alternative political organizations. Independent candidates, third parties, ideological associations — any of the newly flourishing alternatives to the major parties — may offer new routes and stimuli to activity. Very possibly, of course, the new participants may be involved in activity outside of electoral politics. In other words, the new diversity of organizational alternatives may lead to a new diversity of modes of political expression. Demonstrating or legislative lobbying may become for some Americans a more valid mode of political expression — perhaps even a more effective one — than casting a ballot.

Questions of voting and nonvoting remain fundamentally a problem in democracy itself. Even if the incidence of nonvoting were reduced and the parties succeeded in stimulating greater involvement and voting, there is little reason to think that the new voters would add greatly to the rationality of democratic debate or the wisdom of democratic decision. But, on the other hand, democracy involves a set of relationships we generally consider useful: the peaceful settlement of conflict, the processes of accommodation, the healthiness of the democratic safety valve. When large numbers of Americans opt out of politics, they open the way for the well-organized, the interested, and the militant to rush in. They reduce their own political power, and thus contribute to their own sense of powerlessness. And certainly when a pluralistic democracy finds that substantial segments of the society are not exerting their countervailing political influence, that they are in effect abdicating their place in the system, the effectiveness of that democracy as a resolver of social conflict cannot help but be reduced.

[27] For some brief and trenchant proposals along this line, see the report of the Freedom to Vote Task Force of the Democratic National Committee, *That All May Vote* (December 1969). Evidence that the main structural problem is indeed the registration process is contained in Stanley Kelley, Richard E. Ayres, and William G. Bowne, "Registration and Voting: Putting First Things First," *American Political Science Review* 61 (1967): 359–79.

IV

THE POLITICAL PARTIES IN THE ELECTORAL PROCESS

The contesting of elections unites, however briefly, the disparate and fragmented American parties. The choice of a presidential candidate and the following campaign bind the state and local parties into a fleeting semblance of a national party. A statewide election similarly focuses the activities and energies of local organizations and leaders within the state. Furthermore, any election joins the three party sectors into a grand coalition of the party elites and the party clienteles. The contesting for public office is the one time in the life of the party when all its various sectors are united in the pursuit of their varied goals.

The pursuit of victory in elections unites the party for a number of reasons. The election is the event that elevates the business of politics to a visibility and salience that stimulate even the less concerned members of the electorate. The contesting candidates personify and simplify the difficult choices of American politics. Furthermore, the recruitment of resources for the party organization depends on the party's establishing the likelihood, or at least the possibility, of electoral victory. In the long run the incentives that lure resources to the party flow only to those parties that win. Only from electoral victory come the patronage job, the triumph of an interest or an ideology, and even the social and psychological rewards of politics.

The American parties are parties that must win elections; therefore, they must be able to mobilize majorities in the electorate. The conventional references to the American parties as electoral parties are, however, a little too glib and hackneyed. For one thing, these references ought not to imply that the parties carry out their electoral activities with ease. The party organizations find it difficult to control the selection of candidates, to take stands on issues, to fix campaign strategies, even to raise money. Those aspects of the contesting of elections are controlled, in the name of the whole party, by its candidates — its party in government and the candidates hoping to join it. In many parts of the country the party candidates, in fact, have organized their own campaigns, recruited their own workers, hired their own campaign advice, and raised their own campaign funds. If it is true that the party in government controls the central, most visible activities of the party (at the expense of a frustrated party organization), can the party organizations reasonably achieve the goals their activists set for them?

At the same time that the party stages an internal competition over the control of its electoral strategies, it also faces the competitions of other political organizations, which also seek their political goals increasingly in the electoral processes. Over the past twenty years the nonparty political organizations — the interest groups, party factions, personal followings, voluntary campaign committees, ideological organizations — have taken aggressive, overt roles in the nomination and election of candidates. It is not uncommon now to read newspaper accounts of the electoral activities of trade unions, ad hoc campaign organizations such as the Nixon for President Committee, public relations firms, reform groups such as the National Women's Political Caucus, and even a nebulously defined Kennedy organization. As these nonparty organizations grow in electoral influence, the very pattern of party activities is threatened.

Such fundamental issues of control and competition in elections, both within the party and within the broader company of all the political organizations, raise questions to which generalizations and theories about the parties must ultimately be addressed. For these kinds of competition go a long way in determining what the parties are and do in the political system. Throughout the coming chapters runs another theme close to those same basic questions: the impact of political institutions on the forms and activities of the parties. For nowhere are the effects of political institutions on the parties clearer than in the electoral processes. The direct primary, for example, touches every attempt the parties make to control the nomination of candidates. In fact, it is the primary that so often turns the control of nominations from the party organization to the candidates themselves or to other political organizations.

In the chapters of this section, we will observe two sets of distinctions for the sake of orderly exposition. The first is the common one between the nominating of the parties' candidates and the contesting of the general election. Even though the distinction between the two parts of the electing business can be arbitrary and misleading, it is analytically useful. The use of the distinction does not deny that it is a single process we are describing. What a party or a candidate does in one will affect, compel, or limit what it does in the other. Elections may be lost or won in the earliest informal steps to encourage candidates, and the nature of the nomination often depends on the ultimate chances for electoral victory.

The special chapters set aside for the nomination and election of the American president reflect the second distinction. The contest for the presidency is a special case and must be so treated. Although the direct primary dominates the formal nominating machinery for almost all American public offices, the convention it replaced still functions in the nomination of presidential candidates. And the special election machinery of the electoral college sets the presidential election apart from the simpler plurality elections that prevail elsewhere in American politics (Table 1).

TABLE 1   Comparison of Steps in the Nomination-Election Processes in the United States

	Prenomination	Nomination	Election
Presidential elections	Selection of delegates to national convention by state party action or presidential primary	By national party convention	By plurality vote within the states, and majority of votes in electoral college
Other American elections	Access to primary ballot by petition, request, or party action	By direct primary or (in a few cases) by convention	By plurality vote at the general election

Thus Chapters 9 and 10 describe the modal patterns of American electoral machinery and politics. Chapters 11 and 12 deal with the fascinating and peculiar processes by which presidents are chosen. The final chapter of this part discusses the recruitment of the most important resource for the contesting of elections: money.

9

The Naming of the Party Candidates

Few Americans realize how indigenously American the direct primary is. Having devised it and adopted it almost universally for the nomination of candidates for public office, they seem unaware that the rest of the world has not followed their lead. The point is important, not because American political naïveté is unusually great, but because it points up the peculiar and even unique aspects of American politics and political parties. For no other single fact goes so far to explain the differences between the American parties and those of the other Western nations as the direct primary. It has forced on the parties a different set of strategies in making nominations, in contesting elections, and in attempting eventually to maintain responsibility over their successful candidates in office.

In the irresistible advance of the direct primary in the twentieth century no state has been untouched. The great majority of states employ it in all nominations, and the rest use it in most. For the present it should suffice to say that by the direct primary (or more simply the primary) we mean a special election in which the party electorates choose candidates to run for public office under the party labels. At a subsequent general election, the total electorate then makes the final choice from among the nominees of the parties.

Even though the nomination does not formally settle the electoral outcome, its importance is great. At the nomination the major screening of candidates takes place; the choice is reduced to two in most constituencies. At the primary a voter's preferred candidate may be rejected, or in its aftermath he may confront a "Hobson's choice" for the election. Especially in areas of one-party domination the real choice is made at the primary.

For the parties themselves, the consequences of the nomination processes bulk large. The images of the candidates of a party are to some extent its images; the candidates' reputations and stands on public issues become the party's. Furthermore, the candidate with whom the party goes into the election campaign determines to a great extent its ultimate chances for victory. The nomination of candidates, moreover, offers the party a major opportunity for uniting its wings and factions behind acceptable candidates. In short, it is crucial to a political party who its candidates are, both for the success of its electoral competitions and for the building of internal unity and cohesion.

ADVENT OF THE DIRECT PRIMARY

At the beginning of the twentieth century the direct primary had come into use only in scattered communities in scattered states. For the first 110 years of the Republic, first the party caucus and then the party convention dominated the nomination of candidates for public office. Each gave way successively under the weight of criticism that it permitted, if not encouraged, the making of nominations by self-picked and irresponsible party elites. Finally, the primary triumphed on the belief that in a democracy the greatest possible number of "party members" ought to take part in the nomination of the party's candidates. The history of the evolution of nominating methods in the United States, above all, is a story of the progressive victory of the values and symbols of democracy.

Formal systems of nomination developed in the United States along with and as a part of the development of the party system. In fact, parties as parties (rather than as legislative associations) developed and evolved largely as nominators of candidates for public office. At the end of the eighteenth century, local caucuses met to select candidates, and frequently caucuses of like-minded partisans in legislatures met to nominate candidates for governorships and other statewide offices. Similar congressional caucuses met to nominate presidential and vice-presidential candidates. Ultimately the parties developed integrated caucuses, which drew both on local activists and on legislators. But whatever their form, the caucuses were self-selected — there was no machinery, no procedure, for ensuring even the participation of all the powerful in the party. The Jacksonians attacked the caucus relentlessly as an aristocratic device that thwarted popular wishes, and "King Caucus" was indeed an ample target.

In 1832 the Democrats met in a national convention for the first time and, appropriately enough, nominated Andrew Jackson for the presidency. From then on, the convention system quickly triumphed along with Jacksonian popular democracy, the values of which it shared. It dominated the making of nominations for the rest of the nineteenth century. Broadly representative at its best, the nominating convention was composed of delegates chosen by the local party organizations. But even though they were formally representative, the large and chaotic conventions were scarcely that in reality. Both in the picking of delegates and in the management of the conventions, the fine, guiding hands of party leaders were too obvious and oppressive. Party insurgents, unhappy with bossism at the conventions and with the alliance of the bosses and "the interests" — and unhappy with their own failures — belabored the convention system with moral fervor and political cunning. The Progressives led the movement and their journalistic handmaidens, the muckrakers, furnished the often shocking, often piquant, corroborative details.[1]

The cure offered by the Progressives, the direct primary, comported easily with their democratic norms. For it was an article of faith among them that to cure the ills of democracy one needed only to prescribe larger doses of democracy. Appropriately it was one of Progressivism's high priests, Robert M. La Follette, who authored the country's first statewide primary law in Wisconsin in 1902. In the next fifteen years all but four states had adopted the primary, at least in part. In 1955 Connecticut capitulated and became the last state to adopt the primary.

Although the primary was designed to reform the nominating processes by "democratization," many of its supporters saw in it an instrument for crippling the political party itself. For them the primary was an attempt to cut back the power of the parties by striking at their chief activity as a party organization: the nomination of candidates. The party organization had done the nominating under the caucus and convention systems, but primaries took from it the control of who would run under the party name and symbols. Regardless of the motives of the enactors of the primary laws, there is little doubt that they badly hurt the power of party organizations.

The quick success of the direct primary happened during the years of the greatest one-partyism in American history. In the early years of the twentieth century sectionalism was rampant, and one party or the other dominated the politics of many states. One-partyism made the nomination of the dominant party crucial. Although the failings of the conventions might be tolerated when a real choice remained in the general election, they could not be borne when the nomination of one party was equivalent to election. The convention could choose the weariest party hack without fear of challenge from the other party. And so the Progressives, who fought economic monopoly with antitrust legislation, fought political monopoly with the direct primary.

[1] For the story of the convention system and the early years of the direct primary, see Charles E. Merriam and Louise Overacker, *Primary Elections* (Chicago: University of Chicago Press, 1928).

La Follette and the Primary

No one has captured the rhetoric and fervor of the movement for the direct primary as well as its leader, Robert M. La Follette, governor and then United States Senator from Wisconsin. Writing in his autobiography in the chapter "Struggle with the Bosses," La Follette reports a speech of his in February, 1897, at the University of Chicago. Here are some excerpts from the conclusion:

"Put aside the caucus and convention. They have been and will continue to be prostituted to the service of corrupt organization. They answer no purpose further than to give respectable form to political robbery. Abolish the caucus and the convention. Go back to the first principles of democracy; go back to the people. Substitute for both the caucus and the convention a primary election . . . where the citizen may cast his vote directly to nominate the candidate of the party with which he affiliates. . . . The nomination of the party will not be the result of 'compromise' or impulse, or evil design — the 'barrel' and the machine — but the candidates of the majority, honestly and fairly nominated."

Robert M. La Follette, *La Follette's Autobiography* (Madison: R. M. La Follette, 1913), pp. 197–98.

VARIETIES OF THE DIRECT PRIMARY

The primaries of the fifty states are usually divided into three categories. These three differ chiefly in the way they define the party electorate that can vote in them.

The Closed Primary

Found in forty-one states, the closed primary requires that the voter declare his party affiliation so that he may vote only in the primary of his own party. In most of these states voters specify their party affiliation when they register. Then at the primary election they are given only the primary ballot of their party so that they may choose among their fellow partisans who seek nomination. They may always change their party affiliation on the registration rolls, but the states require that this be done sometime ahead of the date of the primary.

In the other closed primary states, voters simply declare their party "membership" — or, more accurately, their party attachments or preference — when they go to the polling place. They are then given the primary ballot of their party. Should their declarations be challenged by one of the party observers at the polls, they may be required to take an oath of party loyalty. These oaths or tests differ (as does virtually all else!) from state to state. Some states require the voter to affirm that he has voted for the candidates of the party in the past; some demand that he declare himself sympathetic at the moment to the candidates and principles of the party; and others ask that he state his intention to vote for the party at the coming general election. Needless to say, the secrecy of the ballot makes it impossible to challenge the worth of such pledges.

The Open and Blanket Primaries

In the seven states of the open primary — Michigan, Minnesota, Montana, North Dakota, Utah, Vermont, and Wisconsin — the voter votes in the primary without disclosing any party affiliation or preference. Upon entering the polling booth voters are given either ballots for every party (one of which is selected in the privacy of the booth) or else a consolidated ballot on which the part with the party of the voter's choice is selected. A voter may not, however, participate in the primary of more than one party.

The distinctions between open and closed primaries are easy to exaggerate. Too simple a distinction ignores the range of nuances and varieties within the closed primary states, which after all do account for 82 percent of the states. There is not a vast difference between an open primary and a closed primary that permits a voter to change party affiliation on the date of the primary by taking a vague, unenforceable pledge that he plans to support its candidates at the approaching election.

The blanket primary, found in Alaska and Washington, goes one step in freedom beyond the open primary. Not only does the voter not need to disclose any party affiliation, but he is free to vote in the primary of more than one party — that is, he may choose among Democrats seeking nomination for one office, among Republicans seeking another nomination (Figure 1). Thus, colloquially, the blanket primary has been called the "free love" primary.

Among these forms of primary the party organizations clearly prefer the closed primary with its party registration prior to the primary. It pays a greater respect to the right of the party itself to make nominations by limiting the party's primary electorate to its own party electorate. And prior registration of party affiliation gives the parties an added bonus: published lists of their partisans. Yet it is not quite that simple. Party registration tends to be at best an approximation of party loyalties at the moment. Especially since people are slow to change their party affiliations, the party totals tend to lag behind the pattern of voting at the moment. Furthermore, the registration figures of the major

FIGURE 1   The Washington "Blanket" Primary Ballot: 1970

SAMPLE
PRIMARY ELECTION BALLOT

THURSTON COUNTY, WASHINGTON   **TUESDAY, SEPTEMBER 15, 1970**

INSTRUCTIONS: To vote for any candidate place an X in the ☐ at the right of the name of such candidate.

FEDERAL

UNITED STATES SENATOR   Vote for One
HENRY M. JACKSON	Democrat	☐
R. J. (BOB) ODMAN	Republican	☐
JOHN (HUGO FRYE) PATRIC	Democrat	☐
WILLIAM H. DAVIS	Republican	☐
CARL MAXEY	Democrat	☐
HOWARD S. REED	Republican	☐
BILL PATRICK	Republican	☐
CHARLES W. ELICKER	Republican	☐
MRS. CLARICE PRIVETTE	Democrat	☐
		☐

REPRESENTATIVE IN CONGRESS
THIRD CONGRESSIONAL DISTRICT   Vote for One
DON STEVENS	Republican	☐
JULIA BUTLER HANSEN	Democrat	☐
R. C. (SKIP) McCONKEY	Republican	☐
		☐

JUDICIAL

JUDGE, STATE SUPREME COURT
POSITION NO. 1   (6 year term)
Non-Partisan   Vote for One
ROBERT T. HUNTER	☐
VAUGHN E. EVANS	☐
	☐

POSITION NO. 2   (6 year term)
Non-Partisan   Vote for One
MARSHALL A. NEILL	☐
	☐

POSITION NO. 3   (6 year term)
Non-Partisan   Vote for One
CHARLES F. STAFFORD	☐
WILLIAM C. GOODLOE	☐
	☐

POSITION NO. 4   (Unexpired 2 Year Term)
Non-Partisan   Vote for One
MORELL E. SHARP	☐
CHARLES T. WRIGHT	☐
	☐

JUDGE, COURT OF APPEALS, Div. 2, Dist. 2
POSITION 1 Non-Partisan   Vote for One
HAROLD J. PETRIE	☐
	☐

JUDGE, SUPERIOR COURT
POSITION NO. 3 (Unexpired 2 Year Term)
Non-Partisan   Vote for One
FRANK E. BAKER	☐
	☐

LEGISLATIVE

STATE REPRESENTATIVE (22nd District)
POSITION NO. 1   Vote for One
HAL WOLF	Republican	☐
CHARLES (CHUCK) A. LINDBERG	Democrat	☐
ELMER KEISKI	Democrat	☐

POSITION NO. 2   Vote for One
MARY STUART LUX	Democrat	☐
WILLIAM M. AMBURGEY	Democrat	☐
BURTON R. JOHNSON	Democrat	☐
FLOYD CONWAY	Republican	☐
		☐

COUNTY

ASSESSOR   Vote for One
DEL PETTIT	Democrat	☐
JOHN M. (JACK) COWAN	Republican	☐
BERTRAN (CARL) NELSON	Democrat	☐
		☐

AUDITOR   Vote for One
C. WESLEY LEACH	Republican	☐
AMY BELL	Democrat	☐
		☐

CLERK   Vote for One
MARK CANTERBURY	Republican	☐
MARY SULLIVAN GOLDENBERGER	Democrat	☐
MARY WOOD	Republican	☐
		☐

CORONER   Vote for One
HOLLIS B. FULTZ	Republican	☐
		☐

PROSECUTING ATTORNEY   Vote for One
JERRY BUZZARD	Republican	☐
SMITH TROY	Democrat	☐
		☐

SHERIFF   Vote for One
DONALD E. ROBERTS	Democrat	☐
PAT HALL	Democrat	☐
TONY SEXTON	Republican	☐
DON REDMOND	Democrat	☐
CLARENCE A. VAN ALLEN	Republican	☐
FRED G. ANDERSON	Republican	☐

Compiled by: C. WESLEY LEACH
Thurston County Auditor
Supervisor of Elections

COUNTY

TREASURER   Vote for One
GEORGE M. HASKETT	Democrat	☐
W. R. (DICK) CHAPMAN	Republican	☐
		☐

JUDGE—Thurston County Justice Court District
Non-Partisan   Vote for One
FRANKLIN K. THORP	☐
	☐

COMMISSIONER
THIRD DISTRICT   Vote for One
WES ESTES	Republican	☐
HOMER HEDGEPETH	Democrat	☐
		☐

SPECIAL ELECTION
THURSTON COUNTY, WASHINGTON
Tuesday, September 15, 1970

INSTRUCTIONS: To vote for or against the proposition, place an
X in the appropriate ☐ following the proposition.

PROPOSITION NO. 1
County Courthouse and Building Bonds
$8,500,000.00

Shall Thurston County, Washington, contract an indebtedness in the sum of not to exceed $8,500,000.00 and issue its negotiable general obligation bonds therefor, to be payable by annual tax levies to be made without limitation as to rate or amount, and to mature in from two to not more than thirty years from date of issue, for County capital purposes only, other than the replacement of equipment, to construct, equip and furnish a new County Courthouse, health facilities and juvenile home on sites presently owned by the County, all as provided in Resolution No. 4080 of the Board of County Commissioners of Thurston County, passed and approved July 31, 1970?

BONDS, YES ☐

BONDS, NO ☐

N. P. BANK NOTE CO. ◄► OF OLYMPIA

or leading party tend also to be swollen by conformists and by a few "political rationalists," who register in it solely to vote in its crucial primary.

But the parties would gladly accept these uncertainties in preference to what they regard as the more serious perils of the open primary. (The blanket primary enjoys even less favor.) Party leaders levy two charges against the open primary: crossing over and raiding. The terms are sometimes used synonymously, but a distinction can be made between them. Crossing over is the practice of voters in choosing to participate in the primary of the party they do not generally support or feel a loyalty to. It is a drifting across party lines in search of the excitement of a primary battle. Raiding is an organized attempt on the part of one party to send its partisans into the primary of the other in order to foist the least attractive candidates on it.

That crossing over happens in open primary states is beyond doubt. Take the case of primary contests in Wisconsin, cradle of the open primary and home of an especially rambunctious political tradition. Its 1952 Republican senatorial primary in which Senator Joseph McCarthy, a highly controversial hunter of domestic communists, sought renomination attracted over 79 percent of the voters. However, only 54.3 percent of the two-party vote in the general election went to McCarthy, the Republican senatorial candidate. There is also considerable evidence to suggest that a substantial number of Republicans crossed party lines to vote for Senator Eugene McCarthy in the state's 1968 presidential primary.[2] Republicans may also have drifted into the Democratic presidential primary in 1972 to support George Wallace. The conditions were certainly right for it: There was no contest in the Republican primary, and a great range of Democrats were on that party's ballot.

As for organized raiding, there is little evidence to suggest that it is more than a worrisome myth. Every party fears that voters drifting to the other party's primary will develop a habit of voting that will carry over to the general election. Furthermore, the party must also be on guard lest the migration from its own primary permit its contests to be settled by unrepresentative or irresponsible minorities. In other words, it has every reason to encourage its loyalists to stay and vote in their own primary.

PRIMARIES: RULES OF THE GAME

The distinctions discussed in the last few pages concern the basic form of the primary election. The states have also found it necessary to cope with problems in the operation of the primaries.

[2] Austin Ranney, "Turnout and Representation in Presidential Primary Elections," *American Political Science Review* 66 (1972): 21–37.

Access to the Primary Ballot

First of all, the states must deal with the problem of how a candidate gets on the primary ballot. Most states permit access to the ballot by petition (called nomination papers in some areas). State statutes fix the number of required signatures, generally either a specific number or a percentage of the vote for the office in the last election. In some cases it is sufficient for the would-be candidate to present himself to the clerk of elections and pay a usually modest fee. Finally, a few states put candidates on the ballot if they have formal party support. In Colorado, for example, any seekers after nomination who poll 20 percent or more of the endorsement vote at party conventions are automatically placed on the primary ballot.

Even such mundane matters as access to the primary ballot have consequences for the parties. The easier the access, the easier it is for crank or dissident candidates to engage the party-supported candidate in a costly primary battle. Such arcane matters as the number of signatures a petition must have, therefore, may materially affect the number of primary contests in the state.[3]

Cross-filing

Occasionally the states have faced the question of whether to limit a candidate to seeking the nomination of a single party. Until 1959 California, alone among the states, permitted candidates to enter both major party primaries, a practice called cross-filing. In 1946, while it was in full flower, Earl Warren won both party nominations for governor; in the general election Earl Warren, Republican, ran without Democratic opposition. Bowing to criticism that cross-filing destroys a party's responsibility for its candidates and, in fact, destroys the basic assumption of nominations by a political party, the state legislature abolished it.[4] The closest remaining practice is New York's willingness to permit cross-filing if — and the "if" is a big one — the second party approves. Since the two major parties do not approve, New York has had no in-

---

[3] Access to the ballot is, along with all other aspects of election law, receiving greater attention by the United States Supreme Court these days. The effect of the scrutiny doubtless will in the long run be to make candidacy easier. For example, in 1972 the Court invalidated a Texas law requiring candidates to pay both a flat fee for candidacy and a share of the cost of the election. The total charges had run as high as $9,000 for a candidate. *Bullock* v. *Carter* (405 U.S. 134, 1972). In March of 1974 the Court also overturned the California scale of filing fees. It did not prohibit filing fees per se, but the justices ruled that states using them must provide an alternative means of access to the ballot (such as a petition) for candidates unable to pay the fee. *Lubin* v. *Panish* (415 U.S. 709, 1974).

[4] R. J. Pitchell, "The Electoral System and Voting Behavior: The Case of California's Cross-Filing," *Western Political Quarterly* 12 (1959): 459–84.

stances of candidates running on both Democratic and Republican tickets. The most common combination is the quest for the two-way nomination on Democratic and Liberal party ballots.

Run-off Primaries

Finally, some states have tried to cope with the issue of primaries that are settled by less than a majority of the voters. In those cases in which candidates are nominated by only 35, 40, or 45 percent, most states simply hope that the general election will produce a majority winner. But the District of Columbia and ten states, all from the South and its borders, have run-off primaries if the winner in the regular primary wins less than 50 percent. In these second primaries the two candidates with the highest vote totals face each other. This southern institution reflects the period of Republican impotence in which the Democratic nomination was in effect election and in which intense Democratic factionalism often produced three, four, or five serious candidates for a single office. Much more recently, another center of one-party domination, New York City, has begun run-off primaries if no candidate in the primary wins 40 percent of the vote. Iowa and South Dakota have approached the same basic problem with a fresh solution. If no primary candidate gets 35 percent of the votes cast, a party convention meets and selects the party's candidate.

The Nonpartisan Primary

Although of lesser importance in a book on American political parties, the nonpartisan primary is the means of nominating thousands of local officials, most judges, and even the legislature of Nebraska. As the nominating system that must accompany the nonpartisan election, the nonpartisan primary groups all candidates for the office on one ballot on which no party designations appear. The two candidates receiving the highest number of votes at the primary become the candidates for the nonpartisan general election. Although there are no party labels on the ballot, the party affiliations of various candidates may be well known. Party organizations may openly endorse and support candidates, especially in nonpartisan mayoralty and city council elections. In those cases the distinction between a partisan and nonpartisan primary may remain only for the voters who have little political information.

THE LINGERING CONVENTIONS

The convention as a device for nominating candidates faded quickly under early inroads by the direct primary. But decline has not meant death, and as of now the convention as a nominating device retains firm control over a significant number of public offices.

Many states exempt the minor parties from the direct primary. The states are not anxious to incur the financial expense, and realism suggests that minor-party nominations are not especially important anyway. Moreover, parties such as the Prohibition and Socialist Labor parties have difficulty enough finding even one candidate to run the futile race. Depending on state law, their candidates may be chosen by party convention or simply by petition. In the one-party days of the South it also became common to give Republican parties the option of holding the primary or of making their nominations in party conventions.

Furthermore, a minority of states still keeps some offices (usually statewide ones) out of the direct primary. In Indiana, nominations for all statewide offices are still made in state party conventions. In other states such as Michigan, candidates for specific statewide offices are so chosen. Until very recently, New York parties chose their statewide candidates in state conventions, in which the ideological and geographic factions of the parties were propitiated and possibly even unified. In 1967, however, New York replaced convention nominations with a system that permits the state committees of the parties to designate their candidates. Other would-be candidates may then challenge the committees' choices in a statewide primary.

Connecticut, the last state to embrace the primary, did so without a conspicuous show of affection. The Connecticut primary is like New York's, a challenge primary, and it combines convention with primary. Each party holds conventions to nominate candidates, and if no other candidate challenges the party nominee, the latter goes directly on the ballot of the general election without an intervening primary. In the event of a challenge, a primary is held, but the challenger must have sought nomination in the convention, must have amassed at least 20 percent of the convention votes, and must later have filed nomination petitions. The first statewide primary took place in 1970, fifteen years after the adoption of the Connecticut primary.

Why has the convention survived in some of the states? It remains in a few states having strong, centralized party organization and a political culture more accepting of the role of parties as robust, self-contained political organizations. As Lockard has written of Connecticut:

> Why such protracted and successful resistance? Connecticut is not immune to political innovation. Although it may be known as "The Land of Steady Habits," it has nonetheless adopted an imposing array of progressive legislation, particularly in matters of labor law and social welfare. Still, matters of party concern are different — at least in Connecticut. For Connecticut parties are different from those of most other states; they are strong, centralized, and highly competitive with each other. The character of Connecticut party leadership —

the power it has and the generally responsible manner in which it uses its power — constitutes the main reason why advocates of the primary made so little progress in Connecticut.[5]

In other words, strong, centralized parties can protect the sources of their strength, for in politics, too, "them that has, gets." Convention nomination enables them to maintain a control over candidates and officeholders and permits them to bargain within the party and to recognize the differences within it without airing them in public combat. And it is certainly no coincidence that in a state such as Connecticut, in which parties as parties still control nominations, party cohesion in the state legislature is just about the strongest in the United States.

THE THREAT OF THE DIRECT PRIMARY

The direct primary does not often substantiate the parties' worst fears, but occasionally it does. In 1962 a political novice from Cleveland with the promising name of Kennedy (Richard D.) managed to win the Democratic nomination for Ohio congressman-at-large in an eleven-cornered primary contest. Not only was he a novice with no support in the Democratic party, but he had run in the primary on a frankly segregationist program. A shocked Democratic party announced that it would not support him in the general election, and Democratic Governor DiSalle said he could not vote for him. Only nominally a Democratic candidate, Mr. Kennedy lost badly in the general election to Robert A. Taft, Jr., the Republican nominee.

Even though such total disaster befalls a party only rarely, the primary often causes it any number of lesser inconveniences, disruptions, and problems. Consider the threats it makes to the well-being of a political party:

1. For the party that wants to influence nominations, the primary greatly escalates the costs of politics. Supporting candidates in a contested primary is usually more expensive than holding a convention.
2. The primary diminishes the power of the party organization to reward its faithful with nomination for public office. It thus makes less certain one of the rewards by which the party can induce service in its ranks.
3. By curbing party control over nominations, the primary denies the party a powerful lever for ensuring the loyalty of its officeholders to the party program. For if the party cannot control or prevent the reelection of the maverick officeholder, it really has no effective sanc-

---

[5] Duane Lockard, *Connecticut's Challenge Primary: A Study in Legislative Politics* (New York: McGraw-Hill, 1960), p. 1.

tion for enforcing loyalty to its programs. The power of European parties to deny renomination to their recalcitrant parliamentarians contributes substantially to their maintenance of party discipline in parliament.

4. The primary permits the nomination of a candidate hostile to the party organization and leadership, opposed to their platforms or programs, or out of key with the public image the party wants to project — or all three! At the worst it may permit the nomination of an individual under the party label who will be, intentionally or not, a severe embarrassment to it.

5. The nature of the primary creates the distinct possibility that the party will find itself saddled with an unbalanced ticket for the general election. In the hypothetical case of an electorate divided into X (50 percent), Y (30 percent), and Z (20 percent) — letting X, Y, and Z represent regions, races, religions, ethnic or national groups — the voters at the primary may select all or most of the candidates from X. (We are assuming considerable bloc voting, but that assumption, after all, lies behind party attempts to balance tickets.) Party leaders unquestionably would feel that a sprinkling of Ys and Zs would make a stronger ticket.

6. Party activists also fear that the primary may produce a loser for the party. The nominee may have appealed to only a shade more than half of the dedicated 20 or 30 percent of the electorate that votes in the party's primary. Such a candidate may be poorly equipped to make the broader appeal necessary in the general election.

In addition to all these specific threats is the more general fear that the primary exacerbates party rifts, splits, factions, feuds, or whatever the headline writers choose to call them. It pits party worker against party worker, party group against party group.

A genuine primary is a fight within the family of the party — and, like any family fight, is apt to be more bitter and leave more enduring wounds than battles with the November enemy. In primaries, ambitions spurt from nowhere; unknown men carve their mark; old men are sent relentlessly to their political graves; bosses and leaders may be humiliated or unseated. At ward, county, or state level, all primaries are fought with spurious family folksiness — and sharp knives.[6]

The resulting wounds are often deep and slow to heal. The cost to the health and strength of the party is considerable.[7]

[6] Theodore H. White, *The Making of the President 1960* (New York: Atheneum, 1961), p. 78.
[7] See Donald B. Johnson and James R. Gibson, "The Divisive Primary Revisited: Party Activists in Iowa," *American Political Science Review* 68 (1974): 67–77. An-

Not even the gloomiest Cassandra expects all these misfortunes to result from any given primary or even a series of them. But they are distinct possibilities for any party, especially the relatively weak and passive one. The parties recognize the danger, but they recognize, too, the futility of a direct assault on the primary. So in the best American tradition of joining 'em if you can't beat 'em, some parties have set out to control the primary. Others have lacked the will or the strength to do so; still others have lost ground to local political cultures that disapprove of a party role in the primary. The result is a range of party responses to the primary that extends from no response at all to complete party domination.

THE PARTY ORGANIZATION FIGHTS BACK

One axiom and a corollary deriving from it govern party strategy in the primary. The axiom is simple to the point of truism: The surest way to control the primary is to prevent competition with the party's choice. And the corollary is equally clear: The party must act as early as possible in the preprimary jockeying of would-be candidates if it is to choke off unwanted competition in the primary.

Within some party organizations a powerful party leader or a few party oligarchs make the preprimary decisions for the party organization. Or it may be a party executive committee or a candidate selection committee. If their sources of information are good, they will know who intends to run and who is merely considering the race. They may arbitrate among them, or they may coax an unwilling man or woman into the primary. If they command a strong and winning organization, their inducements to the nonfavored to withdraw may be considerable. They may be able to offer a patronage position or a chance to run in the future. Any would-be candidate understands the risks in running against a party choice. It is true that some politicians have begun and made political careers by bucking a party choice in a primary, but they are not legion.

This informal and often covert selection of candidates — communicated to the party faithful by the "nod" or by the "word" — has been replaced within more and more parties by representative, publicized party conventions. A few states have formalized them, but in most cases they prevent an unqualified endorsement. Colorado laws provide that all candidates who polled more than 20 percent of a convention endorse-

---

drew Hacker argues to the contrary in "Does a 'Divisive' Primary Harm a Candidate's Election Chances?" *American Political Science Review* 59 (1965): 105–10. To a considerable extent the conflicting conclusions in the two articles are a result of the different consequences studied. Johnson and Gibson study the disaffection of party activists, and Hacker looks at the impact on the general election outcome.

ment vote shall go on the primary ballot in the order of their vote percentage. Utah directs the parties to nominate two candidates for each
office. Conversely, a few states attempt by law to minimize the possibility or the power of endorsing conventions. California in 1963 prohibited party organizations from "officially" endorsing candidates for
office. And other states, such as Wisconsin, have achieved substantially
the same result — albeit with greater subtlety — by requiring party
conventions to meet after the primary is safely past.

In most states, however, party endorsing bodies act informally and
extralegally — that is, without the laws of the state taking notice of them.
In Minnesota, for example, both the Republican party and the Democratic–Farmer-Labor party (the state's version of the Democratic party) hold
conventions to endorse candidates for statewide office and Congress. In
some parts of the state, chiefly the urban areas, they also endorse local
candidates and candidates for the state legislature. The instruments of
endorsement, the conventions, grow out of the local ward and precinct
caucuses mandated by state law. The required vote for endorsement,
set by party rule, is 60 percent within the GOP and two-thirds within
the DFL. The party endorsement, however, is strictly unofficial. The
endorsee must still go through regular procedures to get on the primary
ballot, and the ballot does not mention his endorsement.[8]

If a primary contest does develop despite all plans and strategies, the
party then falls back on its resources in conventional ways. It may
urge party committeepersons to help the anointed candidates circulate
nominating petitions for the necessary signatures and leave the other
candidates to their own devices. It may make available to the chosen
ticket money, know-how, party workers, and the party bureaucracy. It
may print advertisements announcing the party endorsees or issue
handy little reference cards, which the forgetful voter can take right
into the polling booth. On the day of the primary the party organization may help to get the party's voters to the polls. Whether the party
organization acts overtly or covertly in the primary campaign depends
both on the local political culture and on the candidates' own appraisals
of it. The party and/or the candidates may feel that voter sensitivity
to party intervention (i.e., "bossism") may dictate that the candidates
appear untouched by party hands.[9]

Of the frequency of party attempts to manage or influence American
primaries, it is impossible to write authoritatively. Practices vary not

[8] On Minnesota, see G. Theodore Mitau, *Politics in Minnesota*, 2nd ed. (Minneapolis: University of Minnesota Press, 1970).
[9] There have always been dark intimations of another party tactic in the primary:
"dummy candidates." They are candidates induced by the party to enter an already
contested primary in order to divert and divide the support of the unendorsed candidates. The tactic has undoubtedly been employed in American politics, but probably with an incidence far below some suspicions.

One of the Last of the Slatemakers Slates a Slate

Journalists flocked around Mayor Richard Daley of Chicago to watch his attempts and those of his cohorts to determine party nominations in 1972. Perhaps it was out of a sense that they were watching one of the last of a breed engage in an old and dying tribal ritual. From two reports, these excerpts:

"In Illinois, neither major party bothers with the expense and possible disruption of a state nominating convention. Instead, the state organizations create 'slating committees' to recommend their party's slates of candidates. Committee recommendations are reviewed by the state central committees, usually a formality, and those favored become the organization candidates.

"These candidates are still not officially nominated until they are selected by voters in the primary, but here in Illinois, the party organizations are rarely troubled by serious primary opposition."

Seth S. King in the New York Times,
December 7, 1971.

"Slatemaking follows a highly stylized script. Each election year in December, the 'slating committee' — composed of the party's district committeemen, state legislative leaders and a few key Daley observers — repairs to the downstate capital of Springfield to interview prospective candidates. But the Springfield sessions are only warm-ups for the main event: after a few days the Democratic pols pack up and move to the smoky Emerald Room in Chicago, where they are joined by the Cook County panjandrums ... [including] His Honor himself.

"There, some two dozen office seekers arrive to pay court, hoping to be chosen for jobs ranging from U.S. senator to county coroner. Often the screening boils down to three key questions: How much money can you bring to the campaign? Will you support the entire ticket? How will you distribute patronage?"

Newsweek, December 20, 1971.

Postscript: The Mayor's slated candidate for the Democratic nomination for governor, Paul Simon, the incumbent lieutenant governor, was defeated in the primary by insurgent Daniel Walker. Sic transit gloria mundi.

---

only from state to state but within states, and descriptions of local party practice are hard to come by. One is probably safe in generalizing that the most common nominating activity is the recruiting of candidates to seek the nomination. County party leaders in Wisconsin and Oklahoma have freely conceded that they encourage qualified candidates to seek

office. Yet they have not widely attempted to perform the more demanding recruitment activities; only 10 percent of the Wisconsin chairmen,
and less than that in Oklahoma, have tried to dissuade some would-be
nominees.[10] The result is that in most parts of the country the political
party is only one of a number of agencies seeking out and supporting
men and women to run for office. It shares their recruitment with local
business, professional, farm, and labor groups, with civic and community associations, with ethnic, racial, and religious organizations, with
political interest groups, and with officeholders.[11]

There are, however, those party organizations that *do* control the recruitment of candidates and the other preprimary processes. Generally
they are the parties that also intervene in the primary itself. A study
of legislative elections in Pennsylvania constituencies in the late 1950s
found that party organizations regularly attempted to influence the
primary in 74 percent of the 156 primaries (one primary for each party
in each of the seventy-eight districts). In 56 percent of them the interventions in the primary were public and explicit.[12] Such determined attempts to control the primary are not necessarily the norm in other
parts of the country, however. County chairmen in Kansas, Nebraska,
North Dakota, South Dakota, and Iowa disclosed a few years later that
they are not a part of Pennsylvania-style activities in the primaries.
Some 40 percent of them said they never openly supported a candidate
in a primary contest, and about two-thirds of them declared that their
party organizations never endorsed candidates before a primary.[13] Just
what kind of party relationship to the primary was or is now typical
across the United States is anyone's guess.

The role the party organization takes before and during the primary
election appears to be a function of a number of factors. First of all,
all data point to a greater party role in urban and metropolitan areas.
The political ethos of the cities seems to be more tolerant of party
action in the primary; furthermore, the cities are also the sites of the
strong and virile party organizations.[14] Second, at least one study indi-

[10] Leon D. Epstein, *Politics in Wisconsin* (Madison: University of Wisconsin Press,
1958), p. 93; Samuel C. Patterson, "Characteristics of Party Leaders," *Western Political Quarterly* 16 (1963): 348.
[11] Lester G. Seligman, "Political Recruitment and Party Structure: A Case Study,"
American Political Science Review 55 (1961): 77–86. The interaction may also be
reciprocal and complex. J. David Greenstone has illustrated Democratic party influence on trade union endorsements for congressional seats in his "Party Pressure
on Organized Labor in Three Cities," in M. Kent Jennings and L. Harmon Zeigler
(eds.), *The Electoral Process* (Englewood Cliffs: Prentice-Hall, 1966), pp. 55–80.
[12] Frank J. Sorauf, *Party and Representation* (New York: Atherton, 1963), Chap. 5.
[13] Marvin Harder and Thomas Ungs, *Notes Toward A Functional Analysis of Local
Party Organizations* (paper delivered at 1964 meeting of Midwest Political Science
Association).
[14] Sorauf, *Party and Representation*, Chap. 5; Harder and Ungs, *Notes Toward a
Functional Analysis*.

cates that party intervention into the primary is most probable in areas of two-party competitiveness. In one-party areas the majority party may tend to be smugly confident or may be dominated by incumbent office-holders. The minority party tends to be helpless, and primary contests within its ranks are rare.[15] Finally, in the states of the Great Plains, at least, it appears that party control of the primary is more common within the Democratic party, even when one controls for urban-rural differences.[16] That finding suggests differences between the two parties in intraparty expectations and ethos. Commentators on the styles and images of the two parties have often noted the more aggressively parti-san style of the Democrats and the "nonpartisan," middle-class style of the Republicans. Very possibly these differences affect their ap-proaches to the direct primary.

CANDIDATES AND VOTERS IN THE PRIMARIES

What the parties can accomplish in the primaries depends to a consider-able extent on the candidates and on the electorate. And the candidates and voters are often their allies. To put it simply, the primaries are more "manageable" because candidates do not often contest them and because the vast majority of voters do not vote in them. Very possibly one or both of these conditions is of the party's making; the absence of candidates, for example, may reflect the skill of the party's prepri-mary persuading and dissuading. Regardless of cause, however, the result tends to be a nomination politics of limited scope with the nomi-nations more easily controlled by an aggressive party organization.

The Candidates

Simple countings will confirm that in every part of the United States large numbers of primary candidates win nomination without contest. Kirk H. Porter referred to it as the "deserted primary" after finding that in 1944 there had been no contest in either primary for any county office in well over half of Iowa's counties.[17] A number of recent studies of primary contests in state legislative races suggest that matters have changed little since then. For example, in the 1958 primaries for Penn-sylvania legislative elections, 66.2 percent were without contest. Forty-five percent of the legislative primaries in Ohio in 1948 were not con-

---

[15] Patterson, "Characteristics of Party Leaders."
[16] Harder and Ungs, Notes Toward a Functional Analysis.
[17] Kirk H. Porter, "The Deserted Primary in Iowa," American Political Science Re-view 39 (1945): 732–40.

tested.[18] In Wisconsin from 1966 through 1972, 58.9 percent of state legislative primaries were not contested. If one adopts a qualitative standard of the closeness of the competition — to discount hopeless and frivolous candidates — the amount of genuine competition declines even further. In the Pennsylvania data recounted above, about three-fourths of the contests were decided by a margin of less than 30 percent of the vote in the primary.

In the aggregate, competition in American primaries (measured by the number of contestants) is greater under certain rather predictable circumstances: (1) Competition tends to flourish in primaries of the dominant party. In other words, competition tends to increase as the party's electoral prospects do, and aggregately it is greatest among the two parties of a district when they are closely matched. (2) Competition also prospers in primaries in urban areas. It tends to increase with increases in the percentages of voters living in urban or metropolitan places. (3) Finally, competition thrives in primaries in which there is no incumbent officeholder seeking renomination.

There are also other factors influencing competition: the attractiveness of the office and the ease of getting on the ballot, for example. But the chief factor probably is the party's prospects for victory in the general election; large numbers of Americans do not fight for the right to go down to almost certain defeat. As for the power of the incumbent to discourage competition, it is one of the ironies of the primary. The primary really demands the kind of popular appeal and exposure that often only the well-known incumbent can muster. As a result, it creates the conditions that diminish its own effectiveness.[19]

It is also an irony that primary competition is greater in the very urban areas in which the parties are better organized and more apt to engage in preprimary endorsements and recruitment. Of course, it is possible that the number of contestants would be even greater without party activities. Party interventions, however, clearly do not explain the patterns of primary competition. The greater competition of the urban centers may reflect a greater value of public office, a greater desire to seek its social and economic rewards. Or it may reflect a more divided, heterogeneous, diverse society in which major groups tend to spawn their own special candidates. But whatever the explanation, the contesting of primaries clearly is the result of factors far beyond the party system.

[18] Sorauf, *Party and Representation*, p. 111; V. O. Key, *American State Politics* (New York: Knopf, 1956), p. 178.
[19] On the general causes of primary competition, see the references in the preceding footnotes and also William H. Standing and James A. Robinson, "Inter-Party Competition and Primary Contesting: The Case of Indiana," *American Political Science Review* 52 (1958): 1066–77.

The Voters

If candidates are scarce at the primaries, so are voters. All evidence points overwhelmingly to one cardinal fact about the voting behavior of the American electorate at primaries: it does not vote. Take for instance Key's finding about voter participation in the gubernatorial primaries of fifteen nonsouthern states from 1926 to 1952:

In three out of four primaries not more than 35 percent of the potential electorate voted in the primaries of one or the other of the major parties. That is, the total Democratic primary vote plus the total Republican primary vote did not exceed 35 percent of the number of citizens 21 and over.[20]

Or to use another base of measurement, primary turnouts frequently are less than half that at the following general election. For obscure local offices and reasonably noncontroversial judicial races, the turnout may fall a great deal further.

Even though the primary electorate is small, it does have some special characteristics of its own. A substantial sector of it generally comes from the party loyalists and activists (Table 1). Data from the same national survey in 1972 also show that primary voters, as one might expect, have higher levels of political interest and higher educational attainments. Conventional political wisdom has also held that primary voters represent more extreme ideological positions than the party's full electorate. Ranney and Epstein's recent studies in Wisconsin, however, disprove the wisdom for that state.[21] Yet it is probably true that primary voters generally are more concerned with ideologies and issues than nonvoters. If so, they bring those concerns to bear in evaluating possible nominees.

Even this generally interested electorate, in the absence of reliable cues and information, often lapses into erratic voting behavior. For large numbers of voters in the primary, the choice is more difficult than that at the general election. Since all the candidates come from the same party, the voter's party loyalties cannot guide his decision. Nor can any reaction to "ins" and "outs." The primary campaign is brief, the candidates are not well known, and the issues, if any, are often unclear. Therefore, the voter's choice is not so well structured or predictable; the presence of an incumbent in the race may be the only continuing, stabilizing element. Consequently, many voter decisions are made right in the polling booth; the effect of the ballot position and the success

---

[20] Key, *American State Politics*, p. 134 and all of Chap. 5.
[21] Austin Ranney and Leon D. Epstein, "The Two Electorates: Voters and Non-Voters in a Wisconsin Primary," *Journal of Politics* 28 (1966): 598–616; Austin Ranney, "The Representativeness of Primary Electorates," *Midwest Journal of Political Science* 12 (1968): 224–38.

TABLE 1   Party Loyalties of Primary Voters and Nonvoters: 1972

	Strong Democrat	Weak Democrat	Inde- pendent	Weak Repub- lican	Strong Repub- lican
Voted in 1972 primary	70.1%	50.6%	34.3%	58.8%	58.8%
Did not vote in 1972 primary	29.9	49.4	63.5	39.2	38.8
Other responses	—	—	2.2	2.0	2.4
	100.0	100.0	100.0	100.0	100.0

Source Survey Research Center of the University of Michigan; data made available through the Inter-University Consortium for Political Research.

of the famous names indicate that. Small wonder, then, that parties are never confident in primaries and that public opinion pollers prefer not to predict primary outcomes.

THE DIRECT PRIMARY AFTER SIXTY YEARS

More than sixty years have now passed since the introduction of the direct primary into American politics. Thousands of candidates have waged the necessary primary campaigns, and millions of weary voters have puzzled over obscure choices and no choices whatsoever. What difference has it all made? Has the primary democratized the nomination process by taking it out of the hands of party oligarchs? And has it materially increased popular participation and initiative in the selection of candidates for public office?

Basically, the democratic hopes behind the direct primary falter on the lack of competition and low voter turnout. There must be participation — both by candidates and by voters — if there are to be meaningful choices based on meaningful alternatives. But the primary by its nature tends to diminish both. The need for broad public appeal, the cost of a contest, and the sheer difficulty of getting on the primary ballot, among other factors, discourage candidacies. And the multiplicity of primaries with their unstructured, confusing, and unclear choices probably also reduces both the quantity and quality of voter participation. Clearly, if mass participation in the nominating processes was a goal of the reformers who initiated the primary, their hopes have not been realized.

The 1972 primaries for the United States House of Representatives in all the nonsouthern states summarize the amount of choice afforded American voters in one set of primaries (Table 2).[22] In only 42.3 percent of the primaries was there any competition at all. More significantly, in only 18.9 percent of them was there competition enough to prevent the winner from winning by a two-to-one margin. Table 2 also pinpoints the presence of incumbents as a major inhibitor of primary competition. (It also indicates again the tendency for a greater degree of competition in Democratic primaries.) All in all, the opportunities for popular choice in these congressional primaries were considerably limited.

TABLE 2   Competition in Primaries for the House of Representatives: The Non-South in 1972

Primaries	Number	Primaries with some competition	Primaries with "close" competition[a]
Democratic with incumbent	151	66 (43.7%)	21 (13.9%)
Democratic without incumbent	172	79 (45.9%)	50 (29.1%)
Republican with incumbent	142	43 (30.3%)	6 (4.2%)
Republican without incumbent	181	85 (47.0%)	45 (24.9%)
All primaries	646	273 (42.3%)	122 (18.9%)

Source   Richard Scammon, ed., *America Votes 10* (Washington: Governmental Affairs Institute, 1974).

[a] "Close" here means that the winner won by less than a two-to-one margin over his closest competitor.

Second, the goals of the primary reformers have been frustrated also by the controls of the party organizations. If one purpose of the primary was to replace the caucuses and conventions of the party organizations as nominators, the primary fails to some extent when it falls under the sway of those organizations. If it cannot eliminate primary competition, it can often defeat it. The party often commands the money, symbols, and organization essential for primary victory. Also, the party organization often commands the chief political loyalty of a

[22] The data here and in Table 2 are from the 323 congressional districts of the non-South. The inclusion of the 112 districts of the South would further diminish the percentages.

major share of those who vote in the primary. If only 30 or 40 percent of registered voters vote in the primary, some 15 or 20 percent of that electorate is sufficient to nominate. Parties count on the fact that a substantial part of that group is likely to be loyalists who respond to the cues of party leaders or endorsements. So, strong party organizations able to mobilize voters, money, and manpower are still the most effective determiners of primary outcomes.[23]

For a variety of reasons, however, the parties control the primaries only imperfectly. The sheer size of the task deters many of them. The Jacksonian tradition of electing every public official down to the local coroner has confronted them with too great a number of contests. The expense of supporting so many candidates — not to mention the expenditure of organizational energy — forces many organizations to be selective in their primary interventions. In other instances parties stand aside because a role in the primary threatens their internal harmony and cohesion. They may be paralyzed by the fear that their activity in the primary will open wounds or heat up old resentments. Still others are stymied by local political cultures that resist party activity as an improper incursion on the spirit of the primary.

Yet, to argue that the primary has not fulfilled the most optimistic hopes is not to argue that it has had no effect. In competitive districts — especially when an incumbent has stepped down — voters often do play the kind of meaningful role the reformers envisioned. And even for the strong party organization, the primaries set tangible limits. Many no longer find it possible to whisk any "warm body" through the nomination process. The direct primary perhaps can best be thought of both as creating a veto body that passes on the work of party nominators and as affording an opportunity for interparty dissidents to take their case to the party's electorate.

Finally, let us consider the more general impact of the primary on the political parties. V. O. Key argued that the primary leads to one-partyism by drawing both the voters and the attractive, prestigious candidates increasingly to the primary of the dominant party. Little by little the majority party becomes the only viable instrument of political influence and the minority party atrophies, a victim of "the more general proposition that institutional decay follows deprivation of function." [24] The burden of opposition is then shifted to contests within the primary of the majority party. However persuasive the argument, it is as yet unproved. One-partyism has receded in recent years, and much of it

[23] For example, Phillips Cutright and Peter H. Rossi, "Party Organization in Primary Elections," *American Journal of Sociology* 64 (1958): 262–69.
[24] V. O. Key, "The Direct Primary and Party Structure," *American Political Science Review* 48 (1954): 24; the same argument reappears in his *American State Politics*, Chap. 6.

that remains can be explained in terms of changes in the characteristics of the American electorate. It is more likely that the direct primary has caused a general atrophy in party organization in dominant as well as minority parties. Strong, centralized party organization continues noticeably in states in which conventions either nominate candidates or make systematic, crucial, preprimary endorsements. Party organization weakens and contracts in those areas in which it loses vital functions and in which party officials and activists lose their reason for existing.

Furthermore, the direct primary has unquestionably altered the distribution of power within the party. When one speaks of party control of nominations, he means control by the party organization, and any weakening of that control obviously weakens the organization and enhances the power of the party candidates and the party in government. Their ability, especially as incumbents, to defy the organization's wrath and to win primary battles frees them from its discipline and, indeed, often calls them to positions of party leadership. In fact, the inability of party organization in the United States to control the party in government (as it does in so many other democracies) begins with the failure to control the nominations. The direct primary undercuts the ability of the party organization to recruit to public office those partisans who share its goals and accept its discipline.[25] Failure to control nominations, therefore, weakens the party organization vis-à-vis the party in government, and at the same time it deprives the party of a meaningful activity on which the energies and aspirations of its activists might focus.

The goal of the Progressives and the other proponents of the primary was to substitute the party electorate for the party organization as the nominator. With the primary they thwarted the organization's quest for its own goals. Instead of achieving any genuine mass control of party nominations, however, they largely moved the control from the elites of the organization to the elites of the party in government. They succeeded in multiplying the party oligarchies rather than in democratizing them.

Finally, the direct primary has buttressed the prevailing decentralization of power in the American parties. So long as the candidates or incumbents can appeal to a majority of local primary voters, they are free from the control and discipline of a state or national party. Even so powerful a president as Franklin Roosevelt in 1938 met his greatest political defeat in trying to purge a number of Democratic senators and representatives in their local Democratic primaries; only one of his conservative targets was defeated. The primary plays on local loyalties and

---

[25] Leo Snowiss notes differences in ideologies, voting records, political ethos, and party loyalty among congressmen nominated under various degrees of party organization control. See his "Congressional Recruitment and Representation," *American Political Science Review* 60 (1966): 627–39.

appeals to the local electorate, and the vast number of them are extremely difficult for a centralized party organization to control.

If the advocates of the direct primary wanted to aim beyond the nomination process and strike the parties themselves, they found their target. In many instances the direct primary has weakened the parties' control of nominations, robbed their organizations of an important raison d'être, and liberated their officeholders. It has in many important ways made the American political parties what they are today.

10
The
Campaign
for
Election

The formidable Democratic party organization of Pennsylvania had long had a reputation for winning primaries and general elections. At the outset of the campaign in the gubernatorial primary of 1966, few observers gave any chance to Milton Shapp, a Philadelphia industrialist who was challenging the organization's candidate, a thirty-four-year-old lawyer and state legislative leader, Robert B. Casey. But in what was billed as a battle of "exposure versus organization," the Shapp campaign employed some 7,000 spot radio commercials, 34 half-hour television shows on prime time, an assortment of 30 or so pamphlets and leaflets, more than 60 campaign headquarters across the state, and a single mailing of one large brochure to a million and a half voters (estimated cost: $75,000). The total cost of the primary campaign, financed in large part from Shapp's personal fortune, ran over a million dollars. Shapp won the primary.

A similar use of polls, direct mailings, and television — even campaign pictures with well-known athletes, who were paid up to $500 for the picture taking — continued into the general election. Shapp lost that contest, however, to Republican Raymond Schaefer. After it was all over, a reflective Robert Casey observed about the campaign he had lost:

Politics is changing tremendously. The old ways no longer work. From that election, I learned that these days you need a combination of two things. First, the traditional grass-roots effort, the telephoning and the door-knocking. But more than that, you have to do what he did. You have to use the new sophisticated techniques, the polling, the television, the heavy staffing, and the direct mail. You can't rely any more on political organizations. They don't work any more. These days, who wants a job in the courthouse or with the highway department? Why, the sons of courthouse janitors are probably doctors or professional men. You can't give those jobs away any more. We're at the tag end of an era in Pennsylvania.[1]

[1] National Observer, September 26, 1966.

To those reflections one can add two postscripts. The Shapp campaign in 1966 was managed by a young professional campaign manager, Joe Napolitan, who went on in 1968 to help run the Humphrey presidential campaign. And in 1970 Shapp finally succeeded in winning the Pennsylvania governorship, without the help of Napolitan, again defeating Casey in the primary.

Individual cases and illustrations, even feature stories in the nation's newspapers and magazines, do not document a trend. Yet, it is clear that the new professional managers, media specialists, pollsters, and advertising and public relations men have become a new and powerful force in American political campaigning. It is equally clear that they threaten to replace the party organization as the major planner and executor of campaigns. As one urbane former candidate has put it:

> With mass media which use a common language that everyone can read, people no longer need party workers to advise them how to vote. When a citizen can see and hear the candidate on a screen at home, and read news, written by the best journalists from a variety of points of view, about the candidate's public and private life, he does not heed what is told him by the precinct captain on his block. The media have done to the campaign system what the invention of accurate artillery did to the feudal kingdom — destroyed the barons and shifted their power to the masses and the prince. A candidate now pays less attention to district leaders than to opinion polls.[2]

The argument, briefly, is that the party organization has become technologically obsolete — that it has been superseded by newer, more efficient, and more timely avenues and techniques of campaigning. Thus, the argument goes, the party organization has lost an important measure of control over the contesting of American elections and, ultimately, over its candidates elected to public office.

These exotic campaign politics, however, take place within a limiting context of legal regulation and definition. Prior to a discussion of campaigning and changes in it, therefore, it is necessary to discuss the shape of the electoral process itself. The strategies of the electoral game make sense only if one first understands the game itself.

THE ELECTORAL INSTITUTIONS

The legal framework that defines American elections also defines the rules of the game that govern the parties and other political organizations contesting for public office. Each part of that framework, each rule of the game, places a strategic limitation on the campaign. Each adjustment in any one rule may affect one party or candidate more than another.

[2] Stimson Bullitt, *To Be a Politician* (New York: Anchor, 1961), p. 65.

Thus the framework is not an objective influence in the campaign and election.

Political parties around the world have not been slow to realize the possible advantages to be gained by careful, selective tinkering with election law, and the major American parties have been no exception. But Americans have generally tinkered more with the size and shape of the electoral districts; gerrymandering is a peculiarly American art form. The rest of the American electoral rules have remained surprisingly stable, even though they have been complicated by the usual state-to-state variations. The kind of repeated electoral tinkerings common in Europe — the shiftings to systems of proportional representation and back again, and the experiments with second, run-off elections, for instance — have not been common here.

The Secret Ballot

The American ballot is now uniformly secret, but it was not always so. Until the late nineteenth century the oral vote was common in many states and jurisdictions; the voter simply stated to electoral officials which candidates he preferred. During the nineteenth century the oral vote was gradually replaced by ballots printed by the parties or candidates. The voter brought the ballot of his candidate or party to the polling place and deposited it in the box. Since the ballots were by no means identical, his vote was often apparent to observers. Ballot reformers argued for the secret ballot as a way of curbing election corruption, especially vote buying. With the secret ballot, the corrupter could never be sure the vote would be delivered. The secret ballot, named the Australian ballot after the country of its origin, quickly swept the day. By the beginning of the twentieth century its success was complete, and it remains the practice today. It is a ballot printed at public expense by public authorities, and it lists all candidates for office on its single, consolidated form. It is distributed only at the polling places and only to bona fide voters, who then mark it in the seclusion of a voting booth.[3]

Increasingly, especially in large American cities, the voting machine is replacing the paper ballot. It does not, however, alter the basic form and premises of the Australian ballot. Only the mechanics of voting are different. The voter faces the machine within a small, draped enclosure and votes by moving levers next to the names of candidates or parties he chooses. A master lever formally records the votes and at the same time

---

[3] Jerrold Rusk also finds that the introduction of the Australian ballot was accompanied by a sharp increase in split-ticket voting. See his article "The Effect of the Australian Ballot Reform on Split Ticket Voting: 1876–1908," *American Political Science Review* 64 (1970): 1220–38.

opens the drapery for the voter to leave. The advantages of the voting machine, its makers assert, are its long-run reduction of election costs and its speed and accuracy in counting votes. It also thwarts certain forms of ballot box stuffing and dishonest counts. But technology never builds the perfect mousetrap or voting machine, and innovation continues. When the computerized telephone capable of sending messages is perfected, voters may simply dial a polling place and cast their votes by means of sensitized registration cards.

Forms of Ballots

The ballots in use in the United States fall into two main types. About twenty states use the *office-block* ballot, which groups the names of the candidates according to the offices they seek (Figure 1). In the majority of states the *party-column* ballot prevails; it is so named because the candidates of each party are listed together in a vertical column. The names of all candidates for the same office fall in horizontal rows (Figure 2). Thus only in this type of ballot are the candidates of each party grouped so that the voter can perceive them as a party ticket. By their very nature, of course, nonpartisan elections employ the office-block ballot.

All evidence indicates that the parties are correct in their belief that the party-column ballot encourages and facilitates straight-ticket voting (i.e., voting for all of a party's candidates for all the offices being filled at the election). But the amount of straight-ticket voting also hinges on the presence or absence on the ballot of a single square or circle (or a single lever on machines) by which the voter can, in one fell swoop, cast his vote for the entire ticket. These squares or circles are more commonly employed on party-column ballots, but some states combine them with the office-block ballot. Hence the ballot forms can be listed to indicate a diminishing scale of assistance to straight-ticket voting:

1. Party-column ballot with party circle or square.
2. Office-block ballot with party circle or square.
3. Party-column ballot without party circle or square.
4. Office-block ballot without party circle or square.

In this and in other ways the format of the ballot can affect the way the voter sees the electoral contest and the nature of choices in it.

Two other aspects of ballot form deserve mention. Almost every ballot makes some provision for voters to write in the names of persons not listed on the ballot. But the success of write-in candidates is so rare that it is hardly a real question in American politics. Senator J. Strom Thurmond of South Carolina, to be sure, was elected initially in 1954 as a write-in candidate, but one political scientist has referred to that election

FIGURE 1 The Office-Block Ballot: Montana General Election Ballot, November 1970

SAMPLE BALLOT

VOTE IN ALL COLUMNS

STATE AND NATIONAL	COUNTY AND TOWNSHIP	AMENDMENTS
UNITED STATES SENATOR VOTE FOR ONE	**COUNTY COMMISSIONER** VOTE FOR ONE	**Attorney General's Explanatory Statement** This amendment would change the age qualifications for voters from twenty-one (21) years of over to nineteen (19) years or over.
☐ MIKE MANSFIELD — Democrat	☐ AL GASKILL — Democrat	AN ACT TO SUBMIT TO THE ELECTORS OF MONTANA AN AMENDMENT TO SECTION 2, ARTICLE IX OF THE MONTANA CONSTITUTION CHANGING THE VOTING AGE TO NINETEEN YEARS.
☐ HAROLD E. "BUD" WALLACE — Republican	☐ HARRY V. NICHOLS — Republican	BE IT ENACTED BY THE LEGISLATIVE ASSEMBLY OF THE STATE OF MONTANA:
☐	☐ J. B. "JIM" CASEY — Independent	Section 1. Section 2, Article IX of the constitution of the state of Montana is amended to read as follows: "Section 2. Every person of the age of nineteen (19) years or over, possessing the following qualifications, shall be entitled to vote at all general elections and for all officers that now are, or hereafter may be, elective by the people, and, except as hereinafter provided, upon all questions which may be submitted to the vote of the people or electors; First, he shall be a citizen of the United States; second, he shall have resided in this state one year immediately preceding the election at which he offers to vote, and in the town, county or precinct such time as may be prescribed by law. If the question submitted concerns the creation of any levy, debt or liability the person, in addition to possessing the qualifications above mentioned, must also be a taxpayer whose name appears upon the last preceding completed assessment roll, in order to entitle him to vote upon such question. Provided, first, that no person convicted of felony shall have the right to vote unless he has been pardoned or restored to citizenship by the governor: provided, second, that nothing herein contained shall be construed to deprive any person of the right to vote who has such right at the time of the adoption of this constitution; provided, that after the expiration of five years from the time of adoption of this constitution, no person except citizens of the United States shall have the right to vote."
REPRESENTATIVE IN CONGRESS FIRST CONGRESSIONAL DISTRICT VOTE FOR ONE	☐	
☐ ARNOLD OLSEN — Democrat	**COUNTY CLERK AND RECORDER** VOTE FOR ONE	
☐ RICHARD G. "DICK" SHOUP — Republican	☐ HELEN KOVICH — Democrat	
☐	☐	
RAILROAD AND PUBLIC SERVICE COMMISSIONER VOTE FOR ONE	**COUNTY ATTORNEY** VOTE FOR ONE	
☐ PAUL CANNON — Democrat	☐ THOMAS F. DOWLING — Democrat	
☐ ALFRED C. LANGLEY — Republican	☐	
☐	**COUNTY SHERIFF** VOTE FOR ONE	
CLERK OF THE SUPREME COURT VOTE FOR ONE	☐ EARLE K. DAMON — Democrat	
☐ TOM J. KEARNEY — Democrat	☐ DAVE MIDDLEMAS — Republican	☐ For the above amendment
☐	☐	☐ Against the above amendment
CHIEF JUSTICE OF THE SUPREME COURT (FULL TERM—SIX YEARS) VOTE FOR ONE	**COUNTY SUPERINTENDENT OF SCHOOL** VOTE FOR ONE	**Attorney General's Explanatory Statement** Presently, the Constitution of Montana provides that the legislature can submit no more than three (3) constitutional amendments to the voters at the same election. This constitutional amendment would allow the state legislature to submit to the voters at each of the general elections of 1972, 1974 and 1976, an amendment or amendments to the Montana Constitution which provide for the reorganization of the executive branch of state government in addition to the three amendments already permitted under the constitution.
☐ JAMES T. HARRISON — Non-Partisan	☐ DOROTHY H. SIMMONS — Democrat	AN ACT TO SUBMIT TO THE ELECTORS OF MONTANA AN AMENDMENT TO SECTION 9, ARTICLE XIX OF THE CONSTITUTION OF MONTANA WHICH WOULD PERMIT THE LEGISLATIVE ASSEMBLY TO SUBMIT AT THE 1972, 1974 and 1976 GENERAL ELECTIONS, IN ADDITION TO THE THREE AMENDMENTS OTHERWISE AUTHORIZED, AMENDMENTS PROVIDING FOR THE REORGANIZATION OF THE EXECUTIVE DEPARTMENT OF GOVERNMENT.
☐ JOHN M. SCHILTZ — Non-Partisan	☐	
☐	**COUNTY TREASURER** VOTE FOR ONE	BE IT ENACTED BY THE LEGISLATIVE ASSEMBLY OF THE STATE OF MONTANA:
ASSOCIATE JUSTICE NO. 3 OF THE SUPREME COURT (FULL TERM—SIX YEARS) VOTE FOR ONE	☐ EDNA MAE LEONARD — Republican	Section 1. Section 9, Article XIX of the constitution of the State of Montana is amended to read as follows: "Section 9. Amendments to this constitution may be proposed in either house of the legislative assembly, and if the same shall be voted for by two-thirds of the members elected to each house, such proposed amendments, together with the ayes and nays of each house thereon, shall be entered in full on their respective journals; and the secretary of state shall cause the said amendment or amendments to be published in full in at least one newspaper in each county (if such there be) for three months previous to the next general election for members to the legislative assembly; and at said election the said amendment or amendments shall be submitted to the qualified electors of the state for their approval or rejection and such as are approved by a majority of those voting thereon shall become part of the constitution. Should more amendments than one (1) be submitted at the same election, they shall be so prepared and distinguished by numbers or otherwise that each can be voted upon separately. Not more than three amendments to this constitution shall be submitted at the same election, except that there may be submitted at each of the general elections held in the years 1972, 1974 and 1976, in addition to the three amendments otherwise authorized by this section, an amendment or amendments providing for the reorganization of the executive department of government which may include the revision or repeal of sections of this constitution relating to any boards, offices, and departments other than legislative and judicial offices. The reorganization of the executive department is a single subject, and an additional amendment relating to that subject authorized by this section may be submitted to the qualified electors of the state in the form of a title clearly expressing its subject."
☐ WESLEY CASTLES — Non-Partisan	☐ DARLENE O'LEARY — Democrat	
☐ ROBERT W. GABRIEL — Non-Partisan	☐	
☐	**COUNTY AUDITOR** VOTE FOR ONE	
ASSOCIATE JUSTICE NO. 1 OF THE SUPREME COURT (UNEXPIRED TERM—FOUR YEARS) VOTE FOR ONE	☐ WM. J. "BILL" MANNING — Democrat	
☐ GENE B. DALY — Non-Partisan	☐	
☐ HAROLD L. HOLT — Non-Partisan	**COUNTY ASSESSOR** VOTE FOR ONE	
☐	☐ J. NORMAN MATTHEWS — Democrat	
STATE SENATOR SENATORIAL DISTRICT NO. 21 VOTE FOR ONE	☐	
	COUNTY SURVEYOR VOTE FOR ONE	
☐ GLEN L. DRAKE — Republican	☐ OSCAR A. BAARSON — Democrat	
☐ JOE REBER — Democrat	☐	
☐	**PUBLIC ADMINISTRATOR** VOTE FOR ONE	
	☐ MARIE KASPERICK BRAZIER — Democrat	
	☐	

FIGURE 2   The Party-Column Ballot: Michigan General Election Ballot, November 1970

INSTRUCTION BALLOT—INGHAM COUNTY

PARTISAN BALLOT **A**

No. 1461

GENERAL ELECTION, NOVEMBER 3, 1970

CITY OF LANSING, MICHIGAN
COUNTY COMMISSIONER DISTRICT NO. 15

INSTRUCTIONS—To vote a straight party ticket make a cross (X) in the circle under the name of your party. Nothing further need be done. To vote for a candidate not on your party ticket, make a cross (X) in the square ☐ before his name. Candidates for governor and lieutenant governor must be voted for as a unit, and the vote cannot be split. If two or more candidates are to be elected to the same office, and you desire to vote for candidates not on your party ticket, make a cross (X) in the square ☐ before the names of the candidates for whom you desire to vote on the other ticket, and strike out an equal number of names on your party ticket, for that office. If you do not desire to vote any party ticket, do not make a cross (X) in the circle at the head of any ticket, but make a cross (X) in the square ☐ before the name of each candidate for whom you desire to vote. If you wish to vote for a candidate not on any ticket, write or place the name of such candidate on your ticket opposite the name of the office. Before leaving the booth, fold the ballot so that the face of the ballot is not exposed and so that the numbered corner is visible.

NAMES OF OFFICES VOTED FOR:	DEMOCRATIC PARTY	REPUBLICAN	AMERICAN Independent PARTY	SOCIALIST WORKERS PARTY	SOCIALIST LABOR PARTY
STATE GOVERNOR AND LIEUTENANT GOVERNOR	Sander Levin / Edward H. McNamara	William G. Milliken / James H. Brickley	James L. McCormick / Robert E. Cauley	George Boose / Evelyn Kirsch	James C. Horvath / W. Clifford Bentley
SECRETARY OF STATE	Richard H. Austin	Emil Lockwood	Robert E. Miles	John Hawkins	Frank Troha
ATTORNEY GENERAL	Frank J. Kelley	William S. Farr, Jr.		Ronald Roosti	John Zywicki
CONGRESSIONAL UNITED STATES SENATOR	Philip A. Hart	Lenore Romney		Paul Lodico	James Sim
REPRESENTATIVE IN CONGRESS, 6TH DISTRICT	John A. Gihon	Charles E. Chamberlain			
LEGISLATIVE STATE SENATOR, 24TH DISTRICT	Lou Stuttman	Philip O. Pittenger	Leo J. Miles		
REPRESENTATIVE IN STATE LEGISLATURE, 58TH DISTRICT	Thomas C. Walsh	Frederick L. Stackable			
STATE BOARDS MEMBERS OF THE STATE BOARD OF EDUCATION	Thomas J. Brennan	R. Robert Geake			Peter Goonis
VOTE FOR NOT MORE THAN TWO	Annetta Miller	David Robinson II			David Lindsay
MEMBERS OF THE BOARD OF REGENTS OF UNIVERSITY OF MICHIGAN	Paul Brown	Paul G. Goebel, Jr.	George Kindred	P. Thomas Vernier	Vito DeLisi
VOTE FOR NOT MORE THAN TWO	James L. Waters	Jack H. Shuler	Tom Staffin	Marcia Wisch	William Walbridge
MEMBERS OF THE BOARD OF TRUSTEES OF MICHIGAN STATE UNIVERSITY	Patricia M. Carrigan	David D. Diehl	Louise May		Kenneth Kelly
VOTE FOR NOT MORE THAN TWO	Don Stevens	Richard D. Ernst	Carol Smith		Mathew Kovach
MEMBERS OF THE BOARD OF GOVERNORS OF WAYNE STATE UNIVERSITY	Leon H. Atchison	Raymond E. Hayes	Mary Ganiard	Norma Jean Lodico	Terry Lindsay
VOTE FOR NOT MORE THAN TWO	Max J. Pincus	Earl Kennedy	Patrick Tifer	John A. Porter	Lowell E. Miller
COUNTY COMMISSIONER 15TH DISTRICT	James R. Stone	Mildred E. Kallman			

Printed by Authority of the County Election Commission.

as "one of the seven wonders of American politics," noting that "nothing of the sort had ever happened before in the history of the country." [4] Second, the order in which candidates' names appear in the office groupings on office-block ballots may affect the outcome of the election. American voters have shown a notorious disposition to vote for the first name

[4] William Goodman, *The Two-Party System in the United States*, 3rd ed. (Princeton: Van Nostrand, 1964), p. 440.

on a list of candidates.[5] The states differ in their responses to the issue of who is listed first. Some ask the candidates to draw lots for ballot position, others give the incumbent and the other majority party candidate the first and second places, and still others list names alphabetically. Perhaps the most equitable solution is the policy of rotating the names; if there are two candidates, for example, each occupies the first position on 50 percent of the ballots.

Finally, the American ballot is and has always been a long ballot. Its length, to be sure, cannot be controlled merely by electoral or ballot law. It reflects the American tradition of electing, rather than appointing, a great number of state and local officials — judges, coroners, surveyors, sheriffs, jury commissioners, superintendents of public instruction, assessors, public utilities commissioners, clerks of the courts, party committeemen, auditors, and comptrollers. An observable effect of the long ballot, especially in the office-block form, is voter fatigue.[6] Many voters, either tiring or despairing, do not vote in contests at the bottom of the ballot. Partial voting (drop-off) of this sort can be as high as 20 or 30 percent of the voters at a given election.

Structure and Rules of the Choice

Overwhelmingly, American elections are governed by the twin principles of single-member constituencies and plurality election. In other words, we elect only one person per constituency to a city council, to the House or Senate, to the local mayoralty. The candidate who gets the most votes, even if it is not the majority of 50 percent plus one, is elected. Even in those cases of multimember districts — two-, three-, or four-member state legislative districts or at-large elections of local councils or commissions — the principle is not altered.[7] One casts the same number of votes as there are officials to be elected from the district, and the plurality principle still governs. In a two-member state legislative district, for example, each voter casts two votes; the two candidates with the greatest number of votes (i.e., the plurality) are the winners. The effect is little different from that of a single-member district.

The American states have experimented scarcely at all with the systems of *proportional representation* (PR) that so often enchant the other democracies of the world. In these systems, which are of necessity based

[5] Donald S. Hecock and Henry M. Bain, *Ballot Position and Voter's Choice* (Detroit: Wayne State University Press, 1957).
[6] Jack L. Walker, "Ballot Forms and Voter Fatigue: An Analysis of the Office Block and Party Column Ballots," *Midwestern Journal of Political Science* 10 (1966): 448–63.
[7] For a good survey of the effects of various types of district, see Howard D. Hamilton, "Legislative Constituencies: Single-Member Districts, Multi-Member Districts, and Floterial Districts," *Western Political Quarterly* 20 (1967): 321–40.

on multimember constituencies, the voter casts his vote for a party slate of candidates. The parties then share the seats according to the percentage of the votes they polled. In a five-member legislative district, for example:

Party A	60% of vote	3 seats
Party B	23% of vote	1 seat
Party C	17% of vote	1 seat
	100% of vote	5 seats

The possible combinations and modifications are virtually limitless in PR systems, but those endless complexities need not concern us here.[8] What is important is the political result of proportional representation schemes of any form. First, they encourage minor political parties by giving them a share of the elective offices. Ten or 20 percent of the vote will rarely win any public offices in the plurality elections of American politics, but in the Fourth Republic of postwar France (1946–58) it won parliamentary seats and cabinet positions for a number of parties. Second, proportional representation strengthens the hand of the party vis-à-vis its candidates. In strict party list systems especially, the party fixes the order of the party list. To return to the above illustration of the five-man district under simple PR, the leadership of parties A, B, and C draw up the party list of five candidates. By placing a candidate first on the party list the leaders of a party virtually place him in public office; by placing him fifth they consign him to defeat. The prevailing single-member, plurality structure of American elections, on the contrary, reinforces both the two-party system and the independence of candidates and officeholders.

In a few instances, however, American states and localities have experimented with various exotic electoral systems. New York City adopted a variety of proportional representation from 1938 to 1947, with a resulting growth and representation of minor political parties (Table 1). The system was abandoned in 1947 after tension with the Soviet Union made the representation of the local Communist party increasingly intolerable for many New Yorkers. Perhaps the classic case of electoral exoticism has been Illinois' cumulative voting system. Since 1870 the lower house of the Illinois legislature has been elected from three-person constituencies. In order to facilitate representation of the minority party (of the two major parties), the voter is permitted to cast his or her three votes in any one of four different ways: all three for one candidate, one and a half for each of two, one for each of three, and two for one and one for another. Before the election (and the primary), party commit-

---

[8] For an excursion into some of the complexities, see Wolfgang Birke, *European Elections by Direct Suffrage* (Leyden: Sythoff, 1961). See also Douglas W. Rae, *The Political Consequences of Electoral Law* (New Haven: Yale University Press, 1967).

TABLE 1　Effects of Proportional Representation
in the New York City Council Elections: 1945

Party	Percentage of vote	Council seats	
Democratic	59	14	(61%)
Republican	15	3	(13%)
American Labor	10	2	(9%)
Communist	9	2	(9%)
Liberal	7	2	(9%)
		23	(100%)

Source　Belle Zeller and Hugh A. Bone, "The Repeal of Proportional Representation in New York
City — Ten Years in Retrospect," *American Political Science Review* 42 (1948): 1132.

tees in each of the constituencies determine whether the party in the
district will offer one, two, or three candidates for the three seats.
They often decide to contest only a total of three seats (one party offers
two candidates and the other party only one), leaving the voters of the
district no choice in the general election. The nature of the choice in the
system, in other words, has encouraged the parties to adopt cautious,
minimizing strategies that reduce competition between the two parties in
the name of securing representation for both of them.[9]

Date of the Election

In 1845 Congress chose to use its constitutional power to determine the
dates of presidential and congressional elections (Article I, Section 4;
Article II, Section 1). It provided that all states would select their presidential electors on the first Tuesday after the first Monday of November
and that the same date be used for electing members of Congress unless
the state constitution provided otherwise. For many years Maine chose
to hold congressional elections in September, but all fifty states now use
the November date. Since considerations of economy dictate that the
states hold state and local elections at the same time, they have widely

[9] The possibilities of cumulative voting have spurred a sizable scholarly literature,
including: George S. Blair, *Cumulative Voting* (Urbana: University of Illinois Press,
1960); Jack Sawyer and Duncan MacRae, "Game Theory and Cumulative Voting
in Illinois: 1902–1954," *American Political Science Review* 56 (1962): 936–46; and
James Kuklinski, "Cumulative and Plurality Voting: An Analysis of Illinois' Unique
Electoral System," *Western Political Quarterly* 26 (1973): 726–46.

accepted the same date. So uniformity in election date prevails, even though that date in this increasingly urban and industrial country was chosen originally to follow the fall harvests. No such uniformity on primary dates exists, however. Some come in April and May, some not until September. Consequently, the total campaign for public office may be six months or more in some states and two or less in others.

Election Day

The states and localities set the hours and places of elections. In most communities the polls remain open for about twelve or thirteen hours; they open between 6 and 8 A.M. and close at 7, 8, or 9 P.M. The polls usually are located in some public building — a school, a firehouse, a city hall — although they may be found in barbershops, auto showrooms, and private homes in some communities.

In each voting district, usually called the precinct, the administration of the polling place is in the hands of a group of publicly appointed judges, inspectors, or commissioners, as they are variously called. They check the voter's registration, give him ballots or see him into the voting machine, and make sure his vote is cast. Often they remain after the polls have closed to count the ballots, although centralized counting exists in some jurisdictions. The parties or candidates usually have the right to appoint poll watchers to oversee the administration of the balloting and the counting of the ballots.

Voting machines, of course, greatly facilitate the counting of ballots. Final totals are simply read off a set of dials on the back. But in many precincts the job is still a laborious one, often extending into the small hours of the morning. Weary polling officials, often after twelve hours of work at the polls, must decipher unclear marks and apply the often complicated state law on what constitutes an invalid ballot. For example, does a check mark suffice as a substitute for an X? In some states it does, and in some it does not. In a few close cases the count may be challenged, and a partial or total recounting of the ballots may result. The 1962 Minnesota gubernatorial election was in doubt for four months while a special three-man court supervised bipartisan counting officials in a recount of every paper ballot cast in the state. The Democratic candidate finally emerged a ninety-one-vote winner. That and other recounts have testified to three conclusions about the marking and counting of ballots. There has been little or no dishonesty documented, first of all. Second, honest errors in counting and recording do occur: for example, 10s become 100s, digits are inverted, the two parties' totals are reversed. Third, a significant number of voters do not correctly mark their ballots. In the 1962 election in Minnesota, for example, 389 voters voted (invalidly) for two candidates for governor, more than enough to decide the outcome that hinged on ninety-one votes.[10]

Absentee Voting

Most states have some provision for voting by people unable to come to the polls because of illness, travel, service in the armed forces, studies, or an occupation that takes them away from home. There is, however, little uniformity in the details of the provisions for absentee voting. Some states permit it only for specific reasons, some permit it only for certain elections, and some permit it only if the person has left the boundaries of the state. Congress has been under pressure to ensure the serviceman's right to an absentee ballot in the face of the reluctance of some states to provide one. After a more forceful stand during World War II, in which Congress ordered the states to provide servicemen with absentee ballots for presidential and congressional elections, Congress now merely requests the states to permit servicemen to vote.

POLITICAL CONSEQUENCES OF ELECTORAL LAW

Perhaps the broadest impact of American political institutions on the politics of campaigning has been to focus attention on the candidates rather than on the parties. The American electoral process is relatively free from institutions such as parliamentary-cabinet government or proportional representation that encourage the voter to see electoral contests in terms of the greater fortunes and future of political parties. Nonpartisan elections have even further reduced the visibility of the party in elections. Even such details of electoral law as the office-block ballot tend to structure the electoral choice as a series of contests between individual candidates and not as a single, multifaceted campaign between two great parties.

The specific components of the electoral system, therefore, do more than ensure efficiency or good government, or the carrying out of democratic norms, or protection against vote frauds. They carry grave consequences for the parties and for campaign politics in general. In the first place, they may affect the voting behavior of the electorate in the following ways:

1. All evidence suggests that the office-block ballot discourages *straight-ticket voting* and that the party-column ballot encourages it.[11] So,

[10] On recounts, see Ronald F. Stinnett and Charles H. Backstrom, *Recount* (Washington: National Document Publishers, 1964); Samuel J. Eldersveld and A. A. Applegate, *Michigan's Recounts for Governor, 1950 and 1952: A Systematic Analysis of Election Error* (Ann Arbor: University of Michigan Press, 1954).

[11] Angus Campbell et al., *The American Voter* (New York: Wiley, 1960), p. 276.

too, do other electoral details, such as the presence of a party circle or square on the ballot.

2. *Voter fatigue* (or roll-off), the tendency to vote in only some of the contests on the ballot, appears to be in large part the result of the ballot itself. It is greater in areas using the office-block ballot, and it tends to be greater the longer the ballot. The arrangement of the face of the voting machine will also affect it. Studies in the Minneapolis area show, for example, that in those eighteen communities with voting machines in the election of November 1966, only 33.9 to 78.3 percent of the voters voted on a constitutional amendment up for ratification; but in seventeen communities with paper ballots the percentages varied between 92.2 and 100.[12]

3. Every ballot form discourages *write-in voting*, but some discourage it more than others. It is especially difficult on most voting machines; even so small a detail as whether or not the state permits the use of stickers as a way of writing in a candidate's name may be significant.

Such impacts on the voting responses of the electorates to whom the parties and their candidates must appeal obviously affect the parties and the campaign strategies.

The electoral system, however, may have a *direct* impact on the parties and campaign strategy. The states may limit the access of minor parties and their candidates to the ballot by requiring them to file petitions with large numbers of signatures. Electoral systems such as Illinois' cumulative voting, rare though they may be in the United States, drastically alter the nature of the campaign and choices in it; that particular system, paradoxically, has increased the party role in the election by forcing it to decide what number of the three seats in the constituency to contest while at the same time effectively reducing the amount of two-party competition. Even ordinary multimember constituencies invite a party of limited strength to concentrate its voting strength on a single candidate by voting for him and no other candidate (a practice widely referred to as bullet voting).

Most important, the details of American electoral law often do not touch the parties or candidates equally. If voting machines confuse less well-educated, lower SES voters, and if office-block ballots encourage greater voter fatigue (roll-off) among less-educated voters,[13] then the disadvantages may accrue unevenly to the Democratic party. And if the

[12] *Minneapolis Star*, April 11, 1967. The story reports research findings by the Citizens' League of Hennepin and Ramsey Counties. Following that report, the 1967 Minnesota legislature required local governments to put reminders on the machines to alert voters to the amendments. In a subsequent referendum in 1970 the average in voting machine communities went up to 84 percent. It remained at 96 percent in the others.

[13] Walker, "Ballot Forms and Voter Fatigue," makes the latter point.

state refuses absentee ballots to businessmen away on business, the disadvantages may strike mainly the Republicans. Any ballot form that facilitates party-ticket voting works to the advantage of the majority party
in the constituency. And prime ballot position helps the incumbent and
the majority party; so do designations of incumbency printed on the
ballot. Even the hours and places for polling may have some marginal
benefits for one party or the other.

Just how aware the parties and state legislators are of the possible advantages in refining electoral law is not easy to say. It is always difficult
to establish the motives of legislators, especially when those motives may
not be of the highest. But occasionally an attempt is just too persistent,
too transparent, not to reveal the motives of party or political advantage.
Jack L. Walker, for example, comments on Ohio's continuing evolution
of the ballot form:

> In the state of Ohio the ballot has been changed six times during the twen-
> tieth century, and in each case the Republican majority tried to gain an ad-
> vantage for itself by tampering with the election machinery. In 1940 Governor
> Bricker tried to avoid the influences of F.D.R.'s "coattails" by calling a spe-
> cial session of the legislature which approved a separation of the ballot carry-
> ing national races from the one on which state and local races appeared.
> Bricker reasoned that if a normally Republican voter who was determined to
> vote for Roosevelt had to use a second ballot in state races he would be less
> likely to vote a straight Democratic ticket (the ballots were later consolidated
> once again to capitalize on Eisenhower's coattails). In 1949 over $85,000 was
> spent in a campaign to substitute the Office Block ballot for the Party Column
> ballot in an effort to save Senator Robert Taft from defeat in the bitter 1950
> election. . . . The Taft forces thought that by eliminating the party lever they
> would substantially reduce the number of straight Democratic votes and thus
> increase the Senator's chances among normally Democratic, working class
> voters. Key quotes Taft as claiming that the change "was responsible 'for
> something between 100,000 and 200,000' of his total majority of 430,000." [14]

Finally, in one way above all — the drawing of constituency lines —
the American parties have tried repeatedly to steal an advantage in electoral politics. The general tactics have traditionally been two: constituencies of unequal populations and gerrymandered districts. The first and
more obvious of the two, the districts of unequal populations, simply
involved stretching the popular vote of the majority party by putting
fewer people in districts in its strongholds than in the districts located
in the other party's areas of strength. In the past the heavily populated
districts were usually in urban areas, working to the disadvantage of Republicans in the South and Democrats elsewhere. However, in 1952 the
Supreme Court put an end to these inequities. As the courts have applied
the "one man, one vote" rule to constituencies of all varieties, they have

[14] Ibid., pp. 448–49.

A Gerrymander in New York

Usually the gerrymander is easily identifiable by its bizarre shape. The legislative straining for political effect often violates the traditional criteria of "compact and contiguous" districting. The odd outlines invite the observer to see in them all manner of fantastic creatures. State legislatures have, in fact, beginning with Gerry's salamander, produced a veritable political bestiary. The reader can make what he will of the shape of New York's Twelfth Congressional District in the 1950s, but its explanation is less a matter of fantasy:

"There are very few Republicans in Brooklyn, and distributed in ordinarily shaped districts they would never make a majority anywhere. But the Republican legislature strung G.O.P. areas into a district winding through the borough, and the result was Republican victories until this year."

Anthony Lewis, *New York Times,* November 27, 1960.

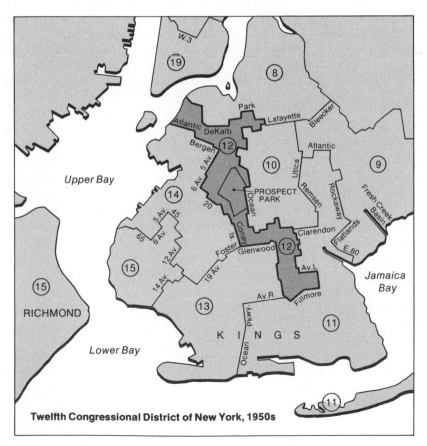

Twelfth Congressional District of New York, 1950s

closed off an indigenously American way of exploiting the rules of the electoral game.[15] The consequences of reapportionment depend on the specific districts being reapportioned. But in the one kind of district that had earlier been the most seriously malapportioned, the state legislative district, reapportionment has on the whole increased Democratic representation.[16]

More subtle and less easy to detect, the gerrymander survives unimpaired. It consists of one party's drawing district lines in such a way as to use its own popular vote most efficiently while forcing the other party to use its vote inefficiently. That goal can be achieved in one of two ways: either by dividing and diluting pockets of the other party's strength to prevent it from winning office, or (if the other party's strength is too great for dilution) by bunching its strength into a few districts and forcing it to win elections by large, wasteful majorities. Frequently but not always, the resulting constituencies, instead of being compact and contiguous, have bizarre and fanciful shapes. (The term "gerrymander" was coined in the early years of the Republic to describe a salamander-shaped congressional district drawn in Massachusetts when Elbridge Gerry was governor.) Which party reaps the advantage of the gerrymander depends entirely on which party controls the legislature that draws the district lines.[17]

CAMPAIGN STRATEGY

The folk wisdom about all aspects of American politics is more than ample, but on the subject of campaign tactics it is overwhelming. Much of it has been brought together into little books on campaigning that read like modern how-to-do-it manuals.[18] Since many of the recent books have been written by advertising and public relations specialists, much of the wisdom has a modern tone. Candidates are advised on dress and make-up for TV, and there is a good deal of emphasis on catchy phrases and slogans.

There is much of value in the assorted wisdom about American campaigning. Generally it represents the distillation of concrete experience.

---

[15] Especially for the political ramifications of apportionment, see Malcolm E. Jewell (ed.), *The Politics of Reapportionment* (New York: Atherton, 1962).
[16] Robert S. Erikson, "The Partisan Impact of State Legislative Reapportionment," *Midwest Journal of Political Science* 15 (1971): 57–71.
[17] For an objective measure of gerrymandering, see Ernest C. Reock, Jr., "Measuring Compactness as a Requirement of Legislative Apportionment," *Midwest Journal of Political Science* 5 (1961): 70–74.
[18] For some recent examples of the how-to-do-it genre, see Edward Schwartzman, *Campaign Craftsmanship: A Professional's Guide to Campaigning for Elective Office* (New York: Universe, 1973); Joe Napolitan, *The Election Game and How To Win It* (Garden City: Doubleday, 1972); and Dick W. Simpson, *Winning Elections: A Handbook in Participatory Politics* (Chicago: Swallow, 1972).

And yet it suffers from two deficiencies that themselves are general warnings about the crafts of political campaigning. The conventional wisdom seems to suggest, first of all, that most political campaigns are run on a master battle plan adhered to with almost military discipline and precision. In reality most American political campaigns lurch along from one improvisation to another, from one immediate crisis to another. They are frequently underorganized, underplanned, and understaffed — and consequently, often played by ear on a surprising lack of information.

The folk wisdom also suggests that there are principles of good campaigning that have an almost universal applicability. In truth, however, optimum campaign strategy depends on a great number of variables, and the only general rule is that there is no general rule. Strategy will vary with the following:

1. *The skills of the candidate:* Does he or she project well on television? How does he handle a press conference or an informal coffee hour?
2. *The nature of the constituency:* Is it several square miles of urban slum or 30,000 square miles of prairie?
3. *The office being sought:* Is it a city councillorship or perhaps a judgeship, which will call for a far more restrained campaign?
4. *The nature of the electoral system:* Is the ballot partisan or nonpartisan? Is the general election two or six months after the primary?
5. *The party organizations in the constituency:* To what extent can their organized resources be counted on? What can they do?
6. *The availability of political resources:* What manpower, skills, and money will be available and when?
7. *The nature of the electorate:* What are the electorate's political norms, party loyalties, perception of issues and candidates? What political styles and tactics do they approve?

There are, of course, other factors. But the chief early task of campaign strategists is the sober evaluation of these variables and of the consequent demands and limits they place on the nature of the campaign.

It is not only campaign situations that differ. So also do candidates and the way they "see" the voters as well as the structure of the campaign and election. Candidates generally seem to believe that campaigns do affect election outcomes, and most of them are tireless campaigners who — not entirely sure of what will "work" in the campaign — spend every available hour and resource trying every conceivable ploy. One study suggests, however, that candidates do differ in their perceptions of what kinds of appeals voters respond to. Winning candidates saw voters as more influenced by issues and candidates, while losers saw them more responsive to party appeals. Candidates may even differ in their understanding of the problem of putting together a majority. The same study found that Democratic candidates tended more than Republicans to see coalitions built of interest groups and organizations rather than individuals.[19] If campaign strategy is essentially a matter of problem solving, then the candidates differ in their understanding of the problem.

The nub of the strategic problem in a campaign is selectivity in the expenditure of scarce time, energy, and resources in order to achieve the maximum effect on the electorate. For a candidate to spread his resources evenly over a constituency is, in effect, no strategy at all. He and his managers must decide how to spend each unit of campaign resources so that it will return the maximum number of votes. Will they work on areas normally loyal to the other party in hopes of cutting losses there, or will they hammer at the party strongholds? They must also decide how to tailor their appeals to different parts of the electorate. For some of the voters there must be stimuli to party loyalty; for others, appeals of issue or personality. The problem is to know the variety and diversity of the voters, the likely bases of their decisions, and the ways of reaching and stimulating them differentially.[20]

The candidate must make these strategic allocations in the face of all kinds of uncertainties and problems.

1. Money and the other resources for the campaign will very likely be in short supply. (Problems of money in elective politics will be considered in Chapter 13.)
2. Information on the efficacy of various campaign techniques will be sharply limited. Given the present state of the art, it is virtually impossible to tell whether a day of coffee parties or a day of handshaking on the street will be more effective — or when it is better to spend $500 on billboards than on a newspaper ad.
3. The campaign will surely confront intractable "givens," about which one can do little. The local press, for example, may be committed to the other candidate and may freeze him out of the publicity he needs.
4. The candidate also will need allies in the campaign, and they will have interests and strategies of their own. Interest groups or other political groups or individuals, for instance, may want assurances on specific issues or programs.

---

[19] John W. Kingdon, *Candidates for Office* (New York: Random House, 1968). It is very possible that the different perceptions of group politics reflect real differences in party traditions.
[20] A number of writers have suggested that the problem of campaign strategy can be approached through "maximization" models such as those of game theory. For example, see John H. Kessel, "A Game Theory Analysis of Campaign Strategy," in M. Kent Jennings and L. Harmon Zeigler (eds.), *The Electoral Process* (Englewood Cliffs: Prentice-Hall, 1966), pp. 290–304. For a more general approach to campaign strategy, see Lewis A. Froman's essay, "A Realistic Approach to Campaign Strategies and Tactics," in the same volume, pp. 1–20.

There is, in other words, uncertainty about the electorate, about the usefulness of the campaign techniques, about the availability of resources, and about the strategies of both the candidate's allies and his opponents. Small wonder that "rational," orderly planning is especially rare in political campaigns.

Actually, the political characteristics of the election race probably do more to set the limits of campaign strategy than any other factors. The presence or absence of an incumbent in the race and the competitiveness of the constituency exceed in significance all other considerations. Those two factors, perhaps, determine whether there is a possibility of victory. They affect the ability of the candidate to recruit workers and resources, to line up the support of groups (which usually have a taste for joining winners), and to attract the attention of voters.[21] In other words, the fact that a candidate is an incumbent running for reelection in a competitive district or a nonincumbent of the losing party in a noncompetitive district, for example, sets some major limits on and imperatives for campaign strategy before the imagination of the candidate and his advisors even begin to work.

THE NEW CAMPAIGNING

Within the past generation, changes amounting to a revolution have altered much of American political campaigning. The skills of the mass media specialists have brought new persuasive techniques to bear on the American electorate — with attendant fears that presidents and lesser officials are now sold to the electorate much as Madison Avenue sells a new mouthwash or toothpaste. And with the new techniques have come the new technicians: the campaign management specialists, a new breed of sophisticated, hard-headed advisors, who as political mercenaries deploy their troops and artillery for a suitable fee.

The archetype of this variety of professional campaign organization in recent years has been Spencer-Roberts, Inc., of Los Angeles, which has been prominent in a number of recent California contests, especially Ronald Reagan's primary and general election campaigns for the governorship of the state in 1966 and 1970. (The fee was reported to be in excess of $100,000.) The assets of an organization like Spencer-Roberts are many and impressive. They have a detached professionalism and experience; they are familiar with the arts of advertising, public relations, and the mass media; they have extensive mailing lists of Republican activists and loyalists in California; and they have good ties to local Republican workers and luminaries. The scope of the firm's operations can best be seen by describing their exertions on behalf of Nelson Rocke-

[21] See David A. Leuthold, *Electioneering in a Democracy* (New York: Wiley, 1968).

feller in the 1964 presidential primary in California. In that election the Goldwater forces had almost completely tied up the regular Republican organization.

With absolutely zero troops of their own to start with, Spencer-Roberts had to use money to recruit troops; by opening 40 to 50 Rockefeller headquarters across the state (6 in Los Angeles alone) to show the flag and banner where moderate volunteers might rally; by publishing a newsletter whose circulation rose from 4,500 to 25,000 in a few months; by direct-mail techniques; by billboards, advertisements, television and the drenching of radio, which in automobile-happy California has a dimension of its own.[22]

In addition, Spencer-Roberts organized local committees for Rockefeller, made all the arrangements for local rallies and handshaking receptions, and set up phone campaigns to reach registered Republicans shortly before the primary date. On major matters of strategy it apparently dealt directly with Rockefeller's New York advisors.

Spencer-Roberts demonstrated its sheer size in 1968 by its involvement in thirty or more campaigns. A good share of those were races for Congress, an involvement which represented the confidence of the Republican Congressional Campaign Committee. By then Spencer-Roberts was aided by its subsidiary organization, Datamatics, which specializes in computer applications of the new campaign technology.

The entire profession of campaign management is by now a crowded one. (It has its own professional association with periodic conventions for the exchange of professional information.) Firms and specialists come in all sizes and shapes. Some are all-purpose organizations such as Spencer-Roberts, which can plan the campaign from the decision to enter through the election-night victory (or condolence) party. Others limit themselves to particular specialties, such as opinion polling or producing tapes for television.[23] But to some extent there is little really new in politics. Much of the new art is a streamlining and sophistication of old campaigning practices. It is generally a more efficient attack on the old demands of any campaign: the assembling of information and the persuading of voters.

New Sources of Information

The development of modern social science has opened up new sources of information and knowledge to the candidate. Computers and data-

---

[22] Theodore H. White, *The Making of the President 1964* (New York: Atheneum, 1965), p. 127.
[23] For a comprehensive survey of the new technicians, see the *Congressional Quarterly* for April 5, 1968. Among the many recent books on the subject see Robert Agranoff (ed.), *The New Style in Election Campaigns* (Boston: Holbrook, 1972); the introductory essay by Agranoff is especially useful.

processing systems permit a party to keep records about constituencies and to process that information rapidly. Carefully kept records usually yield a faster and more accurate answer to "how the twenty-first ward went four years ago" than do even the most conscientious party committeepersons. Then, too, wily parties and candidates have similarly used the scholarly data and findings on the demographic bases of Republican and Democratic strength. The managers of John F. Kennedy's presidential campaign commissioned a simulation of the 1960 electorate as an aid to campaign planning. The simulation attempted, with the aid of computers, to coordinate and correlate knowledge about the American electorate and to project the effects that various events of the campaign might have on it.[24] Other candidates have computerized records of canvasing so that they can quickly compile lists of voters to contact on election day.

No new avenue to political knowledge, however, has been more fully exploited than the public opinion poll. It may be employed at the beginning of a campaign to assess the political issues uppermost in the minds of voters. Questions about leading public issues, about awareness of current problems, or about what issues the voter thinks or worries about will indicate which themes the candidates should develop for greatest effectiveness. Early polls can also develop candidate profiles, information about the way the voting public views the two opponents. If it is found that many voters think a candidate too bookish or intellectual, he may be sent to plowing contests, athletic events, or a weekend fishing trip. Polls can also indicate whether the campaign ought to capitalize on party loyalties or whether the candidate would be better advised to divorce himself from an unpopular party or a presidential or gubernatorial candidate at the top of the ticket. During the campaign a poll or two can chart its progress and impact; it may also indicate where time and resources ought to be concentrated in the waning days of the campaign.

Parties and candidates have not been uniformly willing to avail themselves of such new techniques. Much of the knowledge thus far accumulated, especially of voting behavior, derives chiefly from presidential campaigns and elections and has only limited applicability. Also, many of the techniques are beyond the resources of local campaigns. But the difficulty runs deeper. American political campaigns, despite popular impressions to the contrary, have rarely been run on a solid base of information. Thousands of party organizations around the country never have kept even basic voting data by precincts, wards, townships, cities, and counties. Frequently, what passes for such information are the hazy impressions of a few party officials. So, such a shift to the "new knowl-

[24] Described in Ithiel de Sola Pool, Robert P. Abelson, and Samuel Popkin, *Candidates, Issues, and Strategies* (Cambridge: MIT Press, 1964). A fictionalized version can be found in Eugene Burdick, *The 480* (New York: McGraw-Hill, 1964).

edge" involves a basic commitment to knowledge itself, as well as a willingness to bear the costs of the new knowledge.

New Techniques of Persuasion

Campaigns are basically exercises in mass persuasion, and increasingly the commercial arts of persuasion have been applied to them. There was a time when strong party organizations were the great persuaders in American campaigns, but changes in them and in American politics have diminished that role. Party organizations, even those that continue in something like the form of earlier days, do not "control" votes and turn them out as they once did. And yet they have not been quick to pick up new campaign and communication skills. Into the vacuum have come skilled candidates, their advisors and personal staffs, and the firms specializing in the management of political campaigns.

Predominant among the new techniques is the increasing role of the mass communications media. Frequently now a candidate takes the time and effort to address a rally or meeting largely in the hope that it will produce a news report or a brief film clip on the local TV news. (Of course, the question of whether it produces a news report is not left to chance; the staff prepares news releases and copies of the speech for the local media.) But often candidates have to buy their time and space in the media. Early in the campaign, candidates may vie to commit choice TV time and billboard space for the concluding weeks of the campaign. And as the campaign progresses, the candidates' faces, names, and slogans blossom on billboards, newspaper ads, radio and TV spot announcements — even on lawn signs, automobile bumpers, and construction fences. Full TV or radio coverage of a speech is usually an extravagant waste of money, but candidates may take longer media time for talkathons or "open mike" shows, in which they answer the questions and challenges of all comers.

But to some extent the new techniques are simply new applications of old techniques. Direct mailings, for example, have become increasingly sophisticated means for raising money and reaching voters. In the 1972 presidential campaign of Richard Nixon:

Computers sliced up the nation's census tracts into patterns; the storefront operators in the counties that Malek [Fred Malek of the Committee for the Re-Election of the President] had "prioritized" had identified independents, wavering Democrats and "don't knows"; the 250 telephone batteries in ten key states had poured other names into the computer. And by the end of October the computer was taking over — there would be in the last week eight million "mailgrams" to the nine largest states, cut and coded by county, by age, by income, by Spanish-speaking, by black, by ethnic origin, plus 9,000,000 letters to Republicans. A computer software firm in Texas cut the tapes; mail-list houses around the country sorted names; the Donnelley plant in Chicago printed and mailed — 17,000,000 pieces in all, in the largest single roundhouse swing by mail in American politics.[25]

Indeed, the new techniques may be no more revolutionary than a new hair style or wardrobe, or perhaps a Dale Carnegie course, for the candidate. Or they may be only a new emphasis on a theme or slogan for the campaign. Often, that is, the new campaigning may be little more than a new application of old advertising wisdom about reaching audiences and consumers.

Nelson Rockefeller's campaigns for public office perhaps represent the acme of the new campaigning. His 1966 campaign for the governorship of New York — then called the most expensive nonpresidential campaign in American political history — cost at least $6 million. The campaign, run by a staff of at least 300, put between 3,000 and 4,000 television commercials on the stations of the state.[26] In 1968 his expenditures totaled $8 million — a good deal of it in polling and media charges — in the preconvention search for the Republican nomination. His race for another term in the governorship in 1970 topped his own 1966 record with an outgo modestly estimated at $10 million, making *it* the most expensive campaign. The campaign employed almost continuous polling, a budget of a million and a half for television, and enough brochures, buttons, and broadsides to furnish about three pieces for every voter in the state. Not surprisingly, the Rockefeller campaigns have been the most commented upon nonpresidential elections in American political history (see box on The Rockefeller Campaigns).

All of this is not to argue that the traditional campaign techniques are obsolete. Handshaking on the streets and in the stores, speeches before anyone who will listen, endorsements by local groups and party organizations — all of the old ways are very much alive. The new campaigning is too expensive for many candidates; a minute of prime TV time for a political spot announcement can easily cost $500, and a large billboard in a good city location may well cost the same figure per month. Also, these techniques are inefficient for many local candidates; the radio, television, billboard, and newspaper space they purchase is wasted in great part on readers, viewers, and listeners who cannot vote for them.

Consequently, the new style of American political campaigning has been unevenly used. It is probably employed most often in the campaigns of better financed candidates for state and national office and less often by the candidates for local offices, especially in the less concentrated electorates of the rural areas. At the same time, there is also some reason

---

[25] Theodore H. White, *The Making of the President 1972* (New York: Bantam, 1973), p. 437.
[26] See also James Perry, *The New Politics* (New York: Potter, 1968).

The Rockefeller Campaigns: A Portion and a Commentary

One of the more admired of the Rockefeller TV spots in the 1966 campaign for the New York governorship was entitled "Road to Hawaii." James Perry called it "classic in its simplicity."

Video	Audio
1. *A stretch of road, as viewed from camera mounted on hood of car. Dotted white lines whip by.*	1. *(Road sounds)*
2. *Road whips by.*	2. *(Road sounds under)* — ANNCR *(voice off):* If you took all the roads Governor Rockefeller has built, and all the roads he's widened and straightened and smoothed out . . . if you took all these roads, and laid them end to end, they'd stretch all the way to . . . Hawaii.
3. *Car stops abruptly; covering road ahead, sand.*	3. *(Sound of breakers and Hawaiian music)*
4. *Car backs up, swings around and proceeds forward.*	4. All the way to Hawaii . . .
5. *Remainder of commercial same road is seen, same dotted white line whips by.*	5. . . . and all the way back. *(Road sounds up)*
6. *Super:* A paid political announcement by Friends of the Rockefeller team.	

Taken from *The New Politics* by James M. Perry. © 1968 by James M. Perry. Used with permission of Clarkson N. Potter, Inc.

"Rockefeller must be pouring money into his campaign. I'm beginning to feel an urge to vote for him."

Drawing by Dana Fradon; © 1970 The New Yorker Magazine, Inc.

to think that both party committees and candidate organizations have become more proficient themselves in the new skills and less reliant, therefore, on the professional practitioners. To that extent we may simply be observing the usual process of the diffusion of knowledge.[27]

TO WHAT EFFECT THE CAMPAIGN?

More than one candidate, whether his campaign is old or new style, has wondered about the impact of the campaign's sound and fury. The barrage of words and pictures is staggering, but is anyone listening or watching? Do the spot commercials, the literature, even the canvasing make any difference in the ultimate voting decision? No one really knows for sure.

Logical deduction leads one to some plausible and probably reliable answers. We know that American voters expose themselves to the campaign with great selectivity. First of all, they tend to surround themselves with friends, literature, mass media reports, and even personal experience (such as rallies and meetings) that support their perceptions and loyalties. They tend, furthermore, to perceive what they are exposed to in terms of stable, long-term values, the most stable of which appears to be their loyalty to a political party. Therefore, what we think of as a campaign may to some extent be two campaigns — one party and its candidates shouting at their supporters and the other doing the same. And thus, a good deal of American campaigning has the effect of stimulating, activating, and reinforcing given political predispositions. Far less of it achieves any political conversions. And much of it, too, is directed more to getting people out to vote than to influencing their voting decision.

We can also make some deductions about the impact of campaigns just from the data we have about the exposure of the voter to them. Only a minority of the American adult public reports being contacted by a party worker in presidential election campaigns; for example, only 29 percent report being approached by one of the parties in the 1972 campaign. Media exposure, on the other hand, reaches the great majority of the electorate. Interviewed after the 1972 campaign was past, 57 percent of the respondents reported reading about the campaign in newspapers. Significantly, 88 percent of the respondents watched at least one program about the campaign on TV.[28]

---

[27] At the least, the media now take the professionals more for granted. The flood of articles about them has abated, and *Congressional Quarterly* also appears to have abandoned its reporting of them.

[28] The data of this paragraph come from the Survey Research Center of the University of Michigan; they were made available through the services of the Inter-University Consortium for Political Research. Since the postelection interviews were secured with a reduced subset of the original sample, it is probable that these percentages overstate the experience of the total electorate.

Therefore, most American electoral campaigns are carried on by limited means within limited ranges of attention and perception. And even if it does "reach" a voter, the campaign may not dent his fixed and stable loyalties to a candidate, party, or attitude. Moreover, events outside the campaign — wars, depressions, inflation — may have a far greater impact than the campaign on voting decisions. Therefore, one cannot expect even the most dazzling campaign to achieve a full measure of persuasiveness, for it is a political universe and not a college debating society to which it is directed.

Beyond these generalizations documenting the impact of a campaign is extremely difficult. For one thing, there are all manner of methodological difficulties. The "campaign" is a whole congeries of events and activities; some of them are the activities of the parties and candidates, and some are not. Consequently, it is difficult to say just what part of the total impact can be attributed to any part of the total "campaign." It is also difficult to determine what part of the campaign the individual voter has been aware of and how he or she has perceived it.

Have we, then, no empirical knowledge of the effects of the campaign? Two studies have indicated that personal contacts activate political apathetics more often than mailed propaganda does and that door-to-door canvasing is more successful in affecting voting decisions than telephone calls.[29] The settings of both studies, however, were local elections in which voter turnout and information were low. Other research has shown in varying degrees of conclusiveness that traditional precinct work by party committeepersons does have an impact on voting, producing from a 5 to 10 percent change in the expected or usual party vote. The research suggests further that the effect of precinct work may well be greater in local elections than in media-centered presidential ones. In local elections there are apt to be fewer alternative cues and sources of information.[30] Those conclusions are buttressed by another set of findings that precinct canvasing in a presidential campaign increases turnout but has little effect on voter choice.[31] Finally, recent scholarship finds that active local party organization (before, during, and after the campaign) is associated with a vote increase over the expected norm,[32] and

[29] Samuel J. Eldersveld, "Experimental Propaganda Techniques and Voting Behavior," *American Political Science Review* 50 (1956): 154–65; and John C. Blydenburgh, "A Controlled Experiment to Measure the Effects of Personal Contact Campaigning," *Midwest Journal of Political Science* 15 (1971): 365–81.

[30] Phillips Cutright and Peter H. Rossi, "Grass Roots Politicians and the Vote," *American Sociological Review* 23 (1958): 171–79; Daniel Katz and Samuel J. Eldersveld, "The Impact of Local Party Activity upon the Electorate," *Public Opinion Quarterly* 25 (1961): 1–24; Raymond E. Wolfinger, "The Influence of Precinct Work on Voting Behavior," *Public Opinion Quarterly* 27 (1963): 387–98.

[31] Gerald H. Kramer, "The Effects of Precinct-Level Canvassing on Voter Behavior," *Public Opinion Quarterly* 34 (1970): 560–72.

[32] William J. Crotty, "Party Effort and Its Impact on the Vote," *American Political Science Review* 65 (1971): 439–50.

that specific strategic decisions in campaigns (in this case the decision of some Republican congressional candidates not to associate themselves with Barry Goldwater in 1964) also have an effect on the vote.[33]

To summarize briefly, there are indications that the campaign is more successful in stimulating turnout than in affecting vote. (If that is the case, the implications favor campaigning only among one's probable supporters.) Furthermore, the efficacy of only one kind of campaigning — face-to-face personal contact — seems established, and that appears to be successful under limited circumstances. We know very little about the effectiveness of other techniques, much less about their comparative value. We also have one bit of evidence that campaign strategies do matter. And we have considerable evidence that scholars have a very difficult time measuring the events and techniques of the campaign, and an even harder time accounting for their impact on the electorate. And that is it. For all its vaunted efficiency the new campaign management fraternity has not yet been able to help with any answers.

CAMPAIGN ORGANIZATION

Some American political campaigns are run from under the hat of the candidate. He or she may raise funds (often on his own local credit rating), write his own speeches and press releases, drive his own car from speech to speech. These one-person campaigns are found chiefly in small constituencies, in rural areas, and for less noted offices — for example, the campaign of a rural candidate for state legislator or unimportant county office. A more common and perhaps the modal campaign organization in American politics includes the candidate, the campaign manager, perhaps an office manager, and a small number of faithful political friends, who devote part of their time to major campaign tasks. Together they constitute something of a general council for the campaign. Candidates adopt these modest campaign organizations for one or both of the following reasons: First, an organization costs dearly, and many candidates cannot afford it. Second, for many offices and political cultures, campaigning does not require a large organization; minimal campaigning demands only minimal organization.

The other extreme is the complex campaign organization with full bureaucratic panoply. In its "ideal," textbook form it is headed by a full-time campaign manager, who presides over the functional units that make up the rest of the campaign organization. A research staff examines the political characteristics of the constituency, researches the stands and speeches of the opponent, prepares material for the candidate's speeches, and oversees the gathering of information during the campaign. Can-

[33] Robert A. Schoenberger, "Campaign Strategy and Party Loyalty: The Electoral Relevance of Candidate Decision-Making in the 1964 Congressional Elections," *American Political Science Review* 63 (1969): 515–20.

vasers, often a veritable army of them recruited by the party organization, visit or telephone voters. A speakers' bureau may be necessary to
provide speakers in addition to the candidate. A small group of public
relations and mass media specialists prepares press releases, ads for the
media, and printed literature, and handles the relationships with representatives of the media. A finance committee, possibly supplemented by
a treasurer, centralizes the raising of funds, the budgeting of expenditures, the paying of bills, and the keeping of records. Finally, a bureaucracy of a few secretaries and staff people maintains the candidate's
headquarters, answers the phone and mail, and organizes large mailings.

These full-scale, maximum campaign organizations are certainly not
the norm in American politics. For some campaigns, they must be desirable; for others, they would be organizational overkill. But even when
desirable, for many campaigns a shortage of resources prevents their
establishment. Also, in some instances, they have been replaced by the
organizations of campaign management firms. The candidate with sufficient resources may find it easier to rent a campaign organization. Regardless of the form the campaign organization takes, in most campaigns
the key person remains the campaign manager. Most candidates find it
necessary to shift the burden of directing the campaign so that their
time, energy, and concentration can be spent on the campaign itself.

The larger, the more complex the campaign apparatus, ironically, the
greater the danger of the endemic "disorganization" that marks American campaign organizations. The candidate, his own political following
and friends, the activists of the party organization, the financial contributors, the fund raisers, and the campaign staff all may have different
incentives for participating and different views of what the campaign
should be. What we call "the campaign" may in fact be a number of
campaigns only loosely bound together in a common effort. Many of
the components of the campaign may indeed be pursuing their own
interests, whether they be of ideology, influence, or visibility. A good
deal of time and effort must be paid — often by the candidate — to
integrate and satisfy all segments of the campaign. The candidate may
have to tailor his stands and appeals to satisfy them. And many campaign speeches and statements are beamed more at the campaign organization, or parts of it, than at the broader electorate. Taken as a whole,
however disparate, the campaign organization itself constitutes one of
the major demands on the campaign, its themes, its tone, and its style.

THE PARTY ORGANIZATION'S ROLE

The campaign for the House of Commons in Great Britain is in the
hands of 630 Labour party and 630 Conservative party election "agents."
The parties employ the agents, train them in the direction of campaigns,

and place them in the individual constituencies as managers of the local campaigns for Parliament. English law buttresses their authority by making them legally responsible for the observance of all election laws and for the management of all moneys spent in the campaigns. The parties, therefore, are guaranteed a guiding role in the parliamentary campaigns.

Not so the American party organizations. Nothing, either of law or tradition, assures them even a prominent place in the campaign. They must compete constantly for a role in it, just as they fought to control the nominations. Their adversaries in this struggle are would-be independent candidates, the ad hoc, personal campaign organizations they are wont to create, and the new professional managers of campaigns. Although the realities of American politics force the candidate to run under party symbols that will help him attract the votes of a party electorate, nothing forces him to let the party organization control or even participate in the campaign.

In some parts of the country, however, the party organization still retains assets that make it indispensable for the campaign. If it can command the armies of local workers, it can provide the candidate with a campaign vehicle (or medium) that costs him little while ensuring success. These organizational campaigns occur chiefly in one-party urban areas in which parties control primaries and voters habitually vote the party ticket in the general election. Canvasing and turning out the vote are still relevant there. Furthermore, the urban candidate is much more apt to have been nominated by the party organization through its control of the primary and thus to be its creature in the general election campaign.

Yet, when they can, candidates find it strategically useful to rely on a separate campaign organization composed of friends, followers, and nonparty groups. A personal organization may draw on the time and money of people who are chary of party ties or who consider themselves of the "other" party. It enables the candidate to draw support on the basis of his own personality and charisma. It permits a campaign that surmounts party lines both in its organization and in its impact. Finally, by running his own campaign (and paying for it), the candidate remains free of debt to and hence dependence on the party organization.

And vis-à-vis the party organization the candidate has built-in advantages in competing for control of campaigns. The sheer number of campaigns, coupled with the feebleness of many party organizations, has forced those organizations to surrender control of the campaigns by default. Electoral institutions, from the direct primary to the office-block ballot, have been on the side of the candidates, and so have the political norms of many sections of the American electorate. Furthermore, the candidate now has in his favor a whole new set of campaigning skills for which he does not have to depend on the party organization. Some fifty or sixty years ago the party organizations came close to monopolizing the knowledge, skills, and manpower necessary for a successful campaign. They do so no longer; new sources of knowledge, skills, and manpower are for hire.

It is probably a mistake to conclude, as have some of its victims, that a new-style campaign is indispensable. Campaigns in the Shapp and Rockefeller manner are still very much the exceptions — at least in the magnitude of their reliance on the new knowledge and techniques. It is still possible for the careful candidate to win elections without important help from either the party organization or the media specialists. Many candidates, indeed, are as suspicious of the new practitioners as they are of the party organization. Listen to the campaign manager of a successful congressional candidate:

During our first campaign, some fellows from big P.R. outfits who live out here came around and volunteered their time and their talents. We talked with them and looked at the campaign material they'd put together, and we were scared witless. As far as they were concerned, facts and statistics were simply things to be changed. . . . Basically, the P.R. approach is different. Politics has a deeply negative quality. We're convinced that most people vote against somebody. . . . And that's what we concentrate on — making them vote against our opponent. The P.R. crowd feel they have to sell something positively. . . . We believe in being amateurish. Our brochures look as if they were got up in our basement. But the P.R. men want to put out four-color brochures with dazzling artwork and their idea of how the Gettysburg Address should have read.[34]

All one can say at the present is that the new skills are far more often thrown on the side of the candidate than the party organization. That tends to be true whether they modestly supplement a conventional campaign or shape one largely in their image.

The interests of the candidate and of the party organization in the campaign never completely converge. That is the basic truth behind their struggle for its control. The candidate, unless he has been dragooned to fill a ticket in a lost cause, takes himself and his candidacy seriously. Even the longest shot among candidates tends to think he will win; the degree of his ego involvement in the campaign almost demands it. The party, on the other hand, wants to be selective in its use of campaign resources. It may see some races as lost; these candidates it may be glad to turn loose for their own independent campaigns. Party organizations want to set overall priorities and allocations of scarce resources; they want to eliminate the inefficient and uneconomical parts of the

[34] Richard Harris, "How's It Look?" New Yorker, April 8, 1967, p. 63. The article presents an excellent case study of a congressional campaign that relied neither on party organization nor on the new techniques and specialists.

campaign. Furthermore, the party organization by its nature campaigns to activate party loyalty, and candidates may not care to. It may also want to protect a platform and a program, help a presidential or gubernatorial candidate, or win control of a legislature. But these need not be the goals and interests of individual candidates.

To be sure, there are potent advantages to a party-led series of campaigns on behalf of an entire ticket. Such planning can eliminate the embarrassment and futility of two candidates' competing for audiences in the same small town. It can distribute campaign literature for a number of candidates at the same time. And it alone can mount the major election-day activities: setting up operation headquarters, providing cars and babysitters, checking voter lists to alert the nonvoters late in the day, and providing poll watchers to oversee the balloting and counting. Efficiency and integration of the campaign, however, often threaten the interests of specific candidates. While the party organization may prefer to raise money and prevent unseemly competition for the political buck, an individual candidate may well believe he can raise more on his own. And although the party may prefer billboard posters that celebrate the full party ticket of candidates, some among them may prefer to go it alone.

This distance, even estrangement, between candidate and party organization is apparent also in the expectations of candidates and party officials. In many parts of the country neither group expects the party organizations to run the campaigns. Kingdon finds that only a minority of Wisconsin candidates see the party organization as the most important member of their campaign coalition. A slightly higher percentage, in fact, see interest groups as the most important.[35] And recently the state party chairmen ranked campaign management as the least important of the five responsibilities suggested to them (Table 2).

Out of this pulling and tugging for control of the campaign emerges a great overlapping of campaign organization. In many instances the struggle and tension for control is really a four-cornered one involving the candidate, nonparty groups and specialists, the local party organization, and state or national party organs. Which one dominates depends largely on which one controls the resources — the money, manpower, skills, and information — that the campaign requires. When party organizations can provide candidates the new expertise and skills that the professionals can, and at a lower cost, they will reassert their control over the business of campaigning. But it will require more money than they now have, and it will demand a greater centralization of party organizational authority. It may well be, therefore, that party organizations will be able neither to beat 'em nor to join 'em.

[35] Kingdon, *Candidates for Office*, Chap. 3.

TABLE 2   Rankings of State Party Chairmen Roles: 1966

Role	Republican	Democrat	Both
Raising party funds	2.67	2.97	2.81
Promoting party's image	3.30	3.83	3.55
Administering state party organization	4.42	3.63	4.05
Helping manage campaigns of state candidates	1.75	2.03	1.88
Promoting party's policies	2.90	2.71	2.81

Source Adapted from Charles W. Wiggins and William L. Turk, "State Party Chairmen: A Profile," *Western Political Quarterly* 23 (1970): 329.

Note The values in the table are an average of positions in a rank ordering of the five roles, with first place = 5, second place = 4, etc.

The new campaigning works against the party and the party organization in another way. It reinforces the development of personalism in politics. It is the candidate, not the party, who is sold. The "image" transmitted by TV and the other media is of a person, not of the abstraction known as a political party. The campaign techniques, therefore, foster a tie between candidate and voter — a new personalism in politics — in which the role of party loyalty is less important. The new campaign technicians threaten to displace the party "within" the voter as well as the party organization in the campaign.

Thus the two major American parties are dominated by a concern for contesting elections, but their party organizations have great difficulty in controlling those electoral activities. In many parts of the country the ability of the candidates and the party in government to control them has led to dominance of the party organization itself. If these are electoral parties and if groups other than the party organizations control the electoral processes — the picking of candidates and the staging of campaigns — then those groups control the parties.

The failures of the party organizations inevitably frustrate them. Domination by candidates and incumbent officeholders mattered little when the partisans of the organization wanted only patronage and preference. They and the candidates could agree that electoral victory was their common goal on whatever terms were necessary to win it. The victory itself and its later fruits were all that mattered. But today the tension between these two sectors of the party is far greater as the organization recruits ideological and issue-oriented activists. The electoral goals of the new activists include more than mere electoral victory; they would like to control electoral choices so that they might expound issues and select candidates loyal to them. Thus the inability of the organization to control nominations and election campaigns means simply that it, of all the sectors of the party, has the most difficulty in achieving its goals and rewards at the election.

Through their ability to control nominations and election campaigns, the candidates are freed of organizational domination, both in the affairs of the party and in the decisions of public office. And the failures of the party organizations also enhance the competitive position of the non-party political organizations that want to play electoral politics. It is easier than ever before to influence nominations and elections, for the skills and techniques of electoral politics are more widely available than ever. Whoever bids successfully for them can compete on even terms with the party organization.

11

Presidential Politics: The Preliminaries

It has often been said that the American presidency is the biggest, most demanding job in the world. Its size and responsibilities in part reflect the power and concerns of the government of the United States. They also reflect the unique institution of the presidency itself, for the United States is the only major power of the world that chooses a national executive from a national constituency in free, competitive elections. And as if to match the prodigious demands and responsibilities of the presidency, the American people have evolved a process of nomination and election to that office that for sheer length, expense, attention, and gaudy extravaganza is without peer in the world. It commands front-page coverage in most of the world's newspapers, and in the United States alone media coverage reaches enormous proportions. Between 60 million and 90 million Americans watched the 1968 and 1972 nominating conventions at various prime evening hours.

Furthermore, the quadrennial American presidential campaign and election has become the focal point of all American politics. Its results radiate out to affect other elections — strong presidential winners, for example, carry other candidates into office on their coattails. Its candidates and rhetoric tend to shape party loyalties and identifications, and its regular four-year calendar is the basic pulse of American politics. The presidential election is also the great centralizing moment in American politics, the centripetal force against the decentralizing, centrifugal tendencies. It is the brief but influential hour of the parties as national parties. And, finally, for many American citizens who are often apathetic to local politics, its salience and prominence make it virtually the whole of American politics.

Appropriately, this singular campaign and election process pivots around two singular American political institutions: the nominating conventions of the summer before the presidential election and that constitutional anachronism, the electoral college. Those two institutions combine to create a presidential politics of baroque complexity and an electoral process that remains an insoluble puzzle to many of the world's observers. It is a politics that is, to say the least, peculiarly American.

THE RULES OF THE PRESIDENTIAL GAME

If the American president and vice-president were elected directly by a simple plurality of the American electorate, presidential politics would be vastly different — and vastly simpler. But the presidential constituency, the one national constituency in American politics, is not composed simply of all American adults. It is a complicated constituency from which is chosen an eighteenth-century deliberative body that no longer deliberates. And like any formal electoral system, this one gives a special form to the political competition that goes on within it. Electoral institutions, as we have noted before, are the rules of political competition, and they determine the skills and the strategies of the players.

The electoral college as it is set down in the Constitution rests heavily on the structure of American federalism.[1] Each state receives a number of electors equal to its total representation in the two houses of Congress. In other words, to the fixed quota of two senators one adds the number of the state's representatives in the House. The votes of the states in the electoral college, therefore, extend from a fixed minimum of three (two senators and one representative) to an open-ended maximum, currently the forty-five of California. In addition, since the ratification of the Twenty-third Amendment, the District of Columbia has had three electoral votes. Thus the total membership of the college presently is 538, the sum of the membership of the Senate (100), the House (435), and the three votes of the District of Columbia.

The Constitution further provides that the president and the vice-president must be elected by an absolute majority of the votes of the college; at present that would be 270 votes. Should the electoral college not be able to elect a president by this absolute majority, the Constitution has provided for what is in effect a superelectoral college. Under this plan the election of the president would be settled by the House of Representatives, which would choose among the three candidates with the greatest number of votes in the electoral college. However, while each state delegation in the House is to decide whom its state will support (and is not bound by the popular vote of the state), each state has only a single vote in the balloting. The emergency procedure was twice employed in the early 1800s but not since then. In view of the procedure's uncertainty and its drastic redistribution of political power to the less populous states, the major parties prefer to avoid the necessity for it.

The framers of the Constitution intended the electoral college to be a genuinely deliberative body. The choice of a president, argued Alexander Hamilton,

[1] Article II, Section 1, as amended by the Twelfth and Twenty-third Amendments.

should be made by men most capable of analyzing the qualities adapted to
the station, and acting under circumstances favorable to deliberation, and to
a judicious combination of all the reasons and inducements which were proper
to govern their choice. A small number of persons, selected by their fellow-
citizens from the general mass, will be most likely to possess the information
and discernment requisite to such complicated investigation.[2]

Not all the Founding Fathers were as fearful of direct popular election
as was Hamilton, but the majority seems to have accepted the wisdom
of selection by a body of respected notables. The transformation of the
electoral college began, however, with the rise of political parties. In the
states, slates of electors began to run pledged to support a party's presidential and vice-presidential candidates. In other words, the ties of party
loyalty assured voters that a vote for a specific set of electors was in
effect a vote for party candidates. As soon as that practice of pledged
slates became widespread, the electoral college ceased to function as
an independent, deliberative body. And so the electoral college today is
perhaps the world's most important nonmeeting governmental body. In
most states the electors meet briefly over lunch or dinner in the state
capitol to register their vote formally. Some official of the state then
transmits it to the president of the Senate in Washington, and the collective preferences of the electoral college are recorded without the in-
convenience of a single meeting of the college as a whole.

Party electoral slates and the party loyalty of those on them have had
another transforming effect. The desire of parties to maximize support
for a full slate of electors has undoubtedly influenced the states to make
the popular election of the electors an all-or-nothing race. A plurality
edge for a party, whether of a few votes or many thousand votes, carries all the state's electoral votes. This winner-take-all principle in turn
has had two consequences. First, it has forced the parties and the candidates to appeal to the voters of the large, competitive states with the
big, indivisible blocs of electoral votes. To fail to carry Nevada or Delaware, with their three electoral votes, is not a major loss. But to fail to
win in New York (forty-one electoral votes) or in California (forty-five)
is a major setback. The parties tend, therefore, to pick presidential candidates from the large, pivotal states and to beam a great portion of the
campaign at them. Second, the big-state arithmetic increases the possibility of the loser in the national popular vote being the winner, the
new president. That result can occur if a candidate wins state blocs of
votes by narrow margins and loses others by landslides.[3] Since the Civil

[2] The Federalist, number 68 (New York: Modern Library, 1937), pp. 441–42.
[3] For example, to reduce the problem to three states of equal voting population
and equal electoral vote:

    State A Population of 2,000,000 and ten electoral votes
             Democratic vote: 900,000
             Republican vote: 1,100,000

War two men have been presidential losers even though they led in the popular vote: Samuel J. Tilden in 1876 and Grover Cleveland in 1888.[4]

Although party ties have robbed the electoral college of its deliberative quality, they have not made it completely automatic and predictable. Electors in most states are not legally or constitutionally bound to vote for the presidential candidate under whose name they have run. Four times since World War II individual electors at the "moment of truth" have abandoned the candidate to whom they were pledged. The last one, a Virginia Republican, bolted the Nixon slate in 1972 to vote for the candidate of the Libertarian party.[5] Furthermore, rebellious state parties may exploit this lack of binding tie for their own purposes. They may deny the voters of their state the chance to vote for their party's national candidates by running either a different slate of candidates or an unpledged slate under the state party label. In 1948, for example, J. Strom Thurmond, the Dixiecrat candidate for president, rather than Harry S. Truman, appeared on the ballots as the Democratic candidate for the presidency in a number of southern states. Mississippi Democrats in 1960 and Alabama Democrats in 1960 and 1964 ran unpledged slates of electors under the Democratic party label. A combination of party decentralization and state control over the presidential ballot and election, therefore, limits the development of a national, popular election of the American president.

Each of these characteristics and consequences of the electoral college has produced a body of criticism and reform proposals.[6] One school of thought, concerned about the college's artificiality and the possibility of a "minority" president, has sought to abolish it in favor of a direct, popular election of the president. Others, alarmed by the system's emphasis on the indivisible, big-state votes, have proposed various systems of dividing the electoral votes of the state; most of them involve either

---

State B   Same population and electoral vote
          Democratic vote: 950,000
          Republican vote: 1,050,000
State C   Same population and electoral vote
          Democratic vote: 1,300,000
          Republican vote: 700,000

Here the Republican candidate leads in the electoral vote, twenty to ten, while the Democratic candidate leads in the popular vote by 300,000.

4 Depending on how one counts the Alabama popular vote in 1960 for both pledged and unpledged electors, a case can be made that Richard Nixon won the popular vote in 1960 while losing the vote in the electoral college.

5 The Virginia elector, *mirabile dictu*, was chosen in 1975 to be the Libertarian candidate for the presidency in 1976!

6 On the electoral college generally, see Neal R. Peirce, *The People's President* (New York: Simon and Schuster, 1968); Wallace S. Sayre and Judith H. Parris, *Voting for President* (Washington: Brookings, 1970); and Lawrence D. Longley and Alan G. Braun, *The Politics of Electoral College Reform* (New Haven: Yale University Press, 1972).

dividing the electoral vote proportionally according to the candidates' percentages of the popular vote, or electing some or most of the electors in the congressional districts of the state. (Maine, in fact, decided in 1972 to choose two of its four electors in the state's two congressional districts; the party that carries the state will get two at-large electors, but the loser could conceivably carry one of the districts.) Still others have sought to check the uncertainty of its operation — the possibility of unpledged slates, of state ballots without a national candidate, and of local slates intended solely to deadlock the electoral college. Yet, despite a torrent of polemics and tomes of argumentation, operation of the college remains untouched. It changes today as it has in the past — by custom, tradition, and state law.

Behind all the attempts to reform or abolish the electoral college lie broader questions of political power and ideology. In defining the national constituency of the president and the vice-president, the electoral college enhances the political power of the large, pivotal, urban, industrial states. To state the matter another way, the college creates a presidential constituency that is markedly different from the sum of all the congressional constituencies. Because of the equal state representation in the Senate, regardless of population, the political power of the rural and small-city electorates is magnified in the Congress. In the last generation, the presidents, as a result of the nature of the national constituency, have usually espoused the "liberal" social and economic programs favored by the people of the urban areas. The desire of political conservatives to reduce the power of the large urban, industrial states lies behind some of the attempts to alter the college, especially those proposals that would divide the electoral votes of the individual states.[7] And the desire to preserve that power lies behind a great deal of the opposition to change.

The other chief issue behind reform of the electoral college is no less than direct, popular democracy itself. In the last 130 or 140 years the electoral college has evolved into something very close to a de facto popular election of the presidency. In every presidential election since 1888, it has secured the presidency for the candidate with the greatest number of popular votes in the country. That same period has also seen the spread of democratic norms and a constant broadening of the suffrage. Some of the proposed reforms try to protect and further that evolution either by institutionalizing the popular election of the president and vice-president or by preventing individual electors or state parties from thwarting popular will. Into this category fall both the attempts to abolish the college and those less drastic proposals to limit state party

[7] On this point and also for a general review of the impact of the electoral college, see Allan Sindler, "Presidential Election Methods and Urban-Ethnic Interests," *Law and Contemporary Problems* 27 (1962): 213–33.

control over the ballot choices and to force electors to vote for the candidates they ran pledged to support.

The George Wallace candidacy in 1968 stimulated the most recent concerted attempts to reform the electoral college. The Wallace strategy, a repeat of the Dixiecrat plans of 1948, counted on winning a large enough bloc of states to deny both Richard Nixon and Hubert Humphrey the necessary majority of votes in the electoral college. Wallace would then have been free to bargain with the parties for the electors pledged to him, either in the electoral college vote or subsequently in the "one state, one vote" balloting of the House. Less than a year after the 1968 election, the House of Representatives did approve a constitutional amendment to abolish the electoral college and to elect the president by direct popular vote. The amendment also provided that if no candidate received 40 percent of the popular vote, the two top contenders would be forced into a run-off election. The amendment died subsequently in a Senate filibuster. Southern senators feared national control of elections, small-state senators feared the dilution of small-state power, and other senators feared the encouragement of small, splinter parties.[8]

FIRST STEPS TOWARD THE NOMINATIONS

The national conventions of the two major parties conclude the complicated process of nomination. It is far more difficult, however, to say just when that nominating process begins. For some especially ambitious and far-sighted politicians, it may have begun in their own political career planning some six or eight years before. Within the party defeated at a presidential election, jockeying for the next nomination begins the morning after defeat. In a more formal sense, the nomination process begins as the advance men for would-be candidates straggle into New Hampshire to enter their candidates and delegates in the earliest of the presidential primaries.

Basically, the preconvention part of the nomination process concerns the selection of delegates to the conventions. The major would-be candidates within each party seek delegates bound to them — or at least

---

[8] There are two paradoxes here. The first involves the third-party effect. Generally, the electoral college discourages smaller parties, if only because their support is so difficult to translate into electoral votes. However, a "larger" small party, and especially one whose strength is regionally concentrated, can use the electoral college for its own strategic purposes. The second paradox concerns the effect on the smaller states. The political consequences of the electoral college usually lead to the big-state arithmetic and, conversely, to some slighting of candidates from and campaigns in the smaller states. Formally, however, the electoral college, by including the Senate's equal representation in the formula, does overrepresent the small, usually rural states.

committed or inclined to them. Conversely, heads of state delegations often want delegates to remain uncommitted so that their bargaining power will remain unexpended until the convention meets. Typically in this country, the party organizations control only part of the picking of delegates to their own conventions. The national committee of the party decides what percentage of the total votes in the convention each of the fifty state delegations will have. State legislatures, however, decide the equally crucial matter of how those delegates will be chosen: whether by a presidential primary, by a convention or committee of the party, or by a combination of the two.

Apportionment and Selection of Delegates

The national parties determine the number of votes and delegates each state will have in the Democratic and Republican national conventions. For the first time in a long while the number of votes and delegates to the two national conventions in 1976 will be identical. The Democrats in particular had a tradition of permitting state parties to send more delegates to the national convention than the number of its assigned votes, with the inevitable result that some delegates cast bizarre fractions of a single vote. But no longer, at least for 1976. The number of delegates will equal the number of votes.

To assign the number of votes to each state the national committee or convention of the parties — whichever makes the decision — employs a more than usually complicated formula. The 1972 Republican convention, for example, prescribed the following formula for representation at the 1976 convention:

1. Each state receives six at-large delegates.
2. Each state receives three delegates from each of its congressional districts.
3. Each state receives an additional delegate for a Republican governor and/or senator.
4. Each state whose congressional delegation is at least 50 percent Republican receives an additional delegate.
5. Each state which gave the 1972 presidential candidate its electoral vote receives a number of additional delegates equal to four and one-half plus .6 of the state's electoral vote (rounded to the next whole number).
6. The District of Columbia receives fourteen at-large votes, Puerto Rico eight, the Virgin Islands four, and Guam four.

The formula thus favors heavily the areas of heavy Republican strength; it continues the tradition of overrepresenting the less populous states. Indeed, the 1976 formula was adopted over the strong opposition of about one-third of the 1972 delegates, who wanted to increase the representation of the urban, populous states. But those are the states of liberal Republican strength, and the apportionment of convention delegates in both parties tends to reflect the interests of the dominant groups within them.

The Democrats, however, did break with tradition. In 1968 they adopted a representational formula which represented areas of party strength (the urban, industrial states) more heavily than they had been represented in the past. The seven states of California, Illinois, Michigan, New York, Ohio, Pennsylvania, and Texas jumped from 36 percent of the votes in the Democratic convention of 1968 to 44 percent in 1972. The charter adopted in 1974 provides that delegates to the party's 1976 convention will be allotted on a formula: "giving equal weight to population, which may be measured by electoral vote, and to the Democratic vote in elections for the office of President." The effect is to increase further the relative strength of the areas of electoral strength and to move the Democrats just that much further away from the old norm of apportionment based roughly on representation in the electoral college.

For years the national parties, in preparing for the conventions, had stipulated only the number of delegates the states would have. It was always left to the states or their parties to decide how they would be chosen. In 1968 the Democrats ended that tradition, too. They began to control a number of the other aspects of delegate selection. Best known of those aspects, undoubtedly, was the requirement for 1972 that women, minorities, and young voters would have to be represented in "reasonable" numbers among the delegates. The rules for 1976 back away a bit from that requirement, but not from the commitment of the party to control the selection of delegates. The party charter, adopted in 1974, provides that the selection processes must:

1. Give all Democratic voters "full, timely and equal opportunity to participate."
2. Exclude the use of the unit rule (i.e., winner take all) and, thus, must apportion delegates among candidates according to their strength. (Apparently this stricture does not apply to selection in congressional districts or smaller geographical units.)
3. Not begin before calendar year 1976.
4. Comport with an approved affirmative action program. (The use of mandatory quotas is, however, forbidden.)
5. Be open only to Democrats.

And so ended local autonomy over the selection of delegates to national conventions. The Democratic rules challenged even state election law. Wisconsin and Michigan, with elections of delegates at open primaries, clearly would run afoul of the requirement that selection be limited to

Democrats. Other states had long used the "unit rule"; many of them scrambled in 1974 and 1975 to shift to selection by congressional district.

The Democrats also ended another tradition with their reforms in the late sixties and seventies. Both parties had for a long time followed similar policies in apportioning and selecting their convention delegates. There had, to be sure, been differences between them, but the main structures of representation and selection had been similar. Now increasingly, as a result of the Democratic reforms, they differ on fundamentals. In fact, the representativeness of the national conventions themselves has become a political issue.

The Presidential Primaries

The number of states choosing their convention delegates in presidential primaries continues its steady climb. In 1968, only fifteen states and the District of Columbia elected some or all of their convention delegates in ways that offered voters of the state some opportunity to express a preference for the presidential nominee of the party. Together the delegates from these states and the District of Columbia cast 47 percent of the votes at the Democratic convention and 46 percent at the Republican. Additionally, Alabamans elected unpledged delegates to the Democratic convention. By 1972, twenty-two states and the District of Columbia elected delegates at presidential primaries; Alabama and Arkansas elected unpledged slates at primaries. More than 60 percent of the delegates to the national conventions came from them.[9] In 1976 the total will apparently jump from twenty-two to at least twenty-seven, plus the two states with elections of unpledged delegates. With the addition of Texas for 1976, furthermore, there will be primaries in all of the ten most populous states. It also seems safe to anticipate that more than two-thirds of the delegates at the 1976 conventions will be selected at presidential primaries.

To speak blithely of presidential primaries is, however, an oversimplification. No two are identical. The major source of their variety lies in their two-part character: They can be devices for selecting delegates to the national conventions, and for showing a preference among contestants for the party's nomination. On the basis of the way they combine or divide these two separate functions, the assorted presidential

[9] The twenty-two states with presidential primaries were in 1972: California, Florida, Illinois, Indiana, Maryland, Massachusetts, Michigan, Nebraska, New Hampshire, New Jersey, New Mexico, New York, North Carolina, Ohio, Oregon, Pennsylvania, Rhode Island, South Dakota, Tennessee, West Virginia, and Wisconsin. New York's primary is formally only for the election of delegates, but delegate candidates freely and openly identify with presidential candidates. For 1976 primaries have been added in Georgia, Kentucky, Nevada, Texas, and Vermont.

primaries fall into four categories: primaries in which delegates are chosen, those in which the voters may show a presidential preference, those that integrate the two features, and those that provide for separate delegate selection and presidential preference polls. (See Figure 1 for some sample ballots.)

1. *Delegate selection only.* In Alabama, New York, and Arkansas the primary is solely a vehicle to elect delegates to the national conventions. There is no place on the ballot for the names of the contenders for the party nomination, and the delegates do not run formally pledged to any contender. The ballot is, therefore, innocent of any names except those of men and women who seek election as delegates. In New York, however, delegate candidates have often pledged themselves informally to a presidential contender in the campaign, and the supporters of candidates distribute cards with names of delegates supporting them.

2. *Presidential preference only.* In at least two states, Indiana and North Carolina, the presidential primary is nothing more than a presidential preference poll. The voter is confronted by the names of his party's worthies who have entered the primary, and he merely indicates which he would prefer to represent his party in the November presidential contest. The state committees of the parties then pick the delegates to the respective conventions. Those delegates, however, are required to support the candidacy of the winner of the state's presidential poll.

3. *The two elements combined.* A number of states — California, Ohio, South Dakota, and Wisconsin among them — combine the presidential poll and the election of delegates by a simple device: The delegates pledge themselves to support specific candidates for the party's nomination. That pledge and the name of the national candidate, of course, are linked with the delegate's name on the ballot. In some states every delegate's name on the ballot is associated with a presidential candidate — for example, a statement under each name reads, "Pledged to support John Smith for president." Other states provide that a full slate of delegate-candidates be listed on the ballot under the name of the presidential candidate to which the slate is pledged. On the California ballot, only the names of the presidential candidates appear; a vote for one of them automatically elects the slate of delegates pledged to him.

4. *The two elements separated.* The remaining states — the largest number of them — and the District of Columbia include the two features of the primary but separate them. In these states the ballot has a presidential preference poll in which the party's hopefuls compete for the favor of partisans within the state. In a separate section of the ballot, voters choose delegates to the conventions. Confusion and diversity

FIGURE 1   Assorted Examples of Presidential Primary Ballots:
The Republican Primaries in Oregon (bottom) and New Hampshire (top)
and the Democratic Primary in Wisconsin (middle): 1970

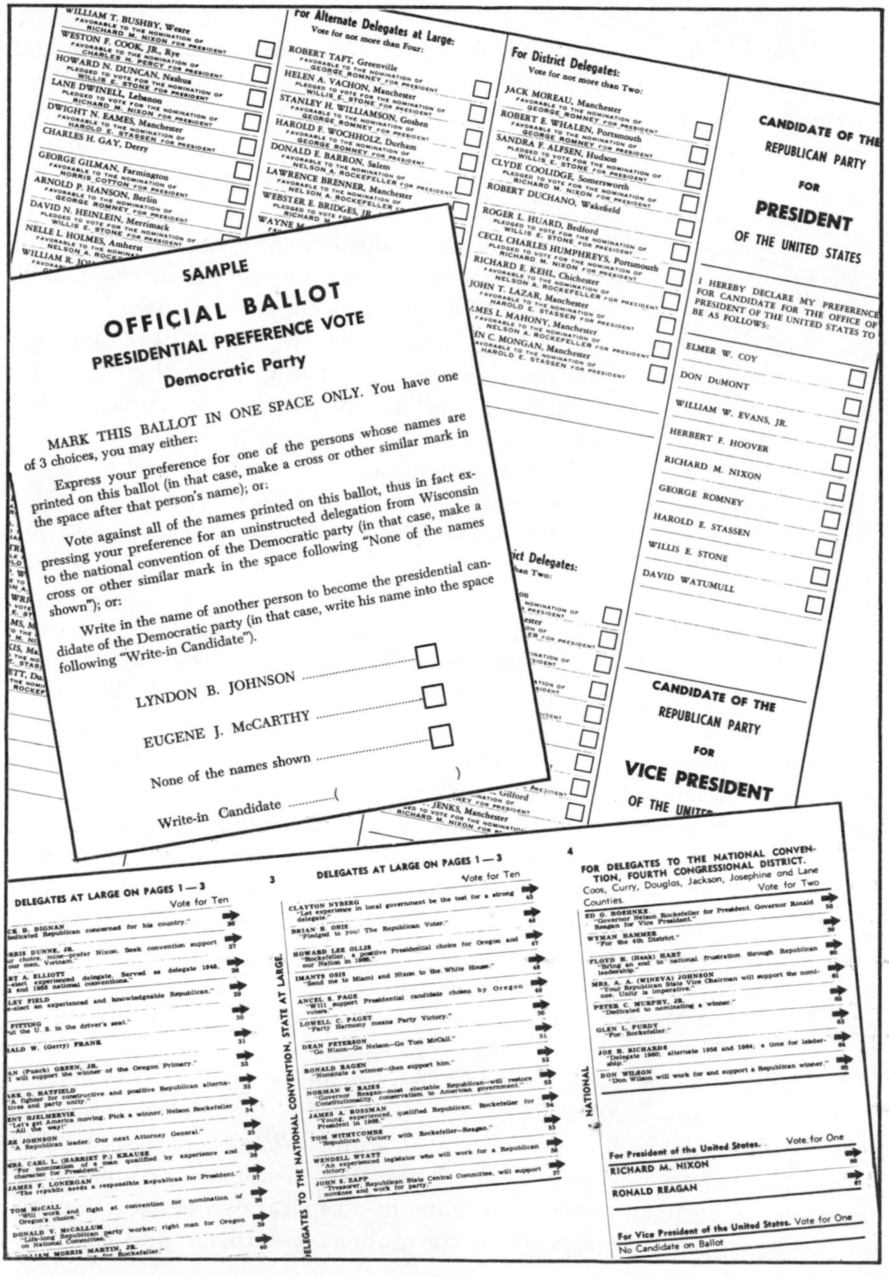

of practice, however, surround the relationship between the two parts. In only some of the states (e.g., Oregon and Tennessee) do the results of the preferential polls bind the delegates selected. In the rest of the states they are only advisory. And in Oregon and some other states the would-be delegates may also choose as individuals to run pledged to a presidential candidate. The result, of course, may be conflicting advice from the voters, and in the case of Oregon the delegate could be bound to a candidate other than the one he pledged himself to.

In outline these are the presidential primaries. There are, though, still other differences among them. First, in some the convention delegates are elected from the state at large; in others, from the individual congressional districts; and in still others, from both. Such a seemingly minor variation, however, can have major political consequences. For example, the chances of a divided state delegation (and its attendant intraparty squabbles) are much greater when delegates are chosen by congressional district. North Carolina also introduced a new twist in 1972. Candidates receiving more than 15 percent of the vote shared the state's delegates proportionately. A large number of primary states, if they are to comply with Democratic rules for 1976, will have to adopt similar plans or shift to election by congressional district.

Second, some states in their primaries elect all the delegates the parties will send to the conventions, and some elect only part of them. In Pennsylvania, for example, about a quarter of the delegates are chosen by the parties' state central committees. Such a provision helps meet one of the parties' major objections to the presidential primary by permitting them to make sure (through their own state committees) that the important leaders of the state organizations will go as delegates to the national conventions of their parties.

Third, the states vary on the issue of whether a presidential hopeful must consent before his name is involved in the state's primary. Most states, but not all, require his approval (or permit his disapproval) before his name may be entered in a presidential preference poll or before delegates run pledged to him. In Oregon the primary law entrusts to a state official the delicate decision of putting on the preference poll the names of all candidates "generally recognized in the national news media" to be candidates for the presidential nomination. Such has been the practice for some time in Oregon, but only since 1965 have Maryland, Nebraska, Nevada, New Mexico, Tennessee, and Wisconsin similarly placed all candidates' names on the ballot. The purpose clearly is to make it less possible for potential candidates to avoid some of the primaries and thus diminish competition and interest in them.[10]

[10] In most of these states a candidate can remove his name by filing a formal disclaimer that he is not and does not intend to be a candidate. It is a step that the coy or dark horse candidate is not anxious to take.

Fourth, the presidential primaries differ in the nature of the commit-ment of the pledged delegates. In some cases the pledge of a delegate to support a certain candidate for the nomination is buttressed only by his enthusiasm for his candidate, by his own code of honor, or by his sense of the political value of integrity. In other states delegates are required by law to take a pledge of loyalty to the candidate. Wisconsin, for instance, specifies by law the content of the pledge:

I will, unless prevented by the death of the candidate, vote for his candidacy on the first ballot; and vote for his candidacy on any additional ballot, unless released by said candidate, until said candidate fails to receive at least one-third of the votes authorized to be cast; and that, thereafter, I shall have the right to cast my convention vote according to my own judgment.[11]

Finally, while all the other states and the District of Columbia have closed primaries, Wisconsin and Michigan hold open primaries. The pos-sibility that voters who would normally support Democratic candidates at the general election will drift into the Republican presidential primary — and vice versa — creates an additional uncertainty and unpredictabil-ity for the candidates.

Delegates Chosen by the Party Organizations

The presidential primaries are dramatic and are reported in the most intricate detail. Nonetheless, the parties of about half the states — as well as the Democratic parties in Guam, and both parties in Puerto Rico and the Virgin Islands — choose delegates by assorted internal party processes. Those processes are usually combinations of state and district conventions. The Democratic parties often simply hold district caucuses during the state convention, but Republican national party rules require the holding of separate district conventions. Generally, the district conventions choose a fixed and equal number of delegates from each district, and the state convention selects the remainder from the state at large. In a few states some or all the delegates are chosen by the state central committee of the party.[12]

Delegates so chosen by party processes may also be instructed by the

[11] *Wisconsin Statutes*, Chap. 8.12. For a general study of the presidential primaries, see James W. Davis, *Presidential Primaries: Road to the White House* (New York: Crowell, 1967).

[12] The mechanics and politics of choosing convention delegates are discussed more fully by Gerald Pomper, *Nominating the President: The Politics of Convention Choice* (Evanston: Northwestern University Press, 1963), Chap. 3. On preconven-tion strategies, see Nelson W. Polsby and Aaron B. Wildavsky, *Presidential Elec-tions*, 3rd ed. (New York: Scribners, 1971), pp. 59–77. For a study of the politics of electing convention delegates in a state convention, see Richard G. Niemi and M. Kent Jennings, "Intraparty Communications and the Selection of Delegates to a National Convention," *Western Political Quarterly* 22 (1969): 29–46.

state party. The mechanics of instruction vary. Some conventions pass resolutions instructing the delegates to support one specific contender for the party nomination. Some, indeed, mandate their delegates to work actively for his nomination in addition to voting for him on the convention roll calls. In other cases the resolution of the convention may state nothing more obligating to the delegates than a preference or recommendation. Often the process of instruction is less formal. The personal loyalties and preferences of the would-be delegates may be well known; they may campaign on the basis of their support for a particular presidential nominee. Again, however, state parties will apparently be in violation of Democratic rules for 1976 if they do not provide for the proportional representation of delegates selected in statewide processes.

THE POLITICS OF SELECTING DELEGATES

The politics of winning a presidential nomination obviously depends on enlisting the support of a majority of the delegates at the national convention. However, the strategies of the presidential aspirants will differ in how and when they make their move for delegate backing. But as front-running candidates increasingly attempt to influence the selection and instruction of delegates, as they try to wrap up the nomination before the convention convenes, the significant part of the politics of nomination shifts to the preconvention phase. The intensive preconvention campaigns for delegates by John F. Kennedy in 1960, Barry Goldwater in 1964, Richard Nixon in 1968, and George McGovern in 1972 assured them of their parties' nominations on the first ballot of the convention.

Even though the intensive preconvention campaign is becoming more common, this strategy makes sense only for some contenders. Front-runners well known to the political public — and who can muster the resources — may feel they have no alternative but to make a show of strength and come to the convention with a majority of delegates firmly in grasp or at least in sight. Other candidates, partially in response to the front-runner's activity, may feel they have to contest the selection of some delegates if only to block the front-runner short of a majority of the delegates. The moral of the dithering inactivity of moderate Republicans in 1964 while Barry Goldwater kept accumulating delegate support is not apt to be forgotten in the near future. Still other candidates may contest the delegate selection in a few states for assorted reasons: to garner enough convention votes to have a substantial voice in its deliberations or to extract a political quid pro quo (the vice-presidential nomination or a cabinet seat, perhaps). Some few candidates, the true dark horses who lack a publicized name and a political following, may avoid contests in the states in order to remain acceptable to all wings of the party should a deadlocked convention think of turning to them.

The pattern of preconvention contesting will be determined within a party by a number of factors, among them:

1. *The presence of a president.* When presidents are eligible for another term, they are in a commanding position to dictate their own renomination and to eliminate competition. Even presidents who are not candidates for renomination (such as Eisenhower in 1960 and Johnson in 1968) may influence the nomination by their late decisions or support for a successor.
2. *The number of candidates and their strength.* Two leading candidates (such as Rockefeller and Goldwater in 1964) force a different form of strategy and counterstrategy than do four or five evenly matched candidates.
3. *The resources of the candidates.* Unquestionably the last-minute campaign of Nelson Rockefeller in 1968, lacking support among the party leaders and organizations and thus dependent on the media, could have been undertaken only by a man of considerable resources.
4. *The degree of commitment of state leaders and parties.* The heavy commitment of most Democratic state leaders to Hubert Humphrey was perhaps the greatest disadvantage that Eugene McCarthy faced in his attempt to win his party's nomination in 1968. Their commitment also led to charges that the party's convention in Chicago was bossed.
5. *Party rules on delegate selection.* The new Democratic rules outlawing the unit rule (and thus forcing some kind of proportional representation) will doubtless encourage more Democratic candidates. Regional or local candidates (favorite sons or daughters) may wish to bring a handful of delegates to the convention for bargaining purposes.

Within these general political configurations, the candidates must also make personal strategic assessments. A candidate may be forced to greater preconvention activity to counter a popular impression that he cannot win or that he does not enjoy party support. Or he may feel compelled to prove to the skeptical that his campaigning skills, his handshake, and his smile (and perhaps those of his wife) are durable enough for the presidential race. He may wish, as George Wallace did, to counter the feeling that his popularity is regional. In 1960 John F. Kennedy entered the presidential primary in Protestant West Virginia to prove that his Catholicism would not hamper him in a presidential campaign. Above all, the candidate's decisions may be governed by his estimates of probable success. No law or political tradition forces a candidate to contest every presidential primary or state convention, and only a foolhardy one would try.

The candidates are not alone in having interests at stake in the selection of delegates to the conventions. So also do the state party organizations and leaders, and their interests often run counter to those of the aspiring presidential nominees. For the local and state parties, a hotly contested selection of delegates is often an occasion of intraparty conflict. Battles between Eugene McCarthy and Hubert Humphrey for Democratic delegates in 1968 — both in primaries and in state conventions — created rifts in the party that have been slow to heal. George McGovern's fight for Democratic delegates in 1972 reopened many of these splits in the Democratic party. The McGovern candidacy — heavily supported by the young, female, minority, and very liberal segments of the party — won little favor among the more staid and traditional leaders of most of the party organizations. And his success in their states, coupled with the party's rules on delegate selection, meant that a good many of them were denied positions as delegates to the national conventions.

The interests and goals of the parties in selecting delegates to the national conventions go further than the avoidance of conflict, however. The state party organization (or one of its leaders) may want to pursue its own goals at the convention. It may want to preserve its bargaining power to affect the platform, to win a cabinet seat for a notable of the state party, to affect the vice-presidential choice, or just to enhance its value in the presidential nomination. Its interests may also be the parochial ones of a state party; a number of state Democratic parties were cool to Kennedy in 1960 for fear of losing the votes of Protestants in the state and thus hurting the party's ticket for statewide office.

For these reasons, the leadership and organization of state parties would often prefer to "depoliticize" the process of selecting delegates. If conflict looms, the party chieftains may prefer an uncommitted slate of delegates or one loyal to a favorite-son candidate rather than chance deep and lasting divisions. Or if there is a presidential primary in the state, they may do as Wisconsin Republicans did in 1964. Faced with intraparty conflict between Goldwater and Rockefeller forces, they negotiated a settlement by which all the major contenders for the GOP nomination agreed to stay out of the Wisconsin presidential primary. Wisconsin Republicans then elected the only slate on the ballot, one carefully composed of Republicans of various loyalties and ideologies and pledged to a favorite-son noncandidate, Congressman John Byrnes. Frequently, therefore, the pressure within the state party for commitment comes from volunteer groups loyal to one national contender or another, from ideologues in the party, and from the contacts and advance men of the contenders. The pragmatic organization men, the pros, tend to oppose it.[13]

Apart from the interests of parties and candidates, however, has it really made any difference whether delegates to the national conventions have been chosen by primary or by party processes? Do the 60 to 70 percent of the delegates chosen by primary behave any differently than do those chosen through party bodies? Do the presidential primaries have an impact on the nominations commensurate with the time and money spent in them?

Not too long ago in American politics the processes of delegate selection were sharply bifurcated. In the states of the presidential primaries a more open, popular, candidate-centered politics worked to the advantage of well-known personalities and generally helped insurgents in the party. In the other states the party organization controlled delegate selection and could apply, with few exceptions, tests of party acceptability both to delegates and ultimately to the seekers after the party's nomination. Estes Kefauver in 1952 and 1956 and Eugene McCarthy in 1968 used the primaries to challenge the party apparatus for the nominations. They failed, as did all other challengers with little support outside the primary states. They failed if for no other reason than that there were not enough primaries; the delegates selected in them were 40 percent or less of the whole. Probably the last great conflict of the two selection modes was that of the Democrats in 1968 (Table 1). Before 1972 the winners of party nominations were those seekers who mixed primary and nonprimary victories, who satisfied both the party organization and the broader party electorate. Hubert Humphrey did, after all, win more than half of all the votes sent by the primary states in 1968.

Much of the difference between primary and nonprimary processes is now diminishing. There are more primaries, and delegate selection is increasingly more open and access easier in the other states. The changes are greater under the Democratic party's rules, but there are changes, too, among the Republicans. George McGovern had successes in both selection modes, even though he and his followers were anathema to many state party organizations. In short, we have had a convergence of the two delegate selection processes into a more lengthy, more homogeneous, more important, and more expensive preconvention politics. It is all a part of a general shift to a more open, mass politics. At least in the Democratic party at present the chief strategic problems are just as likely to be the limits and opportunities under the new party

[13] Theodore H. White's four volumes on the 1960, 1964, 1968, and 1972 elections contain excellent journalistic accounts of the preconvention politics of those years. See *The Making of the President* for those four years, all of them published in New York by Atheneum in the year after the election.

TABLE 1   Humphrey and McCarthy in the Primaries: 1968

	Number of votes candidate won on first ballot, 1968 convention	Percentage of candidate's votes won in fifteen primary states and D.C.	Percentage of total convention votes of primary states and D.C. won by candidate
McCarthy	601	73.0	35.3
Humphrey	1,760	37.4	52.9

rules as the old juggling of separate primary and nonprimary strategies.[14]

Still, the primaries maintain their special role and appeal. Their expansion continues to speak about the way we increasingly view presidential nominating politics. Because of their openness to the voters, their results confer great legitimacy on the winners. Victories acquired in them may still be more important for symbolic purposes than for the number of delegates acquired. And as Eugene McCarthy proved in 1968, victories in them may even help drive an incumbent president from office. The primaries also provide an opportunity for candidates to show their appeals and build a following, and to show their stamina and adaptability under various pressures. And for the successful nominees the primaries build an early name and face recognition which gives them a head start in the election campaign.[15] And, cruelly, too, they help weed out the nonviable candidates. George Romney, for example, dropped from the 1968 Republican race in the face of polls predicting a poor showing in the New Hampshire primary. And Edmund Muskie's withdrawal in 1972 was in considerable part the result of failures in a number of primaries.

A SYSTEM IN NEED OF REFORM?

The briefs against both the presidential primaries and the party selection of delegates are long and weighty. In fact, they seem to so outweigh the briefs in favor that the observer might easily conclude that once again in American politics he must choose between the lesser of two evils. However, the debate has broadened recently to include a third option: a national presidential primary. Although its specific form

[14] For example, see William Cavala, "Changing the Rules Changes the Game: Party Reform and the 1972 California Delegation to the Democratic National Convention," *American Political Science Review* 68 (1974): 27–44.
[15] That seems to be the suggestion of Leonard Weinberg and Joseph Crowley, "Primary Success as a Measure of Presidential Election Victory: A Research Note," *Midwest Journal of Political Science* 14 (1970): 506–13.

varies with different proponents, all proposals outline a single primary election, to be held in all states, in which each party would choose, not delegates, but the presidential nominee himself. Since the single primary would replace the nominating convention, a consideration of it can await the discussion of the convention in the following chapter.

Because the nominating conventions appear likely to remain on the American political scene, the more pertinent question at this point is the selection and mandating of delegates. To put the issue more pointedly, should the presidential primaries as we know them be expanded or abolished? The case against them is impressive:

1. They consume an enormous amount of time, energy, and money before the presidential campaign has ever begun. Leading contenders for the nomination often run through a series of primary campaigns from February through June, arriving at the party convention personally and financially exhausted.
2. They put a tremendous premium on the well-known, familiar name and face — and thus often on the financial and other resources necessary to build that political familiarity. Consequently, their existence makes it difficult for the party to consider less-known or reluctant candidates. (They have not, however, made it impossible; Adlai Stevenson entered nary a primary in 1952.)
3. Their importance may easily be distorted out of all perspective. In the mass of publicity surrounding them, candidates and voters alike fail often to assess them soberly. Wendell Willkie, for example, bowed out of the 1944 Republican contention after a loss to the Dewey slate in Wisconsin; Dewey, however, polled only 33 percent of the Wisconsin Republican vote (conducted in an open primary at that). While primaries are deemed measures of a candidate's popularity, in reality they may be measures of popularity among the voters of the party. They are simply primaries and not general elections.
4. Their results are too often colored by the particular quirks that mark many of them. In some, for example, the candidate may be involved against his wishes. Wisconsin's and Michigan's open primary adds another capricious element. There remain dark suspicions that George Wallace's victory in Michigan's Democratic primary in 1972 was aided by Republican crossovers.
5. Victory in the primaries is won by plurality vote, and if the competitors are numerous, often by a small plurality. George McGovern won the Democratic primary in Wisconsin in 1972 with only 30 percent of the vote. Furthermore, the voter turnout is often disappointingly low. New York's confusing election of convention delegates in 1972 brought only one-fourth of the state's registered Democrats to the polls.

6. The presidential primaries frequently result in internal divisions in state party organizations, warring delegations to the national conventions, and delegates not representative of the party organization and leadership in the state. Like any other primary that takes an important party process out of the control of the party organizations, it weakens them.

The arguments against the presidential primary could be extended, but these are its chief ones.

The charges against the party convention or party committee selection of a state's delegates to the national nominating convention rest on the traditional complaint about party processes — that they are too easily controlled and manipulated by a handful of party oligarchs. That, in any event, has been the charge of the reformers in the Democratic party since 1968. Furthermore, in these states the party electorates and even some of the party activists are excluded from an important and often crucial step in the picking of a president. And it is undoubtedly true that in these states the political ambitions of national figures receive less attention and the interests of the state parties as parties more attention than they do in the presidential primaries.

Debating points aside, however, we seem to be in the middle of a great revival of interest in the primaries. After a period of disenchantment with primaries, the states are returning to them with the enthusiasm they had fifty years ago.[16] Increasing media coverage has spotlighted their role in the nomination process. And their basic rationale — the twin democratic norms of mass popular participation and fear of party oligarchies — seems more powerful than ever. What is most important, the states may think the primaries are becoming more important. Clearly some of the states are venturing into the primaries for the first time to increase their own political leverage or the leverage of some local or regional son. In the case of some of the new southern primaries, at least some state legislators see them enhancing the power of the South in national presidential politics by forcing all candidates to be tested — and possibly tarnished — in those states. If the states think the primaries are becoming more important in presidential nominating politics, they may be helping the prophecy to fulfill itself.

More than just a revival of the primaries, however, the changes in presidential nominating politics reflect the new demands for political openness and mass participation. The spread of the presidential primaries is obviously a part of it. So, too, are the rules of the Democratic party requiring the broadest participation of all segments of the party and

[16] For the early development of the presidential primaries, see Louise Overacker, *The Presidential Primary* (New York: Macmillan, 1926). In 1916 at least twenty-three states had some sort of presidential primary.

(through the abolition of the unit rule) the representation of all shades of opinion and candidate preference. The delegate selection process, that is, is changing in response to the democratic demands of the parties in the electorate. The old control has gradually slipped from the hands of the party organizations and their leaders, so that now we have an open process which reflects the view that the party electorates must be involved in every step to the national nominating conventions. These changes may reshape the entire presidential nominating process. Especially in the Democratic party, and especially with the end of the winner-take-all traditions, we may soon see a fragmented politics in which more candidates will share the convention delegates. In such an eventuality, no candidate will be able to "sew up" the nomination in the preconvention stages. The convention would then be restored to its earlier importance as the candidates and their supporters engaged once again in the old-time bargaining and brokering in order to mass majority support behind a presidential candidate.

The fifty state organizations of the major American parties have only one opportunity every four years to act as a national party. The quest for the presidency is their single national task, and the archaic boundaries set by the electoral college form their single national constituency. Ironically, their attempts to act as a single, unified, national party are disturbed and complicated by a prenomination politics that in length and method divides individual state organizations and sets state party against state party. That friction develops partly from institutions such as the presidential primary. It derives in greatest measure, however, from the fact that the American parties are disunited, heterogeneous conglomerations of state parties and are welded into national parties, even for a brief task, only with the greatest difficulty.

Even at these early stages of presidential politics one also sees the beginning of the repetition of an old theme in American politics. It is difficult for the party organizations to control the presidential nomination, just as it is difficult for them to control other party nominations. In part, again, the presidential primary weakens organizational control and shifts it to the would-be candidates. In part, too, the organizations are weak because they have no means of uniting or coordinating their own preferences prior to the nominating conventions. So candidates with comparatively rational and unified national strategies find it easy to take the initiative from individual state party organizations in this phase of presidential politics. And to the extent that they are able to win the commitments of enough delegates to capture the nominations — as the candidates did in 1960, 1964, 1968, and 1972 — they and the party in government capture the nomination before the party organizations ever gather themselves together to act as a "national party" at the convention.

12

Presidential Politics: The Crucial Decisions

That cynical observer of American politics, H. L. Mencken, especially loved the challenge of reporting a national nominating convention. After ruminating on the Democratic convention of 1924 and the 103 ballots it took to nominate John W. Davis, the Sage of Baltimore wrote:

there is something about a national convention that makes it as fascinating as a revival or a hanging. It is vulgar, it is ugly, it is stupid, it is tedious, it is hard upon both the higher cerebral centers and the *gluteus maximus,* and yet it is somehow charming. One sits through long sessions wishing heartily that all the delegates and alternates were dead and in hell — and then suddenly there comes a show so gaudy and hilarious, so melodramatic and obscene, so unimaginably exhilarating and preposterous that one lives a gorgeous year in an hour.[1]

Former President Dwight D. Eisenhower felt the irritation without experiencing the exhilaration. The conventions, he said, were "a picture of confusion, noise, impossible deportment, and indifference to what is being discussed on the platform." The banner-waving demonstrations that so typify the carnival gaiety of the conventions he dismissed as "spurious demonstration[s] of unwarranted enthusiasm."[2]

Scarcely a convention goes by, indeed, without evoking a series of tongue-clucking appraisals in the serious journals. Calls for convention reform come as regularly as the conventions themselves. And yet the national conventions persist, the chief holdout against the domination of American nominations by the direct primary. How is it that so maligned an institution has so successfully resisted the pressures of change? Has it become an indispensable political institution? And even while offending the canons of taste and decorum, has it really managed to function effectively as a recruiter of presidents?

---

[1] Malcolm Moos (ed.), *H. L. Mencken on Politics* (New York: Vintage, 1960), p. 83.
[2] *New York Times,* June 29, 1965.

THE STRUCTURE OF THE CONVENTION

To a very considerable extent, the conventions are the creatures of the parties themselves. They are subject to no congressional or state regulation, and even the federal courts have been reluctant to intervene in their creation. The responsibility for them falls to the national party committees and their staffs, although an incumbent president inevitably influences the planning for them. Increasingly, too, the previous conventions and, in the case of the Democrats, the mid-term conference are concerned with them.

Planning for the quadrennial conventions begins at least a year before the event. The first harbinger of that work comes with the selection of the host city. That choice reflects a vast number of considerations, from the size of the financial package the bidding cities offer to such usual convention matters as hotel space. Political considerations enter, too. For 1976 the Democrats selected New York as their site in part as an affirmation of the American city, and the Republicans chose Kansas City to symbolize their ties to the "heartland" of the nation.

Months before the convention, too, its major committees emerge. Like all other major American institutions, both political and nonpolitical, the conventions function in part through committees. Generally there have been four of them:

1. *Credentials*. This committee accepts the credentials of delegates and alternates and makes up the official delegate list of the convention. Its prickliest duty is deciding contests (between two delegates or slates vying for the same seats) and challenges (of the qualifications of any delegate or alternate).
2. *Permanent organization*. This committee selects the permanent officials of the convention: the permanent chairman, secretary, and sergeant at arms, for example. Generally its work provokes little controversy.
3. *Rules*. It sets the rules of the convention, most particularly the specific procedures for selecting the presidential nominee. The main procedures have been fixed for some time, but the committee struggles at every convention with rules such as those governing the length and number of nomination speeches, the number of nondelegate demonstrators that will be permitted on the convention floor, and the method of polling delegations should controversy arise within them.
4. *Platform*. This committee's responsibility is to draft the party's platform for action by the convention. It holds open hearings to receive the ideas of citizens, party notables, and the potential presidential nominees.

The chairpersons of these committees are selected by national party officials, who negotiate with state organizations in appointing the other committee members. Early appointment is necessary if only because the committees begin to function before the convention convenes. Platform committees especially have begun to scour the party and the nation for ideas several months before the convention opens.

The first three of these committees — credentials, permanent organization, and rules — make decisions that define the structure and procedures of the convention. These decisions are no less important for being procedural, however. Often they have enormous impact on the substantive decisions the convention makes on the nominees or the platform. The abandonment of the two-thirds rule by the Democratic convention in 1936, to take a prime example, drastically diminished the power of the party's southern wing. Under the rule, two-thirds of the votes of a convention were necessary to nominate, and the strength of the South in the convention was usually sufficient to give it a virtual veto over the presidential nomination. It is precisely because procedural rules such as this so affect the distribution of power at the conventions that state interests, the candidate followings, and the ideological camps within the parties work so hard to win representation on the committees.

In recent years the decisions of the credentials committees have had the greatest repercussions. The 1952 contest for the Republican nomination between Senator Robert Taft and General Dwight Eisenhower hinged in great part on the battle over delegates from Georgia, Louisiana, and Texas. The Credentials Committee voted to seat the pro-Taft delegates from the three states, but in scenes of recrimination the convention as a whole seated the pro-Eisenhower claimants. If Senator Taft had had the votes of those contested delegates, he would have led Eisenhower on the convention's first ballot. In 1972 George McGovern's quest for the Democratic nomination was aided by the convention's decisions to seat the California delegates loyal to him and not to seat the Illinois delegation loyal to Mayor Daley and the local party organization. Similar contests over delegates, reflecting either ideological divisions or different candidate loyalties, have in fact afflicted most conventions. Rarely, however, do they reach the number the Democrats achieved in 1972; in that convention more than a dozen disputes received full floor debate.

A somewhat different problem in credentials has plagued the Democratic conventions since World War II: the unwillingness of some southern state delegations to take the delegate "loyalty oath," the pledge to support the candidates and platform of the convention. In 1948 delegates from Mississippi and Alabama marched out of an evening session of the convention after northern liberals nailed a strong civil rights plank onto the platform. Many of those delegates and their state parties later supported the Dixiecrat party ticket; more heretical than that, four state parties put the Dixiecrat slate on their state presidential ballot as the ticket of the Democratic party. The loyalty issue erupted again at the 1964 convention when the largely black Freedom Democratic party of Mississippi challenged the seating of the Mississippi delegation on the grounds that blacks had been prevented from participating in the selection of national convention delegates. The Mississippi delegates were forced to pledge loyalty to the party ticket, and two at-large delegates of the Freedom Democratic party were seated as regular Mississippi delegates. In 1968 the regular Mississippi delegation and half of the Georgia regulars were barred because they, too, were chosen in processes not fully open to blacks.[3]

Credential fights are the major threat to orderly and seemly conventions. The emotions and the stakes are high, and the recommendations of credentials committees have often been overriden in bitter floor battles. Furthermore, the votes on the floor often fall along ideological lines or lines of support for various candidates. The picture is not one of judicious decision. Under their new party charter the Democrats will now try another approach to disputes over credentials. All such matters will go to a party Judicial Council, a body which will also have to certify earlier that state plans for delegate selection comply with national party rules. But the convention itself, the charter clearly notes, remains the final arbiter of credential disputes.

Finally, to complete the organization of the convention the national committee selects the temporary chairperson, who usually delivers the extravagantly partisan keynote address. His qualifications are only two — an aloofness from the major contestants for the nomination and a telegenic oratorical style — but the candidates are many. They remember that Alben Barkley's oratorical flights in praise of the Democratic party won him the vice-presidential nomination in 1948.[4] But even at lower levels of ambition, the assignment is an ideal publicity showcase, and it does no politician's political future any harm.

The description of the formal structure of the convention, of course, fails to convey anything of its ambience. Born of a rough-and-tumble political tradition and related to the institution of the boisterous convention in other areas of American life, the national party conventions are part carnival, part "fling at the big city," and part (a large part, actually) serious party conclave. At one and the same time they mix phony, well-rehearsed demonstrations of enthusiasm with serious

---

[3] On the issue of the loyalty oath, see Abraham Holtzman, "Party Responsibility and Loyalty: New Rules in the Democratic Party," *Journal of Politics* 22 (1960): 485–501.

[4] On the contrary case they may remember that General of the Army Douglas MacArthur disappointed his supporters by failing to light any fires with his keynote speech before the Republicans in 1952.

thought about presidential stature, the conferences of the powerful king-makers with the aimless amblings of ordinary delegates, the perfunctory afternoon oratorical fillers with the often eloquent messages of the party worthies. The convention is in many ways two conventions: one the surface veneer of bogus fun, hoopla, earnest platitudes, and devotion to party symbols, the other the less public world of bargaining, influence, and negotiation through which agreement is achieved and choices made.

THE DELEGATES

The combination of large numbers of delegates and equally large num-bers of alternative delegates produces gargantuan conventions. The total of delegates and alternates exceeded 6,000 in the Democratic conven-tions of 1968 and 1972, for instance. The national committees are under tremendous pressure from the state party organizations to increase the number of delegates. Party workers in the state cherish the prestige of attending a convention, and the experience of being a delegate also is likely to stimulate them to work in the campaign that follows. Candi-dates and state party organizations have also found that the larger the number of delegates, the fewer difficult choices they have to make and the fewer the number of people they have to disappoint. Large conven-tion size is also increasingly the price of representing the large, populous states in some reasonable ratio to the representation of the small ones. Finally, big conventions create a mass rally atmosphere for television coverage. Especially when the convention is certain to renominate an incumbent president — as the Democrats did in 1964 and the Repub-licans did in 1972 — the rally aspects of the convention replace its deliberative duties.

The delegates to the Democratic and Republican conventions have never been a cross-section of American citizens. Whites, males, and upper income groups have always been overrepresented to some degree. There have also been differences between the two parties. Democratic delegations have had more Catholics, Jews, and trade unionists, the Republicans more Protestants and businessmen. The collective picture of the delegates of each party has, therefore, always resembled a group portrait of its activists and loyal voters. Recently, however, both parties have attempted to broaden the representativeness of their delegations, with the Democrats in 1972 making by far the greater change. For ex-ample, 15 percent of the 1972 Democratic delegates were black, against only 6 percent in 1968, and the proportion of women — 38 percent — was a threefold increase over 1968.[5]

[5] Readers will note that within the Democratic party in 1972 blacks were added to the "overrepresented" populations. The 1970 census counted the black popula-tion at 11 percent of the American total; blacks have, of course, been voting Dem-

Ideologically, the delegates are more committed, more aware of issues and issue positions, than the ordinary voters of their party. They also tend more to the ideological poles than do the electorates of their parties; the Democratic delegates are more apt to be liberal and the Republicans more conservative than even the identifiers of the parties.[6] Furthermore, the ideological commitment of the delegates is increasing. The 1964 Republican and 1972 Democratic conventions clearly broke with the rule of pragmatic compromise and opted for explicitly ideological candidates and programs. The ideological gap between convention delegates and the party's rank-and-file voters results both from the differences between activist and nonactivist and from the way in which the apportionment of delegates at the conventions overrepresents the areas of the party's weakness across the country and thus overrepresents some of the party's electors. That gulf has raised especially acute problems for the Republicans. Ever since 1936 their convention delegates have clearly had their hearts to the right of their candidates. If it had been purely personal choice, they would probably have preferred Senator Taft in the 1940s and 1952, and large numbers were favorably disposed to Senator Goldwater in 1960. In 1964 the heart won out.

Actually, differences among the delegates of a single convention may be more significant than differences between the two party conventions. A number of observers noted the much larger number of clergymen and academics among the McCarthy-Kennedy-McGovern delegates than among the delegates as a whole in the 1968 Democratic convention. Theodore White, in fact, counted twenty-six men of the cloth.[7] The McCarthy delegates also tended in their style and approach to politics to be amateurs similar to those taking over some of the urban organiza-

---

ocratic in recent national elections by a ratio of two or three to one. For slightly different data on 1972 (based on a sample survey) and for comparisons between the two parties, see Joseph H. Boyett, "Background Characteristics of Delegates to the 1972 Conventions: A Summary Report of Findings from a National Sample," *Western Political Quarterly* 27 (1974): 469–78. For example, Boyett finds that 28 percent of the Democratic delegates, against 8 percent of the Republican, were thirty years old or under; that the Democrats had more than three times the percentage of black delegates; that the percentages of male delegates were 57 for the Democrats and 68 for the Republicans; and that 81 percent of the Democrats and 65 percent of the Republicans were attending their first national convention.

[6] Herbert McClosky, Paul J. Hoffman, and Rosemary O'Hara, "Issue Conflict and Consensus among Party Leaders and Followers," *American Political Science Review* 54 (1960): 406–27; John W. Soule and James W. Clarke, "Issue Conflict and Consensus: A Comparative Study of Democratic and Republican Delegates to the 1968 National Conventions," *Journal of Politics* 33 (1971): 72–91.

[7] *The Making of the President 1968* (New York: Atheneum, 1969), p. 272. The White volumes, beginning with the 1960 election, are the major chronicles of recent presidential politics. For an earlier period similar data are often available in Paul T. David, Ralph M. Goldman, and Richard C. Bain, *The Politics of National Party Conventions* (Washington: Brookings, 1960).

tions; the Humphrey delegates were more likely to be professionals —
that is, the McCarthy delegates were more committed to programs and
issues, more insistent on intraparty democracy, less willing to compromise, less committed to the prime importance of winning elections.
Similar differences carried over to the Humphrey and McGovern delegates in 1972.[8] So the two sets of delegates differed not only in their
candidate preference but also in their political styles, their perceptions
of their political role, and their political values and outlooks.

As interesting and important as the individual delegates are, the real
unit of the conventions has historically been the state delegation. Delegates room together at the same hotel and share their experiences with
each other; they also often share the same goals and outlooks. They
caucus periodically, and they are often bound together by loyalty to the
same candidate or party leaders. The 1972 Democratic convention featured the growth of special interest caucuses for blacks, women, youths,
Latins, senior citizens, and Jews. They failed, however, to establish an
influential role.

Perhaps the most critical problem for the group caucuses was that their goals
were sometimes in conflict with those of other organizations, notably candidate organizations. Delegates who had a stake in the nomination of a particular candidate were unlikely to drop their commitment to that candidate in
favor of loyalty to a group caucus.[9]

The state delegations remain the basic unit of even the most unusual of
all conventions. Even the McGovern organization communicated with
delegates as members of their state delegations.

THE BUSINESS OF THE CONVENTION

The convention begins in low key with stiff formalities and the business
of organization. It warms up with the keynote address, tries to maintain
momentum and expectation through consideration of the platform, and
reaches a dramatic peak in the nomination of the presidential and vice-
presidential candidates. This general format remains basically the same
convention after convention. TV coverage has necessitated some re-
arrangement into a more compact convention, with the events of major
interest reserved for prime evening transmission time, but the tempo of
the convention is still governed by the pace of business and the usual

[8] John W. Soule and James W. Clarke, "Amateurs and Professionals: A Study of
Delegates to the 1968 Democratic National Convention," *American Political Science
Review* 64 (1970): pp. 888–98. For a report on "purists" and "professionals" in 1972,
see Dennis G. Sullivan, Jeffrey L. Pressman, Benjamin I. Page, and John J. Lyons,
The Politics of Representation: The Democratic Convention 1972 (New York: St.
Martin's, 1974).
[9] Ibid., p. 68.

dramatic considerations. Ordinarily dramatic suspense is no problem, but it is in the party of a president eligible to succeed himself. The likelihood of his renomination is so great that the spectators know how the play will end. President Lyndon B. Johnson himself solved a good share of the problem in the 1964 Democratic convention by creating suspense and uncertainty over his vice-presidential choice.

Aside from the rites of nomination, the drafting and approval of the platform is the convention's chief business. The platform committees begin hearings long before the convention opens so that the platform will be in draft form for convention hearings. Those hearings before and during the early phases of the convention are often spiced by the appearance of leading contenders for the nomination. The finished document then is presented to the convention for its approval. That approval is not always pro forma, for the platform has occasioned some of the most spirited recent convention battles. In 1968 the forces supporting Hubert H. Humphrey engaged the McCarthy delegates in a virtually unprecedented three-hour floor debate over what the platform would say about the war in Vietnam. The Democrats' discussion of the 1972 platform touched on subjects new to platform discourse (e.g., abortion and gay rights) and set a record for the longest discussion of a platform in American convention history.

Few aspects of American politics so openly invite skepticism and cynicism as do the party platforms. They are long and prolix; the Democratic platform of 1972 ran to 26,000 words, almost twenty times the length of the Declaration of Independence. The platforms are not often read; the congressional party generally ignores them, and even presidential standard-bearers reserve the right to disagree with them. Basically the problem is that platforms are the instruments of ideology, and the two major American parties have not been explicitly ideological. They really have no persistent set of political principles, no total political philosophy that unites their followers. The American party platform, rather than being a statement of the party, is much more apt to be a statement of the presidential candidate and/or the wing of the party in control of the convention. An incumbent president seeking renomination virtually writes the platform himself, and strong contenders for the nomination (such as Barry Goldwater in 1964) can often make sure that their forces are in firm control of the platform committee. And if it happens that the person likely to be nominated disapproves of the platform, he may insist on its modification. Richard Nixon in 1960, clearly about to receive his party's nomination, bowed to the criticisms of the draft platform by Governor Nelson Rockefeller of New York, rushed to New York to confer with him, and then hurried back to Chicago to force revisions on a very unhappy committee.

Part of the cynicism about the platforms grows from the impression that they are exercises in semantic virtuosity. The words and phrases used are sometimes intended to obfuscate rather than clarify, for phrases that mean all things to all people achieve compromises of a sort. But vague or artful as the platforms may be, they do take stands on some issues, and they are not identical. In recent years they have differed over social security, labor-management relations, farm price supports, medicare, racial integration, and war and peace in Vietnam. Above all, the platforms are campaign documents in which the parties pick their issues and positions selectively to promote their goal of assembling a majority coalition. The party platform is important, its leading scholar says,

but not as an inspired gospel to which politicians resort for policy guidance. It is important because it summarizes, crystallizes, and presents to the voters the character of the party coalition. Platform pledges are not simply good ideas, or even original ones. In their programs, Democrats and Republicans are not typically breaking new paths; they are promising to proceed along one or another path which has already become involved in political controversy. The stands taken in the platform clarify the parties' positions on these controversies and reveal the nature of their support and appeals.[10]

Finally, the platforms are what they are largely because they are drafted and approved in conventions mainly concerned with picking a presidential candidate. Every convention vote tends to become a test of the strength of the various candidates.[11]

FINDING A PRESIDENTIAL CANDIDATE

The political pièce de résistance of the convention — the picking of a presidential candidate — begins as the secretary intones the litany of the states: Alabama, Alaska, Arkansas.... As each state is called, the head of the state's delegation responds in one of three ways: by placing the name of a candidate before the convention; by yielding the state's position in the roll call to another state to make a nomination; or by passing. So as the secretary works his way through the states, the contenders for the nomination are entered, each one by a formal speech of nomination and shorter seconding speeches.

It is at this point that the conventions traditionally reached back to a nineteenth-century political style. The speeches of nomination rolled out in great Victorian periods, often seeming to be parodies; seconding speeches, carefully chosen to provide a cross section of the party, were

---

[10] Gerald Pomper, *Elections in America* (New York: Dodd, Mead, 1968), p. 201.
[11] All the party platforms are available in one volume: Kirk H. Porter and Donald B. Johnson, *National Party Platforms, 1840–1964*, 5th ed. (Urbana: University of Illinois Press, 1973). For a broad discussion of platform making, see Paul T. David, "Party Platforms as National Plans," *Public Administration Review* 31 (1971): 303–15.

frequently vest-pocket versions of the main speech. After each set of nomination speeches the supporters of the nominee, usually augmented by young, tireless nondelegates, snaked their way through the crowded aisles of the hall, singing and chanting, waving banners and signs, and generally disporting themselves in the carnival spirit, often for almost an hour.

The first modifications of these hoary traditions began with the advent of television, for the endless hijinks often pushed the most dramatic portions of the convention out of prime evening time. And what seems colorfully old-fashioned in the hall often looks grotesque or vulgar on the TV screen. The Democrats, spurred again by the reform impulses springing from their 1968 convention, made further inroads in 1972. They banned all floor demonstrations, shortened nomination speeches drastically, and made the nomination of favorite-son candidates — those noncontenders with support in only one delegation — vastly more difficult.

Once all the names have been presented to the convention, the task of settling on a single presidential nominee begins in earnest. The secretary of the convention starts again through the states (and the District of Columbia, the territories, and the dependencies), asking each delegation to report how it votes. If no candidate wins the necessary majority of votes, the convention presses on to a second ballot. A number of nominations have been settled on the first ballot, but in 1924 the Democrats plodded through 103 ballots in sultry New York's Madison Square Garden before nominating John W. Davis. Since 1952 no nomination contest in either party has consumed more than one ballot (Table 1). Furthermore, since 1948 the conventions have averaged only two candidates who polled more than 10 percent of the convention votes on any ballot (Table 1). That trend may be attributable to a number of factors: the Democratic party's abandonment of the two-thirds rule, more intensive preconvention campaigning, and the pressures on delegates that result from the increased publicizing of the convention.

The casting of the votes takes place in a context of some of the most compressed political activity in all of American politics. Even before the opening of the convention, representatives of the various contenders have stalked uncommitted or wavering delegates across the country by mail, phone, and personal visit. Once the convention opens, the process is stepped up. Of the 1960 Kennedy organization, Theodore H. White has written:

In all, some forty delegate-shepherds were assigned each to a particular state delegation that was theirs to cultivate; each was given packets of name cards listing the assigned state delegates by name, profession, hobby, children, wife, peculiarity, religion, and sent out to operate. They were instructed, as they found shifts in any delegation, to report such changes to a private tabulating

TABLE 1   Number of Ballots Required to Nominate and Number
of Candidates Polling 10 Percent of Votes in Democratic and
Republican Conventions: 1948–72

| | Democratic Conventions | | Republican Conventions | |
Year	Candidates over 10%	Number of ballots	Candidates over 10%	Number of ballots
1948	2	1	3	3
1952	4	3	2	1
1956	2	1	1	1
1960	2	1	1	1
1964	1	1	2	1
1968	2	1	3	1
1972	2	1	1	1

Source   Data from *Congress and the Nation* (Washington, D.C.: Congressional Quarterly, 1965), and from newspaper accounts of 1968 and 1972 conventions.

headquarters in Room 3308 at the Biltmore; and there, every hour on the hour from Friday through balloting day, a new fresh total, accurate to the hour, was to be prepared. For five days, the shepherds were told, they were not to sleep, see their wives, relax, frolic or be out of touch with 8315. Each morning, for the five Convention days from Saturday to the Wednesday balloting, they were to gather in Room 8315 for a staff survey at nine A.M., then disperse to their tasks.[12]

Such organizational thoroughness probably has never been seen at conventions before or since, but front-runners generally know they must win quickly. The only strategy the other candidates can employ is to join in a coalition to prevent the first-ballot victory. That imperative can join — however temporarily — men of such divergent views as Nelson Rockefeller and Ronald Reagan, who tried unsuccessfully in 1968 to prevent the first-ballot nomination of Richard Nixon.

If the convention has passed through an inconclusive ballot, negotiations renew with even greater intensity. The leading candidates must take care to prevent a chipping away of their supporters — a genuine danger if they fail to increase their votes on a second or third ballot. New support comes most easily from minor candidates or uncommitted delegates, since data suggest that delegates bound to candidates are too loyal to those commitments to be lured away.[13] The favorite-son candidate faces the delicate decision of whether to cast his lot with a front-

[12] White, *The Making of the President 1960* (New York: Atheneum, 1961), p. 157.
[13] David, Goldman, and Bain, *The Politics of National Party Conventions*, p. 379.

runner or to hold tightly and maintain (either alone or in concert) a defensive action. Much of this strategy has, of course, been absent with the first-ballot choices of the last twenty years. The proliferation of presidential primaries, especially of those with election by congressional district, however, may bring bargaining back to the conventions. That is to say, they may make it more difficult for any one candidate to amass the number of committed delegates necessary to win the nomination on the first ballot.[14]

Following the naming of the presidential nominee, the party begins the roll call ritual again to select a vice-presidential nominee. Conventions uniformly ratify the choice of the presidential candidate. Rebellions flash occasionally but always fail; for instance, in the Democratic meetings of 1944 the supporters of Vice-President Henry Wallace tried futilely to resist the decision of President Roosevelt to replace him with Harry S. Truman. And once in recent years the presidential candidate did not indicate his preference. Adlai Stevenson convulsed the 1956 Democratic convention by opening the vice-presidential choice to it; Senator Estes Kefauver was selected on the second ballot. But generally the presidential candidate chooses. The choice, though, is made on very short notice by a tired candidate and his tired advisors on the night of his nomination. The withdrawal of the initial Democratic vice-presidential nominee in 1972 (Senator Thomas Eagleton) and the eventual resignation of Vice-President Spiro Agnew have raised serious questions once again about that selection process.

THE "AVAILABILITY" OF PRESIDENTIAL NOMINEES

There is a bland and misleading term in American politics which describes the personal, social, and political characteristics the parties seek in their presidential nominees. If an individual possesses them, he is said to be *available*. Contrary to its popular use, the word in this idiomatic sense has nothing to do with the candidate's willingness to be a candidate. The assumption seems to be that in that sense every nativeborn American adult is available for the presidency.

The concept of availability sums up the qualities the parties believe make a politically appealing and acceptable — and thus a winning — candidate. In part, the canons of availability reflect the distribution of political power in presidential politics. It is said, for instance, that the presidential candidate must come from a large state — that is, from a state with a large electoral vote that he can be presumed to carry. From 1896 to the present, only five of the twenty-three men originally nomi-

---

[14] On the strategies of presidential politics generally, see Nelson W. Polsby and Aaron B. Wildavsky, *Presidential Elections*, 3rd ed. (New York: Scribner, 1971).

nated for the presidency by a convention came from the smaller states. Seventeen came from seven large states: seven from New York, four from Ohio, two from California, and one each from Illinois, Texas, Massachusetts, and New Jersey. One came from Minnesota, a state that would appear to be "in between." None of the five from the smaller states — Landon of Kansas, Davis of West Virginia, Bryan of Nebraska, Goldwater of Arizona, and McGovern of South Dakota — won the presidency.[15]

In part, too, the concept of availability is a codification of widely held expectations in the American electorate of what a president should be. It is an aggregate of the characteristics the parties think the American electorate would prefer a president to have and would vote for in a candidate. Some years ago it was commonly said that for a person to be considered seriously for the office he had to be a personal success in business or public life; happily married and blessed with an attractive family; a reasonably observant Protestant; a white male in his late forties or fifties; of Anglo-Saxon or North-northwestern Europe ethnic background; the product of small city or rural life.

Although there is considerable validity in such a list as a description of past presidential nominees, to project such requirements into the future would be dangerous. The lore of acceptability shifts with changes in social attitudes. Adlai Stevenson, a divorced man, was nominated in 1952 and 1956; an urban and Catholic candidate, John F. Kennedy, was nominated in 1960. Those nominations probably indicate, at least in part, the declining social stigma attached to divorce, the life of the big city, and Catholicism in contemporary America. In coming decades changing attitudes about women in public life may also strike the male qualification from the formula of availability.

Finally, related to the issue of availability but somewhat different, is the question of career pattern. Although not all presidential candidates have had prior governmental or officeholding experience, most have. Thus the question arises of what positions provide the best jumping-off point and the best training for the presidency. What public positions grace a man with an aura of governmental success and competence and yet give him a good base for building party and public support? From 1900 through 1956, nineteen different men ran for the presidency on the Democratic and Republican tickets; eleven of them had been governors (McKinley, Theodore Roosevelt, Wilson, Hughes, Cox, Coolidge, Smith, Franklin Roosevelt, Landon, Dewey, and Stevenson). Only two, the luckless Harding and Harry Truman, had been senators. It had come to be a commonplace in American politics that the Senate was the graveyard of

[15] If one uses the 1972 electoral vote as a measure, none of the seven "large" states referred to here had an electoral vote smaller than fourteen, and none of the "small" states had one greater than seven. Minnesota had ten.

presidential ambitions. Senators, it was said, were forced to cast too many politically sensitive votes and create too many political enemies; they also were thought to lack the opportunities for national popularity and image.

In 1960, 1964, 1968, and 1972, however, all eight nominees had been senators, and none had been a governor. In the presidential politics of 1972 and after, in fact, even a majority of the unsuccessful seekers for presidential nominations were senators or former senators: Birch Bayh, Lloyd Bentsen, Fred Harris, Hubert Humphrey, Henry Jackson, Edward Kennedy, Eugene McCarthy, Edmund Muskie, and Charles Percy. (After 1972 Representative Morris Udall of Arizona also mounted the first challenge from the House of Representatives in a long time.) The shift to recruiting in the Senate may well reflect changes in the offices of governor and senator and in the public perception of them. Undoubtedly senators find it easier now to keep themselves in the public view, especially with their ready access to the media. Also, the very nationalization of American politics may have convinced large numbers of Americans that a senator's coping with issues of national importance is a good apprenticeship for the presidency. The governors, on the other hand, have found themselves in serious political difficulties in their states in recent years. Problems of taxation and budgeting, racial tension and rioting, and legislative reapportionment — as well as the more conventional political conflict resulting from the spread of two-party competitiveness — have caught many of them in a damaging political crossfire.

Finally, convention delegates do consider the personal qualities of the contenders and their abilities to meet the demands of the presidency. They do so, however, in the context of loyalties to specific candidates and often, too, to specific ideologies. That is to say, the standards for presidential "timber" are not universally agreed upon. Furthermore, delegates may find dilemmas in the fact that the qualities that ensure effective performance in office are not necessarily those that win it in the first place. Difficult as such evaluations of presidential candidates are, they are far less likely to be made in the speed and confusion with which vice-presidential candidates are found. And yet of the six different men who were presidential candidates from 1960 through 1972, three had been chosen as vice-presidents in the hurly-burly of some earlier convention.

CONVENTIONS: YESTERDAY AND TODAY

It is unlikely that small bands of national kingmakers bargaining in smoke-filled rooms ever did control the national conventions to the extent that popular myth has it. Even the celebrated negotiations at the Republican convention of 1920 — in the course of which Warren G. Harding emerged — took place in a convention deadlocked by other candidates with large popular and delegate followings. But whatever power the kingmakers may have had in the past, there is increasing evidence that it is declining. In a number of important ways the national nominating conventions are not what they were a generation or two ago.

New Preconvention Politics

More nominations are decided on the first convention ballot these days, and the chances of a party's picking an unknown candidate diminish. The increased activity of the preconvention period has resulted in increased commitment of delegates. In the preconvention politicking candidates also enlist greater bodies of popular support. It is all the result of a new style of campaigning for delegates that was perhaps ushered in by the 1960 preconvention campaign of John F. Kennedy. More effective organization, greater resources, jet planes, the polls, and expanded media exposure all permit it. The press services keep count of the number of delegates committed to various candidates, and the pollsters periodically report the state of public enthusiasm for them. Both candidates and delegates have fuller information about the entire nomination politics before they get to the convention than they ever did before. Consequently, the crucial bargaining and trading of support, the committing of some and the weeding out of the others, take place increasingly at the preconvention stages. There is some speculation that the new Democratic rules, especially those forbidding the selection of delegates on a winner-take-all basis in statewide conventions or primaries, may fragment the strength of leading contenders enough to prevent one of them from sewing up the nomination before the convention meets. In any event, it is clear that some such restructuring of the rules or processes of presidential selection will be necessary if we are to restore the conventions to the dominant role in the nomination.

New Centers of Power

Political power has to some extent shifted away from the state and local party leaders, who at one time came as ambassadors to the convention for the purpose of negotiating within a fragmented, decentralized system. Power in the parties in the mid-twentieth century is less decentralized as national leadership, national candidates, presidents, and Congresses dominate the political loyalties and perceptions of voters. National party figures and national concerns — and party identifications shaped by national politics — have cut into the complete independence of the state leaders. So, too, has the increased power of potential candidates in the convention, power that is largely a product of their preconvention successes in rounding up delegates. We find, therefore, in many recent nominating conventions a tension among the old and new centers of power. Both Richard Nixon and Hubert Humphrey were in 1968 supported by the leaders of the states and localities; their major challengers, Nelson Rockefeller and Eugene McCarthy, staked their campaigns on national issues and their support in a broader national public. Similarly, the McGovern delegates of 1972 were generally less experienced and influential in their local parties than the Humphrey delegates. In divisions of this sort, bossism and intraparty democracy themselves become issues.

The New Media Coverage

The mass media have increasingly turned the conventions into national political spectaculars, intended as much for the national audience as for the delegates in attendance. Party officials have given key roles to telegenic partisans, speeded up the pace of business somewhat, and virtually eliminated the conduct of serious business in daytime hours. The strategic moves of major candidates, the arrival of powerful figures in the party, and the defection of individual delegates are reported fully. Even the formerly sacrosanct hagglings of platform and credentials committees are done in the public eye. For the party, then, television coverage offers a priceless opportunity to reach voters and party workers and to launch its presidential campaign with maximum impact. So the media spotlight shifts the role of the convention — not completely but perceptibly — from the conduct of party business to the stimulation of wider political audiences.

But media coverage is a two-edged sword, and its results may not be the ones the parties want. A restless television medium searches for excitement and makes news out of the merest incidents and rumors. Often the excitement needs no search; in 1968 scenes of violence in the streets and parks of Chicago provided a running counterpoint to the business of the Democrats within the convention hall. Media exposure is also problematic in other ways. The "openness" of the 1972 Democratic convention kept it far behind its media-oriented schedule. As a result, George McGovern began his acceptance speech at 2:48 A.M. before a TV audience one-fifth what it had been earlier in the evening.[16]

The politics of the national nominating conventions, therefore, have become much more plural, and the roles and expectations in them much more mixed and contradictory. The conventions have lost some of their freedom and deliberative character. The unlikeliness of lightning striking the unknown statesman does not, of course, signal the end of the con-

---

[16] For a fuller study of the impact of television on the conventions, see Herbert Waltzer, "In the Magic Lantern: Television Coverage of the 1964 National Conventions," *Public Opinion Quarterly* 30 (1966): 33–53.

vention. In some years at least, delegates will have to choose from among a small number of candidates who established themselves in the preconvention stages. And when the choice must be made among these well-known hopefuls, it will be made by freer, more open bargaining that involves the majority of delegates as well as the prominent bosses and kingmakers.[17]

Furthermore, the conventions reflect as never before a heterogeneous mix of roles and expectations. There are the old state and local leaders representing the interests of their party organizations, and now there are also new national party leaders, national officeholders, and powerful candidates with blocks of loyal delegates. In addition to the clash of national and local interests, old organizational styles also mix uncomfortably with new styles of media-based politics. Professional party leadership differs in its style and goals from volunteer, amateur party activists. The old electoral pragmatism — the traditional convention emphasis on picking the "winning" candidate — clashes with the ideologists' unwillingness to compromise. In reflecting all these conflicts the conventions only mirror the broader conflicts and divisions of American party politics. But the stresses and strains such conflicts create for the conventions are all too evident.

Taking a broader overview, one may put the matter of change another way. Aided by media-reported campaigning and by the results of periodic polling, the entire process of nominating a president has fallen under the spell and evolving influences of a national, popular democracy. More and more people are becoming aware of the candidates and the choices before the party, and more and more of them are formulating views about those choices. Therefore, to nominate an unknown candidate today is doubly dangerous — first, for the seeming affront to the popularly supported contestants and, second, for the handicap of running an unknown candidate against the well-known candidate of the other party. Even the style, manners, and seriousness of the convention are under a new mass, popular scrutiny. To the extent that secretive or apparently manipulated party conventions are incompatible with the "democratization" of the presidential nominating process, they have to change.[18]

Although change and declining power may beset the conventions, the parties are not about to abandon them. They will gladly make the com-

[17] Gerald Pomper, *Nominating the President* (Evanston: Northwestern University Press, 1963).
[18] William G. Carleton offers another reinterpretation of the national conventions in "The Revolution in the Presidential Nominating Convention," *Political Science Quarterly* 72 (1957): pp. 224–40. William Lucy finds that eventual presidential nominees had in most recent instances been leaders in the opinion polls even before the presidential primaries and suggests that the linkages between mass opinions and convention outcomes have been more direct than we suspect. "Polls, Primaries, and Presidential Nominations," *Journal of Politics* 35 (1973): 830–48.

The County Chairmen and the Conventions

The uncertainties of American politics encourage prediction, and a good share of the amateur prognostication is lavished on the presidential nominations. In making their predictions, most observers rely heavily on the preference polls of a national sample of American adults. Overlooked frequently are the Gallup Polls conducted among the nation's Democratic and Republican county chairmen. The chairmen accurately predicted the parties' nominations in all cases in the 1960s but failed in 1972. (The Gallup organization did not bother to take soundings on incumbent presidents in 1964 and 1972.)

1960	Democrats	John Kennedy	29%
		Stuart Symington	22
		Lyndon Johnson	17
		Adlai Stevenson	14
	Republicans	Richard Nixon	84%
		Nelson Rockefeller	9
1964	Republicans	Barry Goldwater	48%
		Richard Nixon	21
		Henry C. Lodge	13
1968	Democrats	Hubert Humphrey	70%
		Robert Kennedy	16
		Eugene McCarthy	6
	Republicans	Richard Nixon	78%
		Nelson Rockefeller	15
1972	Democrats	Hubert Humphrey	54%
		Edmund Muskie	16
		Edward Kennedy	13
		George McGovern	8
		Others	9

Gallup Polls of October 1959; March 1964;
June 1968; and May 1972.

Even if one is not interested in the political occult, those poll results do suggest something about the politics of winning the presidential nomination.

promises that are necessary to shore up the conventions' credibility. Even in its altered condition the national convention of the 1960s and 1970s is too precious an institution to surrender. It is the only real, palpable existence — the only symptom — of a national political party. It is the only occasion for rediscovery of common traditions and common interests, the only time for common decision making and a coming together to cele-brate old glories and achievements. It stimulates the workers and con-tributors to party labors, and it encourages party candidates in the states and localities. Its rites may not mean a great deal to the majority of Americans passively peering at the TV screen (and a bit sullen over miss-ing the summer reruns), but they do mean something to the men and women of the party organization. They are, in short, a vital, integrative force in the life of the American national parties.

Not surprisingly, the parties have resisted the varying proposals for a national presidential primary advanced over the past several generations. Such a primary would replace the nominating conventions with a na-tional primary for nominating the presidential and vice-presidential can-didates. Its rationale is the general rationale of the direct primary. The objections to the proposals are considerable. First of all, there are the practical problems: a uniform national date, the provision of a run-off primary if candidates are not to be chosen by small pluralities, the impli-cations of such a primary in open primary states. There is, too, the stag-gering burden in time and resources that a nomination campaign in fifty states would place on the parties and candidates. (Very possibly, too, a national primary would encourage a lengthy preprimary politics, in which the leading contenders would seek the endorsement of the state organizations.) But, above all, most scholars and political leaders are not convinced that a national presidential primary would result in the selec-tion of more able candidates for the presidency. It might well result in the nomination of candidates best able — in money and personal charisma — to mount an effective mass-media campaign. From the party's point of view, it might also result in the nomination of candidates less likely to unify the party or appeal to its activists.[19]

THE PRESIDENTIAL CAMPAIGN

Tradition has long dictated that the presidential campaign open in early September. After the July or August conventions, the presidential and vice-presidential candidates rest and map strategy for the approaching campaign. Then it all begins with the Democratic candidate's traditional opening speech on Labor Day.

The campaign for the presidency is in many ways the generic American political campaign "writ large." Its main problems and tasks are different in degree but similar in kind. The candidate and his campaign managers must still raise money, print literature and flyers, contract for ads and media time, schedule travel and speeches, put together an integrated

[19] For a defense of the convention, see Aaron Wildavsky, "On the Superiority of National Conventions," *Review of Politics* 25 (1962): 307–19.

campaign organization, and amass the necessary research. The candidate also faces similar strategic choices. On what mixture of appearances or radio-television speeches will he rely? What timing will he adopt — the full-speed-from-the-beginning strategy of Kennedy in 1960 or the pointed, paced buildup favored by Nixon in the same year? Will he play primarily on the appeal of the party, of the candidate ("I like Ike," "All the way with LBJ"), or of issues and ideology (Barry Goldwater: "In your heart you know he's right")? And like candidates all over the country, he faces problems in presenting himself to voters: Nixon's problem in overcoming a reputation for deviousness; Kennedy's problems of youthfulness, Catholicism, wealth, and family; Goldwater's reputation for impetuous "shooting from the hip"; Johnson's for the ruthless exercise of political power (arm-twisting); Humphrey's for garrulousness; and McGovern's for radicalism.

Yet, many of the usual campaign problems are heightened by the nature of the presidential office and constituency. The candidate's problem of keeping posted on how the campaign is going, on his progress with the electorate, is tremendous. The expanse of the country, the variety of local conditions, and the candidate's isolation from the grass roots make any kind of assessment difficult. In this dilemma the presidential candidates have increasingly relied on professional pollsters to supplement the reports of local politicians. That same expanse of continent plus the length and pace of the campaign put exceptional physical strains on the candidate. Virtually every presidential candidate comes to election day on the fine edge of exhaustion. Finally, there are the special problems of the candidate who must run against an incumbent president and thus run against all the publicity, public exposure, and media attention a president commands. Perhaps these developments in the presidential campaign can best be illustrated by the changes of a century. During the 1860 campaign Abraham Lincoln never left Springfield, Illinois. During the 1960 campaign the two candidates together traveled more than 100,000 miles and gave almost 600 speeches.

The electoral college and the nature of the American parties also shape the presidential campaigns — and the candidates' problems in organizing them. Because of the electoral college, presidential candidates allocate their time and resources in a special way. In all other American constituencies a candidate can pick up useful votes even in his areas of weakness, even in those areas he will lose. Not so in the electoral college, where the candidate gains only if he wins a plurality of the vote in a state. This fact drastically alters the strategy of a presidential campaign, and presidential candidates generally pick a group of states they feel they can carry and then devote their time to them. As a result, presidential campaigns have tended to be concentrated in the close, two-party states, with the candidates largely avoiding each other's areas of strength. At the bottom of virtually every presidential campaign strategy is some reckoning of the states the candidate will surely carry and what combination of additional states (which when added to the safe ones will produce a majority of electoral votes) he has the best chance of carrying.

The rambling, decentralized character of the American parties places special problems of its own on the campaign, chiefly on its organizational aspects. Here one finds the same issues of professional versus amateur, of party committee versus voluntary personal organizations, that one finds in the organization of any campaign. But in the case of the presidential campaign there is the extra complication of the decentralized American party system. Neither the presidential campaign staff nor the national committee controls the whims and activities of the state parties. Most candidates work pragmatically (and inefficiently) through the maze of state and local organizations, finding useful leaders and contacts as best they can. Barry Goldwater in 1964, however, made the best known and best chronicled attempt to establish a single national organization with a comprehensive campaign plan (down to vote quotas for each precinct in the country) and direct lines of authority.[20] By most judgments the loose, untidy nature of the American parties triumphed over the Goldwater desire to impose some order and central planning.

The Nixon administration carried domination of the presidential campaign to new lengths in 1972. Its instrument, innocently entitled Committee for the Reelection of the President, came to be known by a not-so-innocent acronym, CREEP. It was a long step beyond the usual presidential campaign organization in two ways. First, its leadership was limited to personal loyalists of the president; at the outset, at least, it had very few people of any experience in the Republican party. Second, it was controlled by the president's closest aides in the White House; in that way there was virtually no separation of the campaign and the government. Beyond all of that, CREEP achieved a kind of sordid immortality by spawning the major case of corruption in presidential politics in American history. Most of its unwholesome activity actually took place before the nominating conventions and included, inter alia, the break-in and attempted bugging of Democratic National Committee offices (in the Watergate complex), the keeping of intelligence files on Democratic candidates, a vast series of "dirty tricks" in the presidential primaries (e.g., a bogus billboard in Florida purporting to be sponsored by Edmund Muskie and urging "More Busing"), and the collecting and spending of illegal and unreported campaign funds. All in all, the committee's activi-

[20] For two good reports on 1964 campaign organization, see Karl A. Lamb and Paul A. Smith, *Campaign Decision-Making* (Belmont: Wadsworth, 1968); and John H. Kessel, *The Goldwater Coalition* (Indianapolis: Bobbs-Merrill, 1968).

ties helped to bring down a president and to contribute to an already
hefty cynicism in the country about the ethics of campaigning in the
United States.[21]

RADIO, TELEVISION, AND THE THIRD ESTATE

For several special reasons, presidential campaigns depend more heavily
than most others on campaigning through the mass media — radio,
newspaper, and television ads and appearances:

1. Media exposure costs dearly (for example, the two presidential candidates in 1972 spent $28 million on radio and television alone), and
   presidential candidates find it easier to raise large sums of money than
   other candidates.
2. Media exposure is more efficient for presidential candidates. They
   have none of the usual problems of paying for an audience that lies
   partly outside their constituency.
3. The presidential candidates have a more receptive audience for a
   media-centered campaign. The voter who wouldn't pass up a TV
   wrestling show for a congressional candidate may do so for a presidential aspirant.
4. The size of the presidential constituency dictates that this is the only
   practical way for the candidate to reach large numbers of voters. The
   alternative, especially as the states become more competitive, is an
   exhausting travel schedule.

So the dependence of presidential campaigners on the media grows, and
there is no end in sight. To a greater extent than in most other campaigns, the masters of the media — public relations men, pollsters, ad
agencies, TV production experts — form a new political elite in the presidential races.

No candidate can escape the exposure the media provide. A good deal
of it will come without cost or effort; every speech or foray, no matter
how trivial, will be reported. Some of this kind of exposure can be controlled, however. Barry Goldwater's campaign managers persuaded him
to forego press conferences during the 1964 campaign in order not to be
goaded into rash and ill-considered retorts. In their commercial uses of
the media, the candidates have full control. Candidates may choose their
form of exposure: Will it be full speeches or spot announcements? The
former run the danger of boring voters; the latter have been criticized
for merchandising presidents. Richard Nixon in 1968, for instance, de-

---

[21] What we have come to call collectively the Watergate affair, of course, also involved abuses of executive and presidential power far beyond the 1972 campaign.

veloped a novel TV format. He appeared in ten hour-long programs in which he answered questions from panels of six or seven usually friendly questioners. An enthusiastic studio audience watched and cheered.[22]

Something of an apogee in the trend toward the media-centered presidential campaign was reached in the Great Debates of 1960. The networks had laid the way early in 1960 by offering free TV time during the campaign to the Democratic and Republican candidates if Congress would free them from the legal necessity of granting "equal time" to the minor-party presidential candidates. Congress obliged them for the 1960 campaign and that one only. Senator Kennedy proposed the debate format, and Vice-President Nixon agreed; together with network representatives they worked out the protocols. The format was this: four debates, spaced from late September to late October; opening statements from each candidate in the first and last debate; the remainder of these two debates and all the other two debates given over to two-and-a-half-minute responses to the questions of reporters. Some 85 million Americans saw at least one of the debates, and the audiences averaged about 70 million per debate. The composition of the audience was as remarkable as the size. Candidates perpetually face the problem of speaking largely to their committed supporters, but these debates brought each candidate before partisans of the other party and before the self-defined independent and undecided voters.

Most observers seem to agree that the debates of 1960 did more for Kennedy than Nixon. They offered Kennedy the opportunity to close the publicity gap between himself and the better known vice-president. They also afforded him the opportunity of showing his intellectual maturity and grasp of public issues. The debates certainly set no new records for elevated, rational debate of public issues, but they did give the voters a chance to watch the candidates face, under conditions of stress, a series of intellectual demands. A CBS poll conducted by Elmo Roper suggested that a margin of Americans, perhaps as large as 2 million, chose Kennedy over Nixon largely on the basis of the debates alone.[23] President Johnson showed no enthusiasm for the debate format in 1964, and it seems unlikely that incumbent presidents will often be lured into it. Nixon avoided the Humphrey invitations and challenges in 1968. In fact, there may not be many presidential elections in which both candidates will think it to their advantage to debate.

Presidential candidates do not face esoteric campaign problems. Their

---

[22] For a generally acerbic account, see Joe McGinniss, *The Selling of the President 1968* (New York: Trident, 1969).

[23] White, *The Making of the President 1960*, p. 294. On the Great Debates of 1960, see Sidney Kraus (ed.), *The Great Debates* (Bloomington: Indiana University Press, 1962); and Stanley Kelley, "Campaign Debates: Some Facts and Issues," *Public Opinion Quarterly* 26 (1962): 351–66.

problems result more from differences of degree than of kind, of quantity rather than quality, for, despite the exalted magnitude of the office, presidential politics grow out of American political norms, styles, and traditions. And of the entire process of presidential politics, the campaign is probably the most typical and least unusual phase of all. Certainly it is not marked by the special procedures and institutions that the earlier phases are. The art of presidential campaigning is the basic art of American political campaigning — the art of defining the various audiences of the campaign and then reaching them as efficiently and effectively as possible.

THE NATIONAL PARTY

If there is a national party in the United States — despite all the influences that fragment it into fifty state parties and innumerable local ones — it must materialize as the parties contest the one national election in American politics. And it must be able to function as one and to identify some goals and interests beyond those of the state and local parties. Does, then, the quadrennial race for the presidency see the emergence of a national party?

If by the term "national party" one means a national party organization, then clearly there is no national party. The national committees, even during the presidential campaigns, are usually weak, unused auxiliaries of the campaign organizations of the presidential candidates. The candidates have the right to appoint the chairmen of the national committees, and that traditional right in many ways symbolizes both the deference paid to the wishes of the candidate and the subordination of the national committee to him. In fact, in the entire business of nominating and electing a president, the dominance of the candidates is greater even than in the rest of American politics. Hence if there is a national party, it is almost exclusively the party in government, and we have every right and reason to call it the presidential party.

The best indication that the state parties cannot build national organizations or find a national voice comes in the politics before and during the nominating conventions. Even though they are nominally preparing for a national election, the state party activists continue to weigh heavily the interests of state and local parties. In the honest words of a New York delegate to the 1960 Democratic convention:

Politics is business. We figure Senator Kennedy for a winner who will help the local ticket. My first preference is Lyndon Johnson but party considerations come first. DeSapio, who is in trouble back home, and Michael Pendergast are the real leaders. Sure, we have Governor Harriman as the Honorary Chairman and Mayor Wagner as the chairman of the delegation — we had to give Harriman a place of distinction and the mayor just wants publicity and is only protecting his own political future in New York City.[24]

That theme of the dominance of state and local organizational interests is repeated over and over in nominating national candidates and writing national platforms. The delegates want to make sure that the process of choice (both before and during the convention) will not create factions in the organization or in any other way threaten its organizational well-being. They want to protect their bargaining power so that they can maximize the achievement of their particular goals (e.g., promotion of the aspirations of a state leader). And they want to make sure that the presidential candidate and platform of the party will assist the party in winning state and local office.

Much of this localism, even during the period of presidential politics, results from the localism of political incentives. The incentives of patronage and preferment, of political career and social advantage, depend on the winning of state and local elections and the maintenance of an effective state party organization. The goals and incentives of party activists, however, appear to be shifting from these locally rooted incentives to issue, interest, and ideology. And these tend to be national, since the great public policy concerns with which they are involved are national concerns that will be resolved by national political institutions. The party worker, therefore, must look to national politics — to the election of a president and a Congress — for the achievement of these goals. That trend is probably matched by an increasingly national focus within the entire loyal party electorate. The political information and goals of the American voter, as well as his party identification, are increasingly dominated by the personalities and issues of national politics.

Thus there are forces making for a national party and forces resisting it. The conventions themselves illustrate that ambivalence. In some states the state organizations may be strong enough to send to the convention delegates who will protect the interests of the state party. In other cases the delegates may be loyal primarily to a would-be candidate and committed to support him, regardless of the competing interests of the state party. They may even have little experience in the party. The Goldwater delegates in 1964, the McCarthy delegates in 1968, and the McGovern delegates in 1972 generally had less party experience than delegates usually have. The result is an unstable amalgam of state-oriented and national-oriented presidential politics in the conventions.

[24] Quoted by Bert E. Swanson in Paul Tillett (ed.), *Inside Politics: The National Conventions, 1960* (Dobbs Ferry: Oceana, 1962), p. 193. The case studies of the behavior of state delegations to the 1960 conventions reported in this collection are full of similar instances of the strength of state party interests in the nomination process.

With the state party organizations and delegates thus divided between local and national outlook, and with the national committees unable to function effectively, the national party is easily dominated by the presidential candidate and his followers. His is the only organization with purely national goals and incentives. Frequently the party activists whose incentive to action is a national personality or a national ideology find their best avenue to national political involvement in the voluntary organizations (e.g., Citizens for Eisenhower), the campaign organizations, or the personal followings (e.g., the Robert Kennedy personal organization) of the present or potential presidential candidates. So, what is loosely called the national party is really the party of the presidential candidate. His main problem in presidential politics, in fact, is to override and unite all the local, separatist interests and loyalties within the party. He must nationalize the attention of voters and the activities of party activists for at least the brief time of the presidential campaign.

The politics of nominating and electing a president also create for each party a national image. What the party does in nominating a candidate and what he does in the campaign put a stamp on the party, give it profile and salience for millions of Americans. For them the business of presidential politics defines what the party is, what it stands for, and who its supporters are. The creation of that image of the national party is, then, one of the major stakes of the presidential nomination and campaign. In this sense the conservatism of the Goldwater candidacy in 1964 rubbed off on the Republicans, and the painful events of the 1968 Chicago convention had an impact for the Democrats far beyond issues of control within the party. Similarly, the Watergate sins of CREEP in 1972 attached to the Republicans, even though the major sinners had few ties to and little experience in the Republican party organization.

Thus the American party is something of a hierarchical hybrid. It combines a steadfastly decentralized organization with a politics in which the focuses — party identifications, personalities, and issues — are increasingly national and centralized. These centralizing influences, as we have noted, are represented by the candidates, the officeholders, and the issues and conflicts they decide. Taken as a national entity, the American party is an illogical, even contradictory mixture of a decentralized party organization and an increasingly centralized party in government. Such an unlikely combination raises the question of how long the party organizations will be able to remain so determinedly decentralized at a time when all other influences in American government and politics are thrown on the side of centralization.

13

Financing
the Campaigns

At some time in the future it may be possible to draw up a great balance sheet for the parties in which all the resources they recruit — the manpower, skills, and money — are balanced against all the resources they spend. We would then know the sources and the value of all party intakes and the costs and activities on which they were spent. However, that kind of total input-output accounting is beyond us at the moment and so, therefore, is the kind of analysis of party effort that it would sustain.

The resources needed by the parties fall into two main categories: those of the party organization and those of the party in government (Table 1). The discussion in Chapter 4 on the recruitment of manpower and skills into the party organizations approached the question of resources for the organizations. But it dealt almost exclusively with their principal resource, the efforts of active individuals. The party's candidates and public officials — the party in government — recruit and spend another substantial sum of political resources. The party in government needs resources for its political expenses while in public office; congressmen, for example, may collect funds for trips back home for political fence mending. But the vast bulk of the resources the party in government needs are the cash resources for its collective campaigns for election. It is those resources with which this chapter is primarily concerned.

Again, in the best possible of all scholarly worlds, we might be able to account for all the contributions to campaigns for nominations and elections — to account, that is, for all the hours of work, all the goods, all the skills and expertise, and all the cash contributed. But difficult as they may be to identify, the cash contributions are easier to total than the others, and this chapter will be largely limited to them. Although that limitation is forced by sheer lack of information, one can build a substantial rationale for it at the risk of seeming to make a virtue of necessity. While the assets of the party organizations have been largely in valuables other than cash (e.g., goods and services), those of the party in government have been based mainly on cash contributions (Table 1).

TABLE 1   Total Party Resource Needs

	Party organization	Party in government
Type of resource	More services (especially manpower) than cash	More cash than non-cash contributions
Purpose	General expense of maintaining the organization	Largely for election campaigns; lesser amounts for political expenses of officeholders
Time pattern	Continuous	Periodic; at elections

Also, the increasing importance of money as a political resource can be documented easily, another justification for its special consideration here. There is abundant evidence scattered through this chapter that the cash inputs into American political campaigning have risen steeply. As candidates free themselves from the control of campaigns by the party organization, they must get cash to pay for the information, skills, and manpower that the party organization once furnished for no charge (other than a mortgage on their political loyalties). It is doubtful that the noncash inputs are increasing, at least at such a pace. One can only conclude that cash inputs, especially in the campaign activities dominated by the party in government, are increasing in relative importance.

HOW BIG IS THE MONEY?

A forbidding secrecy long veiled the budgets of parties and candidates. Contributors were hesitant to be publicly identified, and candidates feared both an unknowing violation of some law regulating campaigns and the disapproval by a suspicious public of even the most modest expenditures. The 1970s, however, brought extensive requirements to report contributions and expenditures in federal campaigns and in most states. Scholars now face the problems of both the lingering secrecy in some state elections and the enormous proliferation of information elsewhere. And as always there are the analytical problems growing from the very nature of American politics. The welter of overlapping, semi-autonomous party and candidate organizations all have budgets. There are also transfers of funds among them. Furthermore, it is often difficult to allocate expenses to a specific candidate or campaign. How, for example, does one apportion the costs of a billboard or a rally supporting a number of candidates?

Despite these and other difficulties, Alexander Heard and Herbert Alexander, the two most authoritative experts on the question of money in American politics, have estimated that total campaign expenditures — for all offices at all electoral levels, including both nominations and general elections — in the presidential years more than tripled from 1952 to 1972 (see Table 2).[1]

TABLE 2   Total Campaign Expenditures for All Offices in Presidential Years: 1952-72

Year	Sum expended	Percentage increase over previous election
1952	$140,000,000	—
1956	$155,000,000	10.7
1960	$175,000,000	12.9
1964	$200,000,000	14.3
1968	$300,000,000	50.0
1972	$425,000,000	41.7

Source The sources of this data are fully explained in footnote one. Most experts believe that the estimates of Heard and Alexander are, if anything, on the conservative side.

Not surprisingly, the most expensive campaign for public office in the United States is that for the presidency. Just to win the party nomination — that is, the right to run — may cost several million dollars. Governor Nelson Rockefeller of New York spent $7 million in his ill-starred pursuit of the 1968 Republican nomination. The victor in that contest, Richard Nixon, spent $8.5 million. Even the supposedly underfinanced campaign of Eugene McCarthy cost over $11 million. A total of some $40 million was spent to secure the two presidential nominations. With renomination a certainty for President Nixon in 1972, the preconvention contesting was limited to the Democrats. Even so, Democratic candidates spent $37 million before the convention; George McGovern spent almost $12 million of it.

[1] The data from 1952 and 1956 come from Alexander Heard, *The Costs of Democracy* (Chapel Hill: University of North Carolina Press, 1960). Those for 1960, 1964, 1968, and 1972 are from Herbert E. Alexander's four studies: *Financing the 1960 Election* (Princeton: Citizens' Research Foundation, 1962), *Financing the 1964 Election* (Princeton: Citizens' Research Foundation, 1966), *Financing the 1968 Election* (Boston: Heath, 1971), and *Financing the 1972 Election* (Boston: Heath, 1976). Those studies constitute the major body of scholarship on American political finance.

The presidential campaign raises the ante conspicuously (Table 3). Even a third-party candidacy is increasingly expensive; George Wallace spent more than $7 million in 1968. Richard Nixon and his supporters spent about $25 million in 1968 and then went on to set a new presidential campaign record of $68 million in 1972. That latter figure reflects both a prodigious ability to raise political money and the good fortune of not having to spend any of it on a campaign for nomination. The McGovern campaign in 1972 spent approximately $35 million, after having spent $12 million in the preconvention drive. Thus the cost of the national campaign more than doubled in the four years between 1968 and 1972. The division of the two-party expenditures, however, remained constant at a two-to-one Republican advantage.

TABLE 3   National Level of Spending by
Presidential and Party Committees

Year	Amount	Republican percentage of two-party expenditures
1960	$ 19.9 million	49
1964	24.8 million	63
1968	44.2 million	65
1972	103.7 million	67

Source Herbert Alexander, *Financing the 1972 Election* (Boston: Heath, 1976).

It is difficult to generalize about the cost of a race for the Senate, but it is not unheard-of to spend several million dollars in one. Senator John Tower of Texas spent over $2.5 million seeking reelection in 1972. It was the most expensive nonpresidential campaign of the year. More typically, Senate races in fairly competitive states may cost between $300,000 and $800,000. Of course, it is possible for a firmly entrenched senator from a small state to spend considerably less. It is no easier to generalize about the cost of House campaigns. The campaigns of many candidates in competitive urban districts run up costs exceeding $100,000. Other more fortunate candidates may manage for some figure between $10,000 and $100,000. Costs also fluctuate erratically in successive congressional campaigns. It is not unusual for a successful candidate for the House to spend twice as much beating the incumbent than he will in his first defense of the office two years later.

Beyond these quests for national office are the thousands of campaigns for state and local office. Hard information is rare, the generalizations questionable. Many of these campaigns involve almost unbelievably small sums. Each year hundreds of candidates win office in the United States in campaigns that involve cash outlays of a few hundred dollars; on the other hand, the mayoralty campaign in a large American city may cost a candidate and his supporters several hundred thousand dollars. Campaigns for governor of the larger states often exceed $500,000. And Nelson Rockefeller spent more than $10 million winning renomination and reelection in 1970; it was the most expensive nonpresidential campaign in the history of American politics. Campaigns for referenda in California, the home of the most elaborate noncandidate campaigns, have been known to reach a million dollars; the various groups on both sides of the 1964 pay-TV referendum are estimated to have spent over $2 million.

The levels of campaign spending, therefore, are related to a number of factors. Clearly the importance of the office and the size of the constituency are two. Important also is the degree to which the party organization controls campaigning and uses its own apparatus as the chief campaign vehicle. The competitiveness of the race also affects levels of spending. A pair of major-party candidates will generally spend more when and where the election outcome is uncertain.[2]

To repeat, all of these figures reflect only cash outlays. Therefore, they do not reflect the true economic costs of the campaign. They do not usually include the gift or loan of goods or services. Volunteer workers contribute time for canvasing, typing envelopes, plotting campaign strategy, writing press releases, and dozens of other campaign jobs. Partisans may also donate goods: free paper for literature, the use of a plane or auto, or their home and their refreshments for fundraising parties. Nor do these totals include the costs of campaigning borne by the public treasuries. In cities and states with old-style patronage systems, the city hall and county courthouses and all of their employees may be a vortex of campaign activity for the weeks before elections. Senators and congressmen customarily use their offices, their staffs, and even their franking privileges for some campaign help. Heard suggests that these additional contributions, exclusive of part-time volunteer labor, would add another 5 percent to the bill; the value of contributed labor seems greater but it is virtually impossible to estimate.[3] One might venture the opinion, however, that these noncash expenditures form a larger chunk of local campaign costs and that with a shift

[2] For a fuller development of these points, especially the one on competitiveness, see David Adamany, *Financing Politics* (Madison: University of Wisconsin Press, 1969). Adamany's study is the best one on party finance in a single state (Wisconsin). Most of its findings parallel those of Alexander at the national level; that is, the patterns and relationships that prevail nationally also prevail in the main within Wisconsin.

[3] Heard, *The Costs of Democracy*, p. 372.

from party organization campaigning (noncash) to media campaigning (cash), the percentage of noncash costs is, on the aggregate, declining.

The most important fact about the "big money," however, is that it is getting bigger. Heard, writing in 1959, plotted the rises in costs from 1940 through 1956 and concluded that the increases of 54 percent in that period were no greater than increases in the price level — that is, no greater than increases in the general cost of living.[4] Since then, however, the increases have far exceeded the rise in the price level; between 1956 and 1972 the aggregate sums increased by 174 percent, while the price level rose about 54 percent. So although the myth of rising campaign costs is an old one, the phenomenon is actually fairly new. Most observers would attribute the rise to greater dependence on the technology of campaigning: jet travel, opinion polling, computer management of data, and reliance on the media.

These then are preliminary answers to the question of how big the political money is. Unanswered is the more difficult question of how big it *really* is — how big it is when measured by relative values and utilities rather than the fixed measure of the dollar sign. Even in the American economy of 1972 the $425 million figure represented only about .037 of 1 percent of the gross national product. If one is looking for comparative benchmarks, it becomes clear that many smaller countries spend far more on political campaigns (measured by money per voter) than does the United States. A country such as Italy may spend four times what American parties and candidates do per voter, and the two candidates in the Philippine presidential elections of 1965 spent just a bit more than the two American contestants of 1964.[5] And that $425 million total for 1972 is not much more than the $388 million the tobacco industry spent for advertising in 1971.

PATTERNS OF EXPENDITURES

The modern arts of mass communication — and especially the television tube — have revolutionized American political campaigning. In so doing they have, of course, upset and restructured the patterns of expenditures in campaigns. In 1948's presidential election there were no expenditures for television, but twenty years later in 1968 the campaigns of Richard Nixon and Hubert Humphrey together spent $13.5 million for network and local television time. Additions of those magnitudes not only help to explain the absolute rise in campaign costs in recent

[4] Ibid., p. 376.
[5] The entire edition of the *Journal of Politics* for November 1963 (vol. 25, no. 4), was devoted to studies in comparative political finance; see especially the article by Arnold Heidenheimer, "Comparative Party Finance: Notes on Practices and Toward a Theory," pp. 790–811.

years, they also reflect shifts and dislocations in the proportions of campaign budgets going for various purposes.

The reports of the Federal Communications Commission to Congress permit an unusually precise definition of radio and television campaign costs. The total Democratic and Republican election costs for radio and television increased more than four times between 1956 and 1968, from $9.8 million to $40.4 million. The figure for 1968 could be boosted to $58.9 million if one included the nomination expenditures. Part of the increase reflects the spread of television sets and stations; part, however, reflects a growing reliance on TV. The limits placed on media expenditures for the 1972 presidential election, however, altered sharply the pattern of reliance on radio and television (Table 4). Spending by presidential candidates dipped, but the loss there was offset by increases in other campaigns.

TABLE 4   Comparisons in Expenditures for Radio and Television in the 1968 and 1972 Elections

	1968	1972
All presidential candidates, nomination and election	$28.5 million	$14.3 million
Republican presidential ticket	12.6 million	4.3 million
Democratic presidential ticket	6.1 million	6.2 million
All candidates in all elections	58.9 million	59.6 million

Source   Derived from *Congressional Quarterly Weekly Report*, May 12, 1973.

Television and radio expenditures, however, do not fall evenly on all candidates and party levels. Presidential campaigns rely far more heavily on them than do the others. While the 1968 presidential campaign accounted for only 19.8 percent of total campaign costs in that year ($59.4 million out of $300 million), the bills of the presidential campaign ($11 million) explain 33.4 percent of the total radio and TV bill for the 1968 campaign. Some other campaigns do match this concentration of funds on radio and TV. Senator Robert Kennedy allocated over half of his 1964 expenditures for radio spots and television presentations, some $900,000 on TV alone. But campaigns for the Senate and House, not to mention state and local office, rarely rely to such an extent on radio and TV. For many, such as the congressional candidate whose district is a small patch of a great urban center, TV time is a costly, inefficient, buckshot method, striking perhaps one in eight or ten listeners who can vote for him.

Other costs related to the shift to media campaigning are greater in the presidential campaigns. The arts of opinion polling do not come cheaply; in 1968 Nixon and Humphrey together spent $650,000 on polls and surveys. Advertisements on the printed page can also cost thousands of dollars; an eight-page insert in the *Reader's Digest* cost the Goldwater forces about $300,000 in 1964. Given the nature of the presidential office, the campaign for it involves far greater costs for travel and communication; major items are jet fares, postage, long-distance phone bills, and telegrams. The costs of moving presidential entourages — advance men, press contacts, speech writers, diction coaches, friends, advisors, and family — increase not only because of the greater amount of traveling but also because of the higher costs of jet travel itself.

On the other hand, state and local campaigns rely more on newspaper advertisements and campaign literature. Other sources of communication — the lapel button, the bumper sticker, the signs on the lawn or in the window, for example — can also account for a sizable part of the candidate's expenditures. Too, the state and local campaigns bear heavy costs in staff salaries and expenses, and in maintaining headquarters or offices. In almost every campaign, in fact, the major expenses are two: communication costs and overhead and staff costs.

Finally, what difference is there in the expenditure patterns of the two parties? The evidence of recent presidential years suggests that there is not much. Both parties, for example, spend approximately the same percentage of their budget on radio and television. But while general patterns are the same, the level of Republican expenditures has stayed above that of the Democrats. Even if one includes the transfers that Democratic national committees make to state and local committees and the spending of labor on behalf of Democratic candidates, it appears that the Republicans at the national level have been spending between 10 and 20 percent more than the Democrats. What is more, the level of Republican spending held up even in the 1964 campaign, despite the discouraging poll results, while the Democrats' outlays in 1968 under similar circumstances did not. It may well be, however, that greater noncash expenditures by the Democrats — volunteer labor and work by party activists and patronage holders — would narrow the margin if they could be calculated.

SOURCES AND WELLSPRINGS

Political expenditures are comparatively obvious; the voter sees them in the nature of the campaign directed at him. Not so with the political input. While the mechanics of fund raising, the ways in which the parties and candidates get their money, may be no great secret, the contributors have been. To most American political watchers, they are shadowy subjects for speculation, and their motives are the objects of the greatest suspicion.

The techniques by which the parties and candidates raise their funds are limited only by their ingenuity and by the prevailing political norms. The chief methods include the following:

1. *Personal solicitation.* Personal visits, phone calls, personal letters, door-to-door solicitation, or any other personal approach by the candidate himself or his solicitors raise substantial sums for the party. This is the method most generally used to reach the big contributors, the so-called "fat cats" of American politics. The success of these solicitations depends, of course, on the skill of the solicitor and on his access to those willing and able to contribute. Given the well-known propensity of many "fat cats" to give and give again, it may be largely a matter of getting the right list of prospects.

2. *Access arrangements.* Increasingly the parties are dressing up the old-fashioned solicitations with the extra inducement of access to and association with men of power. Both President Kennedy and President Johnson had a President's Club, in which a $1,000-a-year political membership fee entitled the members to periodic dinners with the president and briefings by high-level governmental officials on policy issues of the day. During the Nixon years the Republicans accepted membership in RN Associates at $1,000 per year. Not to be outdone, the House Republican Campaign Committee set up the Boosters Club; $3,000 acquires a founding membership in it, and a sustaining membership costs $1,000.

3. *Mail solicitation.* Appeals by mail, now recognized as the most effective way of raising money in small sums, have enjoyed increasing success. The Goldwater campaign of 1964 established their importance; almost a third of the Goldwater revenue came by way of mail solicitation. George Wallace followed suit in 1968, and George McGovern topped even those successes in 1972. Close to 700,000 contributors gave him about $15 million, close to 60 percent of all the money the McGovern campaign received. The secrets of mail solicitation are the same, whatever the object. The specialists polish carefully the printed message of the candidate, and they are always in search of the profitable list of prospects. (Goldwater's solicitation scored with a list of Americans who had bought an automobile polishing cloth by mail.) The importance of the mail appeal, great already, is likely to increase as new laws prohibit the very large campaign contribution.

4. *Dinners.* As unlikely as it may seem, a considerable amount of the fiscal stability of American politics has been built on a foundation of banquet chicken, mashed potatoes, and half-warm peas. For a "ticket" price, usually between $10 and $100, one has dinner in a large banquet room, listens to endless political exhortations, rubs elbows with the other

party faithful, and perhaps observes a senator, a cabinet member, or a president. It is an occasion, it offers something in return for the contribution, and it may also permit some expense account sleight-of-hand. The sums raised are significant; senators or a state party may net between $50,000 and $250,000 with the right "name" guest as a drawing card. Party committees also traditionally use the dinner for fund raising. The Lincoln Day dinners of the Republicans and the Jefferson-Jackson dinners of the Democrats are traditional annual events all around the country.

5. *Other diversions.* Taking their cue from the success of the political dinner, money raisers have begun to rely on related occasions: the cocktail party, the theater party, the reception, the wine-tasting party, the beach party, and the trip to the races. They are adaptable to all levels of giving and are especially apt for local candidates who cannot risk the pretentiousness of a "dinner."

6. *Patronage.* Although patronage has virtually passed from national politics, there continue to be charges that civil servants are subjected to various indirect forms of pressure to contribute, especially by purchasing tickets to political dinners. There has been little or no evidence of anything more than an occasional overzealous salesman, however. Patronage does yield contributions in many states and localities in which the holder of a public job is expected to contribute a fixed percentage of his salary at campaign time. In Indiana, the state patronage holders are referred to as the "Two Percent Club." Crude as it may seem, the patronage system comes close to governmentally financed campaigns in a few American states. In addition, of course, the patronage workers make an even more substantial noncash contribution in their labors for the party, some of which may occur during the hours of their patronage employment.

7. *Miscellaneous.* One can only suggest the richness of the ingenuity with which other sums are raised. Syracuse Democrats in 1960 offered trading stamps (at a rate higher than that of supermarkets) for contributions. In 1964 the Goldwater enthusiasts opened retail shops in some cities to sell the usual campaign buttons and stickers, Goldwater sweatshirts, tumblers, and pens. At George Wallace rallies in 1968 a Miss Ja-Neen Welch offered her kisses for $20 contributions; the Wallace forces, however, raised greater sums by passing an old-fashioned yellow "sudsbucket." In the late 1960s and the 1970s the Democratic party, drawing on its supporters in the entertainment industry, raised millions of dollars in nationally transmitted "telethons."

Finally, the budget of any single candidate or party committee may show two other sources of campaign funds. One is a transfer from another political committee. Large numbers of candidates for the Senate

and House, for example, receive sums from their party's campaign committees in the Congress. Some, too, may rely in the short run on debt.
But both these sums must ultimately be raised in the ways suggested
above. Some years after the events of 1968 the Democratic National
Committee was still trying to settle debts from that campaign, often on
the basis of a few cents for the dollar.

Whatever may be the form of or the occasion for the contribution,
some individual or group of individuals for some political goal or reason
has added to the political assets of a candidate or party. But who are
these individuals and how many of them are there?

Despite all the innovative techniques of fund raising, candidates and
parties have always relied heavily on the very big contributor. In 1964
about $2.2 million was raised by the two parties in gifts of more than
$10,000 apiece; by 1972 similar gifts totalled $50.7 million. In that same
year there were also some 71,800 contributions of $500 or more, a
threefold increase over 1968. Even at the lower political levels (where
a large contribution often is defined as a minimum of $100 rather than
$500), many state and congressional candidates rely on large contributors
for more than 50 percent of their political campaign funds.[6]

Large contributions also come from organizations. The Committee on
Political Education (COPE) of the AFL-CIO spent more than a million dollars on campaigns — largely Democratic — in 1968, but only
$800,000 in 1972. Those figures do not include large sums spent on
voter registration drives in the same years. Other business, professional,
and ideological groups also contribute; in the 1970s they would include,
for example, the Conservative Victory Fund, the Campaign Fund for
the Environment, the American Medical Political Action Committee, and
the National Committee for an Effective Congress. Their support varies;
some give to candidates, some to party committees, some to Democrats,
some to Republicans, and many to both.

Before 1964 the sporadic efforts to broaden the base of party finance
had not had a notable success. Sometimes the effort was less than enthusiastic, but on occasion, with strong local leadership, it succeeded.
The Democratic National Committee during the 1950s and the 1960s
tried to mount Dollars for Democrats drives, door-to-door solicitations
for party funds. Exact figures on the returns were never published, but
no one seems to have considered them a success.[7] In 1958 a well-adver-
tised campaign for the two parties sponsored by the American Heritage
Foundation and heralded by the Advertising Council yielded a grand

---

[6] Data of this paragraph are from the Alexander studies cited in footnote 1.
[7] Richard F. Schier, "Political Fund Raising and the Small Contributor: A Case
Study," *Western Political Quarterly* 11 (1958): 104–12; and Bernard C. Hennessy, *Dollars for Democrats, 1959* (New York: McGraw-Hill, 1960).

total of less than $500,000 — roughly, what three or four moderately successful dinners might have netted. In 1964 and 1968 the Republicans staged successful solicitations of small amounts by mail, however, and then George McGovern in 1972 raised unimagined sums in small contributions.

The parties and candidates have never ignored the small contributor. His contribution, even if a minor one, is often crucial; moreover, a sure way to recruit a worker is to induce him to make a contribution first. But many Americans will not contribute to their party even if asked. Despite the successes of the national campaigns with mail solicitation, local candidates still find that many of their solicitations do little more

---

A Candidate's Eye View of Campaign Finance

An unusually reflective and customarily candid Hubert H. Humphrey confided to two interviewers, late in 1974, his great distaste for the fund raising a candidate must do. His reflections were especially bitter about the old business of courting the big contributors:

"Campaign financing is a curse. It's the most disgusting, demeaning, disenchanting, debilitating experience of a politician's life. It's stinky, it's lousy. I just can't tell you how much I hate it. I've had to break off in the middle of trying to make a decent, honorable campaign and go up to somebody's parlor or to a room and say, 'Gentlemen and ladies, I'm desperate. You've got to help me. My campaign chairman is here and I'm going to step out of the room.' You even have to go through all that kind of fakery. You ask 'em and you just have to feel like a louse. When you are desperate, these are the things you just have to do.

"...You just have to grovel around in the dirt. And you see people there — a lot of them you don't want to see. And they look at you, and you sit there and you talk to them and tell them what you're for and you need help and, out of the twenty-five who have gathered, four will contribute. And most likely one of them is in trouble and is somebody you shouldn't have had a contribution from....

"When I was in Salt Lake City on Sept. 29, 1968, and wanted to make my first television talk, how did I get on? My campaign committee had to borrow every dime of it. How much did it cost us? A hundred and ninety thousand dollars. Now, I couldn't go out and see all the little cousins and sisters and grandmas and say, 'Your friend Hubert wants to get on television, would you give me your quarters?' No. Your committee borrows it, or you go to someone who says, 'I'll write you a check for $25,000.' "

From "A Candidate's Eye View of Campaign Finance,"
The New York Times, October 13, 1974.
© 1974 by The New York Times Company.
Reprinted by permission.

than cover the costs of printing and postage. The only success other than in presidential campaigns has been that of some senatorial candidates who have been able to tap out-of-state liberal or conservative money in mail solicitations.

COMPETING FOR THE DOLLAR

The solicitation of political money is as decentralized and dispersed as American campaigning is. Chaotic organization, inefficient overlap and multiple solicitations, and even an unseemly scramble for cash ensue. In this competition the parties find themselves hard pressed to raise money as parties; the individual and personal appeal of a candidate or officeholder is far more effective. In part the party organizations' problems are merely a reflection (and a cause) of the basic difficulty the parties have in controlling and coordinating campaigns for office. But the problems also spring from the fact that it is much easier to raise political money for campaigns (the power and goal-oriented activity of the parties) than it is to raise it for the continuing, monthly costs of party organization. Consequently, most American party organizations limp along on small budgets; for example, it is not uncommon for a state party's organizational costs for a year to be just about the cost of a single senatorial campaign (i.e., less than a million dollars). Periodically, parties try to establish a list of regular monthly contributors to a sustaining fund or to make levies on candidates, but in the long run they often fall back on the funds from a few dinners and a handful of loyal contributors.

The competition for the political dollar has another dimension: the uneasy relationships among national, state, and local levels of the party. The interests of the national party organization are two. First, it wants to bring some order out of the chaos of competing party bodies and committees. And second, in the close competition for political gifts, it wants to ensure an adequate source of funds for itself. Behind all of these attempts by the national organizations to exercise some control over the competition for the political dollar there is another, scarcely hidden issue. If the national parties can control more of the business of political finance, they will have strengthened themselves immeasurably against the decentralizing forces of state and local parties.

Historically the Republicans coped more effectively than the Democrats with these intraparty competings. Until the 1960s the Republicans had a reasonably effective system of coordination centering in a Republican National Finance Committee, which negotiated a budget for all the national organs of the party (including the congressional campaign committees) and assessed fund-raising quotas for the state parties. The system, never fully effective, broke down in the conservative domination by Barry Goldwater in 1964 and in the Nixon-centered fund raising of 1968. The Democrats managed a brief and very ineffective attempt at a similar plan in 1960. What little coordination they have enjoyed has come through the personal force and persuasiveness of the treasurer of the national committee.[8] (The present party chairman, Robert Strauss, held that position before assuming the chairmanship.)

The national committees direct their own fund raising both to funds that will sustain their own year-round activities and to those that they can disperse to aid candidates in their campaigns. The former are essential to their existence, but the latter have the potential for drastically altering the basic distribution of power within the party. The implications are tremendous when an incumbent president such as Lyndon Johnson through a vehicle such as his President's Club reverses the direction of monetary flow by collecting funds that might otherwise have gone to local fund raising and then dispersing them back to state and local campaigns. Short of such success, though, the national committees live a hand-to-mouth existence. The Republican National Committee ordinarily can count on the support of large contributors. Democratic contributors tend more to support specific candidates, and the Democratic National Committee has recently had to look to telethons and mail solicitations to raise its funds. Understandably, both have a major stake in public funding of campaigns, especially to the extent that funds are channeled through them.

The main obstacle to centralized party finance, however, remains the voluntary campaign committees. Party organizations may rationalize their solicitation of funds, but they cannot control the solicitations of candidates and their committees. The failures of the party organizations in finance merely reflect their loss of control of electoral politics to the parties in government. The problems of the Republicans in 1960 are typical of those which both parties face at all levels:

The relationship between the Republican Party and the volunteer organizations was typified by the independent fund-raising effort of the latter. Walter N. Thayer, finance chairman of the Volunteers (for Nixon-Lodge), accepted the position on condition that the Volunteers would not be asked to clear potential contributor lists with the regular party finance committees; he indicated the impossibility of adequately financing the Volunteers' effort if the party wanted such clearance. Citizens for Eisenhower lists of contributors from earlier years were used. Over 23,000 persons contributed, and the Volunteers raised $2.3 million, more than $400,000 over their goal.[9]

[8] See Adamany, *Financing Politics,* for the organization of solicitation within the two Wisconsin parties.
[9] Alexander, *Financing the 1960 Election,* p. 51. Former President Dwight D. Eisenhower made a contribution of $500 to the Volunteers.

It is the problem of the party organization against the party in government all over again. And once again the advantage is with the candidates and officeholders. Contributors prefer to give to specific candidates and causes rather than to the umbrella-like concerns of the party organization. They would rather be selective themselves than give the party organizations the power to be selective and, thus, more influential.

REFORM IN CAMPAIGN FINANCE

The regulation of campaign finance in the United States has for a long time been a jerry-built structure of assorted and not very well integrated federal and state statutes. Periodically reformers have attempted to bring order out of that legislation and at the same time to strengthen legal controls over the getting and spending of campaign money. A new episode of reform was under way in the early 1970s, and even produced another fragment of legislation in 1972, when the Watergate scandals broke over the country. The result in 1974 was the most extensive federal legislation on the subject in the history of the Republic.

The 1974 law was, as usual, set down on an already-existing web of legislation, superseding some of it and supplementing some of it. Some of it, in turn, was invalidated by the United States Supreme Court in late January of 1976. The main outlines of all of it, however, fall into two main categories: the limitations on campaign contributions and spending and the provisions setting up a system of public funding of national politics.

Limitations on Contributions and Expenditures

As the country went into the 1976 campaigns the chief provisions of existing federal law were these:

1. *Restrictions on sources of money:*
   Each individual is limited to a contribution of $1,000 per candidate in primary elections and another one of $1,000 per candidate in the ensuing general election. The contributor is also limited to a total of $25,000 in all such contributions in any one calendar year. (In addition, the contributor is also permitted extra expenditures for fund raising and for an advertisement supporting a candidate or candidates.)
   Organizations are limited to contributions of $5,000 to any candidate in any election.
   Corporations and labor unions themselves may not contribute.

Federal employees may not solicit funds from other federal employees
on the job. The same limitation also applies to state or local employees whose activities are financed by federal loans or grants.

The new limits on size of contribution are from the 1974 legislation and
have not, therefore, been tested in an election. There seems no doubt,
though, that they will curb the role of the very large contributor. Even
with the loopholes (and the possibility that all adults in a family can
contribute within the ceiling), there seems no possibility that we will
again see gifts of the magnitude of Clement Stone's $2 million-plus
to Richard Nixon in 1972 or Stewart Mott's in excess of a million to
both McCarthy and McGovern. The Motts and Stones will be unlimited only in their personal, independent efforts on behalf of candidates (e.g., newspaper ads). Organizational gifts will likely become
more important, and surely the contributions of small contributors will.
Candidates already have beaten paths to the doors of the mail solicitation specialists whom they think hold the key to raising money in
small sums.

2. *Restrictions on expenditures:*
   Presidential candidates are limited to $10 million in seeking the
     nomination and $20 million in the election campaign. They are
     also permitted an additional 20 percent for fund raising. Those
     limits will apply, however, only if the candidate accepts public
     funds for the campaign (see below).
   Party committees are permitted to spend sums on behalf of candi-
     dates, those sums being in addition to the expenditures permitted
     the candidate. For instance, the national committee of each major
     party can raise and spend up to 2 cents per voter on the party's
     presidential candidate (that is, a sum between $3 and $4 million).
   Candidates for a federal office are limited in their media expenditures
     (e.g., expenditures for radio, television, magazine, newspaper, and
     billboard advertising) to a total of 10 cents per voter or $50,000.
     That figure will rise, however, for it is tied by statute to rises in
     the Consumer Price Index.

The new limits, again, were passed in 1974 and have yet to be tested in
practice. They seem destined to cut the levels of spending, however. One
need only point out that the $30 million limit for both parts of the presi-
dential campaign is less than half the figure that Richard Nixon spent in
1972. Beyond that, two additional effects may be of importance. The
provision that party committees may raise and spend beyond the candidate's limits may well bolster their role in campaigns. Under the new
limits they can raise and spend, if they are able, close to 10 percent of
the funds for a presidential campaign, far more than they have in the

past. It may help them exercise some control over it. Second, the road
is open to candidates who wish to spurn public financing in return for
unlimited expenditures. The restriction of contributors to $1,000 per
candidate may, however, make that an unlikely choice.

3. *Requirements for accounting and reporting:*
     All contributions to a candidate must go through and be accounted
        for by a single campaign committee.
     Each candidate must file quarterly reports on his finances and then
        supplement them with reports ten days before the election and
        thirty days after it.
     All contributors of $100 or more must be reported and identified.

The publicity provisions of earlier legislation have not been notably
effective. Reports have always been sketchy at best and missing at worst.
But the new legislation may improve the quality of reporting by centralizing candidate responsibility in a single committee. In any event,
whether it is because of the new legislation of 1972 and 1974 or the
post-Watergate sensitivity, experts agree that the elections of the 1970s
will be the most fully reported in recent history.

Public Funding of Presidential Campaigns

Although the Congress has not yet been willing to fund its own challengers from the public treasury, it has embarked on a program of public
support for presidential candidates. The 1976 elections will mark its
inauguration.

Candidates seeking their party nominations will be aided only if they
first pass a private funding "test." They must raise at least $5,000 in
contributions of $250 or less in each of at least twenty states. If they
so establish their eligibility, public funds will match every contribution
up to $250 to a total of $5 million. (Public funds may thus provide up
to 50 percent of a candidate's maximum expenditures of $10 million.)
In addition, each of the major parties can receive up to $2 million to off-
set the costs of its national nominating convention.

Provisions for funding the election campaign are somewhat simpler.
Candidates may draw on a public fund for some or all of their expenses
up to the $20 million ceiling. (That provision, of course, presumes suffi-
cient money in the fund created by voluntary check-offs on each year's
individual income tax return.) Minor parties fare less well. They receive
only a fraction of the $20 million maximum and then only *after* the elec-
tion and after they have received at least 5 percent of the vote. (If they
drew at least 5 percent of the vote in the previous election, they can receive their payment before the election.) It is, in fact, this section deal-

ing with minor parties that has received a major part of the criticism directed at the 1974 statute. Critics charge that it will enfeeble minor parties, certainly making it hard for them to reach major-party status and, in view of the need to pay cash for many campaign expenses, hard even for them to finance a modest campaign.[10]

Immediate Problems

Long before it began to have an impact on campaigns, the 1974 law encountered a number of difficulties. It began life in an aura of inevitable controversy — inevitable because any legislation that so fundamentally alters any part of American politics will surely affect some interests differently than others and thus change the distribution of political power. All estimates of the likely effects of the 1974 law depended to some extent on where the observer stood, but there seemed to be considerable agreement that it would work to the disadvantage of minor parties and wealthy contributors of large sums, and to the advantage of party committees.

Beyond that general debate, problems in implementing the legislation have surfaced quickly. Administration is in the hands of a Federal Election Commission, chaired initially by former Representative Thomas B. Curtis of Missouri. The commission has faced an enormous agenda of difficult questions. For example, if a congressional candidate faces no primary competition, is he free to spend up to the primary limit in anticipation of the general election? Furthermore, the commission's independence was early threatened. Its interpretations could be reversed by congressional action, and the Congress began to view those interpretations with increasing concern. Indeed, it overrode the commission's ruling that congressional office funds should be considered political campaign funds and so reported.

Quickly, too, the opponents of the 1974 legislation took it to the federal courts. The opponents themselves were an unlikely coalition which included former Senator Eugene McCarthy (whose earlier campaigns for the Democratic nomination had been financed by very large contributions), the New York Civil Liberties Union, Conservative Senator James Buckley of New York, and *Human Events*, a right-wing periodical. In their suit the plaintiffs charged that the restrictions on campaign contributions infringed the rights of free speech and political activity and that they discriminated against minor parties. In early 1976 the United

[10] For other approaches to the regulation and subsidization of campaign finance, see the Report of the President's Commission on Campaign Costs (Washington: Government Printing Office, 1962), and Herbert E. Alexander, *Money for Politics: A Miscellany of Ideas*, published by the Citizens' Research Foundation in Princeton, New Jersey.

States Supreme Court upheld the major portion of the law, especially the limitations on campaign contributions and the provisions for public financing of the presidential election. It struck down the spending limits on campaigns for Congress, on candidates' use of their own personal funds and fortunes, and on the independent activity of individuals on behalf of candidates or parties. The Court also gave the Congress thirty days to reconstitute the Federal Election Commission.

Finally, it was soon clear that the new legislation would extract a high cost in compliance from candidates and their supporters. At least at the beginning there was a good deal of uncertainty about many of the provisions. While they waited for clarifications from the Federal Election Commission, candidates often found that they had to make their own best estimates of the law's applicability. They began, too, to bear new costs in bookkeeping and accounting. There were in fact a good many complaints that lawyers and accountants were becoming the new experts in American electoral politics.

State Regulation and Financing

To the maze of federal legislation one must add the even more complicated fabric of state regulation. The states have long set at least some limits to campaign activity. Most, for example, have some law prohibiting certain election-day expenditures; all prohibit bribery and vote buying, and some prohibit such practices as buying a voter a drink on election day. Most states, too, long required the making of reports on campaign contributions and expenditures; but, in general, state regulations never even achieved the modest effectiveness of the old federal legislation.

Watergate spurred a new round of state legislation after 1972. The new state legislation on campaign finance was often set in a broader frame which included legislation requiring registration by lobbyists, open meetings by government bodies, and the disclosure of the personal finances of public officeholders. By the end of 1974, consequently, virtually every state had a disclosure statute which forced reports on campaign giving and spending; many of the states which had long had such requirements tightened them up after Watergate. By the same time about a half of the states had set limits on the sums of expenditures candidates could make. And approximately fifteen of the states had ventured in some way into public financing of campaigns, although none had done so on a scale remotely comparable with the federal plan.[11]

11 *Dollar Politics*, vol. 2 (Washington: Congressional Quarterly, 1974). Generally the publications of the Congressional Quarterly provide the best contemporary reports on recent practice and legislation in political finance.

Predictably, the states present a varied range of legislation, and some of them also display a degree of inventiveness not apparent in federal law. For example, in funding elections, some states have tried the incentive of giving tax credits or deductions on state income tax returns for contributions to candidates (up to a fixed and modest limit). Others have instituted state funds using a check-off system similar to the federal one; others have tried a check-off in which the funds go to the particular party the taxpayer chooses. Generally the reporting provisions are less demanding than the federal requirement of quarterly reports; the majority of states require reports just before and after the election in question. As for the nature of limits to contributions and expenditures, one cannot generalize. For example, the limits states set for gubernatorial elections vary enormously: $50,000 in Alabama, $250,000 in Florida, $500,000 in Kansas, and $1 million in Michigan. Such figures, however, do not reckon with the differences in state law over what expenditures must be reported. Moreover, the Supreme Court's 1976 decision casts considerable doubt on the constitutionality of all of them.

The record of regulation before 1972 was not one of success. Too many loopholes and too little administration led to a conspicuous ineffectiveness. Moreover, the mass of regulatory legislation had unfortunate side effects. It stimulated the proliferation of candidate committees and the decentralization of candidate finance in order to sidestep the limitation on both individual contributions and candidate expenditures. Furthermore, it encouraged — as does any failure in regulation — a cynicism about the motives and the hypocrisies of everyone involved. But the post-Watergate legislation begins a new era in campaign regulation. More and more of the legislation reaches the nomination process in addition to the general election campaign. And both state and federal laws increasingly centralize campaign finance in a single committee and thus include more of the total campaign in their scope. It may well be that the reformist successes of the 1970s will break out of the old cycle of hopeful reform followed by disappointing results, followed soon again by hopeful reform, that has so long characterized the attempts to curb the excesses of American campaign finance.

RESOURCES AND THE FUTURE OF THE PARTIES

Perhaps we will be more successful in future regulation of campaign finance than we have been in the past. But the record of the past is not encouraging, at least in part because of the disposition of large numbers of Americans to view the question of political money with a mixture of unrealism and self-righteousness. They accuse the wealthy candidate who finances his own campaign of buying public office; the Kennedy campaign for the presidency, for example, was dogged by references to "Jack's jack." If the candidate relies on large contributions from labor, business, or professional groups, he may be accused of selling out to special interests. And yet the average voter is generally unwilling to make a political contribution; many indeed will not even allocate a dollar of their income tax payment (at no cost to themselves) to the fund that will support presidential campaigns. One can only suppose that large numbers of Americans think that a political stork brings campaign funds.

Beyond the general problem of voter attitudes, there are three more pervasive problems in campaign finance. The first is the basic one of influence in the parties and electoral processes. Political contributors have political goals and incentives, just as do activists who contribute their skills and labor to the party organization or to a candidate's campaign. Large numbers of Americans wonder what kinds of demands or expectations accompany their financial contributions. Money is obviously a major resource of American politics, and its contributors clearly acquire some form of political influence. What we have not been able to decide is the nature of the influence and the differences, both quantitative and qualitative, between it and the influence that results from nonmoney contributions to the parties and candidates.

It is not easy to specify with certainty the goals or incentives that motivate the financial contributor. Very likely they come from the same range of incentives that stir the activist to contribute his or her time to the party organization: patronage, preferment, a political career; personal, social, or psychological satisfactions; an interest, issue, and ideology. Unquestionably the chief incentive is the combination of interest, issue, and ideology — the desire, that is, to influence the making or administration of some kind of public policy. The goals of financial contributors have shifted in the same way that those of other political activists have. Their desire may be for direct access or for the ear of the powerful. More commonly, it is only a desire to elect public officials with values and preferences that promise a sympathy for the goals of the contributor. Thus the demands of the contributor are largely indirect; certainly very few contributors seek a direct quid pro quo. But it is unlikely that they will continue to support the political career of an officeholder who has indicated preferences out of harmony with theirs.

Two brief footnotes to the subject of financial contributors and their goals ought to be added: (1) These contributors are not a group completely separate from nonmoney contributors; many of the smaller contributors especially are also activists who give time, skills, and labor to the party. It appears likely, however, that a smaller percentage of the large contributors make noncash contributions. (2) The general concern for the goals of contributors is accentuated in American politics because of the failure of the American parties to develop either nonpolitical or widely distributed sources of money. The British Labour party, for example, distributes the burden of finance more widely by means of individual and group payment of membership dues. Some local Labour parties also raise substantial sums by running soccer pools; the advantage of such methods is that contributors to the parties do so indirectly and thus do not make any political demands on them.

Second, in addition to the issue of influence on policy there is the question of power within the party. The status quo in American political finance supports parties in government and helps them maintain their independence from the party organizations. As long as candidates and officeholders continue to finance their own primary and general election campaigns, they block the organizations' control of access to public office. Unquestionably the reluctance of Congress and state legislatures to disturb the present patterns of political finance grows in large part from their satisfaction with the political independence it ensures them. Despite the spate of reforms of recent years, candidate spending — as opposed to party organization spending — remains entrenched. The candidate, rather than the party, gets and spends large sums of money. Even in the sorties into public financing of campaigns, the funds go to candidates and not to party organizations. To be sure, there has been some indirect supporting of a party role — the federal legislation permitting party committees to spend beyond candidate expenditure ceilings, for example — but it is far less than would be necessary to establish strong and disciplined parties with sanctions over their candidates and officeholders.

Third, party reform, especially reform in campaign finance, never affects all individuals and parties alike. It works to some people's advantage and others' disadvantage. The cumulative effect of the reforms of the 1970s will surely be to diminish the influence of wealthy contributors and candidates and to make the "little" contributor more valuable than ever. (And in that respect one ought to note that it is hardly certain that one contributor of $10,000 actually made more effective demands on the recipient than 100 contributors of $100 will.) New advantages may well also accrue to the technicians who can raise small gifts as well as to group contributors and incumbents. New limits on contributions may, indeed, put a new premium on the noncash contribution in politics. The ability of labor to turn out a disciplined vote without a major expenditure of cash may assume a greatly enhanced value. And if we limit expenditures on media advertising, perhaps we similarly enhance the power of the press as it determines who will get "free" media coverage.

The American way of campaign finance reflects the American way of politics. Its costs reflect the vastness of the country, the many elective offices on many levels of government, the localism of American politics, and the unbridled length of our campaigns for office. The domination of spending by candidates reflects our candidate-dominated campaigns, and more generally, the dominance within American parties of the party in government. The importance of the mass media in major American campaigns speaks volumes about the media themselves while it also reflects the sheer size of our constituencies. By contrast, campaign finance in Great Britain involves far smaller sums more firmly in the control of the party organizations. But in Britain there is free time on the government-run BBC and a long-standing tradition of the "soft sell" in all forms of public persuasion. Moreover, the election campaign runs for only about three weeks, and the average constituency in the House of Commons has less than one-fifth as many people as the average American congressional district. And, most significantly, there is no larger constituency, no office with a constituency as vast as most American states, not to mention the American presidency's national constituency.[12]

Aided by institutions such as the direct primary and the office-block ballot and supported by their ability to recruit the resources they need, the American parties in government thus largely escape the control of party organizations. In many states and localities, indeed, they dominate them. But at what price? Certainly at the price of a loss of cohesion as a party in government — for example, in the loss of a unified presence as party representatives in American legislatures. Certainly, too, at the price of a weakening of party organization, not only vis-à-vis the party in government, but also internally in terms of its ability to achieve the goals of its activists. And nowhere in the life of the parties is the competition between party in government and party organization any clearer than in the competition for campaign funds and campaign control. As the costs of campaigning rise and as all participants are forced to shift to a cash economy of enormous magnitude, the future is with the sector of the party with access to those cash resources. So far the advantage is clearly with the candidates and officeholders.

12 For a comparison with the Norwegian experience with political finance, see Jasper B. Shannon, *Money and Politics* (New York: Random House, 1959).

V

THE
PARTY IN
GOVERNMENT

The charge that the American parties cannot govern is an old one, and few scholars of American politics have made it as pungently as E. E. Schattschneider:

Yet, when all is said, it remains true that the roll calls demonstrate that the parties are unable to hold their lines on a controversial public issue when the pressure is on.

The condition . . . constitutes the most important single fact concerning the American parties. He who knows this fact, and knows nothing else, knows more about American parties than he who knows everything except this fact. What kind of party is it that, having won control of government, is unable to govern? [1]

The parties put their resources and energies into a concerted bid for office, and they try to convince the American electorate that it does matter that they, rather than the opposition party, win office. But can it matter that much when the parties in Congress fragment in votes on issues of national policy? For instance, in the roll call votes in the Ninety-third Congress (1973–74) in which a majority of one party disagreed with a majority of the other party, the average Democrat voted with his party only 66 percent of the time and the average Republican only 65 percent.[2]

Yet, in the face of this and other evidence that the American parties do not and cannot govern, it still remains true that party lines, however loosely drawn, are the chief lines in American legislative voting behavior. In the roll calls of Congress and the states, there is a degree of party cohesion that cannot be dismissed. Furthermore, recent scholarship suggests that the party winning the presidency even succeeds in carrying out a goodly portion of its party platform.[3]

The evidence on party government in the United States points in a

---

[1] E. E. Schattschneider, *Party Government* (New York: Rinehart, 1942), pp. 131–32. Italics in the original have been eliminated.
[2] *Congressional Quarterly Almanac* 30 (1974): 1001–02.
[3] Gerald M. Pomper, *Elections in America* (New York: Dodd, Mead, 1968), Chap. 8.

number of directions. It suggests that the parties do not fail entirely in enacting their programs into public policy. And yet it betrays the frequency with which officeholders of the same party disagree on matters of public policy. More surely, it suggests that an individual's assessment of the parties' ability to govern depends on how and to what extent he expects the parties to govern.

Some distinctions are important here. We are talking of *party* government, not merely the governing and policy making of officeholders elected on party tickets. Certainly men and women who seek legislative or executive office do intend to govern, to take their responsibilities seriously, but that is not the issue. We are talking about the ability of public officials of the same party to enact the program of their party. If it is *party* government about which we inquire, which parts of the party do we expect to set policy and which will govern by it? All three sectors, or just the party in government? The entire party in government, or is it possible that the executive party has propensities and abilities to govern different from those of the legislative party?

It is well to remember, too, that although the three sectors of the party are brought together in the search for power at elections, each has its own goals and motives. The activists of the party organization may seek to translate a program or ideology into policy, but they may also seek patronage jobs, other forms of reward or preference, the sensations of victory, or the defeat of incumbents or a hated opposition. The party's voters may be stimulated by an issue, a program, or an ideology, but they also respond to personalities, to the incumbents ("time for a change"), to abstract and traditional loyalties to a candidate or party, or to the urging of friends and family. The candidates and officeholders seek the office, its tangible rewards, its intangible satisfactions, its opportunities to make public decisions. The important point is that none of the three sectors is committed wholly — or possibly even predominantly — to the capture of public office for the purpose of working out party policies or enacting them into law.

The classic American statement on party government (or "party responsibility") was made in the late 1940s by a committee of the American Political Science Association in a report entitled *Toward a More Responsible Two-Party System.*[4] It argued that the American parties ought to articulate more specific and comprehensive policy programs, nominate candidates pledged to those programs, and then see to it that their successful candidates enact the programs while they are in office. In other words, the major parties would serve as the mechanisms through

[4] The report was published by Rinehart in 1950. It also appears as a supplement to the September 1950 issue of the *American Political Science Review.*

which American voters could choose between competing programs, and the winning majority of voters could be assured of the enactment of its choice.

In such terms the question of party government or responsibility concerns not just the nature of the parties but also the nature of the American democracy itself. If the parties were to become policy initiators, they would assume a central representative role in the American democracy. They would bring great, amorphous majorities in the American electorate into alliance with groups of officeholders by means of some kind of party program or platform. They would forge a new representative link between the mass democratic electorate and the powerful few in government. Or, to put the issue another way, responsible parties would bring electorates closer to the choices of government by giving them a way of registering a choice on policy alternatives. In part those choices might be "before the fact" (and thereby represent the mobilization of grass roots support behind proposed programs), and in part they might be post facto judgments on the stewardship of two different, distinguishable parties in government. Behind the proposal is thus an attempt to restore initiative and significant choice to the great number of voters.

The critics of such proposals for party government have concentrated on one insistent theme: the nonideological, heterogeneous, and pragmatic nature of the American parties makes agreement on and enforcement of a coherent policy program very difficult, if not impossible. Yet the party organizations are increasingly oriented toward programs and ideology — and thus toward the uses of governmental authority for specific policy goals. There was a time when the activists of the party organization contested elections for the spoils at stake: jobs, contracts, honors, access, and other forms of special consideration. It made little difference to them what uses public officeholders made of the governmental power in their hands. That time is passing. As more and more citizens are attracted to the party organizations (and also to the party electorates) for reasons of policy, important intraparty pressure builds for some measure or variety of party responsibility.

In other words, the general question of the role of parties within the institutions of government is really two questions. First, it is a question of the party's contribution to the decision making of public officials, of the party's role in a democratic political system. These concerns one may call the issue of the party's impact on the broader political system. But the relationship of party to government is also a question of the government's impact on the party. Political parties, as we have reiterated, are purposive, goal-oriented organizations. The achievement of those goals (the goals of all three sectors) is closely related to the holding of governmental power. But in what way? What, to put it bluntly, does governmental power do for the parties? What kind of rewards does it generate for the men and women who have invested so much in politics and the party? How does it contribute to the health and vitality of the party and its various sectors?

Talk of more programmatic and disciplined political parties leads always to the European parties, especially those of England. Parliamentary institutions foster the kind of legislative cohesion and discipline — the sharply drawn party lines — that the advocates of responsible parties have in mind. Also party leaders in Britain and on the continent, especially those of the parties of the left, seek to organize the party's legislators behind the national party's program. In some cases they have succeeded — in many of the socialist and communist parties, among others. In others they have not, but even in these cases the national party leaders speak powerfully for the party's program. One often sees a concerted effort on the part of the party in government (all of which sits in Parliament) and the party organization to carry out a program that was adopted with the help of the party members at an earlier party conference. Indeed, so strong is party discipline in the legislative process in some European countries that scholars complain about the decline of parliaments, and journalists write darkly of "partyocracy." Ironically, in these circles it is not uncommon to hear envious talk of the flexible, non-dogmatic American parties and undisciplined American legislatures.

The European experience is important for perspective and for the comparison of American party practice with parties in parliamentary regimes. It is additionally important because the European variety of party government, with its focus on parliamentary discipline, has dominated the thinking of many Americans about party government. Reform and change in the American parties toward greater responsibility, however, will probably follow no conventional route, European or otherwise. The role the parties now have in American politics and the roles to which they move will be as uniquely American as the institutional complex of American federalism, separation of powers, and electoral processes. Especially in view of the power of the executive in American government, it is necessary to look beyond the legislature to the executive party for the ability to convert party goals or platforms into public policy.

The first two chapters of this part examine the present role of the political party in the organization and operation of the three branches of government. They are basically concerned with the degrees of party direction or party cohesion in legislative and executive policy decisions. (Needless to say, most Americans would consider party direction in judicial decision making grossly improper.) The chapters deal also with the relationship between party organization and the party in government, especially with the ability of the latter to achieve the goals of the former. In short, they deal with the impact of internalized party loyalties and external party influences on the public officials. The third chapter of this part faces the general question of party government, its desirability and its possibility. It is especially concerned with the question of whether the new programmatic orientations within the party sectors create conditions hospitable to the development of party government.

14
Party
and Partisans in
the Legislature

The political party assumes an obvious, very public form — yet a very shadowy role — in American legislatures. In the legislatures of forty-nine states and in the United States Congress, the political parties organize majority and minority power, and the legislative leaders and committee chairmen are party oligarchs.[1] Yet, despite the appearance and panoply of party power, the voting on crucial issues often crosses party lines, not to mention party pledges and platforms. The party in many forms stalks the American legislatures; yet the effect of party effort and loyalty is often negligible. On this paradox turns much of the scholarly concern and reformist zeal expended on American legislatures.

The character of the American legislative party has been deeply affected by the American separation of powers. In a parliamentary regime, such as that of Great Britain, a majority party or a multiparty coalition in the Parliament must cohere in support of the cabinet (and its government), thus creating a constitutional presumption and pressure on behalf of unity within the legislative party. When the parliamentary majority no longer supports the cabinet, the cabinet falls. Either reorganization of the cabinet or a reshuffling of the legislative coalition supporting it ensues, or else the Parliament is sent home to face a new election.

No such institutional and constitutional pressures weigh on American legislators. They may divide on, dispute with, or reject executive programs, even if that executive is of their own party, without similar consequences. In these American legislatures, the party role has not been institutionalized as it has in parliaments. The American legislature may not run as smoothly without party cohesion and discipline — or without party leadership — but it can run.

[1] The Nebraska legislature is chosen in nonpartisan elections. On the discussion in this chapter, see the bibliography of Charles O. Jones and Randall B. Ripley, *The Role of Political Parties in Congress* (Tucson: University of Arizona Press, 1966).

PARTY ORGANIZATIONS IN LEGISLATURES

In all but one of the fifty state legislatures, the members come to their legislative tasks as elected candidates of a political party. The ways in which they form and behave as a legislative party, however, differ enormously. In some states the legislative party scarcely can be said to exist; in others it dominates the legislative process through an almost daily regimen of party caucuses. And anomalies abound. Party organization is at its weakest in the overwhelmingly dominant party of the one-party states, but in the days of nonpartisanship in Minnesota, the legislators aligned themselves into liberal and conservative caucuses which for all intents and purposes were Democratic and Republican caucuses.

Party organization in the United States Congress stands as something of a benchmark for observations of the American legislatures because the Congress is the best known legislative system. Both parties in both houses of Congress caucus at the beginning of each congressional session to select the party leadership: a party leader, an assistant leader, a whip and assistant whips, and a party policy committee. In addition, the party caucus presents its candidates for the position of Speaker of the House and president pro tempore of the Senate, and it sets up procedures for the appointment of party members to the regular committees of the chamber. In effect, then, the basic unit of party organization, the caucus, begins the business of organizing the chamber; from its decisions rises the machinery of the party as a party (the leaders, whips, policy committees) and the organization of the chamber itself (the presiding officer and the committees).

And yet, for all the party machinery the parties in Congress do not easily organize themselves for action as parties. When the party caucuses (or conferences, as the Republicans prefer to call them) do meet on important issues during the session, they only rarely undertake to bind the individual members. And the parties have not devised any substitute body for setting policy and determining the party legislative strategy. The policy committees set up in the Reorganization Act of 1946 have not succeeded as broadly based instruments of party policy making or strategy setting, even though they were created for the "formulation of overall legislative policy of the respective parties," as the act puts it. One study found that they lacked any internal agreement on party policy and that instead of being a collective party leadership, they had lapsed into the practice of representing the assorted blocs and wings of the party.[2] Despite the original hopes, the policy committees have operated pri-

---

[2] David B. Truman, *The Congressional Party* (New York: Wiley, 1959), pp. 126–30.

marily as advisory boards and channels of communication between the party leaders and influentials and the full party membership.[3]

Dissatisfaction with leadership control of the policy committees breaks out periodically, especially among the liberal Democrats. In 1963 in an attack on the "Senate Establishment" Senator Joseph Clark (Pennsylvania) included strictures about conservative and leadership domination of the Democratic Policy Committee.[4] In the same year the overthrow of Representative Charles Halleck, the Republican leader, by Representative Gerald Ford was accompanied by an increase in the number of younger Republicans on that party's policy committee in the House. But despite the agitation, the policy committees remain at best a means for increasing consultation and communication within the legislative party; they are a very long way from becoming the authors of party policy in the legislature. In the reform of party machinery in the 1970s the House Democrats, however, formed a new Steering and Policy Committee with elected representatives from the caucus. Its future seems uncertain, but since 1975 it has at least begun to function as the party's Committee on Committees. In fact, the Democratic liberals of the House, in the absence of an effective House Democratic policy committee, some years ago formed a policy committee of their own: the Democratic Study Group. The DSG does some staff research, takes policy stands, and represents the liberal views of its members. It has even developed its own whip system.[5]

To the extent that there is "party policy" in the houses of Congress, it is largely set by the party leadership. The floor leaders and the powerful figures of the party consult widely throughout the party, but the final codification of party policy, the sensing of a will or consensus, rests primarily on their judgment. If they are of the president's party, their actions and decisions are limited by his legislative program and his influence within the Congress. Within the nonpresidential party, the leadership in the House and Senate may act not only without a continuing check by the legislative party but also without a continuing check by any party organ or spokesman. Senate party leaders such as Lyndon Johnson in the 1950s and Everett Dirksen in the 1960s, in fact, established themselves as spokesmen for both the legislative and the national parties.[6]

---

[3] For the leading study of one of the policy committees, see Charles O. Jones, *Party and Policy-Making: The House Republican Policy Committee* (New Brunswick, N.J.: Rutgers University Press, 1964).

[4] Joseph S. Clark, *The Senate Establishment* (New York: Hill and Wang, 1963).

[5] See Arthur G. Stevens, Arthur H. Miller, and Thomas E. Mann, "Mobilization of Liberal Strength in the House, 1955–1970: The Democratic Study Group," *American Political Science Review* 68 (1974): 667–81.

[6] More generally on party leadership in the Congress, see Ralph K. Huitt, "Democratic Party Leadership in the Senate," *American Political Science Review* 55 (1961): 333–44; and Randall B. Ripley, "The Party Whip Organizations in the United States House of Representatives," *American Political Science Review* 58 (1964): 561–76.

What emerge as the decisions and priorities of the party leadership, however, are not really "party policy" — except in the sense that they are voiced by leaders of the legislative party. They are rather an amalgam of or a negotiated compromise among the goals of the senior party members (who hold committee power), the party leaders themselves, the rank and file of the legislative party, and (in one party) the president. They rarely flow from any national party program or platform. They speak instead of the powers and perquisites of the legislature, the need to support or oppose a president, and the demands of the legislative constituencies. The party leaders, in other words, do not enforce a prior party policy; they "make" policy for and with their fellow legislators in an ad hoc way. Their party policy is purely that of the legislative party. In view of the party leadership's brokerage role in making it, therefore, it is understandable that studies of congressional roll call votes have placed the party leaders in the fluid middle of the party's voting blocs.[7]

Among the state legislatures are those in which daily caucuses, binding party discipline, and autocratic party leadership make for a party far more potent than exists in the two houses of Congress. But there are also legislatures — especially those of the traditional one-party states — in which party organization is perceptibly weaker than in the Congress. Even in states having a complete apparatus of party organization, the parties fail more frequently than the congressional parties to make it operate effectively. The party caucuses in Congress at least maintain cohesion in their initial organizational tasks; they always agree on candidates for the presiding officers. But in January of 1965, the Democrats of the New York legislature, the majority party in both houses, split so badly that they could not agree on a single set of leadership candidates. After a hiatus of a month, during which the unorganized legislature could conduct no business, the Republicans threw their votes to one of the Democratic factions and thus elected leaders for both chambers. Thus state legislative parties have on occasion found themselves too riven by factionalism even to organize the legislature.

In a one-party state, the party caucus has little excuse for being. Disagreement over organization, leadership positions, and policy issues in these states usually falls along factional lines within the party or along the lines of followings of powerful personages. In the heyday of the Long dynasty in Louisiana, one Democratic faction adhered to the Longs and others followed the competing political kingpins. In this particular case and in others as well, factional lines built on personal and family followings coincide with differing regional loyalties. Alternatively, the legislative caucuses in one-party states may reflect ideological lines; from 1910 to the 1930s in Wisconsin, the La Follette Progressive Republicans

[7] Truman, *The Congressional Party.*

The Party Caucus in Pennsylvania

The party caucuses of the United States legislatures are generally secret, and that secrecy encourages speculation about the grossest forms of party dictation in them. One observer of Pennsylvania politics writes about the legislative caucuses of that state in a way that is closer to the political reality of the caucuses than the dark suspicions of press and public.

"A politically significant part of the caucuses' work is, of course, on policy bills that affect the fortunes of the governor and the parties themselves. Between 10 and 15 per cent of the bills voted on in recent legislative sessions have found the two parties opposed to each other as parties on the floor. Here the caucuses, again principally the majority's caucus, may devote weeks and even months to working out a party position on an issue acceptable to most party members. Negotiation rather than pressure would be the best noun to describe this process. The very slender margin of control each party has had when it has been in control in recent sessions has made it necessary to secure nearly total agreement of the members on a bill. Sometimes the caucus may re-write an unpopular bill that the governor needs to have passed. The House Republican caucus in 1963, for example, scrapped Gov. Scranton's dual proposal for a one-half per cent rise in the state sales tax, and extension of that tax to cover clothing. Instead, it worked up a bill — successfully as it turned out — raising the tax by a full one per cent, but limiting the tax to items previously covered. All but one of the House Republicans supported this measure on the floor. All but two House Democrats voted against it."

Kenneth T. Palmer, "The Pennsylvania General Assembly:
Politics and Prospects," a paper on the state legislatures
prepared for the Pennsylvania Assembly, 1968.

organized one legislative caucus, the conservative Republicans another, and the very feeble Democrats a third.

In a majority of the states, generally in those states of two-party competition, the party caucus prevails as the basic party unit in the legislature. In some they meet no oftener than the congressional caucuses; in others they meet almost every day during the legislative session, often binding their members by majority vote. A state with active party caucuses, such as Pennsylvania, may even spawn caucuses within the party caucuses; both the Pittsburgh and Philadelphia Democrats occasionally caucus separately in addition to attending the Democratic caucus.[8]

Party leadership in the state legislatures assumes a number of forms. The traditional floor leaders and whips exist in most. In others the

[8] On caucuses in state legislatures, see Malcolm E. Jewell, *The State Legislature*, 2nd ed. (New York: Random House, 1969), pp. 48–51.

Speaker of the House or a spokesman for the governor may mobilize the party's legislators. State party officials, unlike the relatively powerless national party officials vis-à-vis Congress, may have a powerful voice in the legislative party. As Lockard reported of the heyday of party control in the Connecticut lower house

the "outside" party leaders are in daily attendance at the capitol and can be seen in corridor conferences with the great and small alike. Each party chairman sits in on his respective party policy conferences and not infrequently he is the real leader of the conference. With few exceptions the men who reach the party pinnacle of the state chairmanship can expect (and they certainly receive) proper deference from their fellows in the legislature. . . .[9]

And the legislative party leaders in the states are no more bound or checked by the rank and file of the legislative party than are their counterparts in Congress. They generally control the caucus in those states in which it meets frequently, and smaller, representative party steering or policy committees are rare in the states.[10]

PARTY ORGANIZATION: EFFECTS AND INFLUENCE

In the United States Congress and many state legislatures the parties have erected imposing organizations. But for what? For organizing party support for a set of party programs or merely for parceling out the perquisites of legislative office? Or does the legislative party seek both policy and perquisites?

The party organizations in the United States Congress have amply illustrated over the last century that they can impose party sanctions on only one issue: the failure of a member of the legislative party to support its presidential candidate. A congressman or senator can freely vote against the party's platform, majority, or leadership — or against the program of his party's president. But he risks punishment if he undercuts his party's presidential candidate. In 1925 the Republican caucus in the Senate expelled Senators La Follette, Ladd, Frazier, and Brookhart after they had supported La Follette and the Progressive ticket in the 1924 elections. That decision also robbed the four senators of their Republican committee assignments and seniority.

In 1965 the Democratic caucus in the House invoked a lesser sanction on two Democrats from the South who had supported the Republican presidential candidate, Barry Goldwater, in the 1964 elections. Although they were not expelled from the party, they were stripped of their legislative seniority and placed below even the new congressmen of the '64

[9] W. Duane Lockard, "Legislative Politics in Connecticut," *American Political Science Review* 48 (1954): 167.
[10] See Belle Zeller (ed.), *American State Legislatures* (New York: Crowell, 1954), pp. 194–95.

class in committee seniority. In 1968 the same fate befell Representative John Rarick, a Democrat of Louisiana, for supporting George Wallace. Disloyalty in presidential elections is not always punished, however. A number of conservative Democratic congressmen rejected the presidential candidacy of George McGovern in 1972 — and a few even supported President Richard Nixon — without suffering any consequences.

Beyond these rare disciplinary actions, the party organizations in Congress also offer vehicles for informal pressure. The president's wishes and influence are often funneled through his party's leaders. They confer with him and carry his proposals to the Congress, and, in fact, they are often called "his" leaders in the Congress. In other instances the legislative leaders may report and transmit the feelings of party leaders outside of the Congress. But as they try to organize consensus within the Congress, they organize it chiefly around the image and interests of the legislative party — around the congressional view of the nation's problems and around its concern for its perquisites and reputation. Their role is classically that of the broker trying to mediate between the local pressures of congressional constituencies and the imperatives of national policy making, and trying also to form majorities out of disparate views and loyalties within the party. The chief limit to their success is always the need of the individual congressman to satisfy a constituency in order to win reelection.[11] Responsiveness to the constituency often outweighs the calls for party unity in Congress.

Attempts to build party discipline in Congress have been undercut in the past by the power of the committees and by a tradition of seniority that awards committee chairmanships to legislators of longest service. The power and independence of the committees places them, as a system of influence, squarely in opposition to any control or influence that the parties might exert. The principle of seniority as a key to power in the committees puts a premium on getting reelected rather than on party loyalty or regularity within Congress. So attempts of the parties to reform seniority and the committee system — such as those of the House Democrats in the 1970s — are nothing less than struggles for control of the business of Congress. The Democrats of the House succeeded by modifying the power of committee chairmen and establishing the principle that the party caucuses would vote every two years to approve the continuance in power of every committee chairman. Indeed, as a result of the reforms three Democratic chairmen who had held their positions by reason of seniority were deposed in 1975. And so, as committee power was diminished, the strength of the party organization was enhanced.

In many state legislatures, party leadership and organization operate

---

[11] David R. Mayhew, *Congress: The Electoral Connection* (New Haven: Yale University Press, 1974).

far more effectively than they do in the Congress. Positions of party leadership and committee power much more frequently go to legislators loyal to the party and to its program. Furthermore, either the party leaders, the party speaking through a periodic caucus decision, or the party's governor or state committee may expect the legislator to support the party program or stand on a particular issue. Whether for an earlier programmatic commitment or for the issue of the moment, they stand ready to enforce party discipline. For example, a survey of the states in the 1950s revealed that in more than a quarter of them the majority caucus in the legislature met frequently and attempted to maintain discipline on behalf of a party program.[12] For excessive lapses of party loyalty state legislators may suffer sanctions inconceivable in the United States Congress. Their influence may wane in the legislature, and they may ultimately lose positions of power. In a patronage state they may find that the applicants they sponsored fare less well than formerly. They may also find in the next election campaign that they no longer receive campaign funds from the state or local party, or worse yet, that the party is supporting competitors in the primaries.

Clearly the parties in some of the competitive, two-party state legislatures have advanced the art of discipline far beyond its state in the Congress. Their contrast with Congress and the less assertive legislative parties of other states affords an opportunity to examine the determinants of such control. Disciplinary success in some state legislatures can be attributed to the following reasons among others.

Absence of Competing Centers of Power

In the Congress the committees have traditionally been the centers of legislative power. A vast amount of the real business of the Congress goes on in them. They are a set of screens that sift through the great mass of legislative proposals for those relatively few nuggets of legislative metal. The result is the creation of important centers of power in the Congress that owe nothing to the parties and do not necessarily reflect the party organization or aims. (In fact, one can argue that since seniority and its power accrue to congressmen from one-party areas, they are definitely unrepresentative of the party in the country at large.)

In the states, on the other hand, legislators accumulate less seniority (turnover is greater), and deference to seniority in allocating positions of power is far less common. A 1950s survey of the state legislatures concluded that seniority "figured prominently" in the selection of committee chairmen in only fourteen senates and twelve lower houses in the states.[13] The parties are freer to appoint their loyalists to positions of

---

[12] Ibid., p. 194.
[13] Belle Zeller (ed.), *American State Legislatures*, p. 197.

legislative power; the committees and other legislative agencies of the states generally operate as instruments of party power in a way they cannot in Congress.

Patronage and Preferences

Patronage and other forms of governmental preference still exist in some states to a far greater extent than they do in the national government. Especially in the hands of a vigorous and determined governor these rewards may be potent inducements to party discipline in state legislatures. The legislator who ignores his party, if it is the party of the governor, may not be able to secure the political appointments that his constituents and local party organization have been waiting for. Conversely, the loyal and faithful party legislator is amply rewarded. In the Congress little such patronage remains with which to induce party discipline. It may well have died there in the early 1930s as Franklin Roosevelt mustered what remained of the federal patronage and told his patronage chief, Postmaster General James A. Farley, not to dole out the jobs until the voting records were in from the first congressional session.

Influence of the State Party Organization

The state legislator is subject to far more sanction and control from his state party organization than is the member of Congress from the feeble national committee of the party. In the states the party organization and the legislative party are far more apt to be allies. State party leaders may inhibit the political ambitions of party mavericks or deny them advancement within the party, especially in states in which they control the nomination processes. They may even prevail on local parties to deny renomination to the disloyal. Indeed, state party leaders may occupy positions of legislative leadership; powerful figures such as the former Democratic Speaker of the California Assembly, Jesse ("Big Daddy") Unruh, combined state party influence with legislative leadership. Lockard reported that the Republicans in Rhode Island had "a policy committee comprised of important senators, a few representatives, the state party chairman, and a few members of the state central committee." [14] By contrast, the national political party is relatively powerless in dealing with its congressional parties. Even so powerful a party figure as Franklin Roosevelt was unable to purge a group of conservative Democrats for failing to support his program. Thus, congressmen are protected by decentralized party power. State legislators are not.

---

[14] W. Duane Lockard, *New England State Politics* (Princeton: Princeton University Press, 1959), p. 218.

Electoral Dependence of State Legislators

State legislators are far more dependent on the local and state party for nomination and election than are the members of Congress. And what the local party has given, it may take away. Congressmen and senators build their own political organizations, their coteries of local supporters, and their own sources of campaign financing. But state legislators are politically unknown and therefore more dependent. In some states the parties control the election of state legislators to such an extent that these positions approach an "elective patronage," which the party awards to loyal toilers in its organizational ranks. (About 70 percent of the candidates for the Pennsylvania House of Representatives in the election of 1958 had held some party office.) [15] Party irregularity may cost the legislator this crucial local support — either through the local party's initiative or at the behest of a powerful state party organization.

Greater Political Homogeneity

Greater party cohesion and discipline in some state legislatures reflect also the greater homogeneity of state parties. While a legislative party in Congress reflects the full range of differences within the nation, that same party in any given state embraces a narrower spectrum of interests and ideologies. This greater political homogeneity of the states produces legislative parties in which the ranges of differences and disagreements are smaller and in which there are fewer sources of internal conflict. The political culture of the state also is more homogeneous, and in some cases more tolerant of party discipline over legislators than is the national constituency. Legislative party strength, for example, has traditionally flourished in the northeastern part of the country (Rhode Island, Connecticut, Pennsylvania, New Jersey, for example), the states of party organizational strength, patronage, weak primaries, and, one infers, a political culture tolerant of the exercise of political muscle.

In summary, the parties in some state legislatures exert far more discipline than they do in other states or in the United States Congress, and these differences may be explained by a number of factors. State legislators may be subject to far more impressive party sanctions: the loss of legislative influence, committee positions, patronage, party influence, a political future, and ultimately even the legislative seat. Second, the party in state legislatures generally faces no competing system of power within the legislature similar to the seniority system in Congress. Finally, the general distribution of political interests and the political culture produce in some states homogeneous, relatively unified parties

[15] Frank J. Sorauf, *Party and Representation* (New York: Atherton, 1963), p. 86.

operating in a political culture that offers more latitude to their legislative discipline.

PARTY COHESION IN LEGISLATIVE VOTING

Party organization in Congress and the state legislatures — with caucuses, leaders, whips, and policy committees — is only the most apparent, overt manifestation of the party in the legislature. Its efforts on
behalf of party unity and discipline among its legislators are tangible,
even if difficult to document. But party influence in the legislature is
broader, more pervasive, than the enforcing activities of the organized
legislative party. Party pressures on legislators come from other sources:
from state parties, from the executive branch, and from the party electorate of the constituency. "Party" in a broader, more figurative sense
also may operate "within" the legislator as a series of internalized loyalties and frameworks for organizing his legislative decisions. To speak
of party only in the organizational sense of leaders and caucuses, therefore, is to miss the richness and complexity of its influence upon the
legislative process.

The multiplicity of party pressures on the national and state legislator
may even create conflicting influences. The cues, even the articulated
demands, a legislator gets from the party electorate in his or her constituency may differ from the demands of the more ideological and
militant souls who make up that constituency's party organization. And
one or both may be at odds with the presidential or gubernatorial voice
in the party. Then, too, party pressures often conflict with nonparty
pressures, including those of nonparty organizations and the legislator's
own belief system. The dilemmas arising from these conflicts are the
staple of legislative conflict. Consider the position of congressional
Republicans in the mid-1970s. The party platform favored cutting back
welfare-state programs generally, and President Gerald Ford shared that
commitment out of both ideology and fiscal prudence. Constituency
pressures, some local party support, and personal inclinations, however,
appeared to work in favor of continued federal aid to education. The
majority of congressional Republicans, therefore, joined Democrats to
continue the program, even to override a Republican president's veto of
it in 1975.

Gauging the various party influences on legislative behavior is no
easy matter. But the collective consequences of party influence ought
logically to be apparent in the actions of the legislative parties. The
proof of the pudding comes as the roll calls begin. If the legislative
party is to govern, it must be able somehow to muster cohesive support
for party positions on votes in the legislature.

Incidence of Party Discipline or Cohesion

Answers always depend on the form of the question, and so it is with the question of just how much cohesion or discipline the American parties generate in legislatures. The answer depends to a considerable extent on the operational definition of the term *discipline*.

One more or less classic measure of party discipline in legislatures has been the "party vote," any legislative roll call in which 90 percent or more of the members of one party vote yes and 90 percent or more of the other party vote no.[16] By such a stringent test, party discipline appears frequently in the British House of Commons but far less often in American legislatures. Julius Turner found that from 1921 through 1948 only 17 percent of the roll calls in the House of Representatives met such a criterion of party discipline. In the 1950s and 1960s it dropped steadily to about 2 or 3 percent. Recently in the British House of Commons the percentage of "party votes" averaged very close to 100.[17]

Although the "90 percent versus 90 percent" standard discriminates between British and American party cohesion, it is too stringent a standard for comparisons within the American experience. Scholars of the American legislatures have opted for less demanding criteria. Whatever the criterion one accepts, it may be used to describe both the overall incidence of cohesion in the legislatures and the party loyalty of individual legislators. In other words, one may make statements about the percentage of instances in which the majority (or 80 percent) of one party opposed a majority (or 80 percent) of the other; and one can also figure the percentage of times that an individual legislator votes with his party when party opposes party. In their study of American legislatures, Jewell and Patterson have collected data from various other studies and sources on party cohesion in state legislatures, drawing on a number of these measures of party cohesion. Table 1 indicates the enormous variation in party cohesion in the decisions of a number of state legislatures. It illustrates also the high degree of cohesion in the urban, two-party states of the northeastern section of the country.[18]

By similar measures the degree of party cohesion in the United States Congress falls somewhere between the extremes of party cohesion among the states. In recent years the two houses of Congress have been pitting

---

[16] The origins of these measures and indices are admirably discussed in Malcolm E. Jewell and Samuel C. Patterson, *The Legislative Process in the United States*, 2nd ed. (New York: Random House, 1973), Chap. 17.

[17] Julius Turner, *Party and Constituency: Pressures on Congress*, rev. ed. by Edward V. Schneier (Baltimore: Johns Hopkins Press, 1970), pp. 16–17.

[18] See also Table 1 of the study by Hugh L. LeBlanc, "Voting in State Senates: Party and Constituency Influences," *Midwest Journal of Political Science* 13 (1969): 36.

TABLE 1   Party Cohesion on Nonunanimous Roll Calls
in Selected State Legislatures (in Different Years)

State and year	Percentage of Roll Calls with Majority vs. Majority		Percentage of Roll Calls with 80% vs. 80%	
	Senate	House	Senate	House
Connecticut				
(1931–51)	90	83	71	77
Ohio				
(1935, 1949, 1955, 1957)	52	40	26	13
Pennsylvania				
(1959)	82	29	—	14
Michigan				
(1962)	56	61	24	43
New York				
(1959)	70	—	—	—
California				
(1967–69)	43	46	11	17
Missouri				
(1955–59)	35	—	—	21
Iowa				
(1955–65)	39	48	—	—

Source Data from Table 17.1 of Malcolm E. Jewell and Samuel C. Patterson, *The Legislative Process in the United States*, 2nd ed. (New York: Random House, 1973), p. 445; and from Charles W. Wiggins, "Party Politics in the Iowa Legislature," *Midwest Journal of Political Science* 11 (1967): 86–97.

majorities of Democrats against majorities of Republicans in 30 to 50 percent of the roll calls (Table 2). And within those votes in which party majority opposed party majority in 1974, the average Democrat in the Senate voted with his party only 63 percent of the time. For the average House Democrat the figure was 62 percent, and it was 59 percent for Senate Republicans and 63 percent for House Republicans.[19]

Occasions for Cohesion

The incidence of cohesive voting among members of the same legislative party varies significantly with the types of issues and questions the legislatures face. Studies in the Congress and the state legislatures find that three kinds of legislative concerns are most likely to stimulate high

[19] *Congressional Quarterly Weekly Report*, January 25, 1975, p. 200.

TABLE 2   Party Cohesion in Congress for 1960–74:
Percentage of Roll Calls with Majority vs. Majority

Year	Both houses	Senate	House
1960	42%	37%	53%
1961	58	62	50
1962	43	41	46
1963	48	47	49
1964	41	36	55
1965	46	42	52
1966	46	50	41
1967	35	35	36
1968	33	32	35
1969	34	36	31
1970	32	35	27
1971	40	42	38
1972	33	36	27
1973	41	40	42
1974	37	44	29

Source Data from *Congressional Quarterly Almanacs* for
each year.

levels of party discipline: those touching the interests of the legislative
party as a group, those involving support of or opposition to an executive program, and those concerning the socioeconomic issues and interests that tend to divide the party electorates.

The interests of the legislative parties as parties — as interest groups,
one might even say — often spur the greatest party unity in legislatures.
The range of this type of issue is broad. It includes, especially in two-
party legislatures, the basic votes to organize the legislative chamber.
In the Congress, for example, one can safely predict 100 percent party
cohesion on the early session votes to elect a Speaker of the House and
a president pro tem of the Senate. Discipline runs high in the state legislatures over issues such as patronage (and merit system reform), the
laws regulating parties and campaigning, the seating of challenged members of the legislative chamber, election and registration laws, or the
creation or alteration of legislative districts. But whatever form these
issues take, they all touch the basic interests of the party as a political
organization. They threaten some aspect of the party status quo: the
party's activists, its internal organizational structure, its system of rewards, its electorate, its assorted activities.

Second, legislators of a party rally around the party's executive, or
they unite against the executive of the other party. Perhaps the reaction

to an executive program is not so predictable as it is in a parliamentary system, for American presidents freely court the support of the other party; nonetheless, it is a significantly partisan issue even in the American context. The *Congressional Quarterly* periodically measures the support the partisans of each legislative party give to the president on those issues that he has clearly designated as a part of his program (Table 3).[20] This executive-oriented cohesion in the Congress and in the state legislatures reflects a number of realities of American politics. It may result from the executive's control of political sanctions — patronage in some states, his personal support in fund raising and campaigning, his support of programs for the legislator's constituency. It also results from the fact that the executive increasingly symbolizes the party and its performance. Legislators of the president's party or the governor's party know that they hurt their party and their own political future if they make the party's executive look ineffective.

TABLE 3   Percentages of Times That Congressmen Supported Bills from President's Program: 1962–74

Party of president	Year	Senate Democrats	Senate Republicans	House Democrats	House Republicans
Democrat	1962	63%	39%	72%	42%
Democrat	1963	63	44	72	32
Democrat	1964	61	45	74	38
Democrat	1965	64	48	74	41
Democrat	1966	57	43	63	37
Democrat	1967	61	53	69	46
Democrat	1968	48	47	64	51
Republican	1969	47	66	48	57
Republican	1970	45	60	53	66
Republican	1971	40	64	47	72
Republican	1972	44	66	47	64
Republican	1973	37	61	35	62
Republican	1974	39	56	44	58

Source   Data from *Congressional Quarterly Almanacs* for each year.

Finally, legislative cohesion remains firm on some policy issues, especially those bearing directly on the socioeconomic interests of the electorate. Certainly in those states in which the SES foundations of party

[20] Truman in *The Congressional Party*, p. 91, finds a similar unity in support of the administration.

loyalties produce an issue-oriented politics, this fact is not surprising. Such issues include labor-management relations, aids to agriculture or other sectors of the economy, programs of social security and insurance, wages and hours legislation, unemployment compensation, and relief and welfare programs. These issues involve, in the oversimplifications of American politics, the welfare state, the whole complex debate over government responsibilities that we sum up in the liberal-conservative dualism. For example, on issues that the AFL-CIO's Committee on Political Education (COPE) considered a test of labor-liberal positions between 1947 and 1966, the Senate Democrats supported the COPE position 72 percent of the time, the Senate Republicans 28 percent of the time.[21] Such substantial cohesion, however, does not obscure the fact that senators differ in the degree of their personal party loyalty. In 1974 Republicans varied from a high of 91 percent (Schweiker of Pennsylvania and Stevens of Alaska) to a low of 10 percent (five, including Barry Goldwater).[22]

To single out these three groups of issues is not to imply that they are the only instances of party cohesion. The structure of the choice itself may encourage or discourage cohesion. In the Congress (and probably in the states, too) party discipline seems to be easier to maintain on the complex, almost invisible procedural issues before the chamber. Apparently the simple, substantive questions attract publicity and thus attract the attention and activities of nonparty pressures. In the House of Representatives, at least, party leadership finds its task easier when it is working on an obscure issue.[23] Also, in the Congress issues of federalism and states' rights produce partisan voting.[24]

Constituency Basis of Cohesion

Party cohesion in legislative voting is greatest in those states of competitive, two-party politics. One-partyism in a state legislature invites the disintegrating squabbles of factions and regional or personal cliques within the dominant party. The South has in recent years been the area of the least cohesive legislative parties. But this is perhaps to labor the obvious; the very concept of cohesive parties and party government

[21] William J. Keefe and Morris S. Ogul, The American Legislative Process: Congress and the States, 3rd ed. (Englewood Cliffs, N.J.: Prentice-Hall, 1973), p. 276. Unquestionably there is considerable overlap between this issue category and the previous one of support for or opposition to the executive; cohesion in reaction to the executive may well be in part an artifact of issue consensus.
[22] Congressional Quarterly Weekly Report, February 22, 1975, p. 388.
[23] See Lewis A. Froman and Randall B. Ripley, "Conditions for Party Leadership: The Case of the House Democrats," American Political Science Review 59 (1965): 52–63.
[24] Turner, Party and Constituency, rev. ed., Chap. 3.

presumes two healthy, competitive parties locked in the struggle to make public policy.

Party cohesion, furthermore, is at its maximum in the legislatures of urban, industrialized states (see Table 1). The key here — and perhaps the key to the entire riddle of legislative party cohesion — is in the types of constituencies the parties represent. In these urban, industrial states the parties tend to divide the constituencies along urban-rural and SES lines, and they develop an issue-oriented politics that reflects those lines. Party cohesion in the legislature, therefore, reflects the relative homogeneity of the interests and constituencies the party represents. It reflects also the fact that the other party represents a different configuration of interests in different constituencies. Also, the legislators of one party may themselves have different background characteristics and life-styles from the legislators of the other party — that is to say, differences in their own values and experience reinforce the party differences in constituencies. So, in many state legislatures an attempt to revise an unemployment compensation program will put two cohesive parties in sharp opposition, with the pro-labor and pro-management sides each reinforced by their roots in their home districts and possibly in their own occupations.

There do exist urban, industrial states with relatively little legislative party cohesion. California has become the most famous example. California's two parties represent districts that by the usual SES measures are fairly mixed. The Democratic party, for instance, has an important rural wing, a possible result of the long-time overrepresentation of rural areas in the state legislature. Similarly in essentially rural and small-city states, such as Iowa and Kansas, the party division of the state's constituencies, even though the division is close, does not reflect a sharp dualism of interests.

Within the legislature of a particular state, the degree of any individual legislator's party loyalty also appears to be related to constituency characteristics. Party cohesion is greater among those legislators who represent the typical or modal constituency when typicality or modality is measured by some index of SES or urbanness. In the example of MacRae's study of the Massachusetts legislature, Republicans tended to represent districts with a high rate of owner-occupied housing; Democrats tended to come from areas in which fewer people owned the homes they lived in. Republicans from low owner-occupancy areas and Democrats from high owner-occupancy districts — that is, legislators from districts not typical of those their party generally represented — tended to be the party mavericks on roll calls.[25] This kind of analysis pointing

[25] Duncan MacRae, "The Relation Between Roll Call Votes and Constituencies in the Massachusetts House of Representatives," *American Political Science Review* 46 (1952): 1046–55.

to the influence and limitations of constituency loyalties is based on the assumption that each party has differing typical districts and that differences are chiefly in SES interests. In short, we appear to be examining here the same constituency effect on the individual legislator that we saw working on entire legislative parties in the paragraph before last.[26]

Clear and unmistakable though the constituency bases of party regularity may be, they do not explain all party cohesion in the state legislatures. The parties as operating political organizations do account for some. Daily caucuses, state party chairmen roaming the legislative corridors, and the party pressures of a vigorous governor do count for something. Even though it is difficult to measure their influence, few observers of the state legislatures deny it. What actual organizational pressure the legislator feels, however, probably comes from the state party, the party in the executive, or the legislative party itself. It rarely comes from the local party, which, if it makes any demands on him at all, generally makes them on purely local, service issues. Limited evidence from Pennsylvania even points out that legislators whose selection was most firmly controlled by the local party — and who, one might suppose, were most beholden to it — showed no greater party cohesion on legislative roll calls than legislators elected without the help of a party organization.[27]

Party regularity also appears to be related to the political competitiveness of the legislator's constituency. Legislators from the unsafe, marginal districts with finely balanced parties are more apt to defect from their fellow partisans in the legislature than are those from the safer districts.[28] To be sure, it is likely that many of these marginal districts are the districts of SES characteristics atypical of the parties' usual constituencies. But marginality may also be a product of the organizational strength of the opposing party or the appeal of its candidates. Hence the legislator winning by small vote margins must be more sensitive to constituency pressures and must therefore permit them to countermand his party loyalties more freely.

---

[26] For a useful exploration of the relationship between party cohesion and constituency variables, see LeBlanc, "Voting in State Senates," pp. 44–53. There is also considerable evidence to suggest that constituency differences lay beneath the high degree of party cohesion in the United States Congress at the turn of the century. See David W. Brady and Phillip Althoff, "Party Voting in the U.S. House of Representatives, 1890–1910: Elements of a Responsible Party System," *Journal of Politics* 36 (1974): 752–75.

[27] Sorauf, *Party and Representation*, p. 144.

[28] The scholarly evidence on this point is not unanimous, but support for it can be found in the MacRae and Sorauf studies and in Samuel C. Patterson, "The Role of the Deviant in the State Legislative System: The Wisconsin Assembly," *Western Political Quarterly* 14 (1961): 460–72; Pertti Pesonen, "Close and Safe State Elections in Massachusetts," *Midwest Journal of Political Science* 7 (1963): 54–70; and Thomas R. Dye, "A Comparison of Constituency Influences in the Upper and Lower Chambers of a State Legislature," *Western Political Quarterly* 14 (1961): 473–80.

In summary, the northeastern states provide the prototype of the state legislature with greatest party cohesion. They are largely competitive, two-party states. Drawing on urban-rural lines and the SES differences of a diverse population, their major parties represent fairly homogeneous and markedly differing clusters of constituencies. They give rise to a politics of issue and even of ideology, which is in turn reinforced by the similar axes of national politics. These are also the states of old-line, vigorous party organizations and party control of nominations. Here, too, one finds that the hardship politics of favors and patronage has armed the parties with impressive arsenals of sanctions and rewards. Organizational strength carries over, too, into the legislative chambers, where regular caucuses and the apparatus of party discipline are often in evidence. Here also party differences and party conflict have a greater salience for the individual legislator (and the individual voter, too). In a now-classic study of four state legislatures, the legislators were asked to indicate the kinds of conflict that were important in their legislature; 96 percent of the members of the New Jersey lower house designated party conflict as "important"; comparable percentages for Ohio, California, and Tennessee were 49, 26, and 23 respectively.[29]

It is not easy to bring the United States Congress into this discussion of the conditions leading to cohesion in legislative voting. There is nothing among the state legislatures to which Congress can be compared. Perhaps it is because of the unique scope of its politics and its powers as a legislature that it does not lend itself to the relatively simple generalizations we have made about the state legislatures. The members of Congress come from fifty different political systems, not one, and the diversity of the constituencies and constituency politics they represent may be too great for a continuous, simple set of party battle lines to encompass. The parties in Congress have a more complex pattern of party cohesion than do the state legislative parties. Because of the special case of the South, the Democratic party achieves varying degrees of cohesion on various issues. The Republicans often manage a greater cohesion on foreign policy issues than on the conventional welfare-state issues of domestic politics. And not until one narrows the members of Congress to the non-Southerners do the constituency bases of party cohesion appear.[30]

In fact, so sticky is the issue of the bases of party cohesion in the Congress that David Truman has suggested that party voting may be better understood in terms of blocs *within* each of the parties. That, of course, is only a sophisticated refinement of the popular wisdom that

[29] John C. Wahlke et al., *The Legislative System* (New York: Wiley, 1962), p. 425.
[30] Lewis A. Froman, *Congressmen and Their Constituencies* (Chicago: Rand McNally, 1963). See also David R. Mayhew, *Party Loyalty Among Congressmen* (Cambridge: Harvard University Press, 1966).

recognizes, for example, that the Democrats often vote as southern and northern Democrats. More generally, these blocs reflect regional differences in economy, attitudes, and political traditions, and they appear to reflect as well the cohesiveness and pressures of state party delegations.[31]

LEGISLATIVE PARTIES AND PARTY GOVERNMENT

Even though party cohesion in American legislatures falls far short of the standards of some parliamentary parties, it remains the most powerful determinant of roll call voting in American legislatures. Party affiliation goes further to explain the legislative behavior of American legislators than any other single factor. Their normal disposition seems to be to support the leadership of their party unless some particularly pressing commitment intervenes. All other things being equal (i.e., being quiescent and not demanding), party loyalty usually gets their votes.

That disposition toward party loyalty on the part of American legislators, however, is easier to identify than explain. Although a good deal of the scholarship on it looks to constituency explanations, no one wants to restrict the explanation to that variable.[32] Obscure though its origins may be, the disposition to party cohesion results from at least five forces:

1. The force of executive, programmatic leadership tends to polarize a legislature "for" and "against" — not only in response to the specific policies proposed but also out of an awareness that success or failure of an executive affects the political fortunes of both parties. And as presidents and governors combine new political and governmental power with greater personal leadership, they increasingly polarize the legislative votes.
2. The national condition of two-party competition itself creates a loyalty to party, a tension between the two parties, and a rejection of the symbols and traditions of the other party.
3. Party discipline may also be enforced or maintained by rewards and punishments. They may be in the hands of an executive (patronage), a party organization (defeat in renomination or a stunted political career), or the legislative leadership (denial of positions of influence or defeat of legislative projects).
4. Loyalty to the legislative party also springs naturally from the group life of the legislature and the legislative party (and in the Congress from the group life of the state delegations within the party). The legislative party's leaders are people of influence and persuasiveness. The

[31] Truman, The Congressional Party, esp. Chap. 3.
[32] Thomas A. Flinn, "Party Responsibility in the States: Some Causal Factors," American Political Science Review 58 (1964): 60–71, makes the point very well.

legislator values their esteem and support as well as the esteem and camaraderie of his legislative colleagues.

5. Finally, the cohesion of the legislative party stems from a homogeneity of interests, outlooks, experiences, and even ideologies within it. In a large number of states the legislators of one party represent a set of political interests different from that of the other party. Those differences may also be reinforced by the differing political styles and cultures they represent — as, for example, in legislatures in which urban Democrats face rural and small-town Republicans.[33]

Yet, despite the relative importance of party cohesion, the fact remains that most American legislative parties achieve only modest levels of cohesiveness — and then only fitfully. Party lines are often obliterated in the coalitions that enact important legislation. Interest groups, powerful governors, local political leaders, the mass media, influential legislative leaders — all contend with the legislative party for the ability to organize legislative majorities. In this system of fragmented legislative power the legislative party governs only occasionally. It often finds itself in conflict with other party voices in the struggle to mobilize majorities in the legislature. The governor or president as a party leader and expounder of the party platform may find himself repeatedly at odds with legislators of his party whose roots are deeply implanted in local, virtually autonomous electorates with local party organizations.

So, the fragmenting institutions of American government once again have their impact. With the separation of powers there is no institutionalized need or pressure for party cohesion, as there is in the parliamentary systems. Two recent studies of Canadian parties suggest, indeed, that the presence of a parliamentary form primarily accounts for the greater cohesion of legislative parties in Canada.[34] It is possible for government in the United States to act, even to govern, without disciplined party support in the legislature. In fact, at those times when one party controls both houses of Congress and the other the presidency — or one controls both houses of the state legislature and the other the governorship — it would be difficult to govern if high levels of cohesion behind an a priori program did prevail in each party.

Even where one finds party cohesion or discipline in an American legislature, however, party government or party responsibility need not result. Cohesion is a necessary but not sufficient condition of responsibility, and that's the rub. The American legislative party tends to have only the most tenuous ties to the various units of the party organization.

---

[33] See also Julius Turner, *Party and Constituency*, rev. ed., esp. Chap. 8.

[34] Leon D. Epstein, "A Comparative Study of Canadian Parties," *American Political Science Review* 58 (1964): 46–59; Allan Kornberg, "Caucus and Cohesion in Canadian Parliamentary Parties," *American Political Science Review* 60 (1966): 83–92.

The legislative parties of Congress do not recognize the equality — much less the superiority — of the party's national committee. Most state legislative parties similarly escape any effective control, or even any persistent influence, by their state party committees. Nor do the legislative parties have a great deal of contact with local party organizations. Many legislators depend on personal organizations for reelection help, and even those who rely on the party at election time receive no continuing advice from the party back home. The local party organizations are usually preoccupied with local issues, local crises, and local services, and, furthermore, they do not often sustain enough activity between elections to keep even the most fleeting supervisory watch over their legislators.

The American legislative party, therefore, has often found it easy to remain aloof from and independent of the party organization and its platforms and program commitments. It creates the major part of its own cohesion, employing its own persuasions, sanctions, and rewards. What discipline it commands generally serves a program or a set of proposals that originate in the executive or within the legislative party itself. Only rarely is the legislative party in any sense redeeming earlier programmatic commitments or accepting the overriding discipline of the party organization. As a legislative party it is politically self-sufficient; it controls its own rewards to a considerable extent. In some cases it attempts also to control its own political future; the party campaign committees of both houses of Congress are good examples. So long as its members can protect their own renomination and reelection, it is able to keep the rest of the party at arm's length.

This freedom — or irresponsibility, if one prefers — of the legislative party grows in large part from its unity and homogeneity of interests in a total party structure where disorder and disunity prevail. The legislative party and executive party are wary and suspicious allies in the party in government, and the decentralized party organization (decentralized even within the states) can define no common goals or programs for them. Even if a group of local party organizations were to establish supervisory relationships with their legislators, no party responsibility would result unless those relationships were unified and integrated within the state as a whole. In other words, there exists no unified political party that could establish some control over and responsibility for the actions of its legislative party. There is only a party divided geographically along the lines of American federalism, functionally along the dimensions of the separation of powers, and politically by the differing goals and commitments its various participants bring to it.

If the legislative party is relatively free to go its own way and pursue its own interests in its legislative activities, what then of the activists of the party organization? Their incentives may not depend on legislative action; patronage and preferment are controlled by executives, and many of the other personal and political incentives are administered by the party organizations themselves. But if their incentives are those of issue and ideology, they do depend on legislative action. The inability of the party to guarantee the commitment of its legislative party on some issues or a simple ideology means frustration and disappointment for them. Their only response and defense is a selectivity of commitment within the party, a willingness to work only for those candidates or causes whose issue positions they are confident of. Since the party cannot vouch for an ideology or a set of issue positions, they attach their loyalty to those within the party who can.

At the most, therefore, the American legislative parties are tied to the rest of their parties by some agreement on an inarticulate ideology of common interests, attitudes, and loyalties. In many state legislatures and in the United States Congress, the mute "ideology" of one party and its majority districts differs enough (even though roughly) from that of the other party to promote the tensions of interparty disagreement and intraparty cohesion. These modal sets of interests and attitudes may or may not find expression in platforms, and they may or may not be articulated or supported by the party organizations. Legislative parties may in the short run even ignore them. Nonetheless, they are there, and they are the chief centripetal force in a political party that has difficulty articulating a central set of goals for all its activists and adherents. Whether this inarticulate ideology can produce a measure of party responsibility, however, is another question, and it will wait until the considerations of Chapter 16.

15

The Party
in the Executive
and Judiciary

The American involvement of the executive and the courts in party politics stems in considerable part from the traditions of nineteenth-century popular democracy. The belief that democratic control and responsibility can best be guaranteed through the ballot box led to the long ballot, on which judges and all manner of administrative officials (from local coroners to state auditors) were elected. Popular election led easily to party influences in those elections. At the same time the dicta of Jacksonian democracy supporting the spoils system, as well as the value of turnover in office, justified the use of party influence in appointments to office. Thus in the name of popular democracy the access of parties to the executive and judicial branches was opened with a frequency quite unknown in the other Western democracies.

It is one thing for the political party to influence — or even control — the recruitment or selection of officeholders and quite another for it to mobilize them in the exercise of their powers of office. The parties have had only limited success in mobilizing American legislatures. The pertinent question here is whether they have had equal success with the executive and judicial branches. To put the matter another way: In the decisions that affect us all, has it made any difference that the men and women making them have been selected by a party? Do they carry out party programs or values? Does the pursuit of public office by the political parties serve only their internal organizational needs for rewards and incentives, or does it also promote the enactment of party programs and platforms?

THE EXECUTIVE AS PARTY LEADER

The twentieth century has often been proclaimed as the century of mass political leadership, in both the democracies and the dictatorships of the world. In the democracies, electorates have expanded to include virtually all adults; at the same time the revolutions in mass media and communications have brought political leaders closer than ever to them. In the

United States these changes have culminated in the personal leadership of the presidency in the twentieth century — a trend summed up merely in the listing of names such as Wilson, Roosevelt, Eisenhower, and Kennedy, names that signify both executive power and a personal tie to millions of American citizens. Not even the post-Watergate reaction against the "imperial presidency" is apt to reverse the trend. Moreover, the parliamentary systems and their prime ministers have been energized by the growth of personal leadership. It is no longer true that the British prime minister is merely "first among equals" in the cabinet, and British elections increasingly are contests for national leadership.

Unquestionably one important ingredient of executive leadership in the United States has been its concomitant leadership of a mass political party. When Andrew Jackson combined the contest for executive office with leadership of a new popular political party, he began a revolution in both the American presidency — and governorship — and the American political party. The presidency ceased to be the repository of elitist good sense and conservatism that Hamilton saw in it and became, slowly and fitfully, an agency of mass political leadership and representation. It was ultimately the president rather than the Congress who became the tribune of the people in the American political system. Popular democracy found its two chief agents — a popularly elected leader and a mass political party — merged in the American chief executive, the power of the office reinforced by the power of the party.

It is easy to speak glibly of the American chief executive as the leader of a party. The chief executive — whether president or governor — wears many hats at once, and one of them surely is the hat of party leadership. Although leadership of his party demands his time and concern, it supports him in his dealings with the legislature and with his administrative underlings. But the specifics of executive leadership of a party are more elusive, for the president and governors are rarely formal party leaders. National and state party chairmen hold that responsibility. The chief executive's role as party leader is really a subtle, complex combination of a number of overlapping partisan roles.

Party Leader as Representative of the Total Constituency

James MacGregor Burns has written of an American four-party system composed of the two "presidential parties" and the two "congressional parties." [1] But even if one does not see the basic divisions of the American party system in executive-legislative differences, it is evident that the president alone represents the national constituency. Even more im-

[1] James M. Burns, *The Deadlock of Democracy* (Englewood Cliffs, N.J.: Prentice-Hall, 1963).

portant, the national constituency he represents differs from the sum total of the congressional constituencies. Whereas their constituencies are local and particularistic ones that collectively overrepresent the rural areas of the country, the president's overrepresents the large, urban, industrial states, on which the electoral college places such a premium. His constituency is more concerned with the problems of the big cities, their industrial workers, and the racial and ethnic minorities that live in them. It is a constituency that makes its incumbent more "liberal," more committed to government social welfare programs, than his congressional party. Furthermore, since his is the only truly national constituency — especially in contrast with the localism of the congressional party — the presidential candidate is the national party. Apart from the party's national convention, he is its only manifestation.

Many of the same observations may be made of the American governors. They, too, represent the entire state in contrast to the local ties of the state legislators. Other public officials may also have statewide constituencies (the constitution-writers of the states have seen fit to elect treasurers, attorneys general, and state insurance commissioners), but unlike these less known and less public fellow executives, the governor embodies the party on the statewide level. He or she is the political executive and is so recognized by the voters of the states. Like the president, most governors must make political and policy records appealing to the voters of the entire state, and like him they symbolize concern for the problems of the whole constituency.

Party Leader as Organizational Leader

At the same time the American executive may choose to be concerned with the organizational affairs of his political party. Some, like President Eisenhower in the 1950s, may choose not to be. But though Eisenhower "preferred to leave the operation of the political machinery to the professionals," [2] not many other recent presidents have.

The opportunities for organizational leadership, however, are generally greater for governors than for the president. Their constituency and political power coincide with a viable level of party organization. In the state party organization there is an organization worth leading and capable of being led. The president, confronted with an often divided and usually futile national committee, is less fortunate. Not all governors assert themselves in positions of party leadership, of course; they may have no taste for party organizational leadership, or they may even represent a dissident faction within the party. But many governors do

[2] Sherman Adams, First-Hand Report (New York: Harper, 1961), p. 25.

lead. Their control of the state patronage establishes them as party leaders, since they control a major element of the party's reward system. Powerful county chairmen must pay them periodic homage.

The president unquestionably asserts his organizational control over his national committee. Its chairman, if not his personal choice, must be acceptable to him. In his relationships with the state and local organizations of his party, he may be less secure. Is it wise for a president to take sides, however covertly, in a deep-seated split within one of the party's state organizations? That unpleasant question confronted both Presidents Kennedy and Johnson in the 1960s as they stepped carefully through the debris of battle between the New York Democratic organizations and the reformers.

The president also faces the question of how to allocate his political resources — the dwindling patronage, his own presence, the prestige of his vice-president or cabinet members — among the parties within his party. Earlier in this century presidents used the cabinet position of the postmaster general as the post for an advisor knowledgeable in the intricacies of the party's many organizations. Franklin Roosevelt relied on James Farley, and Dwight Eisenhower chose Arthur Summerfield; each had extensive party organizational experience, and each served simultaneously as the national party chairman. It was the tradition that Lyndon Johnson honored in 1965 by appointing Lawrence O'Brien, his predecessor's shrewdest political counselor, as his postmaster general. Now that the postal service is reorganized and the postmaster general no longer sits in the cabinet, political advisors hold positions on the White House staff.

Party Leader as Electoral Leader

The chief executive is often a party leader in the additional sense that his electoral successes or failures affect the electoral fortunes of other office seekers within his party. In some cases the effect may be unintentional and unavoidable. Presidential coattails are widely thought to carry into office a certain number of congressional and state candidates. Although specific candidates may be able to isolate themselves from the effect of presidential or gubernatorial success or failure by building their own personal organizations or by cultivating nonparty support, many do not.[3] The basic nature and mechanism of the effect are obscure — is there, for example, a downward coattail effect as well as an upward one? — but the relationship is often present. In the 1964 Democratic

[3] Malcolm Moos, *Politics, Presidents and Coattails* (Baltimore: Johns Hopkins Press, 1952).

landslide, North Dakota Democrats won a house of the state legislature and half of the state's congressional delegation for the first time in history. In Iowa the Johnson sweep turned the state's congressional delegation from six Republicans and one Democrat to six Democrats and one Republican. (Although the president garnered 62 percent of the vote and the popular Democratic governor, Harold E. Hughes, won 68 percent, all of the Democratic congressmen won with less than 54 percent). Thus the glitter of executives or candidates for executives — the candidates at the head of the tickets — can rub off on other party candidates (Table 1). In other words, the short-term judgment on a party that grows out of executive performance or potential can overcome to some extent the patterns of voting that stem from long-term party identifications.[4]

It is, however, easy to exaggerate the ability of presidents and governors to influence the elections of other candidates for office. The executive coattails are not especially strong, especially when they are the coattails of an executive of a "minority" party. The landslide elections of Dwight Eisenhower in 1956 and Richard Nixon in 1972 did help some Republican candidates for the House of Representatives, but they were not enough to prevent Democratic control of the House in both years. Moreover, attempts to spread their coattails in elections in which they are not themselves candidates have not been successful for most executives. For example, despite his personal popularity President Eisenhower's appeal in 1958 for a Republican Congress with which he could work more effectively met total defeat. The Democrats, in fact, increased the margin of their control. Presidents have also failed in most of the few instances in which they have intervened openly in a primary of their own party to try to defeat a disloyal or unacceptable candidate. Governors who control a strong party organization and its resources have succeeded in the task at times, but such victories are not common.

Perhaps the safest conclusion to make is that apart from coattail effects, the impact of the executive on specific primaries and elections is close to negligible unless it is exercised through a party organization. Executive appeals made directly to the voters seem not to have a great deal of effect, no matter how great the popularity and personal strength of the executive. All the traditions and pulls of localism in American politics are against them.

[4] On the general subject of the coattail effect, see the Moos book cited above; also Warren E. Miller, "Presidential Coattails: A Study in Political Myth and Methodology," *Public Opinion Quarterly* 19 (1955): 353–68; Charles Press, "Presidential Coattails and Party Cohesion," *Midwest Journal of Political Science* 7 (1963): 320–35; and Milton C. Cummings, *Congressmen and the Electorate* (New York: Free Press, 1966).

TABLE 1   Johnson Landslide of 1964: Two Legislative Impacts

Elections to the House of Representatives

Year	Percentage of vote cast for Democratic candidates	Percentage of Democrats in House	Percentage of vote cast for Democratic presidential candidate
1962	52.5	59.3	
1964	57.2	67.8	61.1
1966	50.9	56.8	
1968	50.0	55.9	42.7

Elections to the State Legislatures

	Number of states with Republican majority in lower house[a]
Before 1964 election	20
After 1964 election	9

Source   Data from *Statistical Abstract* (1968).
[a] Minnesota and Nebraska excluded because of nonpartisan elections.

Party Leader as Symbol of the Party

Closely related to the role as electoral leader is the executive's role as party symbol, for the president or the governor stands as its most salient representative. In the public's mind, executive programs are party programs. The successes and failures of executives are party successes and failures; their imaginativeness and vigor are the party's. For a public that views politics chiefly in personal terms, a president or a governor is the personification of the party. It is in this sense that chief executives are party leaders by virtue of being chief executives. They can choose not to lead their party organizations, not to lead their party in the legislature, not to intervene in local or congressional elections, not to cater to their special constituency, but they cannot avoid their symbolic impact on their parties. For that impact springs not from their intentions but from the voters' perceptions of their performances.

Again, however, it is easy to overestimate the impact of the executive on the party. During the Eisenhower years, for example, the president's personal popularity rode high; yet the survey data on party identifications for that period indicate only a slight Republican increase — certainly in dimensions far below the president's personal popularity.[5] In the long run, popular chief executives such as President Eisenhower do not convert their personal popularity to their political party *unless* they succeed in altering the voter coalition supporting the party or its organizational structure and leadership.

However, if one looks for presidential impact not on long-run party identifications but on short-run voter choices, the effect is clearer. The material of Table 2 suggests graphically that a sag in a president's popularity may be almost directly reflected in his party's electoral fortunes.

TABLE 2   Relationship between Popularity of President Nixon and Vote Intentions of Voters: 1973–74

	Percentage approving Nixon's conduct of presidency	Percentage intending to vote for Republican congressional candidates
January 1973	68	
April 1973	48	
May 1973		35
September 1973	33	
October 1973		30
December 1973	29	
January 1974		29
April 1974	25	
May 1974		30
August 1974	Nixon resigns	
October 1974		35

Source   Gallup polls for months indicated.

To separate all these closely linked facets of the executive's role as a party leader is to do them violence. They buttress and reinforce each other, and the skillful party leader draws on one to be effective in another. They should more properly be thought of as interdependent aspects of the single phenomenon of executive leadership in the party.

Imposing as these ties between the chief executive and the party may be, they are not without real and tangible limits. First of all, the executive may be limited by his own political experience and taste for political leadership. Some presidents and governors do not want to lead a party,

[5] The point is more fully discussed in the consideration of party identification in Chap. 6.

or they do not think it proper for an executive to do so. And even those who do want to be party leaders may find that the representational demands of the office — the pressures to be a president or governor of "all of the people" — limit their partisan work and identification.

Presidents and governors may also find that they lead only part of a party. For example, governors from one-party states often lead only a party faction. Executives also may share leadership of the party with other partisans. Presidents who are not especially secure in national party affairs may find the more experienced leaders of the congressional party asserting major leadership in the national party. Governors also may find senators and congressmen of their party pressing parallel leadership claims over the state party. These legislators and state party leaders may fear that the governor — or any other single person — will use party control for his own political ambitions.

Both presidents and governors may be limited in party leadership by a paucity of resources on which to base their leadership claims. Patronage is available only to some, and many of the others lack inducements or incentives with which to lead. The president may employ the almost endless prestige of his office and its nearly limitless powers of communication with the electorate, but governors are less able to catch the public eye or ear. And both are limited by the general knowledge that their day on the stage of power is carefully marked out. Whereas a president may have eight years to establish himself as a party leader, one-third of the governors are limited to four years in office.

Nonetheless, the president heads, and occasionally even unifies, the national party. He dominates the national committee and the rest of the national organization, and through a combination of his powers of office and his party leverage he often exerts enough mastery of the legislative party to speak for the party in government. Most important, perhaps, for millions of American voters he is the symbol of the party, its programs, and its performance. The national constituency is his, and his nomination and campaign are the chief activities of the national party. They are the *only* activities with any visibility. Within the state parties, the governors have the same unifying, symbolizing role, and they too have their leverage on legislative parties and state organizations.

Therefore, it is no exaggeration to speak of the American parties as "executive-centered coalitions."

The party primacy of the chief executive lies not only in his advantage in establishing himself as the party leader in the state or nation, but also in the difficulties facing any alternative leader in attempting to do more than limit the impact of his titular status. The loose structure of the party is a coalition which necessarily centers on the chief executive, even though his influence within this coalition may vary widely depending on his skills and opportunities. No other source of party leadership has the legitimacy or the range of sources of influence.[6]

Even in the parties out of power the executive office and its opportunities dominate. Opposition to the other party's executive and his coalition, as well as planning for the next election's assault on the office, provide the chief unifying focus. It is the headless quality of the party out of power that most typifies its melancholy condition.

The executive-centered party to some extent is a coalition of the executive-dominated party in government with the party in the electorate. That leaves the party organization increasingly as the odd man out. The identifications and loyalties of voters are not to the party organization but to the party symbols, meaning for which comes from executives and their programs. The men and women of the party in government often build their own supporting organizations and thus bypass the party organizations in their quest for office. One need only mention once again the fatal strategy of Richard Nixon in 1972. Even in the use of patronage, executives often try to maximize support for their programs and their own political futures rather than to maintain or rebuild the strength of the party organization.

Once in office the executives generally put the leverage they derive from their position as party leaders into the business of governing rather than into any concern for the party per se as an organization. The president, for example, finds himself without sufficient constitutional powers to hold his own in the struggles of the American separation of powers. Indeed, if the proverbial man from Mars should obtain a copy of the United States Constitution, he could not imagine from its niggardly grants of power to the president what the office has come to be. American presidents, faced with that shortage of formal powers, have had to rely heavily on their extraconstitutional powers, such as those they derive from party leadership. They have used that party position especially to help them dominate the legislative branch and to assert their authority over their own executive branch.

PARTY LEADERSHIP AND LEGISLATIVE RELATIONS

For that area of policy making reserved to him, the executive is free to pursue his understanding of public wisdom. But for most executives the area of policy-making autonomy is not large. Aside from the president, who enjoys a primacy in the fields of defense and international relations, little substantial policy is reserved for the executive to set. What impact

[6] Judson L. James, *American Political Parties* (New York: Pegasus, 1969), pp. 163, 169–70.

a governor is to have on the making of policy, on the choosing among alternative programs, or on the enacting of a party program must come about through the formal actions of the legislature. In this pursuit of policy by influencing a legislature, the president and the governors turn repeatedly to their identification with, and embodiment of, their political party.

By far the most important institutional barrier to the coordination of legislative and executive decision making under the aegis of a unifying political party is the separation of powers. Between 1961 and 1969 only thirteen states (Idaho and South Dakota were the only two states of the thirteen outside the South or its border) did not experience at least some period in which one house of the legislature was of a party different from the governor. The reasons for those divided regimes are several: overlapping terms of office, differing constituencies, the impact of a politics of personality and localism, and legislative malapportionment. At such times the executive has no choice but to minimize partisan appeals; and in view of the closeness of the party split in many legislatures and the unreliability of some legislators of his own party, he must always curry the favor of some legislators of the opposing party. Thus the president and governors follow a mixed strategy: partisan appeals and sanctions for their own party and nonpartisan or bipartisan politics for those of the opposition.

The role of the president vis-à-vis the Congress is too well known to bear a great deal of rehearsal here. Presidential power in the party is not usually organizational. Presidents may use a little of the lingering federal patronage for legislative purposes, but they have little leverage that can affect the political career or responses of a senator or representative. Congress responds, however, to the power a president has over the symbols and public prestige of the party. Members of his party know that if they make him look bad, to some extent they also make themselves look bad. They cannot escape the fact that he heads the party's ticket and that therefore he may very well have some impact on their own fortunes and on the fortunes of the party. Indeed, evidence suggests that congressmen who benefited in the past from presidential coattails are somewhat more apt to support the president's programs than those who did not. Legislators thus appear both to anticipate and to react to presidential leadership at the polls.[7]

Governors, on the other hand, are frequently in a position to exercise far greater and more direct party organizational power over the legislators of their own parties. In many states their legislatures are unbound by the traditions of seniority, and governors may take an active part in

---

[7] J. Vincent Buck, "Presidential Coattails and Congressional Loyalty," *American Journal of Political Science* 16 (1972): 460–72.

selecting committee chairmen and influential party floor leaders at the beginning of the session. They often view the party's legislative leaders as "their" leaders, chosen to steer their programs through legislative waters. Governors may also attend party caucuses and even direct the strategy of the party's legislative leaders. They may also lead powerful, ongoing state party organizations. To cross them may be to run the risk of falling from party favor; a legislator's career in the legislature, not to mention his future ambition, may be at the mercy of a determined, politically skillful governor. Thus the average governor has far greater control over party rewards and incentives than a president. But, on the other hand, in the symbolic aspects of party leadership he usually exerts far less influence than a president. Though the governor's party sanctions and organizational power are impressive, he suffers from undersized political coattails.

PARTY POWER AND ADMINISTRATIVE POLICY

Legislatures, under the weight of complex realities, have delegated greater and greater discretion to administrative agencies. Such agencies now regulate vast areas of the economy — the airlines, atomic and nuclear energy, radio and TV, for example — under only the vaguest legislative mandates. Even the question of tariff barriers, long the occasion for bitter, protracted congressional politicking, has largely been sloughed off to the president, the State Department, and the Tariff Commission. Obviously, then, any concept of party responsibility or party government cannot be restricted to legislatures. The administration clearly shapes policy in its application, and party programs require sympathetic administrative leadership to be effective.

There are, however, substantial limits on the executive's ability to unify his administration and hold it responsible to him and to his party's program:

1. The legislature may place administrative positions outside of executive control by stipulating terms of appointment that last beyond a president's or governor's term, by limiting the executive's power of removal, or by placing policy makers under merit system and tenure. It may extend a special legislative protection to others. So potent were the legislative supporters of the director of the Federal Bureau of Investigation, J. Edgar Hoover, that he was independent of presidential authority.
2. Special precautions may also be taken to thwart partisan control of an administrative agency. Federal agencies such as the Securities and Exchange Commission, the Federal Trade Commission, and the Civil Aeronautics Board are headed by five-person commissions or boards,

but not more than three of the members of each may be of the same political party. Republican presidents often meet that formal bipartisan requirement by appointing conservative Democrats, while Democrats seek out liberal Republicans. In the name of bipartisanship, the search often goes on for atypical and unrepresentative partisans.

3. In a number of states the top administrative positions, like the gubernatorial office, are filled by election. At worst that places members of both parties in an uncomfortable alliance. Even if the offices are filled by candidates of the same party, they are often politically and constitutionally independent. They build personal followings, and often the nature of their office allows them to publicize their name or control a minor administrative patronage. They clash with governors over policy matters and guard their administrative independence pugnaciously. In Minnesota, for example, eleven different men held the governorship between 1930 and 1969. In that same period there were only two auditors, four secretaries of state, and six treasurers. Thus the governor may confront a number of entrenched "executive parties" as he enters office; they may even be there as he leaves.

4. Furthermore, American executives suffer some diminution of political power as their terms approach a predetermined halt. The Twenty-second Amendment to the United States Constitution limits the presidential term to between eight and ten years, and twenty-seven of the states limit the gubernatorial time in office, either by providing that the governor cannot succeed himself (eight states) or by limiting him to two terms (nineteen states).

5. Finally, political realities may force executives to share the instruments of party leadership with others. Their appointments may be subject to the close scrutiny of party or legislative leaders; in the case of the president, they must temper their choices to satisfy the dictates of senatorial courtesy should an appointment lie within the boundaries of a state represented by a senator of his party. Other leaders or factions within his party may also press in on him. Senator Robert A. Taft, the leader of the conservative wing of the Republican party, extracted an early commitment from President Eisenhower that in making his appointments he would not discriminate against the Taftites of the party and that he would be "determined to maintain the unity of the entire party by taking counsel with all factions and points of view" [8] within it.

Establishing control of the executive branch is far more complex than simply putting fellow partisans into positions of power. Control over their operations and decisions comes with the greatest difficulty. The

[8] Robert J. Donovan, *Eisenhower: The Inside Story* (New York: Harper, 1956), p. 104.

chief executive faces essentially the same problem in enforcing party discipline on his administrative subordinates that a party leader in the legislature faces. In both cases the problem is prior loyalty to a constituency. Just as the legislators identify with the problems and outlooks of the citizens they know and represent, so administrators often identify with the problems and outlooks of the groups and individuals with which their agencies deal. And just as legislators must depend on the folks back home to protect their political necks, top-level administrators know that the support of client groups is their best personal political protection and the only protection for an agency, its mission, and its budget. In this way the Veterans Administration enjoys the protection of the American Legion and the Veterans of Foreign Wars, and the Environmental Protection Agency depends on the support of organized naturalists and environmentalists. Only with the greatest difficulty does the pressure of party loyalties and party sanctions overcome these loyalties to administrative constituencies. For in the executive as well as the legislative branch, the party has less to give and less to take away than does the constituency.

Only in that part of the administrative establishment closest to the chief executive does the party function as an agency of party responsibility. Through the person of the governor or president, it may hold top administrative officials responsible to a party mandate. At these top administrative levels, the appointee has often been politically active and has associated actively with a political party; he or she has very likely come to recognize the claims of the party organization and developed a commitment to party goals and programs. The cabinet of a president such as Richard Nixon (see box) illustrates the combination of party and governmental experience and loyalty to the president himself. At least seven or eight of the twelve original members of the Nixon cabinet had been close personal political associates of the president. At least half of the twelve had been active in the nominating convention or campaign of 1968.

But when one looks a step below in the administrative structure to the assistant secretary level, party and governmental experience dwindles. These are individuals most often chosen for their skills and experience in administration and only secondarily for their political credentials. The process of their recruitment may have included the political party only incidentally. In fact, in the selection of many of them, the role of the party organization may not have extended beyond determining whether they were politically acceptable (i.e., inoffensive) in their home states. Generally speaking, the partisans who seek these positions through the party organizations lack the basic job qualifications. The party role in appointment suffers, therefore, because executive and managerial considerations weigh more heavily than political ones with most presidents.

The Nixon Cabinet and the Republican Party

The original appointees to the cabinet of Richard Nixon typify the inter-play of both the personal connections to the president and the broader activity within the president's party that one finds in most cabinets. Their political histories indicate party-based recruitment and also a potential on their part for reinforcing the party leadership of the president.

1. William P. Rogers (secretary of state): old friend and advisor of Richard Nixon and fellow campaigner in 1952; attorney general in the Eisenhower administration
2. David M. Kennedy (secretary of treasury): no apparent history of Republican activity
3. Melvin R. Laird (secretary of defense): member of House of Representatives and chairman of House Republican Conference; at least fifteen years on Republican convention platform committees (including 1968)
4. John N. Mitchell (attorney general): campaign manager for the 1968 Nixon-Agnew national campaign
5. Winton M. Blount (postmaster general): active for many years in Republican politics in the South; active in the Nixon campaign in 1960 in the South
6. Walter J. Hickel (secretary of interior): early supporter of Nixon in 1968 as governor of Alaska; cochairman of 1968 Nixon campaign in western states; had earlier been member of Republican National Committee
7. Clifford M. Hardin (secretary of agriculture): no apparent history of Republican activity
8. Maurice H. Stans (secretary of commerce): director of Budget Bureau in Eisenhower administration; chief fund-raiser in the 1968 Nixon campaign
9. George P. Shultz (secretary of labor): no apparent history of Republican activity
10. Robert H. Finch (secretary of health, education, welfare): national campaign manager for Nixon in 1960; active in Nixon's 1962 bid for California governorship; lieutenant governor of California; advisor to Nixon in 1968 campaign
11. George Romney (secretary of housing, urban development): governor of Michigan; early contestant for Republican presidential nomination in 1968
12. John A. Volpe (secretary of transportation): governor of Massachusetts; active in 1968 Nixon campaign as a speaker and as the head of the Nixon-Agnew Nationalities Committee

The hope and assumption that an appointment can at the same time serve both the party organization's reward goals and the executive's need to govern often turn out to be no more than a vain hope.[9]

Unlike the legislative party, the executive party has no explicit form or organization, no caucus or conference, no separate identity as a party group. That is the case largely because the executive party — again unlike the legislative party — has a single powerful leader. The executive party can be called that largely because its members share common experiences in the party of the executive and because they share with him a general concern for the values, programs, outlooks, and symbols of the same party. Those common party ties and loyalties help reinforce their loyalty to the executive and unify them in their support for his programs.

For what purposes, then, do executives use the executive party and their broader leadership role in it? Their power and influence go chiefly for the tasks of governing, of meeting their executive decision-making responsibilities. Only secondarily can they be employed for the goals and interests of the party organization. They may, indeed, make bows in the direction of the party organization. Many governors use some chunk of their patronage purely for party goals, and presidents often use cabinet appointments to assuage and satisfy the need for recognition of various groups or factions within the party. But there is a constant tension between the demands of the party and the need to govern. Concessions such as a cabinet that satisfies the political demands of the party may build party cohesion, but they may also thwart the executive or administrative goals of the president.[10] Not only does the need of the executive to meet his governmental responsibilities depoliticize (or at least de-partify) the executive party, but civil service systems also tend to expand. Moreover, the United States Government and many states severely restrict the political activity of many executive appointees. At the national level, the Hatch Acts effectively prevent some political appointees from continuing their activities within the political party that secured the office for them.

THE MYSTERIOUS CASE OF THE JUDICIAL PARTY

Nothing illustrates quite so clearly the difficulties of evaluating the party in office as the examples of cohesive party voting in American appellate courts. Several recent studies point to the presence of party-rooted blocs in state appellate courts in cases such as those involving workmen's compensation. Another broader study cutting across a number of states finds that Democratic and Republican judges differ significantly in the

---

[9] Dean E. Mann, *The Assistant Secretaries* (Washington, D.C.: Brookings, 1965).
[10] Richard F. Fenno, *The President's Cabinet* (New York: Vintage, 1959), pp. 180–87.

ways they decide certain types of cases. For example, Democrats on the bench tend to decide more frequently for the defendant in criminal cases, for the government in taxation cases, for the regulatory agency in cases involving the regulation of business, and for the claimants in workmen's compensation, unemployment compensation, and auto accident cases.[11] Certainly no one suggests that the incidence of party cohesion in judicial decision making approaches that in legislatures. The relationships appear only in certain types of cases; and the amount of disagreement within an appellate court that can be explained by party division falls far below the amount of legislative division that can be explained by party. But, in any event, there appears to be party cohesion in the American judiciary.

It may infrequently happen that an American judge is swayed by some subtle persuasion of his political party. If it does happen, though, it doesn't happen frequently enough to explain the party cohesion of which we spoke above. The explanation undoubtedly rests in the different sets of values, even the different ideological stances, that the major parties represent. Quite simply, judges of the same party vote together on cases for the same reasons of ideology and outlook that led them to the same political party, or because they have been socialized into the goals and values of the same party. In other words, two judges vote together on an issue of the administrative regulation of utilities because of deep-seated values they share about the relationship of government and the economy. Those same values or perceptions led them some years earlier to join the same political party, or they were developed out of experience in the same political party.

The impact of the party on the decision-making processes of the judiciary, therefore, is indirect. It stems largely from the role of the party as guarantor of its members' commitments. That this should be so ought not to surprise anyone, for the appointment of judges in the United States has classically taken the values and attitudes of judges into account. Although we have only recently accepted in any overt way the notions of judicial law making — the notion that in some instances judges have options and that in these choices they may in part reflect their own prior experiences, perceptions, and values — we have acknowledged it implicitly for some time. President Theodore Roosevelt, considering a replace-

---

[11] On the general subject of party blocs or voting affinities among justices of the same party, see Sidney Ulmer, "The Political Party Variable on the Michigan Supreme Court," *Journal of Public Law* 11 (1962): pp. 352–62; Stuart Nagel, "Political Party Affiliation and Judges' Decisions," *American Political Science Review* 55 (1961): 843–50; Glendon A. Schubert, *Quantitative Analysis of Judicial Behavior* (Glencoe, Ill.: Free Press, 1959), pp. 129–42; and David W. Adamany, "The Party Variable in Judges' Voting: Conceptual Notes and a Case Study," *American Political Science Review* 63 (1969): 57–73. Similar differences in decision making in the federal judiciary are reported in Sheldon Goldman, "Voting Behavior on the United States Courts of Appeals, 1961–1964," *American Political Science Review* 60 (1966): 374–83.

ment for Justice Horace Gray on the Supreme Court, wrote Senator Henry Lodge inquiring about a certain Judge Oliver Wendell Holmes of the Massachusetts Supreme Court:

In the ordinary and low sense which we attach to the words "partisan" and "politician," a judge of the Supreme Court should be neither. But in the higher sense, in the proper sense, he is not in my judgment fitted for the position unless he is a party man, a constructive statesman, constantly keeping in mind his adherence to the principles and policies under which this nation has been built up and in accordance with which it must go on.

Now I should like to know that Judge Holmes was in entire sympathy with our views, that is, with your views and mine and Judge Gray's, just as we know that ex-Attorney General Knowlton is, before I would feel justified in appointing him. Judge Gray has been one of the most valuable members of the Court. I should hold myself as guilty of an irreparable wrong to the nation if I should put in his place any man who was not absolutely sane and sound on the great national policies for which we stand in public life.[12]

Congress, too, has often implicitly examined such issues in approving appointments to the federal judiciary. The Senate in 1969 and 1970 rejected two appointees to the Supreme Court (Clement Haynsworth and G. Harrold Carswell) at least partly because of the general conservatism of their views on race and labor.

Whether or not it should be within the province of a president or a governor to consider such matters in proposing judicial appointments, the appointee's political party loyalties serve as some indication of his values and attitudes. Indeed, it is one of the reasons that in the last century American presidents have appointed to the federal bench a preponderance of men from their own parties. They have generally chosen more than 90 percent of their appointments from the ranks of their own parties, and in every case since Cleveland the percentage has been above 80 (Table 3).

That overwhelming percentage is, to be sure, the result of other pressures. For one, the president's information network and his own personal acquaintanceships — his whole mechanism for recruiting appointees — quite naturally flows through his party and his own contacts in the party. Furthermore, there is an old and honorable tradition in American politics that judicial appointment constitutes one of the most desirable, high-level rewards for good and faithful service to the party or to a candidate of the party. Executives are under strong pressures to make their qualified judicial appointments from within the ranks of the attorneys who have labored for them or for the party.

In the majority of the states, the judiciary is not appointive; it is filled

[12] The Roosevelt letter is quoted more fully in Walter F. Murphy and C. Herman Pritchett, *Courts, Judges, and Politics* (New York: Random House, 1961), pp. 82–83.

TABLE 3   Percentages of Judicial Appointments
from the Party of the President: Grover Cleveland
through Lyndon Johnson

Cleveland	97.3	Coolidge	94.1
Harrison	87.9	Hoover	85.7
McKinley	95.7	F. Roosevelt	96.4
T. Roosevelt	95.8	Truman	90.1
Taft	82.2	Eisenhower	94.1
Wilson	98.6	Kennedy	90.1
Harding	97.7	Johnson	94.6

Source Data from Evan A. Evans, "Political Influences
in the Selection of Federal Judges," *Wisconsin Law Re-
view* (May 1948), pp. 300–51; Hugh A. Bone, *American
Politics and the Party System*, 4th ed. (New York:
McGraw-Hill, 1971), p. 248; and the research of Harold
W. Chase.

by either partisan or nonpartisan elections. In the partisan elections of
seventeen states, of course, the judge is elected as a member or candidate of a party, and one can reasonably suspect that his party tie
represents certain generalized value positions. But the state parties vary
greatly in the active way they contest these elections. In a few states the
party organizations make primary endorsements and actively support en-
ergetic partisans for the judgeships. In other words, they would make the
position a form of elective patronage. Other state parties pay far less
attention to judicial elections; in some cases the same candidate — often
with the endorsement of the state bar association — will run on both
party tickets.

Party pressures and activities are far less obvious and important in the
nonpartisan elections. But regardless of the election process and politics,
the judge still may come to the bench with the values that a party represents, and party lines may even be apparent in the divisions of a nonpartisan judiciary.[13] Judicial terms tend to be so long that many elective
judgeships become appointive. Death often takes a judge off the bench
in midterm, and the vacancy is filled before the next election by a gubernatorial appointment. The political considerations attending such appointments may then prevail, and with the advantage of even a brief

[13] Even in a state in which judges are chosen on a nonpartisan ballot, partisan blocs
may be apparent in some kinds of issues. In Minnesota, for example, the state supreme court has in recent years shown a high degree of party cohesion in two
celebrated, "political" issues: an important question of procedure in the early stages
of the recount of the state's 1962 gubernatorial election and the question of the
authority of the governor to veto a legislative reapportionment.

period of incumbency the appointee usually wins a full, regular term at the next election.[14]

The point, then, is a simple one. There is no way to eliminate the values and preferences, the important frames of reference, that judges bring to their work. Judges have been men and women of the world; they know the issues of their times and the ways the parties relate to them. Furthermore, given the tradition of the political activity of the American lawyer, there is a good chance that the judge has had some active, political party experience. Beyond this, the political party has an opportunity for active and overt influence in the selection process through the initiatives of governors or the president of the party or through the usual processes of a partisan election. In these selection processes, the party has the opportunity, which it sometimes takes advantage of, to select judges who are especially sensitive to the ideological issues for which the party stands and whose ideological positions have been reinforced through years of service to the party.

The use of the federal or state bench as a desirable bit of political patronage obviously politicizes the American courts to a degree unthinkable in many other political cultures. But the relationship between judge and party may even extend beyond the politics of appointment. In some parts of the country the local district or county judge sometimes still retains hidden ties to local politics. In some American counties he is the *éminence grise* of the party, slating candidates behind the scenes, directing party strategy, arbitrating among the conflicting ambitions of the party's candidates. Moreover, the local administration of justice occasionally opens new reservoirs of patronage for the party. The judge who is a loyal member of a political party may parcel out guardianships, receiverships in bankruptcy, and clerkships to loyal lawyers of the party. In the 1966 battle between the party-designated candidate and the reform candidate (supported by Senator Robert Kennedy) for the Democratic nomination for a judgeship in Manhattan's Surrogate Court, it developed that the surrogates had in the preceding year issued 428 guardianships, with lawyers' fees running into many millions, in that one borough of the city alone. Many commentators and journalists, and many party officials, believe that such appointments go chiefly to attorneys active in the party ranks.[15]

How is it that the tie between the judiciary and the parties is so substantial in the United States? The factors are complex and mixed. The

---

[14] The extent to which the nature of the selection or election process either heightens or reduces the party cohesion in judicial decisions is at the moment unknown. See David Adamany's thoughtful analysis in the article cited in footnote 11.

[15] On judicial patronage see Charles E. Merriam and Harold F. Gosnell, *The American Party System*, 4th ed. (New York: Macmillan, 1949); and Herbert Jacob, *Justice in America* (Boston: Little, Brown, 1965), pp. 87–89.

phenomenon of the elective judiciary, compounded by the political appointment process, is one. Then, too, we have no career vocation, no special training process or examination for the judiciary; any lawyer can be a judge. By contrast, in many continental European countries the career of judging requires special preparation, study, and apprenticeship, and one enters it by special civil service examination. In this context, then, the additional factor of the dominance of American politics by the legal profession is free to operate. Lawyers are everywhere in American political and public life, and many of them hope for ultimate reward in appointment to the bench. And within the American tradition, access to the bench is a dream they can realistically entertain. The bench, then, is a part of the universe of rewards and incentives on which the American parties depend.

CONCLUSION

Surprisingly, the influence of the political party on the executives and judiciaries of the American political system differs in degree but not in kind. The main avenue of party influence is indirect, and in both cases it stems from the kinds of commitments and values that membership in a party — or loyalty to one — represents. It depends, in other words, on the ideological impact or presence of the party *within* the men and women who hold administrative or judicial office.

Furthermore, in both the executive and the judiciary one observes the conflict between the policy purpose — even when pursued within the limits of judicial propriety — and the demands of the party. The administrative position and the judgeship are two of the few available positions with which to reward party leaders, and the party is not anxious to have them pass to party nobodies. When that happens the party suffers doubly; no one is rewarded, and even worse the party's inability to use the rewards is spread on the record for all to see. In the filling of positions in both branches, one sees again the struggle between the party's own important need for organizational incentives and the need to recruit people who can best meet the responsibilities of governing. For the American parties it is a dilemma without end or resolution.

16
The
Quest for Party
Government

The political parties are everywhere in American legislatures and executives, and even in American judiciaries. All American executives, all American legislatures but one, and about half the American judiciaries are selected in processes that weigh heavily the party affiliation of the office seeker. Moreover, the appearances of party power are more than plentiful in the party leaders and whips of the legislatures and the clearly partisan cast of many executive appointments. Even the elemental struggle between government and opposition, between ins and outs, largely follows political party lines in the American system, just as if the parties controlled cohesive parties of the government and the opposition. Yet, despite the trappings and portents of power, the American major parties do not govern easily. They find it hard to mobilize cohesive groups of officeholders behind programs and ideologies to which they and especially their organizations and activists have committed themselves.

The discontent with this inability of the American parties to "govern" is an old one within academic political science.[1] But the dissatisfactions are with more than the American parties. They extend to the entire American political system and its fragmented centers of authority, its tendency to blur political alternatives and differences, and its built-in barriers to strong and vigorous governmental initiatives. The critics, many of them admirers of the cohesive parties in the British Parliament, long hoped that by joining electoral majorities and officeholders to party programs they could surmount the diffusion of power in the American polity. The 1950 report, *Toward a More Responsible Two-Party System*,[2] gave the controversy its major recent stimulus. The ensuing academic controversy has slowly simmered down, but it is by no means quiet today.

While the controversy over party responsibility and party government

---

[1] Austin Ranney, *The Doctrine of Responsible Party Government* (Urbana: University of Illinois Press, 1962).
[2] Committee on Political Parties of the American Political Science Association, *Toward a More Responsible Two-Party System* (New York: Rinehart, 1950).

Tweedledee and Tweedledum

It has become a commonplace to compare the similarity of the Democratic and Republican parties on issues to those two identical little fat
men in Lewis Carroll's *Through the Looking Glass*, Tweedledee and
Tweedledum. Carroll borrowed their names from an earlier English poet,
John Byrom, but it was his adoption of them in 1872 that secured their
modern fame. James Bryce, later Lord Bryce, was apparently the first to
use them to describe the American parties; he did so in his *American
Commonwealth* (1888). Some years after Carroll's masterpiece, Tweedledee and Tweedledum also developed a stereotyped appearance — complete with schoolboy caps — doubtless the creation of some influential
illustrator. After all these years, the twins are alive and well in American
politics, as witness the cartoon below. Ironically, the artist is Charles
Addams, best known for his ghoulish and gothic imagination.

Drawings by Chas. Addams;
© 1975 The New Yorker Magazine, Inc.

has embroiled academic political science for the past generation, a parallel concern has agitated the American political world. From the ideologically oriented activists in both parties have come wails of dissatisfaction
with the issuelessness of American politics and the tendency of the major
parties to take similar centrist positions. They complain, much as did
Lord Bryce some seventy years ago, that the American parties are as
similar as Tweedledum and Tweedledee (see box). In 1964 the Republican
conservatives inveighed against the "me-too-ism" of the party's liberals

and moderates; in working for the nomination of Barry Goldwater they pleaded for "a choice, not an echo." Eight years later the major ideological pressures were from the left: The New Left and a coalition of the young, the disadvantaged, and the disaffected spearheaded a movement that won the 1972 Democratic presidential nomination for George Mc-Govern. It, too, rejected the American status quo and the centrist politics of the established leadership of the Democratic party.

At first blush it may seem that the ivory tower controversy over party responsibility has not a great deal to do with the development of distinct programs for the parties. In any event, one would not ordinarily expect such a conjunction of academic debate and popular political controversy. But the two questions are to some extent the same. The groups of scholars favoring party government or responsibility and the ideologues of the left and right in American politics both want the major American parties to present more specific programs that differ more from each other. Both groups also want the parties to govern by carrying their programs into public policy. To the extent that such goals require some degree of consensus on basic values and long-term philosophies within the parties, they both also want greater ideological clarification and commitment within the parties.

THE LOGIC OF THE RESPONSIBLE PARTY

Despite the nomenclature, the doctrines of party government and party responsibility are only secondarily concerned with political parties. They are fundamentally doctrines of democratic government — or, more precisely, doctrines advocating one particular variety of American democracy. Much of the debate over them has been over the kind of democracy we are to have. The whole movement for party government has sprung from a discontent over what some scholars and citizens have seen as the ills of American democracy.

The proponents of party government[3] begin with a belief in strong, positive government as a necessary force for the solution of problems in the American society and economy. And like so many of the advocates of positive government in the context of the American separation of powers, many of them see a need for strong executive leadership if the whole complex governmental apparatus is to move forward with some

---

[3] A word of semantic elaboration may be helpful here. The term "party government" denotes leadership by a majority political party in the important decision-making processes of government; the "responsible" party is one able to organize electoral or popular majorities and officials behind party programs and thus be responsible to its voters for the conduct of office. There is a difference between them, largely in the relationship with the electorate that "party responsibility" suggests. However, it is not much of an oversimplification to use the terms synonymously.

vigor and semblance of unity. Yet, they know all too well that the institutions and traditions of American government diffuse and divide governmental power in ways that prevent the generation of aggressive and responsive governmental programs. Theirs is the old complaint that American political institutions, suited perhaps for the minimal, gingerly governing of the eighteenth and nineteenth centuries, are far less adapted to the present century's need for positive government action. And, clearly, decentralized political parties, each of them divided by a vast diversity of interests and points of view, only accentuate the problem of diffusion.

A second thread of argument runs through the political diagnoses of the proponents of party government: concern for the miniscule influence of individuals in a mass, popular democracy. Contemporary government becomes large, complex, and remote, and individuals find it hard to have the time, attention, and political knowledge for an active role in it. They find it especially difficult to judge or even to know what their elected representatives have been doing in public office. And into the political void resulting from their ineffectiveness and ignorance rush well-organized and well-financed minorities — local elites, interest groups, party bosses, or ad hoc alliances. Consequently, so the argument goes, important decisions are frequently made by public officials and organized minorities without the participation or even the post hoc judgment of the great majority of individual citizens. Individuals drift from one meaningless decision to another; they do not know what the candidate stands for when they first elect him, and they have no standards or information for judging his performance in office when he comes up for reelection.[4]

This sense of alarm about the American democracy, to be sure, is by no means limited to the proponents of party government. It is a more or less standard critique from those quarters of American life committed to the "liberal" confidence in the usefulness of a broad governmental role and to the "liberal" belief in the rationality and desirability of citizen involvement in a popular democracy.[5] It is a position not vastly different from that of critics who would replace establishment elites with a broader participatory democracy. What sets the school of party government apart is its reliance on the organizing and consolidating powers of the competitive political party. A reconstituted (and responsible) pair of political parties, it is hoped, would bring together masses

---

[4] See Ranney, *The Doctrine of Responsible Party Government*, Chaps. 1 and 2, for an analysis of what party government presumes about democracy.
[5] I am using "liberal" in the sense it is used in contemporary American politics. The liberal position favors popular, participatory democracy and positive government. Conservatism, on the other hand, generally connotes a preference for limited government and for the wisdom of political leaders and elites.

of voters behind meaningful party programs and candidates loyal to them and then hold their elected candidates to the obligation of carrying those programs into public policy. The responsible political party thus would bridge the gulf between the politically disoriented individual and the distant, complex institutions of government.

In essence, these are proposals for the reinvigorating and animating of popular democratic institutions through the prime organizing role of the political party. Why the political party for so crucial a role?

> As mobilizers of majorities the parties have claims on the loyalties of the American people superior to the claims of any other forms of political organization. They have extended the area of popular participation in public affairs enormously and have given elections a meaning and importance never before thought possible. . . . Moreover, party government is good democratic doctrine because the parties are the special form of political organization adapted to the mobilization of majorities. How else can the majority get organized? If democracy means anything at all it means that the majority has the right to organize for the purpose of taking over the government.[6]

Only the parties, their supporters believe, are big, stable, and visible enough to carry this representational burden. As the only completely political of the political organizations and the only one with a public or semipublic character, the political party alone has the capacity for developing the essential qualities of responsibility.

The call for responsible political parties, therefore, is a call for political parties with new capacities and new goals. Specifically, the responsible political party must:

1. Evolve and enunciate a reasonably explicit statement of party programs and principles.
2. Nominate candidates loyal to the party program (despite the difficulties of controlling the direct primaries).
3. Conduct its electoral campaigns in such a way that voters will grasp the programmatic differences between it and its opposing party and make their voting decisions substantially on that basis.
4. Guarantee that public officeholders elected under the party label will carry the party program into public policy and thus enable the party to take responsibility for their actions in office.

This much seems necessary if the party is to govern and be responsible to the majorities that chose it to govern. The entire argument rests on the replacement of individual or group responsibility for governmental decisions with the responsibility of the political party.

Concern for developing and enacting programs must infuse all relationships within the party and all steps in the contesting of elections. As

[6] E. E. Schattschneider, *Party Government* (New York: Rinehart, 1942), p. 208.

the report of the committee of the American Political Science Association argues in its very first paragraph:

While in an election the party alternative necessarily takes the form of a choice between candidates, putting a particular candidate into office is not an end in itself. The concern of the parties with candidates, elections and appointments is misunderstood if it is assumed that parties can afford to bring forth aspirants for office without regard to the views of those so selected. Actually, the party struggle is concerned with the direction of public affairs. Party nominations are no more than a means to this end. In short, party politics inevitably involves public policy in one way or another.[7]

The whole idea of party government is policy- and issue-oriented. It is concerned with capturing and using public office for predetermined goals and not merely for the thrill of winning, the division of patronage and spoils, or the reward of the office itself. The winning of public office becomes no more than a means to policy ends.

There still remains, however, a sizable platoon of American political scientists and political leaders who, despite the persuasiveness of the advocates of party government, are definitely unconvinced.[8] The journals of American political science were, in fact, dotted with rejoinders for several years after the publication of the report of the Committee on Political Parties in 1950. Their collective case against party government and responsibility divides into two related but independent arguments: the *undesirability* of party government and its *impossibility* (or at least its *improbability*). Although the two points are related, both logically and polemically, one does not have to make both points to venture one.

On the grounds of undesirability, the skeptics argue across a number of fundamental issues of political philosophy. They fear that an embrace of party government would stimulate a more intense politics of dogmatic commitment — one in which the softenings and majority building of compromise would be more difficult. They fear, too, that by making the political party the prime avenue of political representation, the advocates of party government would destroy the present richness and multiplicity of representational mechanisms in the American democracy. Interest groups and other nonparty political organizations, they feel, are necessary means of political representation in a large and heterogeneous polity. To channel the representation of such a diversity of

---

[7] Committee on Political Parties, *Toward a More Responsible Two-Party System*, p. 15.
[8] The bibliography critical of the concept of party responsibility is a long one. Pendleton Herring's *The Politics of Democracy* (New York: Rinehart, 1940) early presented a view contra the reformers.

interests into the party system would overload its representational capacity. Furthermore, the skeptics are concerned lest party government destroy the deliberative quality of American legislatures, for legislators would cease to be free, independent men and women and would become the mandated, committed representatives of a fixed party position. In short, they fear what European critics often call "partyocracy" — the domination of politics and legislatures by a number of doctrinaire, unyielding political parties, none of them strong enough to govern and none willing to let others govern.

On the related grounds of realism (i.e., the question of possibility and probability) the critics of responsible parties have argued that:

1. The American voter remains insufficiently involved in issues to be coaxed easily into viewing politics and electoral choices in programmatic terms.
2. The complexity of American society and the diversity of interests it generates are too great to be expressed in the simple set of alternatives a two-party system can frame. Consequently, there is some fear that a more programmatic politics would break the bounds of the two-party system and encourage the development of splinter parties.
3. The parties themselves are too diffuse and decentralized — too lacking in central disciplinary authority — ever to take a single national position and then enforce it on their assorted partisans and holders of public office.
4. The institutions of American government stand in the way at a number of crucial points. For example, the direct primary makes it difficult for the parties to choose nominees loyal to their programs, and the separation of powers (and bicameralism) often prevents the control of all executive and legislative authority by a single party.

In other words, at every point the model of the responsible, governing political party appears to the critics to demand too much of the American voters, the major parties, and the institutions of American government.

If the major American parties are to meet the demands and roles of party government, they must find some way to overcome their egregious disunity. The problem is really one of uniting the party organization, the party in the electorate, and the party in office in active and responsible support of a party program — despite their different political goals, different political traditions and interests, and different levels of attention, information, and activity. Three sources of the cohesion or unity necessary for party government appear possible within the range of democratic parties.

1. Cohesion may be promoted by *constitutional imperatives*. The parliamentary system demands that the majority party maintain cohesion in the legislature — and to a lesser extent in the electorate and party organization — if it is to stay in office.[9] In the American system the executive may use his power to achieve united action with the legislative party; it is a force for cohesion, but certainly less effective than parliamentary institutions.

2. Cohesion may also be promoted by *organizational discipline*. A strong party organization may impose its discipline and cohesion on balky partisans in office if it can control renomination to office.[10] The American direct primary, however, makes that a questionable option. Alternatively, powerful party leaders or executives may enforce it through the manipulation of the rewards they control (patronage, preference, access to authority, etc.). But the value of these rewards is shrinking, and political ethics in the United States no longer easily accept an enforced line-toeing. Although the available rewards and a tolerant political culture permit this kind of discipline in some American states and localities, it is impossible in many others.

3. Finally, the cohesion may be produced "naturally" by an all-pervasive, intraparty *agreement on ideology or program*. All three components of the party may reach some consensus on a basic party ideology or program — or at least on a "silent ideology" of interest. The activists and identifiers of the party would then achieve a cohesion arising from common philosophy and goals, and their cohesion to a considerable extent would be a result of internalized and self-enforced commitment to those goals. Distasteful external constraints and restraints would thus be less necessary.

Because it seems that only the third avenue to party government is a likely one for contemporary American parties, the issue of party government becomes one of ideological — or more nearly ideological — politics and parties. A pervasive ideological commitment appears to be the necessary condition for cohesion, which in turn is a necessary condition for responsible governing parties. Organizational discipline may supplement and buttress the ideology, but it does not appear to be an alternative to it.

[9] See Leon D. Epstein, "A Comparative Study of Canadian Parties," *American Political Science Review* 58 (1964): 46–59.
[10] A highly centralized party such as the Indian Congress party can maintain control over nomination and renomination of candidates to the national Parliament and thus exercise a potent sanction upon those parliamentarians of the party who break party discipline. In 1957, for example, the national Parliamentary Board of the party, the agency that selects and approves the candidates for local constituencies, declined to renominate almost one-third of the party's incumbent members of Parliament.

IDEOLOGICAL PARTIES IN THE UNITED STATES

The complaint of the American ideologist with the major American parties is an old and familiar one:

The elections this November will prove totally irrelevant because the American electorate will have no substantive choice among the candidates. Naturally, there will be the traditional rhetoric about the "great liberal policies of the Democratic party" and the "great Republican tradition of fiscal responsibility," but if one pierces the rhetoric of each party, one sees that while each may say varying things, each pursues a common policy, i.e., the preservation of the status quo.[11]

If the complaint is clear, its author and occasion are not. The admonition could be from the political left or the political right, and it could well have been spoken at virtually any national election since World War II. As it happens, it opened an article by a prominent spokesman of the New Left shortly before the 1966 congressional elections.[12] From the conservative right in 1971 came similar sentiments:

I favor the two-party system. But the two parties should represent distinct positions; the reason for the demise of the modern system has been too much sameness and liberal-financed convergence. . . . A "broad-based" party is possible and desirable. To be a "party," an interest, it must have discernible principles, not just a roost for "personalities," engaging or otherwise.[13]

The Democrats and Republicans are guilty, so the charges go, either of suppressing program alternatives subscribed to by significant numbers of Americans or of failing to promote a wide-ranging debate on public issues. In other words, they smother existing ideological differences, and they deny one important opportunity for others to develop.

Both the academic and nonacademic reformers have within their ranks those who seek full-blown, total commitment to ideologies in the parties. But both groups also have those who seek only a crisper, bolder set of programs or issue positions from the parties. The differences between issue and program on the one hand and ideology on the other — and the relationship between them — lie at the heart of the problem. Some distinctions between them are probably overdue.

---

[11] Edward M. Keating, "The New Left: What Does It Mean?" *Saturday Review*, September 24, 1966, p. 25.
[12] The following second paragraph of the essay is also illustrative:

Republicans and Democrats in 1966 are snarling and snapping at each other, vainly attempting to deceive the voter into thinking that there are choices, not echoes, on the political horizon. This is to dissemble. Both parties know that neither will attempt to alter basic American policy, which, on the national level, is to obfuscate the social sickness that is consuming us all, and, on the international level, is intended to extend Americanism to the rest of the world by military blackmail.

[13] Anthony R. Spinelli, "Hooray for the Two-Party System," *New York Times*, July 17, 1971.

Terms such as "issues" and "programs" denote the stands that parties
and politicians take on specific policy options — on defense, foreign
policy, medical care, labor-management relations, and protection of the
environment. Traditionally the parties have, however hesitantly, taken
their programmatic stands in their platforms. Presidents and presidential candidates take theirs in speeches, messages, position papers, and
press conferences. "Ideology," by contrast, denotes the broader values
or philosophies that give rise to coherent sets of stands on issues. Liberalism or conservatism, to illustrate, provides an underlying structure of
values which leads an individual to a logical, even predictable, position
on a number of issues.

In a descriptive sense it is unquestionably true that there are parties
of issue (or program) and parties of more explicit ideology.[14] Certainly
not many of the reformers can hope to develop in the American political context the kind of total *weltanschauung*, the all-embracing concern,
of an East European Communist party or an Asian Moslem party. Theirs
is an ideology encompassing virtually all social relationships, and thus
it spawns a politics of limitless scope and total involvement. Nor, given
the general American agreement on basic institutions, are ideological
differences between the American parties apt to involve dispute over
the Constitution, the general outlines of the American economy, or the
basic fabric of American society. Nor will American parties commit
themselves dogmatically to irrevocable political ideologies in the manner
of some doctrinaire European parties. And so, ideological parties as one
finds them elsewhere — and especially in the bitter class politics of the
European democracies — do not exist in the United States.

However, it would be a mistake to draw the distinction too broadly
between issue stands and ideology. Both are really points on the same
continuous dimension; one blends into the other. Individuals take stands
on specific policy issues, but those stands are often related to some more
basic value or goal. Their disapproval of income taxation (or any taxation) may be related to their desire to toughen eligibility requirements
for welfare programs. In other words, while few Americans develop
total, all-encompassing ideologies, many do develop these rudimentary,
restricted ideologies, which at their minimum are little more than expansions of a single value or interest. It is an ideology — or quasi ideology
— in the sense that it guides the individual to a reasonably logical interrelated set of positions on a group of issues.

The modest form of ideology one finds in American politics perhaps
can be explored and explained in another way. The American parties

[14] Leon D. Epstein, *Political Parties in Western Democracies* (New York: Praeger,
1967), Chap. 10, distinguishes between parties of program and ideology.

have often differed on the major political issues of the moment. In recent years their national platforms have differed over American foreign policy in the Far East, government medical insurance and aid for the aged, fiscal policy and the balanced budget, and government regulation of labor-management relations. Beneath these differences on the policy issues were the different constellations of attitudes, interests, and goals each party had embraced. Each party, in other words, had developed a "silent ideology" based on the commonality of the interests and views (and in a few cases on the full-blown ideologies) of its activists and its party electorate. Its leaders constitute a group of like-minded men and women whose views on public issues separate them from the like-minded leaders of the other party.[15] Such a silent ideology stops short in only one main way from being an ideology in the more conventional sense; it is not usually codified or explicated — either by the party or the individual voter — into a systematic, coherent, and consistent pattern of political values. For the classic American political style focuses the party's attention not on fixed, abstract principles of ideology but on the immediate, concrete issues of public policy that divide the nation.

All these distinctions and definitions are not an arid intellectual exercise. Very likely some degree or kind of ideology is implied in the demand for more programmatic parties. In a heterogeneous society of many conflicting interests, parties cannot take stands on ten or fifteen separate issues if there is no similarity among the coalitions supporting each issue. To do so would be to fragment the party and its electorate. But if the same people take position A on the first issue, position B on the second one, and C on the third one, three issues in effect are reduced to a single cohesive dimension. Such cohesion also reduces the potential cross-cutting disagreement and makes it easier for the party to develop a program. That single cohesive dimension is what ideology in some form brings. But call it what one will (the ASPA report refers at several points to general party principles), greater programmatic commitment in the American parties depends on structures of values or philosophies to reduce the vast number of policy issues to a few dimensions in American politics. Thus results the argument that in the absence of constitutional pressures and sheer organizational discipline, the parties must look to the development of ideology or some approximation of it as the cohesive force necessary for responsible or programmatic parties.

By these modest standards the American major parties have probably never been indistinguishable, but there are ample signs that attention to issues and even ideological concerns within the parties is on the rise.

---

15 Thomas A. Flinn and Frederick M. Wirt, "Local Party Leaders: Groups of Like Minded Men," *Midwest Journal of Political Science* 9 (1965): 77–98.

For example:

1. Men and women are increasingly being drawn to party work out of their involvement with issues and ideologies. The triumph of political ideas and values thus becomes a major incentive to party activity, and to some extent it replaces the older incentives of patronage and preference.[16]
2. Ideologically motivated partisans have increasingly been forming ideological organizations both within and parallel to the party structure. The club-style organizations of some urban Democrats are a case in point. Recently, also, the Republicans have been proliferating extra-party organizations (e.g., the Free Society Association and the Ripon Society), and groups such as the New Democratic Coalition have grown up on the fringes of the Democratic party.
3. The labels of liberal and conservative are freely accepted by increasing numbers of political activists, in contrast to the widely expressed belief of less than a generation ago that to accept the labels, especially the conservative label, was gross political imprudence.
4. In 1964, one of the major political parties chose an avowedly ideological candidate and wrote an unabashedly ideological platform. One observer termed it the end of the "reign of pragmatism" within the GOP.[17] A similar unwillingness to make the usual pragmatic compromises marked the unsuccessful campaign of Eugene McCarthy for the 1968 Democratic nomination and the successful pursuit of the same nomination by George McGovern in 1972.

There are other symptoms of the ideological renaissance. George Wallace ran programmatic campaigns for the presidency in 1968 and 1972. As a number of observers noted, he appealed to a cluster of goals and interests (an ideology?) we often describe as populism, as well as to rather specific racial attitudes. In 1970, a Conservative party candidate for the United States Senate from New York, James Buckley, defeated both the incumbent Republican, Charles Goodell, and a well-heeled Democratic candidate.

Most of these signs of increased ideological concern are visible chiefly among the activists of the party organization. But what of the American voters, especially the less partisan electorate? The existence of ideological political parties does not guarantee an ideological politics. It may very well be that only the small core of party activists is moving to greater ideological sophistication and concerns and that the broad American public is accepting them only selectively and cautiously. There is always the possibility, in other words, that more ideological party cadres

---

[16] See Chap. 4.
[17] James Reichley, quoted by Theodore White, *The Making of the President 1964* (New York: Atheneum, 1965), p. 217.

will bring their new involvement to a deaf or hostile public, that their "ideologizing" will only bore or alienate the majority of the electorate.

The issue of the differences in ideological concern between party organization activists and the electorate is, moreover, not merely a scholarly one. The ideologists of American politics have long claimed that a horde of ideological voters is increasingly alienated by parties unwilling or unable to give them clearly defined ideological alternatives. Much of the 1964 rationale of the Goldwater Republicans, for example, hinged on the argument that a frankly conservative Republican candidate would mobilize the disenchanted, stay-at-home conservative vote.[18] This entire question of whether the American parties are reflecting a nonideological electorate or suppressing an ideological one rests on the stance of the American voter toward issue and ideology.

IDEOLOGY IN THE AMERICAN ELECTORATE

In the late 1950s the authors of *The American Voter* found that by the most generous criteria only about 15 percent of the American electorate employed an ideological framework or ideological terminology as either a primary or marginal means of evaluating parties and candidates.[19] That is to say, less than one in six American voters applied to the presidential politics of the time some ideological abstractions greater than a single issue or group interest. Beneath this thin stratum of ideologists and near ideologists, some 45 percent of the electorate operated on an interest-oriented level — a level that we have earlier called the level of the silent ideology. Their subideological identifications and evaluations were nonsystematic projections of the interests of a group or the fervor of an issue position. For example, they characterized the Democratic party as the party of the worker, the Republican as the party of business or fiscal responsibility.

The 1950s were, however, years of consensus in American politics, a period in which increased affluence seemed to have produced a new politics to replace the SES politics of the New Deal and the 1940s. The consensus was, however, either illusory or short-lived. From 1960 on it became clear that the scholarship of the 1950s had merely reflected a period of unnatural complacency in American politics. It had also probably underestimated the extent of emerging policy disagreements.[20] By the 1970s it was abundantly clear that the differences between Demo-

---

[18] It should be noted, of course, that none materialized in the 1964 elections and that no scholarly study of the American electorate, either before or since those elections, has confirmed the presence of such a body of voters.

[19] See Angus Campbell et al., *The American Voter* (New York: Wiley, 1960), Chap. 10.

[20] John C. Pierce, "Party Identification and the Changing Role of Ideology in American Politics," *Midwest Journal of Political Science* 14 (1970): pp. 25–42.

crats and Republicans on major issues of public policy were increasing. The alternatives they represented were becoming clearer and clearer.[21] Indeed, there was also some reason to think they had also been clearer before the 1950s and that the soundings taken in those years merely represented a dip in the normal level of issue concern and awareness in the American electorate.[22]

The parties in the electorate — whether they are described by party identification or consistency of party voting — differ now most sharply on the traditional areas of economic and social welfare policy. After analyzing the views of Democrats and Republicans on aid to education, medical care, job guarantees, fair employment legislation, school integration, and foreign aid from 1956 to 1968, Pomper concludes: "On five of the six issues — all but foreign aid — party identification meant something by 1968 other than a traditional reaffirmation: it was now related to the policy preferences of the voter." [23] For example, while there had been no differences between the percentage of strong Democrats and strong Republicans supporting the "liberal" position on school integration in 1956, a gap of 27.4 percent had opened by 1968. The similar distance on federal aid to education went from 12.3 percent in 1956 to 41.6 percent in 1968.[24] All the preliminary data from the 1972 election reinforce these conclusions. That election was, in fact, the first presidential election in recent times in which the issues were more important than party identification in the voting. Democratic identifiers, in other words, left the candidate of their party to support Richard Nixon because they saw Nixon as closer to their own positions on the issues than George McGovern was.[25]

It is not only a matter of individual voters perceiving issues. They also increasingly perceive the *parties* as standing for a position on issues (Table 1). Those perceptions fluctuate with the events of the times and with the extent to which campaigns and important figures play on ideological concerns. Hence, the salience of such questions reached a high point in the 1964 presidential campaign, thanks largely to the rhetoric of Barry Goldwater (note, again, Table 1). But regardless of the fluctuations, the long-run trend is to greater citizen perception of the parties as standing for different positions on the major issues of the time. Thus,

[21] Gerald M. Pomper, "From Confusion to Clarity: Issues and American Voters, 1956–1968," *American Political Science Review* 66 (1972): 415–28; see also Pomper's *Voters' Choice* (New York: Dodd, Mead, 1975).
[22] Everett C. Ladd and Charles D. Hadley, "Political Parties and Political Issues: Patterns in Differentiation Since the New Deal," vol. 1 of Sage Professional Papers in American Politics (Beverly Hills: Sage, 1973).
[23] Pomper, "From Confusion to Clarity," p. 418.
[24] Ibid., p. 417.
[25] Arthur Miller, Warren Miller, Alden Raine, and Thad Brown, "A Majority Party in Disarray: Policy Polarization in the 1972 Election," a paper presented at the annual meetings of the American Political Science Association (September 1973).

TABLE 1   Party Identifiers Perceiving Party
Differences on the Desirability of Government
Programs of Medical Care

	1956	1960	1964	1968
Strong Democrat	63%	69%	86%	86%
Weak Democrat	49	59	77	71
Independent	41	45	77	62
Weak Republican	50	69	75	66
Strong Republican	65	67	88	76

Source Adapted from Gerald M. Pomper, "From Confusion to Clarity: Issues and American Voters, 1956–1968,"
American Political Science Review 66 (1972): 418. By permission of the American Political Science Association.

there is one more sign of the increasing ideological content of American
politics.

These commitments and perceptions are not, however, evenly spread
across the American adult population. They are clearly more marked
among college-educated Americans and among political activists.[26] To a
considerable extent, of course, those are the same people; the active elite
in American parties (and in all of American political life) comes heavily
from college graduates. That group differs ideologically in two ways.
First, party activists and the college-educated are more apt to be concerned themselves about issues and ideology; they also tend more often
to see the parties representing alternatives on the issues. But in addition,
they are more apt to locate themselves on the outer ideological reaches.
Ideological Republicans tend to be to the right of other Republicans, and
ideological Democrats also tend, if less certainly, to the left of their cohorts in the party.[27] Thus, while ideology has come to virtually all American voters, it has come with much greater force and with different effect
to those specific American voters most likely to assume positions of leadership in the party.

Whether American adults can go the next step and act on ideological
knowledge by itself is quite another matter. There is evidence to suggest

[26] On the college-educated, see Ladd and Hadley, "Political Parties and Political
Issues." The tie between political activism and ideology has been noted by virtually
all of the scholarly work on voting behavior and political participation; see, for
example, Campbell et al., *The American Voter.*
[27] Ladd and Hadley, "Political Parties and Political Issues"; Herbert McClosky, Paul
J. Hoffmann, Rosemary O'Hara, "Issue Conflict and Consensus Among Party Leaders and Followers," *American Political Science Review* 54 (1960): 406–27; and David
Nexon, "Asymmetry in the Political System: Occasional Activists in the Republican
and Democratic Parties: 1956–1964," *American Political Science Review* 65 (1971):
716–30.

that it is not easy or automatic. The Pierce study of the 1964 events finds that the increase in the numbers of "conceptual" ideologues (those perceiving parties and candidates in ideological terms) was not matched by increases in the numbers of "informational" ideologues (those with specific understanding of ideologies and their distributions in the parties).[28] Thus, voters may lack the information to make specific choices on the basis of issue or ideology. For instance, despite all of Senator Eugene McCarthy's explicit campaigning against American participation in the war in Vietnam in 1968, 60 percent of the people who voted for him in the New Hampshire primary of that year favored a tougher, more hawkish policy on the war! [29] The presidential election of 1972, however, erased all doubts about the possibility of translating ideology into action. Issue concerns dominated the vote decisions as never before in recent American presidential elections. Issues such as the war in Vietnam, unrest on the campuses, and programs for minorities accounted for the major Democratic defections.

In summary, then, there has been an increase in the number of adult Americans who perceive and act politically on the basis of ideological cues and frameworks. The reasons are not hard to deduce. Increased education and literacy among American adults — and new means of communication — make widespread political ideology possible, for ideology is by its nature abstract and intensely verbal. The nationalization of American politics, too, promotes political ideology by focusing political attention on a single, dramatic set of issues or a single ideological dimension and by minimizing the often issueless politics of traditions and personalities. For a politics of ideology is abstract and remote, and it thrives with difficulty in the folksy, face-to-face politics of personal followings, family political traditions, and patronage and preference. It springs more naturally from a depersonalized, urbanized, group-centered politics of influence over governmental activity and programs. Finally, presidential politics between 1960 and 1975 doubtless sensitized millions of Americans to issues and ideologies. Through candidacies such as those of Barry Goldwater, Eugene McCarthy, George McGovern, and George Wallace, ideology begets more ideology.[30]

Yet, sophistication about and involvement in things ideological has not been evenly spread across the American polity. Not many voters can

---

[28] Pierce, "Party Identification and the Changing Role of Ideology."
[29] Philip E. Converse et al., "Continuity and Change in American Politics: Parties and Issues in the 1968 Election," *American Political Science Review* 63 (1969): 1092.
[30] It is very doubtful that the psychological theories are of great use in explaining the rise of ideology; these, of course, range from sophisticated theories about popular paranoia and authoritarian personalities to the garden variety musings about kooks and eccentric old ladies in sneakers. These may well be valid explanations of some ideological responses, but they do not seem to explain the increase in ideological involvement.

sustain the interest or provide the sophistication with abstractions that it demands; theirs is not the ideologist's view of American society. To be sure, many of them do have a capacity to react to an ideological or issue-centered campaign. The Goldwater and Wallace candidacies seem to have shown that. But once the ideological stimulus is past, the concerns abate. At the same time, however, the ideological minority has expanded and entered the major party organizations for the first time. No longer is the ideological elite consigned to esoteric minor parties and genteel, reformist, even antiparty, associations. Its entry into the mainstream of party organizations and activity raises a bevy of questions about the future of American parties.

THE TRIALS OF IDEOLOGY

In general, the uneven rise of ideology risks the development in American politics of a discontinuity between the ideological minority within the parties and the essentially nonideological majority in the electorate. At best, the full electorate is only sporadically given to ideologies. It responds selectively to issues, to be sure, but it also responds to a personality, a deeply felt personal interest, a campaign, a group loyalty, an ancient tradition. To that gulf between the ideological minority and the nonideological majority, the parties and their candidates may respond with appeals on a number of levels — ideological arguments for some parts of the audience, nonideological ones for others. But always there is danger of politically alienating the majority, who are irritated and ultimately repelled by a discourse that is to them obscure, irrelevant, and even fatuous.

More specifically than that, the increasingly ideological political activists and organizations run the risk of alienating even that sector of the party in the electorate that is attuned to the party's ideological themes. Evidence is ample that the ideological positions of the activists need not be those of the party's electorate. McClosky's study, for example, documents the fact that Republican leaders and activists are far more conservative, more unwilling to accept the social welfare reforms of the last generation, than are the rank-and-file loyalists of the party.[31] Caught in the middle of these differences are the party's candidates and officeholders. The only alternatives open to them — conflict with the party's activists, lack of candor with the electorate, or defeat at the polls — are not very attractive.

So it is that a major American party, faced with the development of ideological activists, may develop an internal, private ideology or issue consensus different from the external, public one it shows to the voters.

[31] See McClosky, Hoffman, and O'Hara, "Issue Conflict."

That divergence aggravates, in one more way, the tensions and strains among the party organization, the party in government, and the party in the electorate. There are periodic eruptions of dissatisfaction among the conservatives of the Republican organization with the moderatism of the party in office. Even so conservative a "moderate" as President Gerald Ford found himself rejected by many of the organization Republicans in favor of the more conservative Ronald Reagan. His hand-picked vice-president, Nelson Rockefeller, bowed out of consideration for 1976 in the face of a similar rejection.

For the party as an organization, however, the threats from ideological fervor are also internal. It may presage the factionalism of "true believers" — perhaps the most virulent form of factionalism — since not even victory and victory's fruits will always heal it. It produces scenes of bitterness and irreconcilability such as those of the southern delegations storming from the 1948 Democratic convention after the adoption of a strong civil rights resolution, the closing hours of the conservative triumph in the 1964 Republican convention, and the three-day-long shambles of the 1968 Democratic convention in Chicago. Furthermore, it threatens divisions between the ideologists and the pragmatists. Those differences, of course, rest often on differences of incentive for activity in the party. And their organizational disagreements escalate as charges of sellout and vote buying fly past accusations of dogmatism and extremism.

Party organizations, for all these reasons and many more, seem incapable of containing an expanding ideological ferment. The ideologist quickly becomes disenchanted with the electoral pragmatism of party candidates and with the inability of party organizations to utter anything more than the most muted, even docile statements of principle. The American party organizations are indeed poorly adapted to ideology. They are decentralized and fragmented by American federalism and the separation of powers; lacking unifying structures, they speak in a babel of ideological voices. They have no annual conference and no other instrument for arbitrating the conflicts and fashioning a doctrine. They have no apparatus for political education or socialization; they have no way of propagandizing a doctrine or even an issue position. Their quadrennial platforms are instruments of the presidential campaign for votes rather than lucid declarations of party principles. And the institution of the direct primary makes it impossible for them to ensure the ideological loyalty of their candidates. In short, the major American parties are structurally incapable of controlling — much less monopolizing — the ideological content of American politics.

Discouragement with the party organization and its electoral pragmatism drives some ideologists out of the party and party activity. In other cases it presses them into the quasi-party activity of the Democratic club reformers in New York and California. They affiliate with the party while expressing a distaste and reforming zeal for the regular party organization and its bosses and other pragmatists. Other ideological activists shift the major part of their political concern to organizations less closely tied to the parties. Republican ideologists in the 1960s manned an impressive range of ideological satellite organizations: the Ripon Society (young East Coast liberals), the Free Society Association (Goldwater conservatives), United Republicans of America (conservatives supporting conservative candidates), and Republicans for Progress (liberals and moderates). Ideological factions — like much else about the parties — seem less well organized within the Democratic party. Since late 1967 the dissident Democratic ideologues have tended to work for seekers of the party's presidential nomination rather than in specific and separate organizations. The New Democratic Coalition, a short-lived successor to the 1968 McCarthy candidacy, was the major exception.

Just as the spread of ideology within the American electorate over the past generation has not been uniform, the travails of ideology have not fallen evenly on the two major parties. All other things being about equal, the party out of power has greater spurs to ideology than the party of the president. Ideology is a natural instrument for raising alternatives to the status quo of the majority party. Its unambiguous principles, furthermore, are unhampered by the complex and heavy responsibilities of power. And within a minority party, electoral disappointment invites the recriminations that exaggerate differences in issue positions.

Along with the increase in the sheer quantity of ideological involvement, we have recently seen a slow spread of the scope and breadth of ideology. The debate spurred by the Goldwater candidacy of 1964 seems (perhaps in nostalgic retrospect) almost classic in its simplicity. Most of it turned on a single ideological dimension: the traditional liberal and conservative differences over the proper and useful role of government. It was strong, positive government and the welfare state versus very limited government and individual responsibility. By 1968 and after, however, the ideological dimensions were no longer simple. Differences along an axis of war–peace–defense–military establishment had been added; so, too, had differences touching racial equality, the aspirations of minorities, and aid to the impoverished and disadvantaged. The politics of 1972 added concern for unrest and violence in American society and for the "new morality" and its proposals, for example, of the legalization of abortion and marijuana. What was largely a unidimensional ideological politics in 1964 became a multilevel ideological universe in less than ten years.

Thus ideology comes with many difficulties to the American parties. What is more, it comes increasingly in plural forms that attack the status quo and the consensus of the center. For the parties themselves, the question surely must be whether they can contain that increasing dose of ideological conflict. The threat to the parties is in part one of factionalism, conflict, and splintering — the usual forms of intraparty bickering. Beyond that threat is another: Greater numbers of ideologues threaten the party organizations with an inflexibility of goals that rejects the parties' traditional electoral pragmatism. Many delegates to the Republican convention of 1964 and the Democratic conventions of 1968 and 1972 were prepared to nominate candidates without considering greatly their electability. Some, indeed, preferred defeat with principle to victory with compromise. If the importance of the ideological goal of the party ever crowds out the electioneering role, then the parties themselves will be greatly altered. So, too, will most of American electoral politics.

PARTY RESPONSIBILITY AMERICAN-STYLE

The model of the responsible political party is an ideal. One does not look for it in reality, for no political system yet has developed the cohesion, discipline, and unity that its pure form demands. Even in Great Britain, home of the hopes of the American reformers, practice falls considerably short of the model. Party cohesion in the British Parliament, while significantly greater than in the American Congress, is by no means perfect. British cabinets and parliamentary parties, in fact, have long insisted that constitutional traditions forbade them to be bound by party decision or commitment. Even within the Labour party, traditionally committed to the binding discipline of party decisions, Labour prime ministers have made it clear that although a Labour government will consult with the party's national executive, it cannot be bound by it.

American practice is even further from the model. To be sure, one finds in some state legislatures a high order of party discipline behind or in opposition to the program of the majority or the governor. The programs or principles, however, spring not so much from a party organization or the decision of the electorate — there are rarely mandate elections — as from the initiative of the governor or the party's legislative leadership. What responsibility there is to the voters for their program is established at later elections as the voters reward or punish their programmatic stewardship.[32] Under the best circumstances a sophisticated voter may be able to identify a past policy or decision with a party,

[32] This is substantially the point V. O. Key makes in *The Responsible Electorate* (Cambridge, Mass.: Harvard University Press, 1966). On the American voter's lack of the perceptions and decisions the goals of party responsibility would demand, see Donald E. Stokes and Warren E. Miller, "Party Government and the Saliency of Congress," in Angus Campbell et al., *Elections and the Political Order* (New York: Wiley, 1966), pp. 194–211.

but such a quasi responsibility diverges from the model in one major way: There is little role in it for the party organization, since the legislative party or the executive originates the program and enforces discipline behind it. The responsibility rests not on the overt program of party activists and organizations but on the homogeneous interests of the voters, party leaders, and constituencies supporting the legislative and executive parties. It is a cohesion and responsibility that springs from the silent ideology of common interests.

Occasionally under the stress of crisis or catastrophe, American politics approaches even more closely the model of party responsibility. A strong case can certainly be made that at the presidential election of 1936, the Democrats and Republicans were identified with sharply differing solutions to the nation's economic woes. If their positions were not truly ideological, they were at least determinedly programmatic. The burdens of the depression may have focused voter attention on the hopes and remedies of policy to an unusual degree. Much of the campaign oratory centered around the Roosevelt program for social and economic change and his opponent's charges that he proposed radical changes in the American polity and economy. The combination of programmatic rhetoric and identification, plus high voter attention, may well have produced something close to a mandate election and a mandated congressional contingent of Democrats. If the supposition about the presidential election of 1936 is correct, it indicates that the kind of ideological or programmatic concern necessary for "pure" party responsibility is a product of crisis conditions which have prevailed only for short periods of time in recent American experience. The necessary ideological focus and attention are not expressions of ordinary American politics; rather they are the product of occasional, heightened, extrapolitical crisis.

More common than the case of crisis-stimulated responsibility is the type of responsibility resulting from presidential government. Strong presidential leadership, especially when aided by majorities of the same party in the legislature, produces a somewhat cohesive program that becomes the program of the president's party. Indeed, some presidents have been able to organize the enactment of large parts of the party platforms on which they ran for office.[33] Presidential government, of course, produces only the kind of post hoc responsibility that we noted earlier. And it need not produce the kind of clear programmatic alternative the reformers want. (Platform differences between the two parties, while they can be observed, are not generally great enough to satisfy the same critics.) But presidential government does stamp some differences on the parties, and it does fashion points of reference for the approval or disapproval of voters.

[33] Gerald M. Pomper, *Elections in America* (New York: Dodd, Mead, 1968), Chap. 8.

Can one expect more than this of the American parties? It is true that the new ideological activists, a more sophisticated electorate, a slowly centralizing pair of party organizations, and even the development of nationally recognized issue differences between the parties promise a trend to greater party responsibility. But several notes of caution ought to be mentioned:

1. The American institution of the direct primary (and its undermining of party control of nominations), combined with the decentralizing effect of federalism and the separation of powers, continues to work against party responsibility even in the presence of ideology. It permits the nonideological candidate to become a representative of and spokesman for a party program. It also permits the ideological candidate and officeholder to defend to the political death a program or ideology at odds with that of his party or his president or governor. To be ideological is not necessarily to be "responsible."

2. Much of the increasing ideological or programmatic commitment has not followed the single, unidimensional pattern necessary if ideology (or issue) is to provide the unity essential for party government. If the divisions along SES lines do not coincide with those on minority rights or civil liberties, or with those on foreign policy, the resulting cross-cutting (multidimensional) ideologies divide much more than they unify. Then, for example, hawk-dove differences on Vietnam cut across rather than reinforce liberal-conservative lines on the welfare state. Only if multiple patterns of issue or ideological differences coincide do they offer the basis for two unified, cohesive programmatic parties.[34]

3. Ideology thus far has not been translated into party organizational strength. There are only a few signs of an important growth of authority within the parties; the national committees remain hostages to the traditional decentralization of the parties. Nor has the party cohesion of legislative parties increased. We have not yet developed the mandate elections or the party discipline with which to convert issue unity into public policy.

Thus while the spread of ideology or issue orientation may be a necessary condition for government by responsible parties, it is anything but a sufficient one in and of itself. Especially in the context of fragmenting political institutions — particularly the institutions of federalism and the separation of powers — the growth of ideology may very well work to defeat the goal of party responsibility.

If the advent of ideology will not automatically (or willy-nilly) bring the party to a greater governing role, will the more conscious and overt

---

[34] Donald E. Stokes, "Spatial Models of Party Competition," Campbell et al., *Elections and the Political Order*, pp. 161–79, develops this and related points.

proposals of the reformers? The breadth of the problem of converting
the American major parties into prototypic responsible parties can be
gauged by examining the scope of the reformers' proposals. The Committee on Political Parties of the American Political Science Association,
for example, proposed:[35]

1. *A massive shoring up of the national parties and their organizations.* The committee recommended that the national conventions meet
at least biennially and exercise greater control over the national committees. Above all, it suggested a national party council of some fifty members, which would draft a platform for the national convention, interpret
and apply it to issues between conventions, make "recommendations
... in respect to congressional candidates" and about "conspicuous de-
partures from general party decisions by state or local party organizations," provide a forum for "the discussion of presidential candidacies,"
and coordinate relations among national, state, and local party organizations.

2. *A perfecting of the instruments of ideology.* The committee in essence proposed that the platform mean something and that it bind the
party officeholders and organizations. The platform ought to deal at
least partially with the party's "permanent or long-range philosophy,"
and it ought also to be carefully prepared and systematically interpreted.
"The party programs should be considered generally binding" on both
officeholders and state and local parties.

3. *An asserting of party control over the congressional party.* To
tackle so protean a task, the committee recommended both a consolida-
tion of the present congressional party organizations into a single party
leadership group and the elimination of practices (such as the seniority
system and the traditional power of the House Rules Committee) that
work against party discipline and ultimately against party responsibility.

4. *A remodeling of the American parties into membership, participatory parties.* The committee's hope was perhaps best expressed in its
words:

With increased unity within the party it is likely that party membership will
be given a more explicit basis. Those who claim the right to participate in
framing the party's program and selecting its candidates may be very willing
to support its national program by the payment of regular dues. Once machinery is established which gives the party member and his representatives a

---

[35] The direct quotations in the following list are from the report of the committee,
Toward a More Responsible Two-Party System (New York: Rinehart, 1950). The
italics in the original have been eliminated. One of the members of the committee
has also recently published some reflections on its work; see Evron M. Kirkpatrick,
"Toward a More Responsible Two-Party System: Political Science, Policy Science,
or Pseudo-Science?" *American Political Science Review* 65 (1971): 965–90.

share in framing the party's objectives, once there are safeguards against internal dictation by a few in positions of influence, members and representatives will feel readier to assume an obligation to support the program.[36]

The committee's report ranged beyond these general points. It dealt with other basic inhibitors of party responsibility: the direct primary ("the closed primary deserves preference"), the electoral college (it "fosters the blight of one-party monopoly"), political finance, and barriers to full and meaningful adult suffrage (e.g., the long ballot). In short, it becomes clear that to achieve the goal of government by responsible parties, the committee would undertake — and probably would *have* to undertake — a wholesale reconstruction not only of the American parties but of the American electorate and political environment as well.

However, some other proponents of party responsibility have been more modest in their goals. One of the most persistent and consistent, James MacGregor Burns,[37] touches many of the same themes as the ASPA Committee. There is the same emphasis on the building of grass roots, membership parties, and buttressing of the national party (the presidential party), the reconstructing of a vigorous congressional party; the same recognition of the need for change in the parties' political environment (e.g., the restrictions on adult suffrage and the status quo in political finance). Yet the reforms Burns suggests are less drastic and sweeping and more realistic, even though their direction and their pinpointing of the causes of the present lack of responsibility are not greatly different. Perhaps Burns' relative moderatism springs in part from his recognition of an essentially Madisonian political culture that has not tolerated any instrument — party or other — of national majoritarian political power.

Thus, the agenda of reform is a very long one, and its measures touch the fundamentals of American political life. Even the basic American political institutions work against the development of more responsible parties — against a sweeping reorientation of the role of the parties in the American democracy. They were erected on the principle that one best controls the uses of power by fragmenting that power. So does a political culture suspicious of majoritarian political power marshaled behind programs of action. Nor is there in the American political sys-

---

[36] Committee on Political Parties, *Toward a More Responsible Two-Party System*, p. 70.

[37] See James MacGregor Burns, *The Deadlock of Democracy* (Englewood Cliffs, N.J.: Prentice-Hall, 1963), especially Chap. 14. Note also that Burns is dealing with the parties in terms of his own, somewhat different frame of reference, especially the distinction between the presidential and the congressional parties. See also Stephen K. Bailey, *The Condition of Our National Political Parties* (New York: Fund for the Republic, 1959).

tem a constitutional stimulus to disciplined, governing parties. In the United States, parties do not have to govern to maintain public office as they have to in a parliamentary system.

For the immediate future, barring the special conditions of crisis, it seems likely that the American parties will continue their modest governing role — a post hoc responsibility for carrying out programs that generally promote the interests of the party's activists and loyal electorate. Neither the American parties nor the voters can meet the demands that the classic model of party responsibility would impose on them. It is true, to be sure, that the various sectors of the party are increasingly bound together by a commitment to a set of issue positions which separates the activists, candidates, and voters of one party from those of the other. In a loose, often distressingly imprecise sense, each of the two parties is a distinct group of like-minded men and women. That tentative and limited agreement on issues, reinforced by executive leadership of the party in government, may produce enough cohesion for a modest, variable degree of responsibility. Such a degree of party responsibility will, ironically, be achieved without the central role — drawing up a program and enforcing it on candidates and officeholders — that the reformers planned for party organizations. It will be a party responsibility of the party in government, and that is a very significant difference.

Of the relation between party responsibility and the new ideological and issue concerns in American politics, two things must be kept in mind. Ideology is doubtless a necessary condition for party responsibility, but it is hardly the only one. Second, the kind of ideological awareness and perception increasing in the American polity may not sustain the kind of ideological voting and activism that the doctrines of responsibility seem to presume. That degree of ideological involvement will very likely be limited to a minority of Americans. It is one pattern of relationship that the political party develops with one segment of the electorate. To the nonideological segment the party continues to make appeals on other than ideological grounds — on a mixture of issues, traditions, interests, and personalities. One suspects that even in the classic ideological-responsible party systems, ideological debate and discourse dull the political nerve ends of the majority, who would rather be involved with a dynamic personality or a gut political issue. The danger for parties caught in such a conflict or mixture of appeals — as the parties of Europe have been for at least a generation — is that they either alienate the ideological minority by compromise or bore the majority by dogma.

To conclude, parties in government govern for a great many goals and reasons. They want to satisfy the multiple and complex demands of the electorate. They want to meet the goals — also complex and contra-dictory — of the activists of the party organization. Then, too, they have their own goals to meet, and those goals range all the way from individual desires for power and the perquisites of office to their obliga-tions to public office and trust. In the aggregate, those various goals are extraordinarily complex. Although program or ideology is an important goal for many people in each of the three party sectors, it does not dominate all others. Nor does it dominate the perceptions of the Ameri-can electorate. The present extent of party government — that is, of the parties' ability to enact cohesive programs into public policy — probably reflects the present place of program and ideology in the total structure of the goals and incentives of the American parties.

VI

THE POLITICAL PARTIES: ROLE AND THEORY

Textbooks change with the subjects they treat. Some years ago the concluding chapters in books of this sort invariably discussed the place of the parties in the broader political system and in the smooth operation of American democratic processes and institutions. Those questions are still important and almost obligatory. But political science has changed in the last generation, and a final theoretical "attempt" is probably just as obligatory. Since World War II, political scientists have been caught up in explanations of the empirical behavior, institutions, and processes they study. That new commitment of the profession of political science thus creates a new expectation here: the final theoretical essay.

The theoretical aspirations of political scientists vary greatly. The more confident and optimistic of them aspire to propositions that not only will explain past behavior but also will meet the higher test of predicting future behavior. Less hopeful ones are content with specifying major variables and relationships, with the understanding that the arrangement of them into a final, integrated theoretical pattern of explanations will have to await the collection of more data, more observations, and more explanatory fragments. The pages of these last two chapters will make it clear that the choice here is for the more modest route. The development of theoretical statements about most political institutions and processes is in an early, rudimentary stage, and modesty becomes such a state.

One begins the theoretical task by attempting to explain why the American parties are what they are and why they do what they do. One of the best strategies for this purpose is to observe changes in them over time. As the parties develop new activities, depend on new incentives, take new organizational forms, for example, one is naturally led to wonder how and why the changes came about. What changes in the parties' environment accompanied those changes in the parties? Is there a causal relationship between the changes in the parties and those outside of them? If the decline of patronage accompanies the decline of the old-style urban machine, does it cause that change in the party organization? Or has the decline of the machine reduced the need for patronage and thus caused its demise? We learn much about the parties if we put the changes together into a pattern and adduce explanations for them.

Chapter 17 undertakes this analytical task by examining the changes presently under way in the American parties. It brings together the trends and changes that have been mentioned throughout the book and concludes with an explanation of those changes and a series of projections of what's ahead for the American parties. The central theme — already more than hinted at in earlier chapters — is that the major American parties have begun to lose their powerful, predominant role in American electoral politics. Of necessity, we also face the questions of what produced that change and what electoral politics will look like in their release from party domination.

The last chapter carries the analysis beyond the specific changes presently abroad in the American parties to the level of parties in general and the American parties in other periods of time. In that last chapter, too, the theoretical problems and issues suggested by the contemporary changes will be brought together into some more general categories. The chapter will be concerned with changes in the parties' roles and activities within the larger political system. It concludes, in fact, with the proposal of a developmental approach to the parties, an approach suggesting that parties usually enjoy their heyday when electorates are less educated, less secure, and politically unsophisticated, and that as populations develop political knowledge and sophistication, the parties become less useful and necessary.

One more distinction may help explain what follows in these final two chapters. Following another old scholarly convention, we will in this theoretical exploration look at the parties both as dependent and as independent variables. When we look at the parties as dependent variables, we look at them as the caused; we look at the independent variables acting on them, causing changes in them, altering their activities. On the other hand, when the party becomes the independent variable, we see it as a cause or an explanation of things in the broader political system. In this perspective we see the party or changes in the party causing some behavior or response elsewhere in the political system. The two concerns are separable, but any comprehensive theory of political parties must cope with both.

"Theory" may well be too pretentious a word for the tentative suggestions that follow. At least their goal is a modest one: to raise the understanding of the American political parties beyond the level of analysis of specific events to a more general knowledge that provides insights into continuing trends and into groups of events or phenomena. After a journey through a book such as this, one ought at least to be able to explain why the American parties differ from state to state and from one time to another.

17

The Future
of the American
Parties

A great deal has turned sour for the American parties in the last few years. The late 1960s saw the decline of their prestige; and along with other institutions of American government and politics, they have borne a good deal of the blame for the general malaise and the decline in public confidence that beset American society. From all sides critics blame the parties and the other institutions of the "system" for the ills which afflict American society: the overweening power of established elites, the faulty priorities in public values, and the resistance to change.

Whether or not the parties deserve such disfavor is hard to say. The answer depends in great part on one's estimate of the problems and progress of American society. But whatever may be the current reputation the parties enjoy, their most fundamental problems predate the dip in public esteem. Their time of troubles had started by the 1950s and early 1960s, and, furthermore, their troubles resulted from long-run changes in American society and politics.

CHANGES IN THE THREE SECTORS

The American parties have long been characterized by the loose set of relationships that have bound the three party sectors together. That looseness, or lack of integration, is indeed one of their most fundamental signs. The party organization has not been able either to bring a substantial part of the party electorate into membership or to assert its leadership or discipline over the campaigns and policy making of the party in government. Not surprisingly, therefore, the recent widespread changes in the parties have hit the three sectors separately and differently.

The Party in the Electorate

The American electorate seems to be losing its long-run attachments and loyalties to the American parties. More and more American adults con-

414

sider themselves independents rather than members of or identifiers with a major party. And even among those who profess a loyalty or attachment to a party, the incidence of split-ticket voting is on the rise — that is, the attachment to a political party does not appear to dominate the decision on how to cast the vote as it once did. So we have a decline both in the quantity and the power of party identification in the American public. Since those changes are now more apparent in the eighteen- to thirty-year-old group, they will likely accelerate. The result, obviously, is a shrinking of the size of party electorates and an eroding of the quality of their loyalty. More serious than the loosening of identifications, of course, is the increasing rejection of party altogether, evident perhaps in the declining confidence in the parties and the increased nonvoting of 1968 and 1972.

It has been the stability of party identification, of course, that has undergirded the stability of the two-party system. The unchanging adherence to the party as a reference symbol and an object of loyalties — and operationally as the key to the voter's decisions — has left no opportunities for a new party to gain a foothold in the electorate. Not surprisingly, therefore, the decline of party identification in the American electorate has been reflected in the victories of independents and third parties in increasing numbers since 1960. Independents and third-party candidates won seats in the Senate, an independent was elected governor of Maine, and George Wallace ran with amazing strength as a third-party candidate in 1968. And the threats of independent and third-party candidacies for 1976 raise the possibility of a three- or four-cornered race for the presidency. Furthermore, ticket-splitting and nonparty voting are on the increase. In 1972, for example, the voters in 45 percent of the congressional districts selected presidential and congressional candidates of different parties.[1] And after a long string of presidential elections in which party loyalty governed the outcome, the voters' issue preferences actually accounted for more of their vote decisions in 1972 than did party loyalty.

If the American electorate is not responding as eagerly to its party loyalties, to what does it now respond? Some segments of it are attuned to the new appeals of program and ideology. The Goldwater campaign of 1964, the McCarthy and Wallace appeals of 1968, and the McGovern candidacy of 1972 — along with those of many state and local issue-oriented candidacies — drew on and activated higher levels of issue awareness. General dissatisfaction in some quarters with the issuelessness and similarity of the parties has become more evident in recent years. For less sophisticated voters, the appeals that now register most effectively are candidate personality and image. The handsome faces, ready smiles, and graceful life styles that the television screens convey so

[1] Gerald M. Pomper, *Voters' Choice* (New York: Dodd, Mead, 1975), p. 215.

fully attract some of the support that party symbols once commanded. And since candidates and issues change far more frequently than parties, the consequence is an increasingly unstable, less predictable pattern of voting.

The Party Organizations

In the party organizations, the machines have been passing from the scene, and with them their activists and incentives. Many organizations no longer can depend on the patronage and preferments or the guaranteed election to public office that once recruited their full-time, vocational activists. Instead, they draw the better-educated, part-time leadership, whose incentives more often incline to issues or ideology and who bring with them new demands for intraparty participation. The new party activists tend to seek their payoffs in the triumph of principle or program. Indeed, some among them increasingly reject the politics of compromise, accommodation, and pragmatism that resulted from the assumption that the capture of public office is the alpha and the omega of American politics. And if their ideological goals are not satisfied — or even recognized within the party — they may leave it for particular candidates or other political organizations.

Increasingly, too, the internal, intraorganizational processes cease to be under the organization's control. Under the force of growing participatory expectations, these processes are becoming progressively more public; the private sphere of the party organization shrinks accordingly. The direct primary began the process of taking decisions from the party organization, and some seventy-five years later it continues apace. Also, one can now see the "publicizing" of the national convention processes. The convention is no longer a somewhat closed device for the organization's deliberation and choice making. Its processes are public, and, more important, its options have been sharply restricted in recent years by the activities of the would-be candidates in the preconvention politicking. Even the preconvention scramble for votes increasingly moves from the hands of party organizations as the presidential primaries spread.

At the same time that they are undergoing internal changes, the party organizations are losing their capacity for controlling American electoral politics. No longer do they consistently control either nominations (thanks to the direct primary) or the politics of election campaigning. Candidates increasingly find themselves able to build their own campaign organizations, raise their own campaign funds, and go their own merry ways in the campaign. All the campaign assets they once received from the party organizations and their workers — skills, information, pulse-readings, manpower, exposure — they now can get from pollsters, the media, public relations people, volunteer workers, or even by "renting a party" in the form of a campaign management firm. Especially because the party organizations have been unwilling or unable to provide the new arts for the candidates, they have waned in influence in the contesting of elections. Their fairly primitive campaign skills have been superseded by a new campaign technology, and more and more they are finding themselves among the technologically unemployed.

Furthermore, the party organizations remain decentralized in the face of the increasing centralization of life and politics in the United States. The electorate looks more and more to national political symbols and figures, but the party organizations remain collections of state and local fiefdoms. The futility of national party organization results partly from the suppressing power of the American presidency and partly from the unwillingness of state and local organizations to share incentives and resources with national party organs. The national committees and the national conventions are loose confederations of powerful local organizations and seem destined to remain so. But even those assertive local organizations no longer prosper. They do not easily recruit full-time, concerned leadership with the new incentives, and they do not have (and never did) a competent or ample party bureaucracy to fall back on.

The Party in Government

The men and women of the party in government, freed from reliance on the party organizations by the direct primary, by access to the media, by independent sources of funds, and by supportive personal followers, increasingly establish a direct appeal to the voters. No longer able to rely as heavily on abstract party loyalties, they develop more personal appeals. Indeed, their reliance on independent campaigning and, in some instances, on the media forces them to rely on personal style, physical appearance, even what personal magnetism they can generate. They find in many ways that it is quite a different matter to be sold by media than by party canvasers.

The successful candidates are the parties' contingents in American legislative bodies. And there, in direct relationship to the decline of party loyalties among voters and the decline of party organizations' power over their legislators, they vote as legislative parties with decreasing party cohesion. The instances in the Congress in which a majority of one party opposes a majority of the other in recorded roll call votes have, over the last decade, been at an all-time low. Freed from the party demands of both voters and the party organizations, they are more vulnerable to the nonparty pressures — the local economic interests of the constituency, for example.

But while the legislative party shows signs of losing its cohesion and strength, the executive party has rushed into the vacuum. Presidents and governors enjoy governmental power and leadership of the executive branch at the very time at which they increasingly represent the party and its programs to so many voters. They personify the party and give tangible content to its labels and symbols. In a period when many partisans seek programmatic goals, they alone formulate programs and control policy initiatives. Therefore, it is no exaggeration to speak of the parties as executive-centered coalitions. And nowhere is the phenomenon clearer than in the ability of presidents to dominate the national party organization of their parties, to give life and meaning to the symbol of their parties, and to dominate their congressional parties as they steer a set of initiatives through the Congress.

This much is merely summary of what has been said in greater detail in earlier chapters. The changes cumulatively amount to a vast shift of power within the American political party from the party organization to the executive-led party in government.

The crucial fact, perhaps, is the progressive isolation of the party organization in the American political parties. The organizations had their days of glory in some of the larger cities, but they never succeeded in integrating any significant measure of the party electorate into the organization on a membership basis. Isolated from the electorate and without any broad-based support or participation, they have always been vulnerable to suspicions that they were run by irresponsible oligarchies. The smoke-filled room myths have never died, the cries of bossism are as alive at today's party conventions as they were at the advent of the direct primary at the turn of the century.

What assets the party organizations once had they are losing rapidly. They no longer control the chief incentives for political activity as they did when it was patronage and preference that made the activists go round. They no longer control the resources and technology of campaigning and of electoral politics. And they no longer invoke the feelings of party loyalty in their electorate. But what kind of a party is it in which the party organization loses a preeminent or even equal position? Is not the party organization the only sector of the party that has more at stake than the winning of elections, that offers some possibility of life and principle beyond specific elections and even beyond electoral defeat?

In the case of the American parties, in any event, a coalition of an executive-led party in government and a somewhat restive and fickle party electorate has resulted. The executive rather than the party organization controls and manipulates the party symbols. The alliance of the executive with the party electorate rides on the message of the mass media and political personalism; the organization as a channel of communication no longer matters as much. That coalition is all the easier because party organization has been unable to centralize while the other two party sectors have done so. Especially in national politics, that centralization or nationalization of party messages, cues, and personalities unites the president-led party in government and the large number of voters who react primarily to national issues and faces.

NEW DIRECTIONS AND THE NEW POLITICS

These changes in the contemporary American parties are occurring in the context of broader ferments and upheavals in the American political system. The 1970s see the addition of a volatile young electorate and the new militancy of women, blacks, and other disadvantaged groups. The conserving reactions of middle America and the stable, traditional middle class are no less obvious. Third-party candidacies, and threats of others, flourish along with dissident movements within the parties.

Among these many trends, those which occur within the electoral politics have been characterized by the term "the new politics." A term of considerable variety and looseness, it usually includes:

1. The *new ideological and programmatic concerns* in races for public office.
2. The *infusion of young people* into the parties and campaigns and the consequent end to the domination of the middle generation.
3. A *participatory ethic*, which demands a voice for party activists and an end to authoritarian boss rule.
4. A new emphasis on the *personalism and personal image* so handily transmitted by the communications media.
5. A new strength for *candidacies outside of the two major parties*, whether they are independent candidacies or those of third or minor parties.
6. A fondness for an understated, *low-key political style*, less rhetorical, less partisan, and somewhat more intellectual.

Always implicitly and often explicitly, the new politics also includes a rejection of the traditional pragmatic electoral politics of the past and of those partisans and leaders who would retain them.

In these ways the new politics represents something of a revolution in the mechanisms with which we conduct our politics. At the same time, it brings a revolution in the issues and conflicts — in the substance of those politics, in other words — with which the mechanisms must deal. The range of those conflicts has broadened and deepened perceptibly. The old politics of consensus and compromise appears to have passed. Whether it was based on a genuine social consensus or was the product of suppressed differences need not concern us here. Regardless of its origin, it is less pervasive, at least for now.

This broader range of policy concerns challenges the status quo on a number of policy fronts: foreign and defense policy, the rights of minorities, the preservation of the environment, responses to the decay of the cities, and legislation in areas of personal morality. Beyond these issues are groups questioning more basic values and institutions and the leadership of dominant social groups — questioning the "system" and the "establishment." But specific issues and bywords change, often rapidly. What is important is that a new concern for issues comes to American politics and that this concern involves both a greater number of people and a greater range of issues. The two major parties contained without great strain the narrow range — and rather feeble intensity — of the issue concerns of the old consensus politics. There is now good reason to wonder if they can contain the new issue and ideological input. Possibly that input demands a greater variety and range of political organizations to represent and organize it.

Two caveats about the new politics and the changes in the parties must be entered. The first is merely that predictions about American politics are very perishable. Only a few years ago there were many predictions of sweeping and fundamental changes in American politics, and the turmoil on the campuses and in the streets did indeed seem to promise major changes in other parts of American society. But what seem at the time to be great and lasting changes have a way of turning out to be fleeting events. The issues, causes, and enthusiasms that stir Americans also shift with unexpected speed. Thus the new politics and the contemporary phase in which the American parties find themselves may turn out to be, contrary to expectations, an interlude of no lasting force in American politics.

Second, it is terribly important to realize that these developments in American politics are not of a single piece. They constitute no one movement or logical, coherent program. (Nor should we expect logic or consistency in a politics marked by a history of diversity and accommodation.) To some extent they pull and tug against each other as well as against the traditions of the past. The commitments to issue and ideology flower simultaneously with an increase in personalism, life-style appeals, and media images. Not only is most of the personalism distinctively *not* issue or policy oriented, but in its most attenuated form — the concern for the profile, the smile, the hair, the clothes of the candidate — it is supremely nonpolitical. At its worst, ironically, it is less political than the reliance on party loyalties and identifications that it replaces. The choice made on the basis of party label certainly weighs more political factors than the choice made on the basis of the candidate's charm and self-confidence in front of a TV camera.

Thus, for the parties the advent of the new politics seems to mean a sharp division — in all three of their sectors — between old- and new-style partisans. On the one hand, there are the upper-middle-class ideologues, the so-called amateurs, who demand a politics of differentiation, attention to issues and ideology, and a major participatory role in the party. On the other hand, there are the older, more traditional partisans whose politics are centrist and consensual, whose incentives for activity are varied, and who are willing to accept the old modes of authority in the party organization. It was that difference that lay in good measure behind the battle in the Democratic party in 1972 between the McGovernites and their opponents. But it is a difference beneath an increasing number of factional divisions in the parties, and it promises to remain with them for the foreseeable future.

THE DECLINE OF THE PARTIES

It is one of the comforting beliefs of the conventional wisdom that social systems contain their own self-adjusting mechanisms. The free-market, competitive economic system, which freely adjusts prices and production to changes in supply and demand, offers a ready example. So, too, does the self-correcting system of checks and balances that generations have trusted to keep the American separation of powers in a well-tuned equilibrium. And we have long had similar hopes for the party system. For the ills of unresponsiveness and dissatisfaction in the electorate, the cure is said to be a readjustment of party appeals (spurred by competition) and a consequent realignment of party loyalties in the electorate.

Is it possible that realignment may yet come as a response to the disaffection with the parties? Indeed, it is possible. The external symptoms that ordinarily precede a realignment are evident: a third-party surge named Wallace and the instability of the vote from one election to another, for instance. It may be that the increasing disposition of voters to identify as independents and to split tickets will be reversed by a party realignment restoring the aggregate confidence in and identification with the parties.

The realignment, however, appears to be overdue. Perhaps the most striking aspect of the 1968 and 1972 elections was the fact that in the end there was no realignment, that despite all the ticket-splitting the old party identifications held. Furthermore, an issue or ideological axis on which realignment might take place has not appeared. Burnham suggests that perhaps we are inching toward an alignment of the disadvantaged and the educated successful (the advantaged) against the middle strata.[2] Alternatively, it may be that realignment cannot take place once the voters' confidence in the party system has slipped below a

[2] Walter Dean Burnham, *Critical Elections and the Mainsprings of American Politics* (New York: Norton, 1970), pp. 137–40.

certain point. A considerable number of Americans may simply decide to rely on cues and political organizations outside the parties. Thus they will have no incentive to change party loyalties; new nonparty symbols and loyalties will be added to the old party ties. Perhaps, too, our politics — at least for the moment — are too complex to produce the simple dualism — any dualism — around which voters can cohere in a new alignment. Most of the party realignments of the past formed along the classic lines of "ins" and "outs" at the time of national crisis.[3]

Even if the parties should find an issue and a catalytic event for realignment, however, it is by no means certain that realigning will restore the parties to their political preeminence. Realignment is no solution to the erosion of party organizational capacity to nominate and elect candidates. Nor is it any guarantee that large numbers of Americans will return to an unswerving partisanship or that they will again mark the straight party ticket. The truth is that a party realignment is only a readjustment of the parties to new cleavages in the society. It may even depend on the very kinds of confidence in party and need for party symbols that the American parties appear to be losing.

For the moment, therefore, a good many signs point beyond the cure of realignment to a decline of the parties generally and of party organizations in particular. Both the parties' dominance of our electoral politics and the stability of the two-party system have rested on the acceptance of the party label as a cue for action. Large numbers of voters now have cues and sources of information outside the parties. Many of them also are less and less inclined to accept the omnibus commitments that party loyalty implies. They want to pick and choose among issues and candidates. Party loyalty demands that they buy a whole collection of commitments; in effect, it asks them to divide the political world into two simple categories, ours and theirs. The simple, dichotomized choice that party loyalty within a two-party system demands no longer appeals to an educated, issue-oriented electorate. Knowing, confident, even assertive adults are less and less willing to surrender their selective judgment in favor of an unquestioning loyalty to party.

To look at it another way, the Republican-Democratic loyalties of the American two-party system actually require a politics of low intensity and little involvement in issues. The willingness of millions of voters to buy the diverse bag of candidates and issues assumes that they have no strong feelings about any one of them. Loyalty to the party as a least common denominator can bind diverse populations into one party electorate only when the other lines that divide them are weaker. But what happens when large numbers of voters repeatedly feel more strongly

[3] On realignments, see James L. Sundquist, *Dynamics of the Party System* (Washington: Brookings, 1973).

about a candidate or an issue than they do about a party? What happens when large numbers of voters decide that they no longer need the ready-made, all-purpose, prepackaged judgment of a political party? Above all, what happens when that voter disenchantment takes place at the same time that candidates find ways of communicating with voters outside the usual channels of the party organization?

Those questions are rhetorical, and the answers are indeed implicit in the questions. Yet, it must be clear that all of this is not to predict the imminent decline and fall of the political parties, American or otherwise. There is considerable danger of exaggeration when one draws a series of indicators into one concentrated argument. A good many of the necessary qualifications and counter-indicators get lost. There are, indeed, ample signs that the parties have and will continue to have a creative role in American politics, even if they no longer dominate the channels and resources of our electoral politics. There are hundreds of thriving party organizations, aggregate trends to the contrary notwithstanding. There are still thousands of ardent party loyalists, and millions of voters still cast straight party tickets every four years. When we talk of decline, we do not mean death.

So the parties are alive, if not well, in America. But they will increasingly become a part of a richer, more diverse pattern of American politics. We may well see the repeated emergence of third parties as expressions of deeper discontent with the parties and American society. Eugene McCarthy talks freely of a third-party attempt for the presidency in 1976, and others hint at it cautiously. And some scholars of American politics have also begun to reexamine the long-accepted case against multipartyism.[4] Other political organizations — interest groups, candidate organizations, ideological movements, ad hoc issue organizations — will assume a greater importance in the electoral politics once dominated by the parties. In 1968, in fact, organized labor's efforts registered close to 5 million voters, distributed 115 million pamphlets and leaflets, and recruited almost 100,000 election-day workers. The total bill ran around $10 million.[5] And all these nonparty organizations will reflect and embrace the new ideological politics in a way the parties never could. In this respect it is worth noting that the amateur voluntary organizations within the parties are probably less vital and influential today than they were in the 1950s. Issue-oriented and ideological activists increasingly turn outside the party.

What seems likely, in other words, is a politics of greater fluidity and instability, carried on by a wider range of political organizations. The

[4] See, for example, Lawrence C. Dodd, *Congress and Public Policy* (Morristown: General Learning, 1975).
[5] Theodore H. White, *The Making of the President 1968* (New York: Atheneum, 1969), p. 365.

parties will exert their influence over nominations, elections, and policy making, but so will other political organizations. In many instances the personable candidate — aided by the media — will attract the voter loyalties and activist labors that the party organizations once did. The erosion of the one, stable, long-run loyalty in American politics will contribute to a politics more frequently dominated by the short-term influences of the charismatic candidate or the very salient issue. In its volatility, its lack of continuity, and its lack of predictability, the new electoral politics may increasingly resemble that of the one-party factional and personal politics Key described in the American South in the 1930s and 1940s.[6] Or perhaps it will most closely approximate the nonpartisan politics of school board elections in many American cities.

Diversity and specialization thus characterize the changes in American politics. The diversity of goals and needs, multiplied by the intensity of feelings about them, cannot easily be met by two traditionally pragmatic, compromising political parties. Voters, too, appear to want more specialized cues for political choice and action, and the activists among them want to discriminate among the causes and people for whom they will work. All of that leads to an increased specialization and division of labor among the political organizations. Just what specialized role we may anticipate for the parties is not altogether clear. Some voters will still find the party a useful cue-giver and an effective vehicle for their political goals. Indeed, there will be locales in which the party organizations maintain control of nominations and elections and in which the party loyalty of the electorate remains firm — that is, the old party roles persist. Where the parties do lose some measure of those traditional roles, they may well turn into more ideological, issue-oriented parties. The changes will be less marked in areas in which the electorates are less educated and less politicized. Where voters are politically more sophisticated and less dependent on party symbols, ideological activists will more often control the party organization.

AFTER THE REIGN OF THE PARTIES

Political life in the United States without the guiding dominance of two assertive political parties is not unthinkable. Much of our local politics has been nonpartisan in reality as well as in name for some time. But a diminished role for the parties throughout much more of electoral politics suggests impacts of a greater magnitude. The question of the consequences not only for the political processes but for the quality of American democracy itself troubles many observers.

[6] V. O. Key, *Southern Politics* (New York: Knopf, 1950).

Burnham has put the concern directly and simply:

Political parties, with all their well-known human and structural shortcomings, are the only devices thus far invented by the wit of Western man that can, with some effectiveness, generate countervailing collective power on behalf of the many individually powerless against the relatively few who are individually or organizationally powerful. Their disappearance as active intermediaries, if not as preliminary screening devices, would only entail the unchallenged ascendancy of the already powerful, unless new structures of collective power were somehow developed to replace them, and unless conditions in America's social structure and political culture came to be such that they could be effectively used.[7]

The American parties — and all others for that matter — mobilize sheer numbers against organized minorities with other political resources, and they do so in the one avenue of political action in which numbers of individuals count most heavily — elections. Thus the parties have classically been the mechanisms by which newly enfranchised and powerless electorates rose to power. The old-style urban machine in the United States, for example, was the tool by which the powerless, often recently arrived, urban masses won control of their cities from older, largely "Wasp" elites. In a more fluid politics of bargaining among a larger number of political organizations and millions more uncommitted voters, the fear is that the advantage will be on the side of the well-organized minorities with other political resources.

The decline of the parties, therefore, could have ironic elitist consequences. The educated, sophisticated, involved political minority may help impose a new kind of political tyranny on the less involved, lower SES segments of the electorate. It increasingly imposes an ideological politics that lacks salience and may indeed be incomprehensible to the less sophisticated. At the same time it contributes to the decline of the most useful cue-giver, the major political party. The removal of the political party as an organizer and a symbol in our present nonpartisan elections helps upper SES elites, both of the right and the left, to dominate those politics. The political party, in other words, is the political organization of the masses who lack the cues and information — as well as the political resources of status, skills, and money — to make a major impact on public decisions via other means. The diminished power of the parties makes the game of politics more difficult for them to play and win.

A continued decline of the parties also threatens to rob the political system of an important builder of majorities. Although imperfectly, the major American parties have pieced together majority coalitions. Amer-

---

[7] Walter Dean Burnham, "The End of American Party Politics," *Trans-action*, December 1969, p. 20.

ican presidents have enjoyed the legitimacy of majority coalitions most of the time, and the party majority in legislatures has at least permitted them to organize for action. With weakened parties, how are we to find majorities in a fragmented politics? Are we to rely on the personal appeals and promises of national candidates? Or do we face the kind of political immobilism that has resulted elsewhere from the splintering of intransigent groups and deeply felt loyalties and sentiments? To be sure, it is easy to overestimate what the parties have traditionally contributed to our politics, but the contributions, if more modest than many believe, are real and important. Certainly, a mature political system can and will work out its adaptations. There are indeed alternatives to stable, two-party systems which dominate electoral choice. The issue is whether they can pull together the separate pieces of American politics and political institutions as effectively as the parties did.

It may be that the parties will come out of their present decline in ways and to degrees we cannot foresee. Were the party organizations to acquire the resources for distributing the new campaigning skills to candidates, they would redress their recent losses to the new campaign technicians and to other political organizations. The key to the future of the parties is clearly in a recaptured ability to control the major resources of American politics: money, organization, people, and know-how. Perhaps, too, the parties would fare better if the current mood of national self-doubt and political cynicism were to lift. But for the short run, at least, important trends are afoot in the parties and in American politics. Regardless of whether they last, they will have their short-run effects, and the long run is often nothing more than a series of short-run trends. These trends also suggest a great deal about the mechanisms by which parties change and adapt, and those explorations are the subject of the next and last chapter.

18
Toward
a Theory
of the Political
Party

The political parties have never been able to contain the splendid diversity of American politics. Americans have always pursued alternate routes to influence by dealing directly with public officials, by working through interest groups and other political organizations, even by various forms of direct demonstrations and civil disobedience. It has never been the case, in other words, that all our politics has gone on through the political parties. Indeed, the parties have not even monopolized our *electoral* politics. They have indeed been an important element in American politics; they certainly have assisted the development of mass, popular democracy in the United States. But a good deal of scholarship on the American parties attributes to them a role far more central and impressive than they have played in reality.

At the least, this myth of party primacy exaggerates the influence of the parties in American politics. It is as if the sheer pervasiveness of the party label in American elections and public office guarantees a political role for the parties. But in reality parties do not easily control nominations or elections, nor do they readily govern on behalf of party programs. In a more extended form, the myth leads many Americans to think of the parties as the "indispensable instruments of government," [1] even as the originators of democratic forms and processes. This point of view finds it hard to imagine American democracy without the parties in something like their present form. It also frequently argues that stronger, vital political parties are the best tonic for the ills of the democratic order. This point of view, of course, pervades the arguments on behalf of central, guiding roles for "responsible" parties in the American political system.

Behind the assumptions of party primacy is a false *theoretical* assump-

[1] Committee on Political Parties of the American Political Science Association, *Toward a More Responsible Two-Party System* (New York: Rinehart, 1950), p. 15.

tion, which is what concerns us here. It is that the parties are causes rather than effects, that they are perpetually independent rather than dependent variables. They appear to cause, to shape, to produce; the fact that they themselves are caused, shaped, produced is neglected. Simply because the rise of parties accompanies the rise of democratic institutions and the expansion of adult suffrage, we have no basis for assuming either the causal role of the parties or the necessity of parties' accompanying democracy for all time. Very likely both parties and contemporary democratic institutions were "caused" more or less simultaneously by the same general social forces and conditions. Parties do, indeed, have their impact on political processes and institutions, but other political and nonpolitical factors in turn have their effects on them. The parties are "in" and "of" the political system, and one cannot expect that they alone among political institutions can escape the influences that shape everything around them.

The mission of this chapter, therefore, is to identify the reasons why political parties — especially the American parties — develop as they do. What shapes the particular structure of the parties, the relationships among their sectors and various activists? What determines their role or activities in the political system? And what accounts for change in them over time, and for variation in them from place to place? The answers, if we have them, should provide at least the outlines of a theory about the political parties. Thus we look for summary statements that explain how and why the parties became what they are and how and why they continue to evolve today.

THE IMPACT OF THE PARTY'S ENVIRONMENT

In the first chapter of this book we briefly discussed the major environmental influences that impinge on the political parties, among them:

1. The political institutions, such as federalism and the separation of powers.
2. The statutory regulations of the parties.
3. Electoral institutions and processes.
4. The definition of the electorate.
5. The political culture and its subcultures.
6. The broader, nonpolitical environment.

In the chapters between that one and this there are numerous examples of the impact of these components of the parties' environment. For instance, the effect of the direct primary on the parties' role in the nomination process has been set out in some detail. So has the effect of the separation of powers on legislative party cohesion and on the national committees.[2]

The effects of these categories of influences, therefore, are already apparent. In the aggregate they shape both the nature of the party system and the roles and activities of the parties (Figure 1). Thus the left side of Figure 1 merely recapitulates the general view of the second chapter that the American party system — and probably others, too — reflects the interests and cleavages of the society and also specific political institutions and electoral systems. The right side suggests the impact of the various environmental components on the roles and activities of the parties. It indicates an important and basic assumption in all this theorizing: that the external environment impinges most directly on the parties by shaping demands for what they do and how they do it. Those demands in turn shape party structures and the balances among the three sectors to ensure the meeting of the demands.

Let us look at the same question in another way. Along with other political organizations, the parties are essentially engaged in the business of aggregating influence. How they aggregate and for whom they aggregate are what their environment determines. In other words, the pattern or style of their activities, functions, roles, or what have you, is set by complicated influences outside the parties themselves. Those environmental influences shape the following four kinds of intermediary factors which in turn shape the parties' activities:

1. *Mechanisms or avenues of aggregation:* the nature of the electoral processes, the structure of representation, the nature of nonelectoral avenues, the kinds of public decisions and choices open to the citizen, and the structure of majority building in government.
2. *Needs and demands to be aggregated:* characteristics of the citizens, their numbers, the franchise, the interests of the electorate, citizen culture and expectations, needs for cues and symbols for political choice, and demands for participation and activity in politics.
3. *Structure and resources of the parties:* the legal position of the parties, the resources (personnel and other) that they control, their organization and internal relationships, the incentives they command, and their political capacity.
4. *Structure and resources of competing political organizations:* their legal positions, resources, form, and incentives; their competitive position regarding the parties and other political organizations.

---

[2] One very extensive attempt to treat the political parties as a dependent variable — a "caused" — has of course been the persistent American movement to reform them. Austin Ranney in *Curing the Mischiefs of Faction: Party Reform in America* (Berkeley: University of California Press, 1975) describes the attempts with enormous insight.

FIGURE 1   Environmental Influences on the Parties

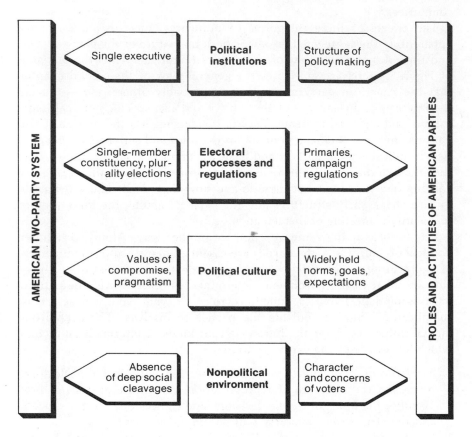

Among these categories it is the first, the mechanisms or avenues of aggregation, that remain relatively fixed, because they result largely from
the institutional determinants (such as the basic governmental forms,
electoral law, etc.). The second group, the needs and demands, change
most rapidly and obviously, for they reflect changes in the complex,
nonpolitical environment of the parties: levels of education, degrees of
political information, standard of living, and issues of public policy, for
example.

Changes in the third and fourth categories — the parallel ones of the
structure and resources of parties and their nonparty competitors —
tend to occur secondarily — that is, they are often determined by the
avenues and the needs and demands. Changes in the needs of candidates
for campaign help or in the demands of voters for cues to the choices
they face are reflected back on the parties and alternate organizations.
To oversimplify greatly, the causal influence moves primarily from the

needs-demands to the structure and resources of the political party. To take a contemporary example, the new demand of activists for a participatory role and open party decisions is affecting the form and even the capacity for action of the American party organizations.

Because we do not readily see the changes wrought on the avenues of aggregation by political institutions, it is easy to underestimate the effect of these institutions. A comparison of the American parties with those of other political systems, however, makes it clear. It suggests that the presence of a parliamentary form of government or, alternatively, of the American-style presidential form is the single most powerful determinant of the nature of the parties. The institutional factors in a party environment, of course, are not completely unchanging. We considered but ultimately rejected the elimination of the electoral college in 1969 and 1970. Interestingly enough, one of the most persuasive arguments made against the abolition of the electoral college hinged on its effect on the party system, especially the possible encouragement of third-party movements.

Basically, the rapid, frequent changes in the party environment — the ones that explain the recent developments in the American parties — are those that change the needs and demands of the various actors in the aggregative political processes: the candidates, the citizen voters, and the political activists.[3] These actors have goals and demands for which the party is a possible means or instrument. To what extent do these people need the party to achieve their goals? Are there alternative means, other political organizations, that will be more effective? To seek public office, candidates need assorted help and resources. Can they get the necessary skills and resources from the party at the lowest price? The voters want their choices — voting and otherwise — to achieve certain goals with a minimum expenditure of time, effort, ego, and anxieties. Do the cues of the party aid them for less cost than the cues of their neighbors, daily papers, unions, or professional associations? The party activists, too, have their goals. If patronage is high among them, the chances are that there is no viable alternative to work within the party. If the goals are ideological or issue-centered, the alternatives are more promising.

As Table 1 suggests, the pattern of needs and demands on the parties shapes not only their roles and activities but ultimately the party structures and their available resources. For the sake of simplicity, the table is limited to two polar types of party: one set of needs and demands produces a strong governing party not unlike that championed by the advocates of party responsibility; the other, a fragmented party that functions far less assertively among other political organizations. We

[3] Anthony Downs in *An Economic Theory of Democracy* (New York: Harper, 1957) develops the maximizing approach systematically.

TABLE 1   Relationship of Political Needs and Demands
to Types of Parties

	Types of Parties	
Needs and demands of	Dominant, policy-making parties	Weak, fragmented parties
Political, governmental institutions	Parliamentary form, or institutional imperatives for cohesion in policy making; unitary form	Fragmented governmental institutions (federalism, separation of powers, etc.); numerous points of access to policy-making process
Candidates, party in government	Need party for nomination and access to ballot, for resources and skills of campaigning, for its control of a loyal electorate	Need broad support for nomination (as at primary); easy access to ballot; need skills and resources for campaign that party does not control
Political activists, workers of party organization	Seek rewards (whether material or other) which party controls	Seek rewards that can be achieved in work outside the party
Voters, members of party electorate	Depend on an integrated and simple system of cues on candidate and issue; need to reduce decisional costs	Seek differentiated cues; have plural reference groups and symbols; willing to bear higher decisional costs

deal here with exaggerated, polar types — with pure forms — which perhaps do not exist in reality. But it is clear that change in the American party system is clearly from the governing party on the left toward the fragmented party on the right.

THE PARTY STRUCTURES

A second, somewhat derivative level of a theory of the parties concerns the parties themselves: their three sectors and the relationships among them. What the parties are as political organizations depends on the expressed needs for the aggregation of political interests and on the capacities the parties have for aggregating them. In other words, the parties as structures are the creatures of the services they must perform to satisfy the demands of their various clienteles.

To take a specific example, the traditional American urban machine of the late nineteenth or early twentieth century has passed slowly from the scene because the services it performed are no longer widely demanded. Public agencies and programs took over its social service activities, and an expanding industrial economy provided better, more lucrative jobs than it did. As the immigrant populations became integrated into American life, they needed the help and protection of the city machine less and less. Similarly, the declining need of many city voters for an all-purpose political symbol eroded party identifications and thus the size and loyalty of party electorates.

Once we settle that question of the interface between the party and the aggregative politics of the broader political system, we move to the sketching of alternative models of the parties themselves. As Table 1 indicates, there are two: the strong, governing party and the more fragmented one. Figures 2 and 3 spell out those party types in terms of their internal characteristics (rather than their party activities) and show that the stronger type is dominated by the party organization and the fragmented one by the party in government. The American parties, of course, appear to be moving increasingly to the form headed by the party in government. Although they may have never been as organization-dominated as many parties of the rest of the world, they did approach it more closely than they now do.

The two party models differ also in the degree of integration of the three sectors. In the organization-centered model the three sectors are bound closely by ties of loyalty and discipline. A substantial part of the party electorate, in fact, joins the organization as members, and the debts of candidates and officeholders for nomination and election assistance bind them to the party organization. The key to the organization-centered party, in fact, lies in the ability of the organization to unite the party in government to it and to the goals of its activists. In the patronage and preference party of the classic urban machine, both sectors were united in the overarching goal of electoral victory and the electoral pragmatism it demanded. Alternatively, the two sectors might be united, as the "party responsibilitarians" argue, by loyalty to the same principles or issue positions. The substantial difficulties with that possibility were discussed at length several chapters ago. Finally, in some party systems the organization's superiority is ensured by institutional structures such as a proportional representation electoral system, in which it controls the party list of candidates. That third possibility, however, seems to be completely unavailable to American party organizations.

In the party controlled by the party in government — typified by the American executive-centered coalition — there is far less integration of

FIGURE 2   Party Dominated by Party Organization

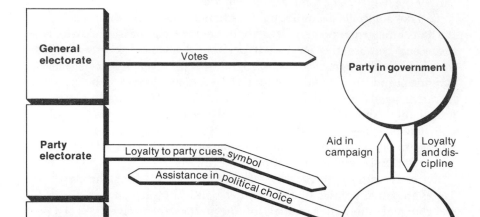

the three sectors. None of the direct, binding ties really exists — everything depends on the pragmatic alliances of convenience at election time. The dominant party in government, in fact, is free to form alliances with nonparty organizations, such as interest groups, rather than work with its own party organization. The substantial distance between the congressional parties and the national committees illustrates the point. The party in government, in other words, establishes contact with the party electorates without relying greatly on the party organization.

The issue of the integration of the three party sectors probes the fundamental question of what a political party is. Can a party in which the party in government freely makes pragmatic electoral bargains maintain any meaning and stability for the party symbol? Does a political party have to be something more than the sum total of the candidates choosing to run on its label? At the least it seems unlikely that the party led by its party in government can provide the continuity and breadth that sets the party apart from other political organizations. The parties we call strong for their ability to dominate or monopolize certain forms of political activity have been those led by the organizational sector. Only the party organization has the breadth of skills and resources, as well as the commitment to all party goals and even to the party itself, to fill this leadership role within the party.

It is possible, of course, that a strong executive can dominate the party

FIGURE 3 Party Dominated by Party in Government

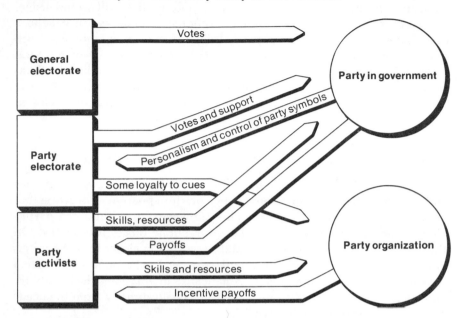

in government and through it the political party. He may even dominate the party organization, often at the cost of vitiating it. Presidents may succeed in that role, but it is not so clear that the less visible and powerful executives of state and local governments can. But even assuming they can, do we then have anything more than the political triumph of increasingly powerful executives? The point of the argument in behalf of strong parties exerting policy leadership as well as leadership in the recruitment of public officials — or in merely providing a stable cue to millions of voters — is that the party augments the officeholder's electoral responsibility to the people who elected him. The crucial question is whether a party controlled by executives in government does that — or whether the executive-centered coalition is not an alternative to, or a mutation of, the more traditional political party.

What contributes to the decline of party organizations? In the first place, the American party organizations, unlike many of their counterparts elsewhere, do not have legal or institutional guarantees of a superior position. European party organizations often do — in the form of proportional representation electoral systems, controls over campaign funds, control over nomination for office, or constitutional imperatives for legislative discipline. Because of the precarious position of the American party organization, the advent of ideology as the goal of the organizational activists separates the party organization increasingly from the electoral pragmatists of the party in government. Second, the party organization is increasingly losing its monopoly of the skills, knowledge, and resources necessary for winning elections; candidates can get those necessaries elsewhere. The party in government makes alliance with nonparty groups and individuals more attuned to its goal of electoral victory. Finally, the American party organization appears to be the victim of restrictions and controls intended to democratize it. Even though those regulations merely shift power from one set of party oligarchs to another, the party organizations are usually the losers.

PARTY AND THE SOCIAL PSYCHOLOGY OF THE VOTER

When one reexamines and refines all the differences between parties and other political organizations, many of the apparent differences between them disappear. One difference, however, does not. The parties alone attach their name to candidates for public office in elections. On the surface, it appears to be a trivial difference. On closer look, however, one sees that it involves the willingness or need to respond to that label on the part of large numbers of Americans. In this way the durability and special character of the political parties result directly from the needs and perceptions of the American voter.

In fact, an argument can be made that the political party results in major part from the need of most voters to reduce the many costs of voting and other forms of political participation. Voters require a guide, a set of symbolic shortcuts, to the confusing, often trackless political terrain. The parties' labels, personages, and activities run as a constant, clearly perceptible thread through the confusing jumble of political conflict and the baffling proliferation of American elections. The fact that the party label is stable and extensive enough to do so — combined with its advantage of appearing on the ballot itself — sets it apart from other political organizations. When that cue-giving service, in addition, produces voter loyalties or identifications with the party, when those loyalties are as enduring as they have been in the United States, and when they dominate so many voting decisions, it determines much of the character of the parties and the party system. In fact, the conclusion that this pattern of reliance and loyalty is the primary determinant of the American party system is difficult to escape.

In addition to the importance of the party cue, loyalty to it, and its use in the voting decision, however, other crucial voter perceptions, values, and attitudes shape (and sustain) the parties. The stability of the two-party system is based on the parties' assumption that many voters value this system, especially its comfortable continuity, understandable choices, and associations with democratic processes. To some extent the parties, as we have known them, assume also that voters (as well as candidates) will adopt a strategy of electoral pragmatism, that they will be willing to choose between unpleasant alternatives and take the lesser evil. Similarly, they expect that few citizens will "throw their votes away" by voting for candidates who have no chance of victory. The party system also assumes that voters will not long support a chronically noncompetitive party, thus forcing it to make the repairs necessary to improve its competitive position.

At a more general level, parties are also strongly shaped by the levels of support and approval in the mass public. General confidence in them will protect them from restrictive legislation. That kind of confidence, however, the American parties have rarely enjoyed. More often they have had to contend with public fears of party oligarchs in smoke-filled rooms and consequent statutory controls, loss of party control over nominations, and demands for opening and publicizing party processes. Looming behind that widespread suspicion of the parties is the possibility that a deeper, newer cynicism about them, especially among young citizens, will lead to their rejection.

In a general sense, too, parties reflect the political-psychological needs of voters. The rise of personalism in political campaigning is a case in point. It is easy — too easy — to attribute this personalism to the new campaign technology and reliance on the mass media. Behind the personalism is the need of many citizens for personal leadership, for flesh-and-blood embodiment of distant government, even for the vicarious ego-strength of a confident public figure. Perhaps, too, the new personalism reflects a dissatisfaction with the parties as lifeless abstractions and impersonal organizations.

To argue that popular needs, perceptions, values, and expectations shape the parties is perhaps to argue for little more than the impact of the political culture. The political culture, however, works in subtle ways, and it is wise to specify them. The large coalition, majority parties we know in the United States are to an inordinate extent the product of the political subculture of one group of citizens: the less involved and less political. It is the less active, less confident, less influential, less informed citizens who most need the parties and whose reliance on them and their symbols have made them what they are. To a great extent the political party, here and elsewhere, is preeminently the organization of the politically marginal man and woman.

PARTIES, POLITICS, AND DEMOCRACY

That the origin and rise to importance of the political parties is intimately bound up with the sweep and spread of democracy is abundantly evident. The parties grew as the first mobilizers of electoral power while electorates expanded. The relationship of the parties to democracy, however, extends beyond their origins and initial growth. Democracy presupposes a degree of citizen participation and choice. By definition it involves a broad distribution of political power and requires organizational intermediaries to mobilize the political power of individuals in order to make it effective. The entire development of the parties reflects these imperatives of democracy, and changes in the parties have mirrored changes in the very nature of democracy and its institutions and electorates.

It is this close relationship that leads to assertions of the importance, even the indispensability, of the parties. The closeness of the identification of the political party with democracy, however, depends on how one defines democracy and on the ability of a society to meet its assumptions. Traditionally in the United States, democracy has meant the building of majorities by compromise, accommodation, and brokerage among the groups of American society. In many ways it is a gentle, middle-class politics, one which tinkers and adjusts to maintain a broad consensus and which ultimately makes only incremental changes in the status quo. It is a politics of reasonableness and moderation — and is possible, therefore, only among groups and individuals whose differences, not being very wide or deeply felt, are easily compromised. For that kind of democracy the major American parties have been ideally suited. They have been open, permeable organizations whose political pragmatism ably built the majority coalitions.

That model of pluralist American democracy, the critics of the new politics charge, has outlived its time. Their preference is for a politics of more explicit conflict, a greater diversity of policy alternatives, and a more frequent and fundamental reexamination of the status quo. They see the rich diversity of classes, generations, and races participating actively on behalf of their diverse interests. Their politics are also more ideological and issue-oriented, more committed and less pragmatic, yielding, or compromising. If large numbers of people join them in rejecting the democratic politics of compromise and accommodation, then the parties, too, must change. To those new kinds of democratic expectations, political parties — the American ones especially — do not easily respond. All their structures and traditions are keyed to other expectations.

The democracy of the mass political parties, therefore, is not necessarily democracy's pure or final realization. Democratic expectations, institutions, and processes change, and with them so do the parties. The parties may have been essential, as many have suggested, during the initial politicization of the uneducated, economically disadvantaged masses. But when education and affluence open new channels of political information and of political mobilization, then competitors arise with new organizational forms, new appeals, and new political resources. The assumption that only the parties can aggregate or mobilize political influence effectively no longer has the ring of truth.

Furthermore, the relationship of the changes in the parties to those in democratic processes is closer than we might infer from mere assertions that everything changes. In the United States and many of the Western democracies, the changes in the parties occur in phases related to the development of democratic politics and modern political institutions. Three phases are apparent:[4]

1. Initially the parties began in most of the Western democracies as parties of limited access and narrow appeal. Originated at a time of a restricted, aristocratic suffrage, they were limited in personnel, confined largely to electioneering activities, and closed to mass participation. This was their formative, premodern period.
2. As the electorates expanded, the parties also expanded their organizational forms to include larger numbers of activists and members (although the American parties resisted more than most the development of mass membership). The aggregation or mobilization of the large numbers of new citizens came to occupy much of the parties' attention. The parties dominated the political loyalties and even the political socialization of the new, mass electorate. As the dominant political organization of a citizenry marked by relatively low levels of political information and sophistication, they became the chief givers of political cues. (In many of the new nations of Asia and Africa, which began with virtually complete adult suffrage, the parties entered stage two very quickly.)
3. Finally, as in the United States today, as electorates mature along with democratic processes, as political loyalties and interests become more complex and heterogeneous, politics becomes more diverse and differentiated. The political party in this stage becomes more of a *primus inter pares*. Its sole control of the mobilization of power ends amid growing competition from other political organizations. The party remains both a potent organization and a powerful reference symbol, but it loses its monopoly of the resources, skills, and information in electoral politics.

These stages in party development reflect no organic, natural growth or life cycle. They are direct responses to changes in democratic electorates and processes, and they certainly do not appear to be limited to the United States. Parties in Western Europe, for example, are losing mem-

[4] For another developmental approach to political parties, see Samuel P. Huntington, *Political Order in Changing Societies* (New Haven: Yale University Press, 1968), especially Chap. 7. His four stages seem to coincide with the first two here.

bership and appear to be entering the third phase, too.[5] It may be, in fact, that when an electorate reaches a certain point of politicization, parties and party loyalties are no longer as useful as they once were to large numbers of voters.

Are the American parties becoming relics of an earlier and simpler political age? Will their decline continue indefinitely? Those questions force speculations about the unknown tomorrows of American politics. Possibly other stages will follow the third. But for the moment at least, it does not look as though the parties will disappear. They are deeply rooted in American law, and the advantages they afford in political organizing — largely a result of their statutory and ballot status — would alone guarantee their continued life. They also remain deeply set as important reference symbols in the political worlds within countless citizens. Thus many political processes and numerous political expectations are too deeply set for the parties simply to pass away.

The major problem for the American parties today arises from the increased differentiation in American aggregative politics. As the American electorate continues to develop more complex interests, it acquires more differentiated loyalties and responds to more differentiated cues. It maintains identifications with parties, but it responds also to candidates and to issues, programs, and ideologies. It responds differentially to specific elections and political levels. The ultimate consequence is a more diverse, complex politics that no single set of loyalties, and thus no single set of political organizations, can easily contain and manage.

So the American parties find it increasingly difficult to be all things to all citizens. There probably will never again be a dominant, all-purpose political organization in our politics. The parties especially cannot easily meet the expectations of ideological politics and pragmatic electoral politics at the same time. And their symbols cannot continue to work their old magic on all elements of so diverse a political population. The new challenge for them in a fragmented politics is to be selective in their appeals and activities. For the first time in their histories they must define a clientele exactly and reach it. That may well be the greatest challenge of the next phase in their development.

[5] Anthony King discusses this and related points in his excellent essay "Political Parties in Western Democracies," *Polity* 2 (1969): 111–41.

INDEX